P9-EDF-437

ALARM SYSTEMS AND THEFT PREVENTION

Second Edition

ALARM SYSTEMS AND THEFT PREVENTION

Second Edition

Thad L. Weber

BUTTERWORTH PUBLISHERS
Boston • London
Sydney • Wellington • Durban • Toronto

All references in this book to personnel of male gender are used for convenience only and shall be regarded as including both males and females.

Library of Congress Cataloging in Publication Data

Weber, Thad L.
Alarm systems and theft prevention.

Includes index.
1. Burglary protection. 2. Burglar-alarms. I. Title.
TH9705.W42 1985 621.389'2 84-29319
ISBN 0-409-95175-7

Butterworth Publishers
80 Montvale Avenue
Stoneham, MA 02180

10 9 8 7 6 5 4 3 2 1

Printed in the United States of America

Contents

Preface and Acknowledgments

For the most part, this is not a technical book. Written in layman's language, it is intended to be read by people who supply, use, or need security services and equipment.

In large measure, this book recounts the sometimes sad, sometimes humorous, and nearly always unfortunate experiences of manufacturers, distributors, retailers, and individuals who have lost valuable merchandise, money, jewelry, or securities to criminal attacks.

In most cases the losses occurred because there was a weak link: a vulnerability in the total security defense. The criminal succeeded because he studied, investigated, and researched his target's defenses and found means of avoiding, defeating, or outrunning the defenses.

In many cases, the weaknesses were due to the inexperience of the target. In some cases they were due to defects or oversights by the alarm service company or other security contractors in the planning of alarm systems or in the security procedures followed.

It is hoped that, in reading this book, you will profit from the mistakes of others—learn how to eliminate security weaknesses and reduce vulnerability to criminal attack techniques. While this book is not a "whodunit," it does at times challenge the reader's security experience and imagination. Where the shoe fits, please balance any chagrin, indignation, and frustration with a resolution to begin a more earnest and comprehensive devotion to security by taking that essential step: thinking like a thief.

Every effort is made to present in practical terms those weaknesses in physical security, alarm systems, or related security procedures that, when blended together, resulted in vulnerability. In addition to analyzing these cases and identifying the key elements of vulnerability, remedies for curing the weakness are also offered.

Other sections of this book deal with the application, strengths, and limitations of security equipment. For the most part, equipment is presented from the practical viewpoint—what a security device or system will do (or not do) and how it should be applied and operated, rather than the detail of mechanical design, electrical circuitry, or laboratory theories. Thus, the reader will search in vain for pictures, schematics, and technical bibliography.

This second edition includes revisions and expansion of the original text and addresses changes and innovations in technology, improved criminal attack techniques, and growing-pains subjects such as unnecessary alarms, changes in alarm contract formats, and a look at the future of the alarm industry. New chapters deal with the application of passive infrared sensors, wireless sensing devices, multiplex and other mediums for transmitting alarm signals, and new techniques for the installation, service, and supervision of sensors via application of microcomputer technology to alarm control circuits. Revisions cover significant advances in the areas of safe and vault construction and related new UL (Underwriters' Laboratories) standards as well as improvements in line security circuits.

New or improved criminal techniques as they relate to burglary and robbery are described with suggestions for reducing or eliminating vulnerability to these MOs (modus operandi). The author notes with some concern the increasing mobility of specialists in the burglary field and their opportunistic approach to weaknesses in alarm response procedures.

A look into the future of the alarm industry includes suggestions for reducing unnecessary alarms and predictions of new methods of signal transmission and their potential effect on the structure of the alarm industry. The alarm system of the future may well be fully redundant, operationally fail-safe, and supervised via satellite at a computerized central station a thousand miles from the protected premises.

Space-age sensing techniques, digital communicators, municipal ordinances, suburban and residential security requirements, and competition have effected a myriad of variations in the extent and the quality of alarm systems and services that may be considered for the protection of a given premises. A new chapter discusses the format of alarm system contracts that have evolved as a result of these changes to assist the subscriber and the alarm contractor to achieve agreements that will provide effective deterrents to burglary and robbery attack.

Finally, a security checklist has been added after the text section. This checklist is intended to assist the subscriber in improving his security against burglary, robbery, and theft and may be used by the alarm contractor to analyze a prospective subscriber's premises as to alarm system requirements or to evaluate existing systems to develop recommendations for improving such services.

Although the criminal must be acknowledged for providing us with many unhappy learning experiences, the author is deeply appreciative of the contributions to crime prevention and to this book provided by many experts from the security world, including law enforcement officers, former associates in the alarm industry, and corporate security directors. I would also like to express a special thank you to Mr. Gerald Van Dorn and Mr. James B. White; their expertise and dedication to crime prevention has been inspiring.

Thad L. Weber

ALARM SYSTEMS AND THEFT PREVENTION

Second Edition

1

Introduction

"B.T." (Before the Telephone)

Even within the alarm industry, few people are aware that the electric burglar alarm, invented in 1853, antedates the telephone (1876) and the electric light (1879). It was, in fact, virtually the earliest commercial application of electricity except for the telegraph, which was first demonstrated in 1844.

As a matter of fact, Edwin Holmes, founder of the New York City company that still bears his name, pioneered in the development of both the electric burglar alarm and the first telephone exchange. Holmes invented the first automatic telephone disconnect switch—the weight of the telephone speaker on its cradle disconnected the circuit, the same principle used today—and held many patents that formed the backbone of the telephone communications system. Professor Alexander Graham Bell, Thomas Edison, and other notable inventors came to him for advice.

PIONEERING IN ALARM INTRODUCTION

Holmes pioneered the commercial use of alarm and telephone systems under difficult conditions, not the least of which was the complete absence of manufacturers of electrical equipment. Holmes found it necessary to manufacture the world's first insulated electric wire conductor and to install his own connecting circuits (poles and wiring) between alarm-protected premises and his central office.

First Central Office

Holmes's first central electric protection offices, established in 1858 in both Boston and New York, soon served an impressive list of residential and banking customers, including the Bowery Bank, the Manufacturers' Bank, the Bank of Montreal, Equitable Life, Phelps Dodge and Company, John Jacob Astor, and Tiffany. In 1872 Holmes developed the electrical safe cabinet, providing jewelers and bankers with a protected safe enclosure to safeguard their safe and vault assets. This service became so popular that he was soon forced to relocate his New York central office nearer to the concentration of these customers.

First Telephone Office

In 1873 Alexander Graham Bell and his financial backers came to Holmes with a prototype of the telephone. At Holmes's suggestion, the facilities of the Holmes burglar alarm central office and the circuit wires connecting it to Holmes's customers were utilized to provide the first telephone intercommunication through a switchboard between two or more commercial premises miles apart. This practical demonstration was so successful that Holmes was asked to build the first commercial telephone exchange, which he completed in New York in May 1877. By August of that year, over 700 commercial phones were connected through the Holmes telephone exchange. At that time, the Bell Telephone Association, forerunner of the American Telephone & Telegraph Company (AT&T), was formed. Mr. Holmes was one of the first officers and directors of that company. He also became the first president and an original stockholder in the New York Bell Telephone Company and was instrumental in the company's success in establishing telephone service in the New York metropolitan area.

First Demonstration of Skilled Attack

From the memoirs of Mr. Holmes's son (E. T. Holmes, Jr.), entitled *A Wonderful Fifty Years* and published privately in 1917 by Atkins Press, we learn that as early as the turn of this century the equivalent of today's burning bar was available to the criminal underworld. During the primitive days of electricity, it was possible to develop a temperature of 5,000 degrees F using an electrical arc device that could be operated from an ordinary lighting circuit with the simple addition of a heavier fuse link. Since it requires only 700 degrees F to boil the toughest steel like water in a tea kettle, Holmes's electrical arc demonstration dramatically proved the ease with which a safe or vault could be penetrated—and sold his electric burglar alarm service to significant banking customers. Holmes demonstrated burning a 1½- to 2-inch hole in 12 inches of solid steel in 30 minutes or less. At the same time, he recognized the inevitability of progress in criminal attacks.

As Holmes prophetically put it in *A Wonderful Fifty Years*, "The whole history of bank burglary and vault building is competitive; and in the same manner that a new system is devised to protect armor plate, so the burglar finds or devises a new method of attack."

A CONTINUING CHALLENGE

In closing what he termed a successful 50 years, Holmes observed that the challenge to the security world, an industry older than telephone service, was to continue to improve its product and its service to prevent crime. Basic to Holmes's life were his forthrightness, his dedication to his business, and above all, his belief in the electric burglar alarm system. In March 1880, he sold his stock in AT&T for $100,000. Its worth today is incalculable, but Holmes held a firm conviction that "the burglar alarm industry held a greater potential than the telephone." *(A Wonderful Fifty Years)* Reflecting on this prediction in the cold light of crime today, on the significant growth of the security industry in the past 20 years, and on rising federal attention to crime prevention, it is not impossible that by the turn of this century the security industry may fulfill Holmes's firm belief, challenging in size and assets the great telephone communications industry.

While Holmes's projections for the future were optimistic, the security industry has grown over the years to be a vital element in economic progress throughout the nation, and crime prevention and deterrence have become important national problems.

As the following pages will illustrate, electric protective systems—alarm systems—despite their occasional vulnerability have made and will continue to make significant contributions toward the prevention of crime. These contributions, coupled with advances in the strength and resistance of mechanical barriers and with the unremitting vigilance of an alert business community, could win the battle against the criminal.

2

Basic Burglary

The Burglar as Specialist

Contrary to widely held opinion, the United States does not lead the world in all phases of crime. For example, Tokyo's rate of reported burglaries per capita exceeds that of New York or any other major U.S. city. However, the principal city with the *lowest* rate of reported holdup (robbery) attacks per capita is—you guessed it—Tokyo. To use armed force against an individual of one's own race and religion violates basic tenets of Oriental culture.

CRIMINAL SPECIALIZATION

While Western civilization does not reflect such an excellent deterrent to holdup, a significant difference still exists between the professionals of burglary and of robbery. Rarely do police records reveal criminals who are both robbers and burglars; the robber seldom has the finesse of the burglar, and the burglar rarely has the psychological makeup of the bandit. Indeed, the classic burglar disdains violence, does not like to be seen, and will rarely arm himself with anything more substantial than a screwdriver, a celluloid strip, or a bank calendar.

It is possible that external forces have contributed to this clear distinction between the two so-called professionals. Our society has ordained that the penalties be significantly different. The robber faces rather severe first-offense penalties. For example, the sentence for armed robbery in California is indeterminate, while in Texas, a conservative state, the sentence is 99 years or more.

LEGAL ADVANTAGES OF BURGLARY

Bad Luck Arrests

In contrast, a burglar captured with tools such as a screwdriver, a plastic bank calendar, a flashlight, or a small hammer will probably be able to fight his way through a number of bad luck arrests with no more on his record than breaking and entering (first offense, suspended sentence), unlawful entry (case dismissed), vagrancy, loitering, and intoxication. Of course, if this poor unfortunate is so inept as to be captured several times in rapid succession, he might suffer indignities such as a three-month sentence in the workhouse (suspended), six months in county jail, or—were he so foolish as to be captured in possession of a knife or gun—he might receive a one- to three-year sentence.

Low Apprehension Rate

Few burglars are so inept. The percentage of arrests in cases of burglary—as reported by law enforcement agencies, Underwriters' Laboratories (UL), and the Small Business Administration's *Report on Crime Against Small Business*—is typically 2 to 4 percent; fewer than 5 out of 100 instances of attack. In most cases the professional burglar plans his activities so well as to never be captured, though he may occasionally have to exit quickly and empty handed.

PROFESSIONAL VS. AMATEUR

The professional burglar is not to be confused with the amateur, particularly the addict who, pressed for daily cash and "under the influence," is unpredictable and can be dangerous. Amateurs, both addicts and opportunists, are responsible for the very great majority of instances of ordinary burglary. However, as experience and skills increase, so does the value of the "take," and the top professionals of burglary can be credited with the successful attacks against formidable targets, with the "scores" running into six and even seven figures.

ROLE OF ORGANIZED CRIME

For the most part, the professional burglar prefers to work alone or, where necessary, with a small group of trusted associates. Links with organized crime arise because of the necessity for realizing cash from the results of burglary through the disposal of the merchandise to a professional fence—often an arm of organized crime. While the burglary team includes its own specialists in planning, administration, communications, electronics, safe and vault construction (or destruction), transportation, and brute force, much of the "take" from these professional attacks is useless (unless they are directed at banks or cash proceeds) without a means of converting the loot into safe, ready cash. This need leads the professional burglar to the crime corporation and, in turn, puts him within the sphere of influence of organized crime. Professional burglars may not like the influence that organized crime enjoys over their activities, but—for reasons of health—they seldom argue these points with their contacts in the crime syndicate.

While the crime corporation shares in the profits from burglary (sometimes taking the major portion), organized crime is concerned with its public relations image and is therefore sensitive to the size and frequency of criminal activity in areas where it is dominant and to Justice Department and income tax investigations as well as ethnic labels. Syndicate elements seek a low profile and avoid publicity wherever possible. They recognize that major burglaries are front-page copy and an unfortunate reminder to John Q. Public that professional crime is all around. In most cities, organized crime does not willingly jeopardize its major income—from narcotics, gambling, and prostitution—for even a major share of a haul of diamonds.

Many legislators are proponents of legislation that would substantially increase the penalties for fencing stolen goods. The theory is sound. If the fence risks long-term imprisonment and treble civil damages, fencing could become a rare practice among those criminal elements whose wide-ranging connections make large-loss thefts profitable.

3

Sophisticated Burglary

Big Bank Burglary

In the burglary "league," any successful bank burglary[1] is considered "top drawer." Though some jewelry and fur burglaries represent higher dollar-loss figures, they don't offer the challenge, the immediate full-value cash product, or the prestige of successfully attacking one of the most important and sensitive responsibilities of law enforcement and security.

The rating scale of the denizens of the burglary world even recognizes the distinction in difficulty between attacks on branch banking locations and on a bank's main office—its highest and best protected risk.

BRANCH BANKS AND MODERN STORE CONSTRUCTION

A modern branch bank is usually located in a suburban or retail-residential environment with a lower crime rate and, not surprisingly, lighter police patrol service. Evening and weekend mobile patrol checks of the premises are infrequent, while the opportunities for police observation of suspicious characters loitering in the vicinity of the branch are rare.

Following World War II, as the banking industry followed the rapidly expanding growth in suburban areas, branch banking facilities were designed to conform to the lightweight construction adapted by retail stores similarly located. During that period, it was not unusual for branch banks to have vaults constructed of steel plate and cinder or gypsum block rather than reinforced concrete. During the 1960s and early 1970s, such structures were singled out for burglary attack. As a result, federal regulations governing banking security were amended in 1976 to require as a minimum standard that bank vault walls, floors, and ceilings contain 12 or more inches of reinforced concrete and be equipped with steel vault doors at least 3½ inches thick.

[1] Bank *burglary*, the breaking and entering of the premises when closed, is to be distinguished from bank *robbery*, which does not carry the same underworld prestige, except in the rare instance of a large "haul" by a gang of professionals.

However, lightweight vaults in existence at the time the regulations were upgraded were, by law, "grandfathered" and some remain in use today. One may even find (as substitutes for vaults) freestanding burglary-resistant safes and, occasionally, only a fire-resistant safe, a security weakness almost common in stores and offices.

As a matter of fact, in safes fire resistance and burglary resistance are antithetical; that is, a fire-resistant safe is relatively easy to burglarize, while a burglary-resistant safe cannot usually protect its contents from the heat of a serious fire. Thus, when the need to protect safe contents from both fire and burglary is recognized, it has been common practice to install a burglary-resistant steel strongbox inside a fire-resistant safe. Only in recent years has the UL approved the listing of a safe featuring both fire- and burglary-resistant qualities, the latter at a relatively low burglary-resistance level, however.

Lower physical security at the branch bank was originally balanced by banking policies and controls that were expected to maintain lower cash assets on hand, thus reducing the loss risk and consequently lessening the need for security. However, when new dollar volumes, cash assets, and safety deposit rentals soar beyond the planning for the branch location, bank directors smile—and sometimes fail to recognize the increased risk. Suburban and branch stores enjoying booming business experience a parallel increase in cash, stock, and risk.

MAIN BANKS—THE FORTRESS

As a target for burglary, the main banking office of a major financial institution is very different from the shopping center branch bank. First, the main bank with its related offices is usually located in a downtown business district where a significantly higher crime rate draws a concentration of police patrols from a metropolitan police force, offering skilled investigation and other resources not readily available in suburban communities.

Further, the bank structure is usually imposing, often having massive window grilles and heavy entrance doors. The building is a multi-story monument to security, standing well away from its neighbors. This fortress image was once believed to be important in attracting customer deposits, a concept now out of style. An image of friendliness and accessibility is the current vogue—and an admitted factor in bank robbery. Yesterday's main banking location did not house other business tenants, and even today the bank's floors are designed to be well secured during closed hours.

Main banking offices house one or more massive steel-reinforced concrete vaults, each complete with an eye-filling vault door with time and combination locks securing its seven inches or more of attack-resistant steel and space-age alloys—a security masterpiece in burnished steel. The vault door is still often placed as an architectural focal point to stress the security of customers' assets.

The professional burglar regards the assets in the main vault of the main banking office as the "jewel in the eye of the tiger"! The following case is primarily valuable as an example of highly skilled professional burglary attack using sophisticated methods. Equal and identical skills, organization, and techniques have been evidenced in burglary attacks against a wide variety of high risks.

A CASE OF MAIN BANK BURGLARY

Tom was first contacted some six weeks before the target date for the burglary. A member in good standing of an elite burglary ring, with a record of successful participation in similar burglary attacks, he was asked to survey ("case") a fortresslike main vault of a major bank in a city of approximately 250,000 population.

The street-level bank vault was constructed of 24-inch steel-reinforced concrete; ¾-inch steel lining and ½-inch steel plate covering the entire vault exterior added to the structure's physical security. When locked, the vault was sealed by a rugged torch-resistant, drill-resistant, explosives-resistant vault door 10 inches thick and equipped with dual combinations, relocking devices, time locks, and other approved vault door security design features.

It was a dual-purpose vault safeguarding both the bank's funds and 700 safe deposit boxes rented by bank customers. The safe deposit boxes contained cash, securities (some negotiable, some not), valuable jewelry, and irreplaceable items of indeterminate value.

Tom was briefed by the gang's ringleaders. The basic planning that preceded his invitation to participate had been developed by review of the published assets of the institution and careful observation of the bank's security policies and cash patterns. This examination indicated the "jackpot" should be at least $1.5 million cash, plus another $2 million or more in proceeds from the safe deposit boxes. This would make it a record burglary haul and offered a strong incentive for tackling the formidable vault and its sophisticated alarm system.

Planning

The preparatory planning had involved several members of the gang with skills for the following:

- Selection of likely targets;
- Detailed study of the physical plant, security procedures, and alarm

systems to determine ways and means of defeating the total security system;
- Identification of alternative points of entry and exit from the location;
- Development of getaway routes;
- Timing, including the day of the week and the hour of the day. Attack timing (as we shall see in this and other skilled attacks) is often split-second in nature and is essential to the success of the operation;
- Selection, from a large acquaintance of experienced criminals, of the best attack team for the particular target;
- Communications for use before, during, and after the attack;
- Administration, including the pre-attack investment in equipment (for both the electronic and the physical assault), living and travel expenses, and division of profits.

While some of these points may appear to border on melodrama, one must remember that professional burglars are rarely unknown to law enforcement officials. Quarrels over expenses and the division of profits afford informants and, subsequently, police with the information and evidence necessary to reconstruct the crime. As a result, the professionals of the criminal world recognize the necessity for careful selection of team members and for clear-cut policies that will enable the gang to work together confidently, successfully, and harmoniously.

The Specialist

Tom was invited to participate because of his long-standing record of reliability in two areas of specialization vital to this specific burglary attack. First, Tom was skilled in oxyacetylene torch attack against the variety of steel alloys that may be encountered in a vault door. Tom had a cataloglike memory of the internal design of safe and vault doors by leading manufacturers and was thoroughly familiar with safe and vault construction.

If the attack were to take place at all, however, Tom's other skill, making keys by impression, would be essential since the gang needed a key to the street door that enters onto the banking floor. Since this bank entrance was on a heavily traveled avenue within the close observation of frequent police patrols, lock picking to defeat the door lock cylinder was too dangerous because the length of time required to pick a lock varies from minutes to hours. The prolonged presence of a "pick man" at the bank entrance door might be suspicious to passersby and reported to the police.

There was an even more compelling need for a key to this entrance door: the scope and complexity of this burglary would require a number of visits to the banking floor prior to "B-Day" in order to obtain firsthand information on the alarm system and the vault construction. This necessity also ruled out the pick-lock approach; to pick the lock repeatedly under tense conditions, overlooked by traffic and police patrols, would be taking too great a chance.

A key made by impression, however, would permit frequent, quick entries to the banking premises. The impression method had one other advantage: there was little danger of damage to the entrance door lock. Lock picking, in contrast, sometimes damages cylinder pins, necessitating an unexpected change in lock cylinders, and, in any event, leaves microscopic evidence of the picking.

On-Site Inspection

Tom met frequently with the gang leaders to familiarize himself with the bank's layout and the methods to be employed in the actual attack operation. He visited the banking institution during open hours, both alone and in the company of the gang's leader, to satisfy himself that conditions for the attack were favorable—that the odds for success were heavily in favor of the burglars. Most important, he sought sure alternate means of escape in the event something went wrong and police or alarm system supervisors detected either the burglary in progress or trouble with the alarm system at the banking site. Tom knew either signal would bring an armed response.

These visits were not easily accomplished. While the gang members were not residents of the city in which the attack was to be made, their descriptions and their "profession" were known to local police. To avoid being identified while reconnoitering, gang members used a number of different automobiles for their visits to the city. While there they also changed license plates regularly to avoid positive identification in the event they were noted as suspicious persons. On each visit they wore different clothing and traveled in and out of the city as quickly as possible. When it was necessary to remain overnight, they varied motel locations with each visit, never congregating at a single place.

The making of a key for the entrance door lock cylinder did not prove to be an easy task. Tom was forced to visit the entrance door a number of times to take impressions and had to cut or modify several keys. Some fifteen visits to the door were required to produce a key that readily operated the lock.

Casing the Alarm System

Once the key was ready, the most skilled phase of the attack commenced. This phase required the minute and knowledgeable examination of telephone alarm line circuit wiring, the alarm system, and the related protective alarm devices to determine the approach necessary to compromise electrically the ability of the alarm system to signal the burglary attack. For this purpose the leaders added Dick to their entourage.

Dick was a true specialist, one of the few professional burglars who possesses the knowledge and skill necessary to defeat the central station alarm system. Once the alarm system was neutralized, the only barrier to their success would be the physical strength of the vault. Dick's experience was well known to the gang; indeed, his skills had been essential to them in a number of similar and successful attacks against highly sophisticated central station alarm systems.

The gang began their surreptitious entries into the bank about a week before the scheduled attack date. Initial visits to the premises were made to determine the exact nature and type of alarm system in use. Dick established that the bank vault was protected by a complete sound-sensitive electric protective circuit recognized by insurance authorities as one of the highest forms of vault alarm protection available. The sensors within the vault were capable of signaling an alarm from a drill and hammer attack before any significant penetration could be made into the vault. In addition, heat detection devices and vault door alarm circuitry would detect a torch or tool attack against the vault door itself. The alarm control instruments and associated power supplies were wired, in accordance with recognized standards, to register an alarm in the event of any known method of attack against the alarm circuit wiring at or between the control unit and the vault sensors.

Alarm Attack

Standard circuit security requirements for such an alarm system afford substantial resistance to attack. Indeed, thousands of similar systems had deterred and detected every attack by professional burglars for 50 years or more. Not until late 1965 was an instance of underworld defeat of such an alarm system recorded in the United States.

In the case under consideration here, the alarm serving the bank was connected via a high-security[2] direct-line telephone circuit running from the control instrument to the offices of a central station alarm company. This link was additionally defended by a special line security device protecting the alarm system at the telephone circuit terminal box, vulnerable since 1965.

Direct-Line Vulnerability

Let's digress for a moment to discuss line security and the vulnerability that has been found to exist in conventional direct-line alarm systems. The alarm systems designed for high-risk vaults afford a virtually "crook-proof"

[2] "High security" is used in the relative sense; a direct line is high security by comparison to the less expensive, party-line (McCulloh) central alarm circuit.

circuitry as far as the security of the sensors and the wiring on or in the vault are concerned. However, since local bells will not always frighten the burglar away or bring police response in time to prevent a loss, it is necessary to monitor (supervise) the alarm system. To accomplish this, the vault protection devices are connected via the alarm system control instrument to a remote supervisory location (a central station) monitored 24 hours a day, 7 days a week.

Exclusive, unshared telephone circuits are used to link the alarm system to the central station. These telephone circuits consist of two or more wires connected to the alarm system control instrument at the banking location. From there they run exposed on the exterior walls and ceilings or in shafts or conduits provided for such purposes to a telephone wiring distribution point (telephone terminal box) located inside the building or (in some unfortunate instances) mounted on the exterior of the building. Alarm system telephone connections are the same as for commercial telephone circuits, and the telephone alarm is carried by conventional underground or overhead telephone cables through the number of telephone company central offices necessary to reach the central station alarm company.

Once a telephone terminal junction box having alarm line connections is located and accessed, the "electronic burglar" has certain means to distinguish the burglar alarm system lines from commercial telephone circuits. Even though a burglar will need time and access to a building to trace wiring patterns, many commercial buildings neither are properly secured at night nor maintain controlled access and identification procedures during the day.

Labeled Wiring

In many locations, telephone company practices unwittingly assist the burglars. Standard operating procedure provides for the installation of red insulating sleeves (rubber, bakelite, or plastic material) as covers over alarm circuit terminal posts. This is done to reduce the chance of unnecessary alarms by telephone repairmen or installers accidentally disconnecting, shorting, or grounding the alarm circuit.

In other instances, overzealous telephone company installers have further simplified the burglar's task by hanging durable white linen tags on alarm circuit wires at the telephone terminal boxes. On these are written convenient declarations such as "XYZ Alarm Company circuit—Jones Company silver vault—second floor, east wall." These road maps are often invaluable to the burglar since they solve the problem presented when several alarm circuits, all with identical electrical characteristics, run through one telephone terminal box. Without tags, considerably more time is required to identify the alarm circuits protecting the target safe or vault, and it would be necessary to create a number of false alarms in order to identify the correct circuit by observing police and alarm company guard response. Moreover, a hunt-and-peck method is considered unhelpful since bank security supervisors should react to a sudden flurry of false alarms from normally trouble-free safe or vault alarm systems by increasing security measures and improving alarm response procedures.

Simulation Key to Direct-Line Attack

Having located the correct telephone circuit, the electronic burglar uses meters and other test equipment to measure the electrical characteristics of the alarm line circuit and the changes that occur when central station personnel perform periodic tests from the central office of the telephone circuits and the alarm control instrument, sometimes testing individual protective devices as well.

Such tests are made by central station personnel in order to detect skilled attacks or other tampering with the alarm system. In a semiskilled attack the alarm company may detect a lack of response or an incorrect response from the protected premises. In a highly skilled attack, however, the burglar measures the changing electrical characteristics of the correct test response and simulates these when the test is performed from the central station.

Despite the difficulty of simulation, for over five years skilled electronic burglars have occasionally been able to defeat such central-station-tested alarm systems. While it is impossible to state definitely the frequency of success, known cases indicate that attackers fail in as many as five of seven attempts to defeat direct-line central station alarm systems.

Pre-attack Electronic Preparations

Dick knew he must be able to respond quickly to the central station's tests at irregular intervals, but this he had done successfully in earlier defeats of well-operated central station direct-line alarm systems. True, he had made a mistake or two on some jobs, but then circuit characteristics and timing are not easily simulated with the necessary accuracy; just a slight electrical variation or a brief delay in the test response will cause an alarm signal at the central office.

In this case Dick faced an additional challenge. The main vault's alarm system had been upgraded with *line security* that produces additional, difficult-to-simulate electrical impulses, providing greater protection against compromise by increasing the extent and difficulty of simulation required (see Chapter 16).

Advance planning and visits to the bank's basement utility areas had enabled the gang to ascertain that line security equipment did indeed protect these telephone alarm line circuits. Fortunately for the gang, Dick had previous experience in attempting to defeat such systems and, in his home workshop, had been successful in substituting signal-generating devices that accurately simulated the signals produced by this particular type of line security equipment.

Nevertheless, this compromise could not be performed with certainty on a single try. Dick needed to install his compromise equipment on the alarm system's telephone circuit and practice with it. He needed to learn the changes in circuit characteristics that occurred when a remote test was performed by the central station, the timing of such testing (if indeed the central station followed any set pattern), and the voltage variations that might occur over a 24- to 48-hour period.

Dick knew that some necessary alteration of the alarm circuit wiring at the telephone terminal box would be permanent and, at the very least, would arouse the curiosity of telephone company or alarm company personnel should they visit the basement telephone terminal box in the days preceding the actual attack. Further, the bulk and nature of the compromise equipment would be obvious if it were installed anywhere in the vicinity of the telephone terminal box.

But Dick was equal to the challenge. On B-Day-minus-four, he entered the bank building with the gang's key and, together with his apprentices, proceeded to the basement telephone terminal box and the previously identified telephone circuits connecting the bank's main vault alarm to the alarm company's central station. From there, he proceeded to the roof of the bank building in order to install a long extension cable through an unused chimney flue from the roof to the basement. This cable he connected into the vault's telephone alarm line circuits. The roof end of the cable extended across to the accessible roof of an adjacent vacant commercial building. From there the cable ran through a roof skylight and down a stairwell to a location on the first floor of the unoccupied building.

The Burglary Command Post

Dick had now established an electronic command post close by, safely out of the way, in a building that offered additional escape routes. Dick was careful to use weatherproof insulated cable and to install it with tender loving care since any break or ground in this cable would be fatal to his compromise operations.[3]

With the cable connecting the compromise equipment at the command post with the vault's alarm line circuit, Dick was now in a position to monitor the circuit characteristics and the periodic central station tests remotely and safely. In a few days he was able to simulate the correct response to all tests. The alarm system was defeated; his work successful.

---

[3] A similar sophisticated attack in New York was discovered when rain short-circuited a cable.

Dick also installed a second concealed cable over the same route, this time to the main banking floor, to provide communications with the gang at work in the bank building. This was important since the electronic command post in the vacant building would be monitoring police radio receivers, and warnings would have to be communicated to the attackers at the vault. The communications cable provided a link secure against the gang's being accidentally overheard.

During the nights preceding the actual attack, Dick's compromise system was occasionally misoperated in order to create alarm signals; the gang wanted to observe the response time and activities of alarm company agents and the police. Bold, daring, artful, and well organized, this gang operated with the confidence and precision of a smoothly functioning business organization.

The gang was fortunate in that the telephone terminal box was located in a rarely used, unchecked area of the bank building basement. To determine whether anyone visited this area, Dick simply placed a slip of white paper in the jamb of the door leading to the telephone equipment room. On his return visits, Dick checked to see that the white paper was still in place. If it had been missing, he would know someone had entered the telephone equipment room in the preceding period. No one did. Dick's final task was to set up and test two-way hand-held radio equipment to be used for communications between the next-door command post and the gang's outside lookout.

Logistics of the Physical Attack

The delivery of the heavy-duty equipment necessary for the physical attack on the vault presented a problem. The "bill of materials" prepared by Tom, the torch expert, called for a large and heavy oxygen tank and an equally bulky acetylene gas tank, fuel necessary for burning through the vault door or through the steel surrounding and lining the concrete vault.

The torch attack also required an assembly of burning torches, a welder's mask, insulated gloves, a supply of thermic lances (also called "burning bars"),[4] oxyacetylene tank gauges, and other related items. In addition, the planning required forcible entry tools such as sledgehammers, jimmies, heavy-duty electric drills, a large supply of carbide-tip drill bits, chisels, punches, and hand tools. The checklist also provided for large canvas covers to hang from the ceiling outside the vault (to prevent observation of the burning from the exterior of the premises) and an endoscopic microscope (to view the interior of the vault through a burned or drilled hole).

So much equipment would require a small truck or van, and the delivery

[4] Actually, the thermic lance rods were brought along as reserve burning power, and Tom did not expect to have to use this equipment.

of such unusual gear through a main entrance on a main thoroughfare could arouse the suspicions of even the usually unobservant pedestrian traffic. Delivery of the equipment without detection would seem to be at least a very risky proposition and at best problematical. However, again this well-organized gang displayed strength in planning and ingenuity; they took a tip from Edgar Allan Poe and did the obvious. They established B-Day-minus-one as the delivery date and the late hours of the night marking the end of a traditional pre-Lenten carnival as the time. While revelers moved tipsily and wearily through the crowded streets towards a Sunday morning hangover, "delivery men" pulled up to the front entrance of the bank in a small truck, and five men nonchalantly carried the equipment into the bank. No passersby saw anything suspicious.

With the vault alarm system compromised, the heavy-duty equipment in place, and the vault shielded from view, the attack team leaders, Tom and Harry, were joined by the other three members of the assault group, physically strong individuals with prior experience in force attacks against safes, safe deposit boxes, and vaults. While there were many hours of hard labor ahead of all of them, the rewards would be great.

Daylight Attack

The actual assault was timed for early Sunday morning, when daylight would minimize the possibility that the torches' distinctive blue light would be seen by passersby. The preceding night of Saturday/Sunday was spent digging an escape tunnel through the wall separating the basements of the bank and the adjoining vacant building where Dick's electronics command and communications post was located. This tunnel proved more difficult to accomplish than original planning had indicated, and when dawn broke the tunnel was still incomplete. The gang made the decision to proceed with the vault attack even though the escape tunnel planned would not be available. When the automobile lookout had arrived and established himself at the appointed location near the bank building, the command post reported all conditions were "go," and the vault attack began.

HOW DID IT HAPPEN?

Since our objectives are to deter and prevent crime, the events that followed are not particularly relevant. Readers familiar with the case will know the ending, while others may conjecture that the vault door was strong enough to withstand this torch and tool attack and wonder how such a well-organized gang could have committed so monumental a blunder as to overestimate their ability to penetrate the vault structure.

Other alternative endings include the successful penetration of the vault, the theft of the assets, and an unsolved crime or that some unforeseen event, perhaps following the completion of the burglary, undid the gang's best efforts. *What is vitally important to readers is the vulnerability that set the stage for this attack.*

What, in your opinion, were the significant weaknesses in the banking structure, the premises surrounding the vault, the alarm system, and the security procedures related to the defense of these assets? How would you have reduced these vulnerabilities or strengthened the defenses to a level where the attack would have stood little or no chance of success? What might the police or the alarm service contractor have done to prevent this attack? Could this happen to you tomorrow? *Why not take a moment and jot down your points of view before you read on.*

MISSING DETERRENTS

There were a number of ways in which this attack could have been prevented. *Deterred* would be a better word since the presence of several practical defenses would have persuaded the gang's advance scouts that this bank vault was not the best target for them, and the attack would never have occurred.

Discarding costly and therefore commercially unacceptable ideas such as an even stronger vault structure or a 24-hour guard force on the premises, let's begin by agreeing that—since telephone lines entered the building from an underground source and fed directly into the basement and the cable was properly shielded against physical attack—motion-detection alarm devices protecting the interior would have signaled the earliest entry of the gang, preventing their access to the telephone terminal box. (A simple perimeter alarm system consisting of alarm contact devices on accessible doors and windows would not have been adequate against an attack this sophisticated.)

Other steps that would have discouraged, if not prevented, advance scouting include tighter security precautions during business hours to prevent access by unauthorized persons to any area other than the customer banking floor. A highly pick-resistant lock cylinder in the building entrance lock also would have made it more difficult, if not impossible, for the gang to make the necessary surreptitious advance visits to the premises during closed periods. Pick-resistant cylinders are less susceptible, if not immune, to impressioning.

The vulnerability of telephone circuits could have been reduced by the elimination of identifying tags and insulating sleeves, by the installation of alarm devices on the telephone terminal box and in the area immediately surrounding it, and by additional high line security equipment. While alarm contractors do not claim that high line security devices make central-station-reporting alarm systems invulnerable to skilled attack (line security equipment can only make the compromise attempt much more difficult), there are specific forms of pseudorandom direct-line and multiplex line security circuits in use today that have been attacked but not defeated.

THE ECONOMICS OF PROTECTION

While the combination of intruder motion-detection equipment and improved line security would have deterred or spoiled this attack, other questions arise: How expensive are such systems? Can they be defeated? Are there other considerations? We answer some questions concerning the defeat of motion-detection equipment in Chapter 7.

On the one hand, installation of motion-detection equipment throughout a banking floor and in vulnerable basement areas would represent a fairly substantial installation and service investment. On the other hand, in this case, partial motion-detection protection could have provided coverage around the vault exterior and in the area where vital telephone lines linking the alarm control instrument to the basement terminal box were exposed.

In addition to motion-detection equipment in the area around the vault, consideration could also have been given to the installation of combustion detection devices outside the vault to detect the torch attack early in the attempt rather than after the vault was pierced. The combustion detection devices could have been connected to a separate alarm circuit or an outside bell alarm. If this step had been taken, there is a strong possibility that efforts to compromise the vault system might have overlooked the separate system serving the combustion detection devices or that the process of compromising all systems simultaneously—double line security plus the separate circuit—might have proved too difficult for Dick's skills.

In recent years, many users of high-risk alarms have adopted policies requiring the use of two separate central monitoring stations, each providing high line security to the effective protection of safes and vaults. This strategy has proven highly successful in deterring or detecting compromise burglary attempts.

THE GEOGRAPHY OF PROTECTION

One aspect of this situation was unusual. The availability of the vacant adjoining building made the bank vault far more attractive and vulnerable as a target. When considering the security of one's own premises it is a good idea to determine whether the security of an adjoining structure is satisfactory or whether its weaknesses might be increasing one's own vulnerability to burglary attack.

In passing, we might also note that something can and should be done to improve the security of police radio communications regarding burglar alarms. Provisions can be made for coded transmissions that do not identify the alarm system in trouble and thus do not alert the burglar to the fact that the police are on their way.

LESSONS FOR THE SECURITY-RESPONSIBLE EXECUTIVE

There are two other lessons to be learned from this story. First, this was a well-organized, professional, skilled attack by a criminal corporation. They did almost everything right. They planned well and developed accurate critical timing. However, when a minor problem (the wall that resisted escape route tunneling) was encountered and a command decision was necessary—whether to go ahead, delay, postpone, or abandon the attack—the extraordinary profit to be gained was an overriding factor in the decision to sacrifice the burglar's most important requirement: a sure escape route.

This decision is paralleled every day in corporate business operations, where decisions are so often based on short-term profits rather than on sound, long-term security. Persons with the security responsibility have the task of driving home, with as much vigor, enthusiasm, and persuasiveness as they can muster, the argument for enough security to prevent the major catastrophe and the information necessary to ensure that management knows the risks involved in shortcuts in security.

There is a second moral to this story. No one person can be expert in all phases of security at all times. Even the underworld corporation employs specialists to achieve maximum performance in each phase of each planned attack. Take a tip from the professional criminals, and periodically seek the advice of specialists to make sure you are kept informed of current methods of attack and of the most effective methods for deterring such attacks.

4

Burglary Through Unprotected Points

Think Like an Agile Thief

The Los Angeles Zoo is truly a marvelous sight. The animals enjoy comforts seldom found in captivity and, more important, are protected from the human animal who delights in visiting their home. Great planning and understanding went into the development of the zoo—natural landscape, craggy terrain, comfortable caves, clear water, and moats surround and protect the inhabitants. The intent is to permit the larger animals a sense of freedom, while still preventing their escape.

But is this always the case? Suppose that one fine day, as Mama Rhino lay comfortably warm in the bright sunlight, she gazed soulfully across the waterless moat and said to Papa Rhino, "You know, this is a great life—no fear, no worry about food, ideal weather—but wouldn't it be nice to just once take a stroll around the park? Pity they won't let us out for a walk." What if Papa Rhino thought briefly and quietly said, "Well, then, if you'd like to take a stroll, I'll arrange it." Moving carefully into the shallow end of the moat in front of his mate, he might stand, forming a natural bridge between the level of the pit and the outer edge of the moat. "Walk across," he might smile, and Mama could tiptoe gently across Papa's back, step gingerly onto the turf beyond, and nuzzle up against the most surprised zookeeper in Los Angeles. Of course, this can't happen; animals are not capable of such intelligence. Nevertheless, the zoo anchors the logs that form caves for the bears and the chimps.

The human animal certainly recognizes subtle opportunities, although he usually directs his ingenuity toward getting in rather than getting out. What you and I would consider to be inaccessible openings into areas containing valuable merchandise become a challenge and an opportunity to ingenious thieves.

WHAT IS INACCESSIBLE?

For example, you would think windows several stories above street level or adjoining rooftops are inaccessible, right? A long ladder is needed to reach these windows legitimately. Nevertheless, an agile thief can gain access by many ways. Only a few examples follow:

1. The offset or ledge, which need merely be wide enough to permit a foothold or a handhold, can be used by the rope burglar who descends from the window of an unprotected premises a floor above or from the always accessible roof structure, attaching his rope to beams or standpipes.
2. Unprotected windows can be entered from an adjacent premises. One need only remember the agility with which the efficient window washer uses his equipment to move from window to window outside the building.
3. A construction elevator incorporated in temporary scaffolding and unprotected during the closed period requires only a little knowledge of motors and ropes and relatively appropriate garb to use this means to ascend or descend to the chosen floor.
4. How about reaching that third-story window from the roof of a truck trailer "innocently" parked in the alley?
5. Steeplejacks and daredevils have ascended the exterior of the World Trade Center with nothing but their agility and the small hand- and footholds provided by the masonry and brick structure. But what if he slips? An Indian "rigger" once told me a basic truth: It hurts just as much to fall 25 feet as it does to fall 25 stories.
6. Boards and ladders may be laid across from unprotected windows or nearby buildings or from fire escapes adjacent to unprotected windows and fire exits.

Undetected Exit and Entry

These same supposedly inaccessible—and unprotected—windows and other openings can also be used to exit without triggering an alarm signal, permitting the hide-in intruder to escape without detection. True, these are not easy exits for the thief carrying a heavy load of loot, but they are quite convenient when small, lightweight, valuable merchandise is involved. And when both entry and exit go undetected, the thief can chalk up a good prospect for a return visit.

Similarly, these exits may also be used as escape routes by the smash-and-run attacker who knows responding police and alarm company agents will be approaching by elevator or stairway.

Shafts, Ducts, Disused Doors, Crawlspaces, Trap Doors, New Adjacencies

What other unprotected openings may lead to your premises? How about an elevator shaft, a dumbwaiter, an old chimney flue, or air conditioner ducts?

Are the openings between blades of that big roof fan large enough to permit a skinny fellow to crawl through?

Does that modern drop ceiling hide between it and the real ceiling a crawlspace connecting your premises with an unprotected tenancy?

Is that wall between you and the premises of your neighbor solid, or is there a concealed opening? These forgotten openings are also used to ship goods illegally during the open-for-business period.

Did you find a trap door in the floor or in the ceiling of a closet?

Have you re-evaluated your accessibility since that new building rose several feet away?

SOLUTIONS DIFFER

What needs to be done about these possibilities depends upon the nature of your business, your insurance requirements, your location, and your degree of optimism. In most instances, openings can readily be either permanently sealed or secured with good pick-resistant locking devices and protected with appropriate alarm devices. Where the openings serve no purpose and no fire safety ordinances are involved, it is most economical to seal these openings permanently. The materials used to block the opening should be of sufficient strength to deter forced entry or exit and should be installed with mortar or with fasteners that, unlike conventional screws, cannot be removed.

Only a meticulous search and survey will reveal the number and types of unprotected accessible openings in an occupancy. And in case you're concerned as to what you may have missed in your premises, why not spend an hour or two at the Los Angeles Zoo? Those stacked logs may provide you with another clue. Don't you think it's time that you began to think like an agile thief?

5

Underwriters' Laboratories

UL—What Does It Really Stand For?

In 1972, the author accepted an appointment to the Burglary Protection Council of the Underwriters' Laboratories (UL). This invitation was one of several extended to persons having no direct commercial interest in the activities of the Burglary Protection Council, a measure taken to broaden the interests represented by the council. The reader is assured that this appointment does not prejudice the author's outlook concerning UL's contribution to the prevention of burglary, robbery, and theft. This chapter is written to assist the reader in a better understanding of the role of UL in the overall prevention of crime.

ORIGIN OF UL

UL was founded in 1894, immediately following the introduction of Edison's electric light at the Columbian Exposition. UL's founder, William H. Merrill, recognized that behind the glitter and excitement of the electric light lurked several dangers. Fire, smoke, explosion, and electric shock were hazards that could snuff out this promising light.

Merrill set out to develop effective safety standards for electrical equipment. His efforts soon interested those manufacturers who faced competitors marketing cheap, often unsafe equipment to an uninformed public. When his tests uncovered serious fire and shock hazards, manufacturers quickly recognized the benefits that standards and testing facilities offered them as well as the public. Today, UL's slogan is still "Testing for Public Safety."

Merrill's program incorporated both standards for laboratory testing and quality-control inspection of manufactured products at the factory, and this too continues today. Merrill's fire and shock prevention standards and testing rapidly expanded, and his work was soon sponsored by the National Board of Fire Underwriters. By 1901 the company, then known as Underwriters' Laboratories, Inc., had expanded beyond electrical equipment and was testing products such as fuel-consuming heaters, fire extinguishers, and building construction materials.

Today UL is an independent nonprofit service corporation employing

3,000 people, operating four test facilities, and exercising testing and inspection expertise in the fields of electrical, accident, and burglary prevention equipment; fire- and burglary-signaling systems; fire-extinguishing devices and systems, building materials, gas and oil equipment, chemical products and processes, and X-ray and other medical and dental electrical equipment. UL derives its revenue from a wide range of industry (over 10,000 manufacturers and government bodies) by means of charges for testing and inspection services.

UL SERVICES

UL is frequently and erroneously thought of as a research and development laboratory. It is not, though suggestions made by UL engineers often enable the manufacturer to improve an existing product. Nevertheless, UL's function is to apply its existing safety and testing standards to the product submitted by the manufacturer for listing. Thus, it is the alarm industry, not UL, to which we must look for new and improved devices and systems in the burglary-, fire-, and security-signaling field.

It is important to understand that the UL label on a product usually indicates its design, and the manufactured item itself, meet certain UL standards. In order to meet criteria for alarm system certification, protective devices, control units, circuitry, and so on must in addition meet specific UL burglary prevention and detection standards. The mere presence of a UL label on a component (such as a power cord, plug, transformer, and so forth) of a burglary alarm system or holdup alarm system does not necessarily mean that the alarm system is or can be a UL-certified system meeting crime prevention standards.

The Burglary Protection and Signaling Department of UL compiles Field Service Records that reflect in some measure the experience record of UL-certified systems in burglary attack. However, these records solely concern the performance of some 75,000 certified alarm systems (of the estimated millions of U.S. alarm systems in service) and is dependent upon the voluntary submission of experience reports by UL-listed local and central station alarm service companies.

These voluntary reports of performance by UL-certified systems indicated that criminals attacked approximately one in sixteen of these systems then in use. The UL report cannot accurately reflect the success of these attacks since reports of losses are often vague or, for one reason or another, omitted from contractors' reports. Further, UL evaluates the alarm system in terms of detection of the attack rather than the prevention of loss since there must be adequate physical deterrents to prevent most losses.

Nevertheless, since these UL-certificated alarms protect the country's leading high-risk industries, even a small incidence of success in these attacks must reflect millions of dollars in losses to crime. The most frequent targets of burglary attack in recent years analyzed were men's clothing, jewelry, liquor, appliances, money,[1] drugs, women's clothing, electronic devices, food, automobile accessories, and tools and hardware. Others near the top included camera and optical goods, tobacco, furs, office machines, guns, and sporting equipment.

Although UL's Field Service Records do not provide loss figures, recent reports prepared in the '70s mention attack methods that reflect the advance of the criminal's ability to defeat or circumvent the UL-certified systems. Included are telephone line tampering, phone line compromise, failure of motion detection devices, interior devices avoided, tampering with and defeating bell housings and alarm system control units, lock-ins, "jump-outs" (compromise of individual door contacts, lacing, or foil), kidnappings, and so on.

THE CASE FOR PROGRESS

While UL-certified alarm systems afford substantially better protection than unlisted systems, the experience of these certified systems largely determines the experience of the insurance industry. Since it is the insurance industry that effectively dictates to its risks the extent of the security to be provided, including and in particular UL-certified alarm systems, the parallel is hardly surprising.

A reasonable degree of change in the crime economy is long overdue. Improved security (safes, vaults, building structures, alarm systems, and security procedures), whether offset in part or in full by lower insurance premiums, would reduce crime losses and benefit the user, the economy, the gross national product, tax revenues, and the public. Any genuine setback to the crime industry dissuades individuals from seeking employment in that field and persuades some of those now engaged in criminal activity into early retirement.

This brings us to the crux of the matter: Can we continue to base our security on insurers' after-the-fact recommendations, derived from weaknesses already exploited by the underworld? Or should some body—UL, the alarm industry, or the federal government—accept the responsibility for research and development of more effective security systems?

Clearly, UL cannot be considered at fault in this. UL performs very well in its function, which is the testing of alarm components and systems against its standards and the inspection of field installations, manufacturing processes, and alarm company operations. It is the insurance industry that has lagged.

In practice, the insurance industry raises its security sights in response

---

[1] UL records indicate less than 25 percent of bank alarm systems are certified. Since banking institutions are historically insured against burglary and robbery losses under a broad blanket bond policy for which underwriters do not require UL certificates as a condition, most bank alarm system installations are not covered by certificates.

to an increase in pay-outs covering theft losses. However, their experience lags behind the actual events by one to two years. In a rising crime era, this produces too-little-too-late security measures. Indeed, some people contend that it is not in the best interest of the insurance industry to take bold, progressive leadership toward security systems capable of sharply reducing criminal attack and the attendant insurance claim pay-outs. After all, they contend, a risk whose defenses against loss are statistically certain to be effective hardly needs insurance or, at best, needs only insurance against catastrophic loss.

Actually, UL is best equipped and experienced for the task of developing improved security systems and procedures. For example, in recent years, insurers have required high risks to use burglary-resistant safes and to construct bank-type vaults. This demand has led to a vigorous UL testing program applicable to safes, vault doors, and materials used for vault wall construction. The UL rating levels were expanded and toughened. Many domestic and international manufacturers not surprisingly have improved their design and obtained UL listings for their products. Given such means and incentive (through assistance from industry or government), UL could quickly contribute to the advance of security at all levels. However, it is unlikely that current government programs, set up to establish separate standards and competitive (to UL) testing facilities, will appreciably change the security picture.

Why hasn't UL taken this initiative independently? Few alarm contractors or security equipment manufacturers would participate in the cost of developing higher levels of security because, until the improved security systems win widespread recognition, specification, and sales, competitors will continue to sell an uninformed market inferior, less costly service and equipment at a substantial competitive advantage. What is probably needed is a federal business tax credit for investment in improved security. This would be a workable, positive incentive program, capable of quickly creating a genuine end-user market for improved security systems.

UL ACTIVITIES IN CRIME PREVENTION: LISTING

Before we explore what UL might do in the crime prevention field in the future, let's review what it does at present. A company desiring UL Burglary Department listing as an approved Burglar Alarm Installation and Service Contractor submits its applications to UL and indicates, in addition to data related to its business experience, the class of recognition desired.

UL approval is usually first achieved in recognition of the standards applicable to "Local Alarm" system installations. Until recently, the Local Alarm classification was further subdivided into Mercantile or Financial alarm system installations and the protection of premises or safe or vault alarm systems. Certification for the installation of holdup alarms is usually limited to installations incorporating bandit-resisting enclosures that will automatically alarm if an attempt is made to enter by climbing over a side of the enclosure or if any entrance to the enclosure is opened.

There are also UL equipment and certification standards for residential burglary alarm systems. No certification is given for surveillance cameras. However, some UL equipment standards applicable to camera detection systems would permit the user to require the installer to warrant that the UL equipment standards have been met.

LOCAL ALARM SERVICE STANDARDS

On receipt of an alarm-installing company's application for listing, UL conducts an investigation that includes on-site inspection of four or more local burglary alarm systems, the service and maintenance facilities, supplies of replacement parts, and office and record-keeping procedures of the applicant company.

When it has been determined that the inspected installations equal or exceed UL's standards, a listing is promulgated indicating that the contractor is approved to furnish certified Local Alarm installation and maintenance service. The alarm contractor then acts as an agent for UL in issuing, for its qualifying installations, the certificate that specifies the standards that have been met.

UL also periodically conducts field inspections of new and existing installations for which certificates have been issued by listed companies to ensure continuing compliance with UL standards. UL may investigate complaints by users as to the quality of service provided by the contractor, and when circumstances warrant it, the authorization to issue UL certificates is withdrawn.

However, it does not follow that a UL-approved alarm contractor must install only systems meeting UL standards. As a matter of record, less than one-quarter of the systems installed by UL-approved contractors (both those approved for local and for central station systems installation) are certified.

Apart from maintaining UL standards where applicable to the installation of alarm systems, a Local Alarm contractor's obligations as an approved agent consist mainly of maintaining ethical business practices and of providing competent maintenance. When repair service required by a local alarm system defect is reported to the alarm company before noon, the contractor must make the repairs before the close of business on the same day; otherwise he must provide service within 24 hours of the time of the request on or during a normal business day; That is, a service request received after 12 noon but before 5:00 P.M. on a Monday must be acted upon by 5:00 P.M. on Tuesday, while a request for service received at 3:00 P.M. on Friday in most cases need not be answered until 3:00 P.M. Monday. In practice, however, alarm companies may provide around-the-clock alarm service as a competitive sales tool, although this service is not required by any certification standard.

UL CENTRAL STATION SERVICE STANDARDS

When an alarm contractor desires UL approval to provide central station services to UL standards for premises, safe, or vault alarm systems, he must meet standards for the operation of the central station itself. Typically, these requirements include the following:

1. The central station must be housed in a well-constructed fire-resistant structure.
2. The operating (alarm signal supervisory center) and guard rooms must be protected against unauthorized entry and attack at all times. A holdup alarm system within the central station must be directly connected with another central station or a police facility.
3. Central station alarm monitoring equipment, including computers, must be fail-safe—any outages must register as alarms of some kind.
4. The number and types of alarm circuits that may be supervised by individual electrical monitoring units are limited.
5. Emergency lighting and fire-extinguishing equipment must be at hand.
6. Electric time clocks or date-time stamps must be used to record the receipt of alarm signals, opening and closing times, and so on.
7. The electrical power for the alarm circuits must include provision for at least 24 hours' standby power without recourse to conventional power sources for recharging battery circuits. Auxiliary fuel-powered generators for standby operation must be maintained in good order.
8. Central station operations must have been performed satisfactorily for a period of at least 90 days prior to UL inspection of the facility.
9. During the recognized alarm-closed period (defined as those hours in which 25 percent or more of the company's subscribers have their place of business closed and the alarm set), central station operations must meet the following minimums:

   Alarm systems requiring a remote test shall be tested at intervals not exceeding three hours during the closed period.

   The company shall have on duty at all such times, in addition to at least one trained operator (to supervise the switchboard signal monitoring equipment), at least two employees trained to act as guards. In cities where excellent police cooperation and response are available, the minimum guard-on-hand requirement is reduced to one, except that guard forces are to be in proportion to the number of customers served. (UL inspections may well result in recommendations to increase the number of on-hand guards to a level that will ensure a minimum of delay in response to UL-certified premises alarm and trouble signals.)

   Guards must be equipped with uniforms, identification, and firearms or night stick.

Procedures must be established for determining individual customers' daily opening and closing schedules and the response to alarm signals received at unscheduled times. Code signals or other special identification procedures must be required for irregular and special openings.

Response to alarm signals must be specifically planned, including procedures for safeguarding customers' keys and identifying customers found on the premises. Permanent records must be kept of all significant transactions.

The foregoing requirements are minimum standards that are applicable, as far as UL is concerned, only to certified alarm systems.

In practice, some alarm companies have operating standards that exceed the UL minimum, and some provide equal levels of service for noncertified alarm system customers. Wherever a noncertified alarm system or service is involved, however, the alarm company is under no legal or moral obligation to provide any service other than that defined in the company's written contractual agreement with the user.

If a subscriber wishes noncertified alarm service, he would be well advised to study and, if necessary, to obtain legal advice clarifying the agreement presented by the alarm company. Where necessary, the user should require the alarm contractor to add additional warranties covering the operation of the central office, the maintenance of alarm system records, maintenance performance, and so forth. If the alarm company is itself UL approved, such additional warranties should not add to the expense of the system, or at least not materially.

GRADES OF SERVICE

An approved central station contractor still cannot issue Central Station UL Certificates for approved alarm systems installations unless the guard(s) responding to an alarm signal during the closed period hours can regularly arrive at the premises within a specified period of time. These time response periods are defined in the following sections.

Grade C Service

Under normal conditions, the time required to reach an alarm system shall not exceed 30 minutes from the receipt of an alarm or unauthorized opening signal. The arrival time of the guard shall be understood to be the time recorded by an operator in the central station of a signal[2] given by the guard(s) upon arrival at the premises.

Times when the arrival signal is delayed abnormally, and are therefore not truly representative of the service, may be excluded. These abnormal runs are defined as those that include delays caused by fires, riots, burglary attempts, change in subscribers' keys without notification to the alarm company, traffic accidents, cable breakdowns, and open lines or other trouble that prevents signaling.

Individual alarm systems that cannot be reached in 30 minutes shall not be considered within the range of Grade C service and cannot be certified as central station service by the alarm contractor. However, if said system is equipped with an approved outside sounding device, the system may be certified as a local alarm system.

Grade B Service

The time required to reach the alarm system and to signal shall not exceed 20 minutes. The conditions concerning exceptions to this signal time response requirement are the same as those outlined for Grade C service.

Grade A Service

The time required to reach the alarm system and to signal shall not exceed 15 minutes. Again, the conditions applicable to Grade A service are the same as the others, except as follows: Transmitter alarm systems (McCulloh, or party-line, circuits) may not be classified as Grade A unless they meet the standards for a combination of transmitter and local alarm system with an approved outside sounding device and the time for the guard to respond and signal is within 20 minutes.

Grade AA Service

Only Grade A alarm systems employing UL-approved line security devices or systems may be given a Grade AA rating certificate. The sole additional requirement necessary for a Grade AA rating is that the connecting line (alarm telephone circuit) between the central station and the alarm system shall be so supervised as to detect automatically a compromise attempt by means of resistance substitution, potential (voltage) substitution, substitu-

---

[2] *Signal* is generally understood to mean that the guard communicates in code or by voice over the alarm telephone circuit to the central station supervisor. However, in cases where the alarm company is not furnished the keys to the premises, the signaling is in practice accomplished by a telephone call from a point adjacent to the premises or by communication over a mobile radio transmitter.

tion of randomly selected equipment, reintroduction of signal information transmitted between the protected premises and the central station (by tape recording), or by introduction of a synthesized signal into the alarm signal transmission circuit. A compromise attempt by any one of these methods shall cause a locked-in alarm signal that demands attention by central station personnel. Grade BB and CC certificates may also be issued where response time meets those standards.

KEYS OR NO KEYS

Alarms from all certified key installations shall require a complete search of the premises and adjacent locations that are accessible. A *key installation* is one for which the operating company holds the necessary keys to permit immediate access of guard(s) from the street to a protected interior or to the interior of a premises enclosing a protected point—a mercantile vault, safe, or stockroom. UL requirements for the safeguarding of subscribers' keys are designed to control their use, to account for the dates and the period in which these keys are exposed through use, and to minimize the possibility that keys may be lost or duplicated by unauthorized persons.

Alarms from no-key installations shall require a complete exterior search of the premises by guard(s) who shall remain at the premises if the subscriber, upon being notified, advises that he will arrive within one hour to admit the guard for a search and to restore alarm services. Even though a system may be UL-certificated, no-key guard response will clearly be much less effective in detecting an intruder or in preventing or minimizing the extent of loss. An obvious example would be a premises located above grade level with access from exits or other points of entry not visible to the guard making an exterior search. It is also more difficult to establish the actual response time in no-key installations.

LEVEL OF PROTECTION

UL has also established standards grading the level or extent of the protection afforded by a premises, safe, vault or stockroom *installation*, as described in the following sections.

No. 3 Installation

This alarm system must protect with screens (or tinfoil and trap devices) all accessible windows,[3] doors, transoms, skylights, and other openings leading from the premises.

[3] Until late 1971, accessible stationary show windows visible from streets or highways did not require alarm protection as a condition of certification. However, since that date all show

Alternatively, a No. 3 installation may also be achieved by protecting all movable accessible openings with alarm contacts (electrical switches) and, in addition, by providing one or more invisible channels of radiation (the minimum overall length of the rays or radiation being equivalent to the longest dimension of the area or areas) so as to detect movement within the area so protected. A further alternative No. 3 installation provides for alarm contacts only on the doors leading from the protected area or areas, together with a system of invisible radiation to all sections of the enclosed area, to detect four-step movement.[4]

Invisible rays or *channels* refer to photoelectric or infrared beams and directional types of microwave or ultrasonic detection systems. *Radiation to all sections* is achieved by the use of conventional ultrasonic, radar, microwave, or passive infrared detection systems.

Volumetric-type sound detection units may be used for certification. However, the use of such detection devices must be limited to buildings or substantial constructions in which a forcible entry through roof, walls, or floors will create a significant amount of sound energy. In addition, the construction must reduce extraneous outside noise. Normally, this standard restricts application of volumetric sound detection systems to buildings or areas that are constructed of masonry, metal, and glass. Sound detectors must not be spaced more than 50 feet apart, regardless of the square footage area covered, and there must be at least one sound detector installed in each enclosed or semi-enclosed area.

No. 2 Installation

In addition to the standards established for a No. 3 system, a No. 2 system requires that all inaccessible windows, all ceilings and floors not constructed of concrete, and all halls, partitions, and party walls enclosing the premises be protected with traps. If invisible radiation is employed, an alternate means of providing a No. 2 level of certification, then alarm contacts must be installed on all movable openings leading from the premises, while the invisible radiation intrusion-detection system must extend to all sections of the enclosed area so as to detect four-step movement.[5]

---

windows that are a part of new certified alarm systems must be protected with shock sensors, electrical foil properly spaced or, as an alternative, must have UL-approved burglary-resistant glazing. Since UL certificates for alarm systems installed before 1971 are subject to expiration, this protection must be added before UL renewal certificates are issued for older systems.

[4] When channels of radiation are used, as in a No. 3 installation, it is expected that the system will be so installed and sensitive that an alarm signal will be initiated when a person walks four consecutive steps across each channel at any point at the rate of one step per second.

[5] When full-area coverage is required, as in a No. 2 installation, the motion-detection system shall respond to the movement of a person walking four consecutive steps at the rate of one step per second. Each such four-step movement is considered a trial. A sufficient number of detection units must be installed so that, upon test (made by moving progressively throughout the protected area), an alarm will be initiated in three out of every four such trials.

A No. 2 installation may also be provided by protecting all inaccessible windows with alarm contacts and all accessible windows, doors, transoms, skylights, and other openings with screens or foils and traps. This must be supplemented with a network of invisible beams that, in effect, subdivides the floor space (or each section of the protected area) into three approximately equal areas. More divisions may be necessary; there must be at least one subdivision of protection per thousand square feet of floor space. The principle is that the intruder must necessarily move through the beams in order to carry out his attack, even though he may be able to force entry into the premises through an unprotected point.

No. 1 Installation

A No. 1 installation provides for the complete electrical protection of the entire premises, except for building walls exposed to the street or public highway and that part of any building wall that is two stories or more above the roof of an adjoining building. In this case, *complete protection* refers to the installation of electrical foil or wiring on all surfaces of the premises—floor, walls, and ceilings—and for the installation of contacts and foil or electrical wiring on all doors, windows, and any other openings, accessible or inaccessible.

In practice, a No. 1 installation is rarely made except for the certification of small, completely enclosed stockrooms. No. 1 installations also apply only to central-station-related service, never to Local Alarm systems.

SAFE AND VAULT CERTIFICATION

Partial Protection

Safe or vault alarm systems may be certified for *partial protection* when the outer doors or lock and bolt mechanism are protected with approved devices. Partial protection would not detect attack through the body of a safe or through the walls, floor, or ceiling of a vault.

Complete Protection

In addition to partial protection, *Complete protection* requires that the top, bottom, and all sides of the safes or vaults be electrically protected—that is, by the installation of electrical wiring (lacing), by UL-approved proximity (capacitance) systems, and by UL-approved sound or vibration sensing systems (see Chapter 25).

ALARM SYSTEM CERTIFICATION

When an alarm contractor has completed and tested an alarm system to the requirements of one of these categories, he may issue a certificate. This may be labeled a Grade A Local Premises No. 2 or No. 3, Grade A Local Safe or Vault Partial (or Complete) Protective System, or as a Central Station System One, Two, or Three (referring to the extent of the protective wire and sensor system installed), or Partial or Complete (as applied to safes and vaults) with a corresponding central station designation as Grades C, B, A, CC, BB, or AA. All the applicable certification levels are entered on a prenumbered certificate furnished the alarm contractor by UL for issuance to the user.

The certificate also lists the name and address of the user, the type and model number of the alarm equipment installed, whether the installation is a key or a no-key system, and the issue and expiration dates of the certificate. UL certificates may be issued for periods of one to five years and are renewed at the expiration date if the system meets current requirements for that level of UL certification.

By issuance of the UL certificate, the alarm contractor warrants (to a greater extent than is stipulated in his standard alarm contract) that the alarm system meets certain minimum standards and that service in responding to, supervising, and maintaining the alarm system shall be in accordance with at least the minimum standards set forth by UL for that grade. For this reason some alarm companies may withhold the certificate, even though the installation and service meets a UL certification level, unless the certificate is specifically requested by the user or his insurance underwriter. It would be prudent for every user of a local or central station alarm system to determine whether his system meets UL standards and, if so, whether a valid UL certificate has been issued and is currently in force. In new installations and renewals of existing agreements, any understanding that UL certification is to be provided by the alarm contractor should be included in any sales proposal letter and written into the formal alarm contract with specifications as to the number of certificates and the levels or extent of protection to be provided. In many cases it would be wise to upgrade the alarm system to certificate standards, both for the benefits to be derived from the improved security of a better system and for insurance premium discounts that may be available to users of certified alarm systems.

MAXIMIZING CERTIFICATION

Since a certified system should be inspected at least annually, where UL certification is in force it may be prudent for the user to request that the contractor annually issue a supporting letter indicating that the system has been inspected and repaired where necessary and that the system meets then-current standards of the UL certificate. Over a period of years, emergency repairs performed during closed periods, for example, may result in inadvertent changes or damage to the alarm system that negate the protection it was intended to provide and that constitute a violation of the certification standards.

For example, when inspections were not performed on schedule, banks of windows and rows of overhead doors cut out of the alarm circuit during emergency repair periods have inadvertently remained out of service for long periods of time. Indeed, substantial uninsured (because of certificate violation) losses have occurred due to burglary attacks through supposedly protected points.

Two or more protective systems may be combined to signal over one central-station-supervised telephone circuit or to a single local bell. For example, it is possible to combine Partial or Complete safe or vault protection with a certified premises alarm. In this case the alarm company can issue certificates covering, let us say, both the No. 3 premises installation and Complete protection of the vault. This serves the user as an additional warranty as to the propriety of the installation and the central station service and may afford the user additional insurance premium credits. The same would be true of a completely protected (No. 1) stockroom combined with a No. 3 or No. 2 premises alarm circuit; two separate certificates should be issued.

However, in any situation where more than one alarm signal goes out over a single alarm telephone circuit, there are certain security disadvantages that may not be tolerable in a high-risk application. For example, operating safe or vault protective systems on alarm telephone and central station supervisory circuits separate from premises alarm systems permits the user to keep the safe or vault closed and alarmed until the full staff is at hand and the normal business day has commenced. Similarly, the user can prudently lock the safe or vault and turn on that alarm system as soon as the premises doors are closed to the public. Both measures significantly reduce the attraction of armed robbery against safe or vault contents during the high-risk minimum-staff period.

UL APPROVAL OF ALARM DEVICES AND SYSTEMS

In addition to standards for the installation of alarm systems and for services by alarm contractors, UL also tests and lists those alarm sensors and systems submitted by alarm equipment manufacturers and by alarm contractors who manufacture equipment for their own use. These are tested against established standards, and their production is periodically inspected by sampling to ensure that the same standards still apply.

Alarm equipment is rated as to effectiveness, reliability, and resistance to defeat as far as protection of the premises, safe, or vault is concerned. Only UL-approved alarm devices and systems can be incorporated in a UL-certified premises, safe, or vault installation. Use of unapproved components is a violation of certification standards and nullifies the certificate.

UL BURGLARY DEPARTMENT FIELD INSPECTIONS

In addition, UL Burglary Department requires from approved contractors periodic reports about the performance of the alarm systems, the maintenance of records, attacks against certified premises, and so on. Further, UL field inspection personnel regularly audit alarm contractors' records, inspect new and existing installations (over 8,000 inspections annually), and on occasion, conduct surprise closed-period tests of specific alarm systems to measure the response and service provided by the central station. However, in this author's opinion, the number of the UL Burglary Department's closed-period compliance inspections is limited and should be substantially expanded. Further, in the absence of parallel security engineering and inspection forces from the insurance industry, an activity that has slowly decreased, there is all too little overall field inspection and compliance activity.

It must be stressed again that UL certification standards are—necessarily—based on the existing capabilities of the average alarm-contracting firm and the environmental problems of actual field conditions. One example is the length of time permitted for response to an alarm signal. In crowded heavily trafficked city and suburban areas, this may be longer than the time required for a burglar to attack a substandard safe, vault, or premises structure successfully. And while some companies actually do provide services superior to UL standards, there is little or no incentive for the alarm contractor to provide a better grade of service, either in terms of UL standards recognition or in insurance premium credits.

PROPOSAL FOR EXPANSION

UL standards for security—those mentioned notwithstanding—are far superior to those that might be established by local law enforcement or government agencies or any other known less-experienced, less-established group. Further, as far as the alarm contractor is concerned, the UL standards are much more encompassing. It is the author's firm opinion that UL Burglary Inspection Department is the agency to which assistance and encouragement should be given if we are to develop higher standards of security to meet the criminal threat of today and tomorrow.

The UL program might most effectively be expanded in the following areas:

Recognition of improved safe and vault structures by new ratings (classifications) that clarify the real extent of the protection they afford against burglary.

Development of additional time-response classifications—for example, to recognize the value of a 5-minute guard response in the protection of a substandard vault. Recognition, by the user and by insurers, of the security offered by better response would encourage the expansion of central station service and guard facilities, a key factor in the prevention of loss.

Development of new certificate standards that recognize the user's total security system. This envisions cumulative ratings that would recognize the installation of UL-approved pick-resistant lock cylinders, deadlocks with bolts that resist cutting, burglary-resistant glazing material, burglary-resistant safes or vaults, and alarm systems appropriate to the risk—a total security system.

Present standards fall far short because structural design and barrier materials are not factors in UL certification. For example, a sheetrock or plywood partition does not require protection because penetration would leave evidence of forced entry. This requirement does not exist despite the fact that it is well known that this material affords no delay barrier to prevent hit-and-run attack.

Increased field inspection of certified installations and alarm services, with emphasis on surprise closed-period alarm tests to determine realistically actual guard and police response in terms of time, search procedures, and alarm service restoration.

Development of improved alarm operational security procedures to eliminate weaknesses presently exploited by criminals. These changes would apply to alarm opening and closing procedures, the exchange of code signals, written authorizations, key seals, and so on.

Formation of a UL Burglary Department research and development facility for the purposes of improving security systems and devices, reducing false alarms, applying motion-detection techniques (presently known but not utilized) more effectively, and standarding alarm components and systems.

Development of UL standards for training, installation, and service manuals applicable to motion-detection equipment. Motion-detection systems, for the most part, employ sophisticated solid-state electronics circuitry foreign both to the conventional burglar alarm system and to the conventional installer. Misapplication, errors in installation, and poor service or maintenance of this equipment are contributing heavily to the increasing rate of false alarms. These problems are due in large part to a lack of information and of adequate training for installation and service personnel, needs that should be satisfied before the wide-scale introduction of any sophisticated product.

Public information services. In recent years UL has increased its participation in industry seminars oriented to the alarm contractor and by publication of information for the industry. Pamphlets designed to explain the value of UL certification to residential alarm system users have been issued. Such educational services should be expanded to alert contractors to the pitfalls of inappropriate sensor application and the performance benefits of UL-tested/listed devices and to stress the obligations of the alarm user in the proper operation of an alarm system to reduce the incidence of unnecessary alarms.

The UL report system should be expanded to include *quarterly reports from equipment users.* Information on the number of alarms, time response, and service effectiveness would enable UL to improve field inspection and accountability.

A complaint department should be established to provide users with a recourse when installation or service becomes a problem. This department might also develop a user's service guide, in layman's language, providing information to assist the user in procuring improved alarm systems and services and in improving security practices.

Where would expansion in these areas lead? Expanded and improved UL services can only result in a higher level of security service with a corresponding reduction in crime losses. It is anticipated that an expanded UL role would lead to increased insurance company recognition in the form of premium savings for users, just as the insurance industry once recognized the benefits offered by the services of UL's founder, Merrill. The alarm industry is presently beset by attacks not only from the criminal side but also from police agencies aggravated by the rising alarm rate and from federal agencies determined to make a dent in the crime picture. The advantages of expanded UL activity would be obvious to them. Indeed, a UL research and development laboratory could enable many alarm contractors to reduce present research and development budgets, while benefiting many smaller alarm contractors who can't afford such activities.

In short, Underwriters' Laboratories Burglary Department began as the leader in the alarm industry, and its leadership should be maintained and expanded.

6

Ultrasonic Intrusion Alarm Systems

Ultra-attack

Sid, a prosperous tobacco wholesaler, one day discovered that, despite the U.S. Surgeon General's attack on the perils of cigarette consumption, his business was so flourishing that it had outgrown its tenth-floor warehouse space in a lower Manhattan loft building. (It could have been any urban area.) With hopes for further expansion and success, Sid searched for larger quarters located more centrally in relation to his current and future customers.

He soon found that Manhattan real estate bore the most expensive square foot cost, while his account concentration could be better served from a Brooklyn or Queens facility. Weeks of searching made his choice clear: He could stay where he was (and limit the size of his business), or he could move to one of many larger single-story detached buildings in Brooklyn or Queens. In these outlying locations, though, he would be faced with the necessity of purchasing a building, installing heating and warehousing facilities, offices, and cashier's areas, as well as accepting considerably more warehouse space than would be needed to meet foreseeable expansion. In the end, Sid's sense of entrepreneurship prevailed and he took the big plunge. He purchased a large existing warehouse conveniently located between two major expressways, near airport and railroad terminals. The building had a column-free lightweight roof in which were installed many ventilation fans.

THE COST THAT BROKE THE CAMEL'S BACK

The shocks of moving were many and the overall expense a burden. There were many surprises and hidden costs, but the straw that broke the camel's back was protection.

Sid's insurance broker, when notified of the pending move, promptly replied by letter that a substantial burglar alarm system would be required to bring the new building's security to the level required for insurance in the high-risk tobacco-wholesaling business. The broker indicated that a No. 2 premises central station burglar alarm system[1] would be equivalent to the protection at the old location. Sid was unconcerned since there had been no substantial installation or service costs connected with the burglar alarm system in Manhattan.

Sid failed to see significant differences between the two situations. When he moved into the Manhattan loft, there had been an existing central station alarm system and, because of the tenth-floor location, most of the windows were rated inaccessible[2] and consequently had not required alarm contacts or foil tape. The floors, ceilings, and building walls had not required protection either, since they were constructed of 12-inch reinforced concrete or equivalent masonry. Only the passenger and freight elevators and the doors and walls of the fire tower had required "bugging." Not only had the installation at the old location cost Sid very little, but also the alarm company's monthly service rate for the single alarm system was modest. Protection thus had not been a major expense in Sid's experience.

NEW BUILDING, NEW PROBLEMS

The new building in Brooklyn was a different cup of tea, however. To meet UL standards for a No. 2 certified central station premises alarm, it would be necessary to protect fully (with alarm contacts and foil) all movable doors, windows, skylights, and other accessible openings, as well as (with wiring or other devices) the entire ceiling of the warehouse. On top of that, there were loading doors and loading doors and loading doors—one entire end of the building was made just for a fleet of delivery trucks. If full alarm system protection were not provided, these doors would provide very convenient access for emptying the warehouse on a quiet Sunday afternoon.

The need for extensive protection stemmed from the fact that the entire facility was at ground level; all exterior points were accessible by UL standards. In addition, there were factory-type windows the entire length (on opposite sides) of the 200 by 300 foot building, and many contained cracked or broken panes of glass. A number of the loading doors also were damaged and were poorly fitted to their overhead tracks, while the building walls were of cinder block construction. Although these walls would not require electric protection to meet UL standards for a No. 2 classification, they certainly constituted no formidable barrier against attack.

To protect the new premises to insurance underwriters' requirements, two methods could be considered: One type of installation would use conventional alarm-actuating devices, foil tapes and foil panels on doors and win-

---

[1] See Chapter 5.

[2] See Chapters 4 and 5.

dows, and extensive—and expensive—ceiling wiring circuitry covering the entire 60,000 square feet.

An alternative method would involve the installation of alarm-actuating devices only on movable doors and windows (all considered accessible) plus the installation of so-called invisible rays, or motion-detection devices, throughout the interior of the entire building. These devices could be UL approved photoelectric, ultrasonic, or microwave intruder motion-detection systems. For reasons that will become evident, ultrasonic motion-detection equipment appeared to be best suited to the building environment.

THE ECONOMICS OF ALARM SYSTEM CHOICE

Between the cost of the conventional alarm system and that of the alternative proposal utilizing "sophisticated"—as the salesman put it—intruder motion-detection equipment, there was a substantial difference. Actually, the salesman produced compelling arguments in recommending ultrasonic motion-detection equipment, not the least of which was a lower installation cost. Conventional wiring techniques and skilled installers capable of wiring ceilings and windows are fast becoming extinct, installers remaining enjoy substantially higher wages than did the ones who wired Sid's Manhattan loft years before. The alarm company, confronted with a shortage of installation personnel with the skills necessary to perform such work efficiently, naturally stressed "the effective application" of motion-detection devices. In this case, the cost of a conventional installation would have been three times that of the ultrasonic system. Besides, the shortage of skilled conventional installers would have delayed completion of the installation far beyond the date Sid was scheduled to begin operations at the new location.

In addition, the salesman recognized that the alarm company could realize significant cost savings if the installation were commenced promptly and completed prior to the installation of shelving and warehouse stock fixtures. He based his quotation on an installation schedule that would produce these labor savings, passing some of the cost savings on to Sid. Even so, the final contract price was a staggering sum, and the salesman was not sure of the sale. Consequently, he made little reference to the fact that Sid would be expected to repair all faulty and ill-fitting doors, replace all broken or cracked glass, and furnish special AC outlets (on separate circuits) for the ultrasonic systems.

Despite the fact that the installation price would be one-third the cost of conventional wiring, and therefore seemed to be a bargain, the monthly service rate (in which the alarm company had to include amortization of the more expensive ultrasonic equipment) would be considerably higher than Sid's old service rates had been. There were certain shortcuts the salesman could and did take to keep the service rate down. One shortcut, for example, later defined as poor judgment, put vast areas of protection on a single alarm control circuit. In fact, the entire 60,000-square-foot warehouse was to have only three alarm systems.

ADVANTAGES OF ULTRASONIC

To be sure, there seemed to be distinct advantages in the use of motion-detection systems in this location:

1. In this wide-open empty warehouse, ultrasonic equipment would (in theory) detect the entry of an intruder through the cinder block walls, the panels in the wooden loading doors, or the roof.
2. This method of protection would also give short shrift to anyone who hid in the premises, planning to loot the building after business hours and to give an alarm signal only as he left the premises with his haul.
3. Unlike skylight wiring or foil wiring on windows and exterior doors, ultrasonic devices are not affected by heavy rains or the moisture of condensation, which affect the stability of conventional alarm wiring circuits.
4. In a tobacco-wholesaling operation, the less wire the better; while rodents prefer candy, they will also chew on wiring insulation.
5. Ultrasonic systems are self-restoring—that is, while they are upset into an alarm condition when an intruder moves through the invisible wave path, the system rebalances itself when motion stops. Thus, with this circuit arrangement, the sensors will continue to register additional alarm signals if movement recurs.
6. Finally, the use of ultrasonic eliminated the need to construct electric alarm screens for certain relatively large air conditioning ducts, a feature of conventional protection.

There are also disadvantages connected with the use of ultrasonic detection devices in large warehouse areas of this type, but Sid didn't listen to these very carefully when the alarm company sales engineer made his final pitch.

In late September Sid signed an agreement calling for the completion of the installation within three months—by New Year's Day. Sid furnished the salesman with a blueprint of the empty building and suggested that the alarm company begin work promptly—this was no time for procrastination. The stage was set for trouble.

Now it's your turn as experts to speculate on what happened New Year's Day. Did the year start off with a bang, or is there something missing? Why did the salesman prefer ultrasonic to photoelectric or audio detection equipment? Would microwave or passive infrared have done as well? What disadvantages were there to the use of ultrasonic equipment in so extensive an installation? What is a walk test? Why would zones have been helpful?

PROBLEMS OF ALTERNATIVES

There were certain basic disadvantages to the use of photoelectric beams in this application. In fact, most alarm company policies prohibit the use of photoelectric systems as the major means of warehouse interior space protection. Such protection would be particularly hazardous in a tobacco warehouse, where there are sharp seasonal peaks when merchandise is piled ceiling high and when workers, some on tow motor units, dash frantically back and forth through the aisles moving merchandise in and out at breakneck speed, with little regard to the alignment of photoelectric units—or the security such devices represent.

Audio (sound) detection equipment in a warehouse of lightweight construction, located between two heavily traveled highways near a major airport, would have resulted in prohibitively high unnecessary alarm ratios (trucks, aircraft, rain on the roof, and so on).

Microwave detection equipment might have served equally well, but the salesman felt that the flexing of the lightweight metal roof in high winds would create false alarms, as could the row-on-row fluorescent fixtures.

Passive infrared sensors would have been as effective. However, the salesman was less familiar with that then-new device and was concerned that these sensors would be affected by the numerous space heaters.

THEN THE TROUBLE STARTED

Lack of communication, procrastination, or pressure to complete other overdue alarm installations took their toll. Before you could say "set the alarm," Sid was on the telephone justifiably complaining that only 30 days remained until he must move his valuable stock into the new warehouse, and the alarm company hadn't even begun the installation.

A week later, after several similar calls, the installers arrived on the scene. To their dismay, racks, shelving, and the first shipments of low-value candy had preceded them. Other workmen were swarming over the premises installing lighting fixtures, partitions, floor covering, plumbing, and so forth. In the midst of these obstacles, the alarm installation was begun and continued at a slow pace.

The alarm company's original instruction for the repair of poor-fitting doors and windows and broken glass had gone unheeded; little had been done to correct the situation. The installers, embarrassed at being behind in their work and doubtful of meeting the deadline, decided not to remind the already angry Sid of his commitments to repair the building.

Despite all these problems, but with significant additional labor costs for the alarm company (many hours of premium pay for overtime work on Saturdays and Sundays), the deadline was met and the alarm installation completed on New Year's Day. The test of the alarm was postponed, however, until the following week, since it had proved impossible to command the attention of Sid or any of his supervisors, all of whom were too concerned with a million other problems occurring in the last throes of the move.

When finally tested, the conventional alarm devices on the movable doors and windows passed easily. The ultrasonic coverage, however, was unsatisfactory from the start. Air turbulence, created by drafts through broken windows and the many roof ventilators, kept the ultrasonic transducers in a constant state of imbalance. The alarm could not be set, and Sid was forced to employ a watchman at premium short-term rates to guard the premises.

PRACTICE MAKES IMPERFECT

During the weeks that followed, ultrasonic units were relocated away from roof ventilators and space-heating equipment, and sensitivity levels were reduced to secure a stabilized passing grade for the system. It was even necessary to relocate one unit away from a telephone that upset the system when it rang during closed hours.

Then Sid finally got around to installing partitions to provide private office space for the warehouse manager and various supervisors. The partitions ran from floor to ceiling so in those offices without an ultrasonic transmitter and a receiver there now was, in fact, no protection at all.

To reduce internal losses, Sid soon found it necessary to construct interior wire cages and stockrooms for attractive merchandise like cigarettes, small appliances, and high-value items. In some of these cage areas, merchandise was stocked to the ceilings, creating accidental barriers behind which alarm protection again disappeared. This came to light when someone removed a ventilator head one night and helped himself to a truckload of cigarettes. No alarm was registered because the thief passed the cigarettes up through the skylight—cigarettes are light enough for this method.

Still no one remembered to warn Sid that it was unsafe to stack merchandise against exterior perimeter walls since a penetration from the outside of the building would not cause an alarm unless the burglars moved onto the warehouse floor. So one night someone knocked out some cinder blocks and removed $20,000 in cigarettes from stock stacked against the west wall. No alarm was registered.

About this time Sid discovered ultrasonic alarm systems are not self-testing and that the effectiveness of all transducers cannot be tested from the alarm company central station. (An alarm test from the central office during the closed period only proves that at that precise moment at least one sensor is functioning, but even this test does not measure the sensitivity level of any of the individual detection units.)

20-20 HINDSIGHT

After several significant losses and numerous false alarms caused when loading doors were damaged and wintry blasts howled through the night, Sid agreed to replace the broken windows and to have the alarm company revamp the installation to provide for an increase in the number of individual alarm systems from three to ten. This move would permit individual systems to be set and tested, as well as allow the alarm company to detect more accurately the presence of intruders in one section of the building as distinguished from another. (In some prior burglaries, alarm company agents had fruitlessly searched one end of the building while the burglars apparently continued thieving in another.)

Modifications were also made to include walk-test devices that would allow Sid to conduct periodic tests of each system to make certain that each ultrasonic sensor was functioning properly, and to determine the location of "dead" spots created whenever incoming merchandise was stacked ceiling high or stock was relocated. In addition, several multi-position annunciator panels were added to the system. These devices locked in a visual indication of the status of each sensor so that the cause of an alarm could be pinpointed to a specific unit. These zone indicators were located just inside the entrance to the premises. The indicators permitted police and others, arriving in response to an alarm, to pinpoint the location of the trouble and also provided, if several sensors were activated, a strong indication of the presence of intruders.

Despite these improvements, Sid still had a problem: if he was to use wall space for storage, some form of wall protection would be necessary. To achieve this Sid authorized the installation of vibration detectors. These supplemental devices, unlike UL-listed shock sensors, Sid later learned, were not foolproof.

Sid also learned that ultrasonic systems may not detect motion if the intruder moves at a very slow pace or if a knowledgeable hide-in intruder is careful to remain within aisle spaces not adequately covered by ultrasonic. In addition, soft goods such as cardboard or clothing absorb ultrasonic wave patterns, he discovered, further reducing the effectiveness of the system. In retrospect, passive infrared sensors would have been more effective in the detection of the movement of intruders in this environment, and their detection range would not have been reduced by the addition of soft goods inventory.

THE HIGH COST OF DIVORCE

Sid and his alarm company are still "married"—neither can afford a divorce. Sid doesn't have enough spare cash to install conventional protection, and the alarm company is always hopeful that once they get the system settled down, their cost of service will make the contract profitable at last. But one thing is certain: Sid is an unhappy customer who still doesn't understand why things aren't what they used to be. Most of their problems could have been avoided, however, if negotiations had been full and frank and if complete construction plans—including prints of proposed warehouse and office layouts—had been furnished initially.

7

Microwave Motion Detection

A Sensitive Detector

As the market for security-related equipment expanded explosively in the late 1960s, many electronic manufacturing, research, and development companies vigorously sought commercial security applications for the sophisticated electronic devices and systems they had developed for the U.S. space program and the Vietnam war. The application of microwave-transmitting-and-receiving equipment to the detection of the movement of intruders was one of the earliest and most successful applications of existing technology.

The microwave motion-detection equipment adapted for alarm system use transmits and receives radio energy at a frequency of 10.5 billion cycles per second (10,525 MHz). Use of motion-detection equipment of this ultrahigh-frequency (UHF) subjects the installer and manufacturer to licensing requirements under FCC rules and standards. These FCC regulations cover the design, manufacture, installation, and maintenance of this equipment in order to minimize radio transmission interference effects. These rules foster high standards of design and performance that should benefit the user by reducing false alarms and equipment problems.

SPECIAL REQUIREMENTS

The introduction of radio frequency (RF) energy-transmitting-and-receiving devices operating at these ultrahigh frequencies did saddle manufacturers and alarm contractors with three unique problems:

1. For this equipment to operate reliably at 10.5 billion cycles per second, its electronic components must remain very stable during long periods of use.
2. Personnel handling these devices must be trained if they are to be competent to deal with the equipment's special installation and service requirements.
3. Alarm contractor sales and engineering personnel must be as aware of the security limitations of microwave as of its special capabilities.

INTRODUCTION OF MICROWAVE

One firm that pioneered the application of microwave equipment to the security field met most of the stability requirements by the use of solid-state components and achieved the compatibility necessary for the units to work with conventional alarm control instruments and circuitry. Nevertheless, their first microwave units (installed in 1967–1968) suffered component failures that resulted in a significantly high rate of false alarms. Although the manufacturer made every effort to replace or exchange faulty equipment promptly, the credibility of microwave as a reliable detector had been damaged with some installers, police, and users. This was, indeed, a case in point for extended performance and life tests under field conditions prior to production and wide-scale commercial use of any new detection devices or systems.

This pioneering equipment manufacturer developed detailed installation and service manuals and—to an extent heretofore unheard of in the alarm industry—offered training seminars to alarm contractors. In sampling the opinions of alarm contractors as to the field performance of microwave equipment, it quickly became apparent that those contractors who participated in the initial training program have been successful in the use of microwave equipment. In contrast, contractors who expressed dissatisfaction with microwave performance seemed to lack knowledge as to the proper application and the limitations of microwave systems.

NEED FOR STANDARDS AND INSPECTION

Clearly, this sampling illustrates the need for standards of application and installation and for the subsequent inspection of motion-detection system installations as an expanded function of Burglary Protection Division. UL field inspections of certified alarm system installations do uncover improper installations and equipment misapplications. However, while UL's limited field inspection was adequate for conventional hard-wired perimeter detection devices and predictable photoelectric beams, today's volumetric (or area) motion-detection systems are far more vulnerable to installation error and, accordingly, should be subject to detailed inspection by a competent neutral party like UL.

An effective motion-detection system program would include the inspection of each alarm system and, prior to the certification of any of the alarm contractor's field installations, evidence of a proper training program for sales, installation, and service employees. This training program should be a joint effort of the manufacturer or supplier of specified equipment and of the alarm contractor. (This general problem is expanded upon in Chapter 5.)

The same principle—adequate pre-installation training—should of course apply to any special equipment tested, approved, certified, or rated, whether by another independent testing laboratory, a government agency, or an insurance underwriter.

TECHNICAL PLUSES AND MINUSES

The principal argument for microwave as a reliable volumetric or space-intruder detector is based on the fact that UHF radio signals are less subject to RF interference from mobile radio-equipped vehicles, citizens' band (CB) transmitters, aircraft, diathermy equipment, and so on. This is generally true, and microwave equipment does have a better track record than systems operating in the radar band—915 million cycles. However, microwave equipment is sensitive to certain kinds of interference that do produce false alarms, and proper installation techniques are most important to prevent this. For example, where microwave signal overlap may occur, as in major aisle areas, sensors operating on different frequencies might be installed to eliminate interference between units. Similarly, the operating principles of microwave as an intruder detector must be fully understood if installations are to be genuinely effective for security.

OPERATING PRINCIPLES

The microwave detection unit consists of a RF transmitter and a receiver. RF signals are beamed from the transmitter into the area to be protected, striking stationary objects within the area and reflecting back to the receiver. Each receiver may be considered as being programmed to disregard these known reflections from stationary objects. When an intruder moves through the area within the field of coverage, however, the signals reflect back to the receiver at a different rate (the Doppler principle), and the unit's intelligence circuit is activated by the change in frequency to signal an alarm status. Interfacing relays transmit the alarm signal through conventional burglar alarm control instrument circuits to a central station or a police station or sound a local bell.

Two unique characteristics of UHF signals are the basis for the feasibility of microwave detection systems. First, UHF signals may be transmitted in a variety of relatively precise directional patterns, enabling the alarm contractor to cover premises layouts of widely varying sizes and configurations. Second, microwave signals are not affected by either air turbulence or low-frequency noise, both present to some degree in most mercantile premises locations and prime causes of false alarms.

SPECIALIZED COVERAGES

In order to adapt microwave equipment to different premises requirements, manufacturers have developed various signal transmitters, or transmitting "horns." Earlier models resembled the old-fashioned phonograph horn; later versions are somewhat smaller and vary in shape. Depending upon the size and shape of these transmitting horns (the sophisticated term is *antenna*), one may project narrow microwave beams down long narrow corridors 20 to 300 feet in length or transmit broad elliptical beam patterns to saturate areas up to 10,000 square feet in size.

Microwave sensors utilizing a transmitter and a receiving unit have particular application in the protection of aisles up to 500 feet in length. Unlike the narrow photoelectric beam coverage, such microwave units provide detection areas of coverage 4 to 8 feet in diameter at a point equidistant from transmitter and receiver. This technology also has application outdoors behind fencing and gates.

By the use of special antennas, both beam- and saturation-type patterns can be provided in an integrated microwave system. Such an arrangement could cover both an open warehouse area and vulnerable perimeter walls. Another special antenna, the Y-type, provides beamlike protection of two corridors or perimeter walls at right angles to one another.

The field of coverage of microwave transmitters may be compared to the field of view provided by different camera lenses. For example, a long narrow microwave beam pattern is comparable to the field of view provided by a telephoto lens, while a broad elliptical antenna pattern compares to the view provided by a wide-angle lens.

CONTAINING MICROWAVE SIGNALS

This analogy to photography might be extended to state that neither microwave transmitters nor camera lenses see through substantial solid objects. In a warehouse, aisle spaces where the view of the microwave transmitter is blocked by stacks of merchandise are in a shadow area, and intruders moving solely within these aisles are not likely to be detected by the system. Actually, however, this aspect of microwave requires detailed explanation.

Solid exterior walls and uninterrupted barriers of concrete, masonry, or metal substances will fully block microwave signals, and when these materials completely enclose an area, they contain the microwave signals and reduce false alarms due to external causes. However, since few enclosures are so constructed (other than special stockrooms and vaults), it is important to recognize that microwave signals can and do pass through glass doors and windows and through lightweight walls or partitions constructed of plywood, glass, Sheetrock, or fiberboard. While this pass-through property affords the installer the ability to protect rooms and partitioned areas within a single premises with only one microwave system, pass-through represents a great potential for false alarms and leads to the following installation precautions:

1. When the exact area to be protected is only a portion of the total premises, care must be taken to ensure that microwave signals do not pass

through wood or glass partitions into an area that will be occupied after the protected area is closed because any movements in the secondary area will be sensed. An example would be a manufacturing or warehouse operation where that operation is secured (and the alarm system set) before the departure of employees working in adjoining office areas. This problem can be avoided by a transmitter-mounting location that will beam the microwave signals away from the office area.

2. Care must be taken to ensure that the microwave transmitters are installed so they will not look through glass show windows, entrance doors, or lightweight nonmetallic partitions into unprotected areas. Where it is not possible to locate transmitters looking away from glass or other penetrable materials, it is necessary to reduce the microwave signal strength until it falls short (by 15 to 20 feet) of doors, windows, and walls of penetrable composition. When this is done, the alarm contractor must recognize that intruders can break and enter show windows and otherwise penetrate some distance into the premises before disturbing the microwave system. Under these circumstances, either other devices should be provided to detect such entries or valuables must be removed from the no-security zone for the closed period.

3. Microwave signals are reflected back from metal surfaces. On occasion, the bounce of the signal off a metal plate, office partition, or display sign may actually pass through a window or lightweight partition on an opposite wall with enough strength to detect motion in the unprotected area beyond. This is another potential false alarm hazard that can be eliminated—once it has been recognized—by reducing microwave signal strength or by repositioning the detector.

PROBLEMS OF HIGH MOUNTING

For the protection of a large warehouse or factory area, a wide-angle microwave beam pattern, transmitted from a unit mounted near the ceiling, will see over the top of stacked merchandise and thus be effective in detecting burglary attack through the roof. However, while microwave equipment is unaffected by audio or ultrasonic noise, it has its own idiosyncrasies. For example, a sheet metal roof flexing due to air turbulence will change the microwave signal pattern received and be read as an intruder, causing false alarms. The same condition may occur when high winds cause metal loading doors (curtain as well as sectional types) to flex. Similarly, if the microwave transmitter is beamed to look at rotating fan blades, such as of a roof ventilator or a space heater, it will signal an alarm. Another reason for locating microwave units somewhat below ceiling level is that fluorescent lights within the beam pattern may cause false alarms.

MASS AND BULK IN FALSE ALARMS

The bulk or mass of a moving object outside a protected area is also a factor in false alarm potential: a trailer truck passing close by exterior walls of 6-inch cinder block or, similarly, a railroad car moving along a siding adjacent to a building may reflect a sufficient amount of signal back to the receiver to produce a false alarm under circumstances where an animal or a passerby may not.

Clearly, microwave's unique false alarm potentials, as well as the special requirements of microwave system layout and applications, create a necessity for careful consideration and expert knowledge. Installation should always be preceded by practical tests utilizing portable equipment to establish the extent of coverage and to solve all special problems before the system is finally installed.

CONTINUING INTERFERENCE

Microwave discriminator circuits are incorporated to compensate for random external motion of small objects such as windows and exterior doors shaken by wind or vibration or the continuous vibration of motor-driven fans. However, while these discriminator circuits do reduce false alarms due to minor changes in background noise vibration levels, continuing interference within a specific period of time may accumulate in the discriminator circuit and increase the circuit's sensitivity to such interference until the threshold is reached and an alarm is registered. Thus, it is important at all times to secure doors, windows, and other sources of motion and vibration properly within the protected area.

Care must also be taken to ensure that the transmitter and receiver (usually one self-contained unit) are firmly mounted on a vibration-free column or wall. Mounting devices or brackets securing the transmitter must be flexible to permit the correct directioning of the beam pattern, but they must be mechanically sound. Once adjusted, the bracket must securely lock the unit in the selected orientation.

ADJUSTMENT AND TESTING

Microwave system sensitivity controls permit adjustment of the range of the microwave signal. This is particularly important because the sensitivity level (range of coverage) may change due to any of a variety of reasons, including defective components, variations in voltage, and the addition or removal of equipment or stock within the protected area. For this reason it is imperative for the user to test the range of the system periodically to be certain that the field of coverage has not extended to a distance that will result in false alarms or been reduced to leave areas unprotected.

Most microwave equipment manufacturers incorporate a walk-test capability enabling the user to perform this check in a period of a few minutes prior to securing the premises. The person walk-testing an area must pause approximately one minute to permit the system to restabilize itself before proceeding to walk-test another area of the premises. Without this precaution, the test will overstate the actual sensitivity, or range, of the system.

GENERAL PRECAUTIONS

Like other forms of motion detection, microwave units cannot distinguish between human and other moving objects, and the movement of dogs, cats, rats, and animals of similar size will be sensed. Birds flying through the protected areas may also produce false alarms; a bird flying in or near the transmitter-receiver unit will certainly do so.

Other general alarm installation requirements applicable to microwave equipment include:

- Mounting 8 to 12 feet above floor level to reduce the chance of the unit being damaged or knocked out of alignment (by forklifts, for example) during business hours;
- Standby battery power to provide for uninterrupted operation in the event of power failure, momentary or prolonged;
- "No-parking zones" for materials (particularly metal) to prevent the build-up of temporary dead spots in critical areas.

Microwave signals readily pass through acoustic ceiling tiles, affording the installer a good place to hide the detection device. Where this is done, the microwave units should be mounted at least 2 feet above the dropped ceiling to avoid surface reflections caused by too-close proximity of the ceiling tile to the detection unit.

SPECIAL PRECAUTIONS FOR HIGH-VALUE RISKS

In recent years there has been substantial application of microwave to the protection of high-value stocks. Under these circumstances the possibility of planned attack against the microwave units must be considered, and special precautions are appropriate as follows:

1. As noted, the field of coverage provided by microwave equipment is not constant and may change. While the use of the walk-test determines

the coverage at the moment the test is made, this cannot assure consistency of coverage during the closed period. (Remember that closed period may be one night, a three-day holiday, or a two- or three-week plant shutdown.) To meet this problem, special RF signal-measuring devices can be located in vital areas to create an alarm if the microwave signal drops below a certain level.

2. The field of coverage provided by the microwave transmitter depends upon the direction of the antenna as determined by its position at the mounting bracket. In high-risk situations, the locking devices that secure the unit at the bracket should be electrically "trapped" to provide an alarm or trouble signal if someone changes the unit's orientation during an open-for-business period when the microwave detector is either turned off or the alarm supervisory circuit is disconnected. (When properly installed, the unit is automatically protected against tampering whenever the detector and the alarm supervisory circuit are in the alarm-on condition.)

3. Since solid metal and masonry effectively block and reflect microwave signals, security procedures should include physically checking the protected areas at the close of business each day (whether or not a walk-test is performed) to ensure that no one has moved a large object or mass into the microwave beam pattern, effectively reducing the coverage. Metallic substances such as tin foil and tacks placed in the microwave horns will also change the beam pattern, as will metal screens hung in the field of coverage.

4. When high-risk areas requiring protection are extensive, individual microwave units should be segregated into two or more zones or control circuits to pinpoint the area from which the alarm signal is generated. When a zone indicator can be strategically located at the premises, a single remote (central station or police station) supervisory circuit may suffice. However, separate alarm supervisory circuits often afford the central station supervisor the opportunity to detect and follow the movement of an intruder through separately alarmed areas and to direct the police and company guards to a capture.

5. For the high-value risk, line security equipment to protect the telephone alarm line circuits linking the microwave alarm systems to the remote supervisory point is also recommended.

OTHER FORMS AND GENERAL COSTS

We have devoted considerable coverage to the applications and idiosyncrasies of microwave equipment because it is likely that this versatile method of protection will continue in use for many years. Properly installed, microwave is suitable for residential, retail, warehouse, factory, museum, school, and church applications. Presently available microwave equipment includes, as well as the more versatile equipment discussed here, portable units suitable to temporary and changing protection requirements and minimicrowave equipment to detect vandals and afford limited protection to small areas.

While the cost to install microwave equipment is considerably less than wiring doors, windows, and walls and less than the cost of installing ultrasonic or audio systems (for which more detection units are required), the cost of microwave equipment itself is higher.

Although it is not possible to give specific microwave installation cost norms, the alarm contractor will invest approximately $500 for a microwave system to cover an area of 10,000 square feet. Whether the user purchases such equipment outright or leases the equipment from his alarm service company, he must recognize that the cost of sophisticated intruder motion-detection equipment is substantial—all the more reason for making certain the system is properly engineered and installed, both to detect intruders and to be as free of false alarms as possible.

8

Passive Infrared Technology

The Phenomenal Intrusion Detector

In less than a decade, passive infrared technology has become the installer's choice for application to intrusion-detection layouts. This acceptance is based on the sensor's versatility in terms of patterns of coverage, installation ease, and immunity to false alarms due to the environment.

DESCRIPTION

A passive infrared intrusion-sensing device consists of a pyroelectric heat-sensing element, an optical lens system, a low-current power supply, and a logic circuit or analyzer. The device can accomplish the following:

- Measures temperature (infrared energy) changes,
- Relates a temperature change to an increment of time,
- Compares the change in temperature within that time frame with the existing or ambient temperature within the range of the sensor,
- Transmits an alarm signal if this coefficient of change exceeds the logic circuit standard of acceptable temperature-time change. This sensitivity factor varies by manufacturer and model number. The most sensitive equipment available today may detect a change of 1 degree Celsius caused by an intruder moving as slowly as 2 inches per second.

Thus, the passive infrared sensor, unlike ultrasonic, microwave, or photoelectric beams, does not transmit any energy into the area it protects. Instead, the heat-sensing element sees or looks through an optically defined finger-shaped area of space within which it measures minute changes in infrared energy or temperature.

Within designed limits, the energy-sensing element and the related logic circuit accept the existing ambient or background temperature seen within the finger of detection as the norm within its detection range. The sensor then continuously detects and measures increases or decreases in temperature and compares this with the background temperature. The analytical circuit also measures the changes in temperature against units of time, permitting the acceptance of normal changes that may occur in an area during a closed period when, for example, heating or air conditioning systems have been turned off or adjusted to moderate temperature settings. Thus, when the passive infrared element senses temperature changes per unit of time in excess of the designed or programmed allowable norms, the analyzer translates the excessive changes in temperature into alarm signals.

BASIC ADVANTAGES

Passive infrared sensors do not respond to the most common closed-period gremlins found to occupy a factory, warehouse, or office space when their occupants are away. Neither noise made by time clocks, ringing telephones, clanging pipes or radiators, or doorbells nor moving mechanical objects such as ventilation louvers, display banners, fan blades, or large metal surfaces like those presented by exterior overhead doors activate a passive infrared sensor. Similarly, vibrations caused by low-flying planes, railroad cars, 18-wheelers, or ground tremors may vibrate the passive infrared sensor through its mounting structure, but since the device transmits no energy, its operation is seldom affected by these vibrations. In contrast, an ultrasonic, microwave, or photoelectric beam device's field of energy is changed by such vibrations, and these devices then transmit false alarm signals.

It is also noted that sound-absorbing materials such as drapes, curtains, rugs, and acoustical tiles, which do absorb ultrasonic energy and subsequently reduce the sensitivity of those devices, do not have any significant impact on passive infrared sensors. Therefore, a passive infrared sensor properly installed during premises construction is likely to perform on the same sensitivity levels after these interior furnishings are added.

USES OF PASSIVE INFRARED DEVICES

Within each finger of detection, a passive infrared sensor will detect a human being, an animal, or a bird moving into or out of that zone. Although small animals radiate less infrared energy, alarm levels may also be reached based on the sensitivity of the unit, the number of animals seen, and their speed of movement into or out of the finger of detection. Close proximity to the sensor is usually not a factor in the detection levels since the optical systems are designed to compensate for that factor. However, mini-type passive infrared units, designed for flush-mount, wide-angle coverage, have shorter lenses and higher electronic sensitivity levels and may, therefore, register small objects moving in close proximity to the sensor.

CAUSES OF FALSE ALARMS

Significant changes in temperature may also be created by mechanical means, and if this occurs, a false alarm may be transmitted. Examples include the infrared energy output of a space heater or furnace located within a finger of detection or the exhaust output from an air conditioner or commercial refrigerator/freezer. Sharp changes in temperature resulting from mechanical failure of heating and air conditioning units or drafts created by broken windows during the closed period may also cause false alarms. Fire, explosion, violent chemical reactions, and leaking gas may cause alarms that would be described as welcome rather than false.

Natural energy created by sunlight and mechanical energy resulting from vehicle or train headlights, spotlights, or heavy duty flashlights shining directly or reflected into an optical detection zone may also cause an alarm signal. Mirrors or metal surfaces may reflect or radiate infrared energy into a field of detection.

In most applications, proper positioning of the passive infrared sensor and adjustments to the optical system and sensitivity will minimize the incidence of false alarms from sunlight, artificial light, and reflected or radiated energy. However, since one or more of those potential false alarm sources may exist outside the premises, the installer must take into consideration the possibility of these undesirable elements' being transmitted through windows or metal wall surfaces. "What ifs" like the energy reflected from a 40-foot aluminum trailer parked in the yard outside the show window when the sun sets on Sunday must be part of the installer's analysis in dealing with passive infrared sensor application.

RF energy, like that externally transmitted by mobile radios, diathermy equipment, and perhaps, internally by induction furnaces, fluorescent lights, or faulty ballasts, may cause false alarms as they are picked up in the electrical logic circuit, just as they affect ultrasonic and microwave circuitry. These potential false alarm causes are reduced somewhat if the sensors are shielded. However, the transmission cable may still be vulnerable to this problem. Similarly, strong electrical noise caused by lightning or loose power connectors may create false alarm conditions.

CONTROLLING OR REDUCING UNWANTED ALARM SIGNALS

Two characteristics of the passive infrared sensing device, the optical system and the very low power requirement of the sensing element, combine to permit precise sensitivity and area of detection limits that tend to be more constant over long closed (armed) periods as compared to the practical operating limits of ultrasonic or microwave sensors. In addition, these advantages permit the use of dual sensing elements that can be programmed to permit comparison of the conditions that exist in two precisely aligned adjacent fingers of detection so as to require a measurable difference between the two fingers of infrared energy levels, thus avoiding the translation of a momentary change into an alarm condition. This dual-element-sensing concept may be valuable in cancelling out false-alarm-generating interference such as that caused by lightning, other electrical noise, and reflected or direct exterior light (headlights and sunset, for example).

OTHER ADVANTAGES

Since passive infrared sensors do not transmit sound, ultrasonic, RF, light, or infrared energy into the area of protection, the power required to operate the energy-sensing and the signal analysis circuitry is substantially less than that required for other intruder-sensing devices. This advantage translates to less use (and lower cost) of AC power outlets and transformers; the extended use of remote sensors, powered by a master control unit power supply; and longer standby battery performance in instances where the basic power supply is interrupted. Alternately, the sensor may also be operated by DC power.

Further, the lower power advantage extends to the use of *wireless* passive infrared sensors that may operate up to a year on 9-volt DC batteries and that may be equipped with an audible low-battery indicator. To the author's knowledge, passive infrared sensors are the only intruder movement-detection devices that may be installed as wireless units.

A variety of unique optical lens configurations permit manufacturers the variation in the angles and lengths of the shaped fingers of detection. However, field adjustment of sensor optical fields is not usually possible. Instead, unit-mounting adjustments enable the installer to adjust coverage to precise distances. As a result, these factors provide for unique applications. For example, in one application passive infrared sensors are installed to provide complete intrusion-detection coverage of a manufacturing area where gold-chain-making machines run unattended, while open aisles surrounding the banks of chain machines are in fact unprotected and permit the movement of cleaners and other employees immediately adjacent to the protected area without concern about the generation of false alarms due to changes in passive infrared coverage patterns. This application would be difficult to impossible to achieve if ultrasonic or microwave sensors were applied under similar conditions.

Since passive infrared sensors transmit no energy, sensors installed to overlap each other to provide saturation coverage within an area do not interfere with each other. By comparison, it is noted that some microwave units do interfere unless overlapping coverage is achieved by the use of sensors operating on different radio frequencies.

Since passive infrared sensors are less subject to problems related to the vibration of the building structure than other devices, there is not as much need to locate sensors on rigid building columns or to install expensive floor mounts. Thus, the installation and location of these sensors are both economical and flexible.

Passive infrared sensors are also smaller than other devices and, therefore, lend themselves to a variety of cabinets that are aesthetically pleasing. These cabinets also permit use of decorator colors and application of wallpaper to the trim plates. The small sensing apertures are concealed by plastic lens screens. These size and style features enhance the appearance factor for such devices in residence and office applications.

Since directional adjustments are simplified and accessible when the trim and lens cover are removed, there is versatility in mounting possibilities that permits the installer to flush mount, recess, or locate the unit in or on a ceiling. Residential units are also available for installation in electrical outlet boxes and may be disguised as a common duplexed electrical outlet. Electrically trapped (connected into the 24-hour circuit) cover plates permit this variety of mounting configurations while reducing the vulnerability to tampering with range or directional coverage patterns during the open-for-business period.

It should be noted that a ceiling-mounted passive infrared sensor affords an umbrellalike 360-degree detection area of coverage that may be particularly suitable for providing protection in the narrow aisles of a stockroom where valuable merchandise is stored on multiple racks. Such racks would otherwise block out the protection intended by wall-mounted sensors.

However, it should be noted that passive infrared sensors, like standalone ultrasonic or microwave units, are unsupervised as to range of coverage. If, for example, an object that is capable of blocking out infrared energy is placed within the field of view of one or more of the sensor's fingers of detection, it will to some extent eliminate the area of coverage provided by that sensor. In an extreme case, attaching a thick sheet of plastic or cardboard over the lens opening during the open-for-business period may negate the entire protection pattern. Thus, the installer should normally mount sensors 8 feet above floor level, and the subscriber should visually check each sensor for tampering or obstructions when securing the premises each night.

It follows that passive infrared sensors require the same due diligence in walk-testing the areas of coverage on a frequent basis. Fortunately, available equipment includes a variety of visual alarm indicators that permit a subscriber to walk-test the unit under controlled conditions so that employees and others visiting the premises are not privy to the extent or limitation of detection coverage. Similarly, optional remote zone indicators permit a subscriber to determine which sensor caused the alarm signal to which he is responding.

Most of the equipment currently marketed includes background detection circuitry that permits the installer to determine if stationary heat sources or variations in ambient background temperature will result in the unstable operation of an individual sensor. This feature permits relocation or readjustment of the sensor to eliminate the potential for false alarms.

Passive infrared sensors may also be mixed with ultrasonic or microwave standalone sensors using the same analytical or logic transmission cables. This mixing permits the installer the efficiency to utilize individual devices best suited to specific areas of a protected premises as dictated by the length or width of aisles and the potential interference sources within a given area. For example, an ultrasonic device could be substituted for passive infrared in an industrial process area where unusually high temperatures persist or where automated process equipment produces sharp changes in temperature during the normally closed period.

DUAL DETECTION

Some manufacturers have combined passive infrared and microwave sensors in a single unit with a common signal transmission cable circuit. This dual detection technique requires both movement and the transmission of body heat in order to create an alarm signal. This concept, which provides for identical patterns of detection coverage, is superior to the redundancy achieved by the installation of two separately operated intruder-detection sensors and is most certainly a more efficient way of achieving the primary objective: fewer false alarms. However, it should be noted that where dual sensing systems are employed and one sensor (for example, microwave) has a longer range of detection, the actual transmission of the alarm signal will not occur until the intruder comes within the detection field of the sensor having the shortest range. While the cost of this equipment is somewhat higher than single intruder-detection devices, the manufacturers feel the savings resulting from the reduction of unnecessary alarms will far exceed the equipment cost. The author agrees with this theory. As municipalities enact more stringent alarm response ordinances, the charges for such police service will likely rise to what-the-traffic-will-bear levels. Given the alternative of substituting additional private security agents for police, it would seem that effective redundant detection sensing is the only efficient answer to the alarm response problem. Clearly, the development of passive infrared sensing provides a further means by which the alarm industry can effectively address this most critical problem.

PROBLEM AREAS

The extraordinary demand for passive infrared sensing has created a market into which many suppliers have rushed. Inevitably, this demand has led to instances where newly designed sensors have had limited field test application and random rather than 100 percent quality control and inspection. As a result, some of the products shipped to installers have been subject to unusually high sensing element failure rates—in excess of 10 percent in some cases. If such failure rates are not detected at the factory, the potential for false alarms, as well as undetected intrusions, is significant.

There is a concern when passive infrared sensors are installed in areas where ambient temperature levels are high. Although manufacturers' specifications normally state the operating range to be between 32 and 120 degrees F, some sensors tend to suffer from reductions in range and sensitivity when ambient temperatures are 95 degrees or higher. This problem is of greater concern in environments where, during closed periods when air conditioning and ventilators are closed down, the ambient temperature may rise slowly to levels in the 100-130 degree range. If such temperature conditions occur, particularly in warehouse and factory environments in warmer climates, intrusion may go undetected. In these environments it is suggested that walk-tests be performed at opening time on the first business day following a weekend or holiday period shutdown.

Humidity is also an important factor in sensor performance. Some manufacturers do not specify the operational humidity limits, while others state a 90 percent maximum relative humidity. When humidity is a major problem, performance tests should be made prior to installation of the sensors and, if necessary, alternate sensing techniques employed to solve that problem.

Care must also be taken to analyze potential sources of indirect reflected energy. Thus, heat generated outside the protected area that is radiated into the field of detection through glass or reflected into the field of detection by mirrors or metal surfaces located outside or within the protected premises must be avoided.

When passive infrared sensors were first introduced into the security marketplace, some observers contended that a burglar in a wet suit or otherwise insulated to prevent infrared energy from radiating from the body was, or might be, a means of defeating the concept. As a practical matter, the high detection sensitivity capability—the ability of the energy sensor to distinguish as small a change as 1 degree C in targets moving less than 2 inches per second, makes the wet suit theory a dubious one for the burglar to undertake. As a practical matter, we know of no confirmed successful burglaries involving this technique.

SUMMARY

In less than a decade, the acceptance by alarm contractors has established passive infrared as the most popular intrusion-detection sensor presently available. No doubt the contractors' position has been influenced by the sensor's versatility in terms of patterns of coverage, an apparent reduction in false alarm incidence as compared to other sensors, and ease of installation, as well as savings in the cost of installing these sensors. As volume permits suppliers to achieve further efficiency in the manufacture of passive infrared sensors, such cost advantages might become even more significant.

9

Environmental Causes of False Alarms

Things That Go Bump in the Night

The design and installation of an alarm system invariably takes place during the daylight open-for-business hours of Monday through Friday. Frequently, "Act I, Scene 1" of the alarm installation is staged in an empty premises being readied for business occupancy or in a vacant area under construction or renovation.

Even where the premises is already occupied, the true environment in which the alarm system must function is not always apparent. In an occupied area things such as people's work activity and the flow of supplies often conceal the conditions that exist during the closed periods of both day (weekends and holidays) and night.

When an alarm system survey is made of a premises in full operational swing, the occasion is often the need to install or to add on to an alarm system following burglary attack or to meet additional insurance company requirements arising from the insurer's current business experience. When an addition to an alarm system is required, it may well involve an intrusion motion-detection system. These electronic devices are most susceptible to false alarms due to conditions not clearly evident during normal business hours. The following sections illustrate how closed-period environmental conditions can cause alarms.

STEAM

Photoelectric beams are installed along the perimeter walls in an electroplating plant. Large floor vats contain chemical solutions maintained during the day at temperatures close to their boiling points. The plant closes at 4:00 P.M. and, in the winter, room temperatures drop rapidly as cool air pours through broken factory windowpanes and openings around poorly fitted loading dock doors. The solutions in the vats cool less rapidly, however, and steam soon rises from their surface. As this cloud of steam is sucked into the air circulation patterns, it drifts across the photoelectric beam path, momentarily blocking its light source, and a false alarm occurs.

NOISE

At another location, ultrasonic motion-detection devices are installed in the office and warehouse area adjacent to the machine shop. This system has functioned satisfactorily for several years with few or no false alarm problems. Recently, however, a small section of the machine shop was enclosed in a heavy-duty wire cage to protect tools and dies that had been mysteriously disappearing. The ultrasonic system was easily extended to provide coverage in this enclosure.

Since there was no known air turbulence in the area, and no one worked in the cage during the periods the warehouse alarm was on, no concern was felt over false alarm possibilities. During the first weekend following the installation of the additional ultrasonic sensing devices, however, there were false alarms at precisely 7:00 A.M. (starting time), 10:00 A.M. (coffee break), the beginning and end of the workday lunch hour, and washup and quitting times. The repetition of false alarms at precise times (plus the close proximity of the newly installed ultrasonic sensors to a bell operated automatically by the electric time clock) established the cause of the trouble.

It should be noted, however, that in instances where bell or chime-type annunciators (or even telephones) are located farther away from the ultrasonic devices, false alarms may or may not occur. As a result, the alarms appear to be coming at random intervals, and it is more difficult to determine that ringing bells and chimes are the cause.

BOUNCE

In a small retail occupancy, a microwave detection system was installed above the entrance door looking back into the retail area and (through a partition) into the rear of the store. This application was theoretically correct since the microwaves would not be projected toward the penetrable glass show windows. The installer did not know, though, that the wallpaper on the partition separating the retail section from the rear stockroom was metallicized. The proprietor had not mentioned the wallpaper, if indeed he knew it contained some metallic substance.

In operation, the microwave signals struck the partition and were reflected back from the metallicized surface rather than penetrating through to the stockroom as intended. Since the original protection planning assumed some microwave coverage in the stockroom area, this presented a security problem. Fortunately, no loss occurred as a result of this environmental problem. What did develop was a series of widely spaced false alarms occurring most often on Wednesdays and Saturdays, usually between 11:00 and 11:35 P.M. After months of false alarms and fruitless system tests, an alarm company guard in a patrol car happened to be passing the troubled premises at the exact moment his dispatcher reported an alarm from the premises. For the first time someone was on the scene at the time of the alarm and could report a large crowd of late-night moviegoers leaving the theater and walking en masse past the store show windows.

Supplied with this information, the alarm company engineer correctly deduced that the bounce of microwave signal energy off the metal wallpaper and back out through the show window did not normally produce a high enough energy pattern for individual pedestrians walking past the premises to upset the alarm circuit. However, when the theater army filed by the windows in close-order drill, the moving mass was large enough to disturb this unintended alarm field, causing the false alarms.

Each reader undoubtedly has his or her own favorite false alarm story. One of the author's memorable puzzles was finally attributed to a giant cockroach whose personal passageway between the dining room and a restaurant kitchen was a small opening cut through a partition to extend the range of a photoelectric beam!

EXPECT THE UNEXPECTED

If a relatively trouble-free alarm system is to be achieved, individuals planning security—whether user, salesmen, or installers—must anticipate unusual closed-period conditions. To assist in this, we have compiled a list of some common environmental alarm causes. Table 9.1 lists these trouble sources by types of motion-detection equipment. In actual practice, some of these causes are "iffy"; proper care in the location of the sensing devices and in dressing or shielding the lead wires connecting the sensor units to the control equipment may reduce the probability of false alarms to an acceptable level.

The key to trouble-free systems lies in developing Sherlock Holmesian deductive thinking in order to anticipate the possibilities and to plan layouts and install in a way that provides sound security while precluding false alarms.

PLAN AHEAD

While the alarm contractor has the primary responsibility of the original system layout and planning, the alarm user is responsible for false alarms or loss of alarm effectiveness that results from deficiencies in security procedures or from structural changes in (and additions to) the premises. An example of security impaired by the alarm user would be the erection of

Table 9.1 The Relationships of False-Alarm-Generating Conditions to Premises Motion-Detection Systems

Alarm-Generating Conditions	*Photo-electric*	*Infrared*	*Ultra-sonic*	*Sound Detection*	*Radar*	*Microwave*	*Passive Infrared*
Air Turbulence Factors							
Fluttering venetian blinds/shades	0[a]	0	X	X	0	X[b]	0[a]
Gravity-fed roof vents	0	0	X	X	X[b]	X[b]	0
Cycling air blowers/ducts and steam or hot water radiators	0	0	X	0	0	0	0
Loose-fitting doors/windows	0[a]	0[a]	X	X	X[b]	X[b]	0
Factory bell time systems	0	0	X	X	0	0	0
Telephones	0	0	X	X	0	0	0
High winds	0	0	X	X	0	0	0
Noise-Only Factors							
Internal							
Unattended teletype	0	0	0	X	0	0	0
Cooling radiators	0	0	0	X	0	0	0
Clocks/chimes	0	0	X[c]	X	0	0	0
Floor contraction	X[d]	X[d]	0	X	0	0	0
Elevator annunciators	0	0	0	X	0	0	0
Barking dog	0	0	0	X	0	0	0
External							
Low-flying aircraft	0	0	0	X	X	X	0
Trucks and buses	0	0	0	X	X	X	0
Demolition work	0	0	0	X	0	0	0
Police sirens, horns	0	0	0	X	0	0	0
Rain, hail, thunder	0	0	0	X	0	0	0
Gunshots	0	0	0	X	0	0	0
Moving Parts							
Internal							
Motors, generators	0	0	0	0	X	X	0

Industrial machinery	0	0	0	0	X	X	0
Elevators	0	0	?	0	X	X	0
Space heaters	0	0	X	X	X	X	X
Ovens	0	0	0	0	X	X	X
Automatic pumps	0	0	0	X	X	X	0
External							
Elevators	0	0	0	0	X	X	0
Subways	0	0	0	0	X	X	0
Window-cleaning equipment	0	0	0	X	X	X	0
Electrical							
Transformers	0	0	0	0	X	X	X
Arcing	0	0	0	X	X	X	X
Fluorescent lights	0	0	0	0	X	X	0
Voltage drops	X	X	X	X	X	X	X
Power failure	X	X	X	X	X	X	X
Temperature change	0	0	0	0	0	0	0
Lightning	X	X	X	X	X	X	X
Changes in lighting	X	0	0	0	0	0	0
RF line transients	X	X	X	X	X	X	X
Obstructions							
Falling cartons	X	X	X	X	X	X	0
Shadows created by stacking of additional merchandise, shelving, and so on	X	0[e]	0	0	0	0	0
Smoke	X	X	0	0	0	0	0
Dust	X	X	0	0	0	0	0
Steam	X	X	X	0	0	0	X
Gases	0	0	0	0	0	0	0
Animal Objects							
Night watchman	X	X	X	X	X	X	X
Lock-in intruders	X	X	X	X	X	X	X

Table 9.1 (*continued*)

Alarm-Generating Conditions	*Photo-electric*	*Infrared*	*Ultra-sonic*	*Sound Detection*	*Radar*	*Microwave*	*Passive Infrared*
Birds	X	X	X	?	X	X	?
Rodents, insects	X	X	0	?	X	0	?
Cats, dogs	X	X	X	?	X	X	X
Miscellaneous							
Heavy vibration (machinery on other floors, etc.)	X	X	X	X	X	X	0
Telephone circuit interruption	X	X	X	X	X	X	X
Humidity	0	0	X	0	0	0	X

0 indicates immune; X indicates potential false alarm; ? indicates uncertain.
[a] Unless movement extends into beam path.
[b] If metal extends into beam path.
[c] Might be a problem in a clock shop.
[d] If floor mounted.
[e] Self-contained units without reflectors.

Notes: Capacitance, air pressure differential, vibration, and sound detection systems designed primarily for safe and vault protection were omitted from this analysis to avoid invalid comparisons.

In some instances where some motion-detection systems were unaffected by alarm makers, this is actually a disadvantage since it indicates a weakness that may easily be exploited by the intruder. An example of this is listed under "Obstruction"—stacking merchandise or adding shelving creates serious dead spots insofar as volumetric motion-detection systems are concerned. Conversely, the beam-type systems will only detect if obstructions are actually placed in their path, and they are effective only when they fully circle heavy, bulky stock that cannot be moved over or under the beam paths.

Over the years, equipment suppliers have produced several variations of redundant or dual-type motion-detection systems. In the past, such equipment proved to be more costly as compared to single detection sensors, and their application in reducing false alarms was not sufficient to gain their acceptance. More recently, manufacturers have introduced dual systems that combine passive infrared and microwave sensing devices. Solid-state technology provided some reduction in the costs of these dual units, and tests indicate the combined sensing circuit is, in fact, less susceptible to false alarm factors than any individual sensor. In fact, the dual sensor responds to the conditions introduced by an intruder who provides body heat and movement and ignores most environmental conditions, other than extreme vibration, RF line transients, lightning, and under extreme conditions, moving metal surfaces that both reflect microwave energy and conduct or radiate heat. Perhaps, as the penalties associated with false alarms become more costly, dual sensing systems will be used more extensively. Expanded application of other dual detectors utilizing ultrasonic and passive infrared sensors is also anticipated.

interior office partitions, thus reducing the area protected by existing motion-detection devices (see Chapter 6).

Protective coverage provided by ultrasonic, audio, and passive infrared motion-sensing devices is contained by glass, drywall, and wooden partitions, panels, and walls. The effectiveness of audio and ultrasonic devices is impaired by the installation of sound-absorbing materials such as acoustic ceilings, draperies, and carpeting. Microwave and radar intrusion-sensing devices can fall victim to metal partitions, wire mesh screens, fluorescent lighting, and aluminum and foil display signs.

Cases in which motion-detection devices were shut out by alterations include instances where dropped ceilings were installed, leaving ultrasonic or passive infrared sensing units protecting only the crawlspace, and where a new forklift was used to double stack appliances, reducing microwave sensing ranges to 15 to 25 feet. Finally, there is the relocating of high-risk stock to an unprotected area and forgetting to move the sensing devices to the new location. To avoid any of these pitfalls, one must plan ahead.

10

Alarm Defeat by Lock Picking

Take Your Pick

J.C. had operated a camera shop in a central city shopping area for many years without ever becoming a burglary statistic. There was good reason for this.

For one, J.C. had had carefully installed and maintained what his insurance broker fondly described as a Grade A No. 3 Local Premises Burglar Alarm System. At night and on weekends, a loud bell installed over the entrance door rang if a door or window was opened. J.C.'s second-floor tenants, who lived directly over the store, were in fact his own private supervisory force. If the bell sounded (and if they were home), they'd promptly call police. Naturally, the tenants had learned not to hit the panic button at 8 A.M., Monday through Saturday, when J.C.'s clerk opened the entrance door prior to turning the alarm system to the off position.

INSURER-REQUIRED CHANGE

In the wake of the civil disorders of 1965–1968, J.C.'s insurance company concluded that this basic local bell burglar alarm system was ineffective in deterring losses under riot conditions. Because they were not supervised from a remote point by police or by central station alarm company personnel, the local alarm could not, they felt, reliably bring police to stop looters. Despite the fact that J.C. had never suffered a burglary loss under any circumstances, they insisted that a condition for renewal of his insurance policy would be the installation of a central station burglar alarm system.

Unhappy and dismayed, J.C. shopped around and soon discovered that central station service would mean tripling his present monthly service and maintenance charges. However, he was pleased to learn his local police department would accept a connection from his premises, via telephone circuits, to a monitoring device installed in the police station—and at very little additional expense. J.C. had little experience in this area, and to him this seemed a solution to his problem. The fact that the insurance company was willing to accept this compromise of their request settled the issue; the alarm system would be connected to the police station.

POLICE-REQUIRED CHANGES

Remove Bell

There was one small hitch. The police department would not agree to supervise J.C.'s alarm system unless he disconnected the outside bell. The police knew that there would be times when circumstances beyond their control would delay their response. When such delays occurred, local residents measured their annoyance by the length of time the bell sounded, often making formal complaints to the police commissioner. The police also had a second reason for wanting the bell to go: they preferred to apprehend burglars; their experience was that bells do frighten some scared, easy-to-catch intruders away from the scene of the crime before police can arrive.

So the bell was removed. J.C. didn't fight this very hard because it had been his responsibility to get out of a warm bed and hurry to the premises with the keys any time the police called to say the local alarm bell was ringing. Now if the police arrived in response to an alarm and found no obvious signs of breaking and entering, J.C. could authorize them to leave the alarm system out of service for the night, permitting him to stay at home, warm and comfortable, rather than make the worrisome trip downtown and back. J.C. knew that an entry through the roof, ceiling, or walls of the premises might not be visible to the patrolmen, but then his bed was warm and comfortable.

No Opening Signal

J.C. also found that the police would not tolerate an alarm signal at the police station when he opened his entrance door each morning or when he closed at night. To solve this problem, his alarm contractor suggested that an alarm shuntlock switch could be installed in the doorframe outside the entrance. J.C. learned that an alarm shuntlock was a combination of a lock and an electrical switch. With it, J.C. could turn the alarm protective device(s) attached to the entrance door on or off, permitting an authorized person to enter or leave when the burglar alarm system was on, without causing an alarm signal.[1]

ALARM SHUNTLOCK AND KEY CONVENIENCE

J.C. also learned that the lock cylinder (and therefore the key) used with the shuntlock would be identical to the keyswitch in his alarm control instru-

[1] Alarm shuntlocks are most commonly used in conjunction with local (bell) alarm systems and with local alarm systems connected with police stations. They are seldom used with central alarm systems, and as a matter of fact, the use of shuntlocks is not permissible in a UL-certified central station premises alarm system.

ment inside the premises, the point at which the entire system was turned on and off and, in the old days, the means by which the local bell was tested. J.C. knew that the odd tubular key of this type of lock cylinder offered some degree of security against picking the lock. The alarm contractor did tell him about a securer lock cylinder with an unusual double-bitted key, but retaining the same tubular key was recommended for convenience to avoid an addition to the already substantial number of keys J.C. carried.

The alarm contractor did not feel it necessary to tell J.C. that, by keying these locks alike, the contractor also reduced the number of keys his repairmen and inspectors would have to carry in response to alarm and trouble signals from J.C.'s premises. To be absolutely frank (which the alarm contractor decided not to be), he ordered all his alarm shuntlocks and alarm control switches keyed alike—one key enabled any of his employees to go about their business servicing any of his subscribers. Besides, for larger quantities of lock cylinders keyed alike, the manufacturer afforded the contractor an additional discount from the price for small-quantity, individually keyed orders.

Convenient for Whom?

Neither J.C. nor his alarm contractor saw the weakness they were creating. However, a burglar did and less than a month later proved the point with one night's work.

When J.C. arrived at his premises one Monday morning, he had some difficulty engaging the key in the shuntlock switch. He failed to notice that, instead of turning the alarm protection device off by turning the key 90 degrees to the right, he was actually turning the protective device on by turning his key 90 degrees to the left. He did notice, however, when he started to insert his door key, that the door lock cylinder was damaged. The cylinder had been "pulled" (forced out of the door) and then jammed back in. To his surprise, the door opened at a touch. J.C. entered the premises to find his camera showcases cleaned out and a small alarm-protected safe at the rear of the store battered and forced open. Gone were his cash receipts from a busy Saturday.

Though J.C. did turn the shuntlock switch to "on," there was no police response to his entering. The burglar had repeated the feat of picking the alarm shuntlock switch outside by picking the premises alarm control instrument keyswitch to the "off" position. That deactivated the protection on the safe and permitted the thief to score heavily in the cash department.

Unfortunately, J.C.'s tenants had been visiting friends at the shore that weekend, and there had been no one to hear the pounding on the safe. Coincidence? Maybe.

Duplicate Key?

Recovering from his shock, J.C. called the police, his insurance broker, and the alarm contractor—in that order. The investigating police detective held that the alarm shuntlock switch had been defeated either by a special lock-picking tool manufactured primarily for the use of locksmiths or by a duplicate key. Since the attacker had found it necessary to remove forcibly the less pick-resistant entrance door lock cylinder, the detective felt that the attacker could not have real skill in the manipulation of lock-picking tools used by experts.

Either of the detective's theories could have been correct since the duplicate key would have worked against the keyed-alike alarm control instrument switch as would the special locksmith's tool designed for this tubular keyway. Once the attacker had adjusted the tool to defeat the shunt-lock switch outside the premises, the same setting would have enabled him to turn off the alarm system at the control instrument.

The insurance company grudgingly settled the loss in full, unaware that they had created their own monster. The local alarm system originally employed by J.C. might have been more effective against this type of attack than the new arrangement the insurance company had, in effect, forced upon him.

WEAKNESSES OF ALARM SHUNTLOCKS

If it had not been for his inquisitive nature and his interest in switches and gadgets, J.C. would have permitted his locksmith and his alarm contractor simply to replace the damaged locks with identical locks, setting himself up for a repeat attack. But J.C. spent some considerable time in analyzing what had happened to permit this burglary to occur.

Perhaps we should pause a minute and jot down our thoughts on the weaknesses that exist under these conditions and the steps that could be taken to reduce this vulnerability and to deter similar attacks. What are your thoughts?

J.C.'s thoughts ran along these lines: He reasoned correctly that almost any type of locking cylinder can be defeated by a skillful picklock, and he immediately set about to determine what steps could be taken to make this shuntlock switch arrangement less vulnerable, either by using a highly pick-resistant cylinder or by eliminating the outside switch arrangement entirely.

He first discovered that there is a relatively inexpensive collar that installs permanently over the tubular lockswitch cylinder and makes it impossible to insert the special locksmith's tool designed to pick this type of cylinder. But since the collar would not prevent the use of a duplicate key, J.C. discarded this as a less than satisfactory solution.

Further investigation by J.C. and the alarm contractor revealed that there is indeed a UL-approved version of this shuntlock switch cylinder that is more difficult to pick and that is not vulnerable to this particular lock-picking tool. (Indeed, to his dismay the alarm contractor learned that his original use of a non-UL-approved lockswitch could not be proper in any UL-certified local alarm system and, further, that the use of any exterior alarm shunt switch was prohibited in a UL-certified central station alarm.)

J.C. discarded the pick-resistant cylinder approach because it too could be defeated by use of a duplicate key. J.C. rightly concluded that he must either remove the switch from outside the protected system or install further protective devices within the premises.

PROTECTIVE DELAY

J.C. saw finally that any switch mounted outside the premises had one inherent weakness—an attacker could practice defeating the shuntlock keyway for hours on end, and time and again, as long as he was not suspect to passersby. No alarm condition would be signaled by his efforts to pick the shuntlock.

Being a camera bug, J.C. solved the problem by the application of a timer device, utilizing the same principle that permits one to photograph oneself. J.C. had the alarm contractor move the shuntlock to the interior side of the door and install a timer. This allowed J.C. a period of 30 seconds in which to leave the premises after the key was turned or an alarm signal would be registered. Similarly, the timer gave J.C. 30 seconds in which to enter the premises and turn off the switch when he opened in the morning. Now anyone who hoped to pick the alarm shuntlock would have to do so within a 30-second period, or the alarm signal triggered by the opening of the door would be transmitted to the police station.

Still concerned over the use of duplicate keys and over the fact that he could not envision the alarm contractor changing his policies on keyed-alike systems for many subscribers, J.C. first considered protecting his alarm control instrument by the installation of a highly pick-resistant lock cylinder of a different type but then decided upon a keyless digital pad device that he felt afforded an even higher level of security.

OTHER SOLUTIONS

J.C. made some mental notes about other steps he might consider at a later date if inventory values and his cash-on-hand risks increased. These steps include the periodic change of the lock cylinders in the entrance door as well as in the keyswitches, the installation of intruder motion-detection devices to detect a different type of entry (through the unprotected ceiling or party walls), and the ultimate step to a central station system. Then there would be no key weakness because the alarm company would supervise opening and closing at scheduled times by the acceptance and exchange of special coded signals.

Some police departments are more flexible in their acceptance of alarm signals at appointed opening times on business days as well as in their willingness to permit the retailer to continue the use of the outside bell. If his police department had accepted the local bell and an opening ring, J.C. could have obtained a special alarm attachment for the entrance door: a shunt magnetic door contact. These contacts permit an authorized individual to exit when the alarm system is turned on without activating the local bell or signaling the police. However, when the retailer opens his premises in the morning, the bell rings (a good test) and the police do receive an alarm signal. Usually the procedure is to accept this as a proper opening of the premises if it occurs within an agreed-upon period of time.

APPROPRIATE NON-ALARM MEASURES

Special credits go to those of you who suggested that J.C.'s habit of keeping large Saturday retail business cash receipts in the safe might have marked him as a good target. J.C. should have made arrangements for the deposit of his Saturday cash receipts—or, for that matter, any other business day receipts—in his bank's night depository or by making a deposit during the business day.

J.C. might also have considered the installation of a grille gate inside the entrance. A gate would provide a physical delay after any entry that would trigger the alarm before the burglar could gain access to valuable stock.

11

Problems of Police-Connected Alarms

Who Has the Key?

Sometimes the news media—TV, radio, and newspapers—have difficulty obtaining the facts concerning sophisticated burglaries, and the facts they do get are sometimes difficult to comprehend. Add to this the press of time involved in reporting tomorrow's headlines today, and some media crime reports become ludicrously inaccurate.

Not so this recent case, which did not come to the attention of the press until a full week after the crime had taken place. Given that much time to get the facts, the following newspaper report should be accurate. Let's call our jewelry store proprietor "Ruth Jones."

ENTRY AND ALARM

To quote the newspaper story, Ruth had "all kinds of protection—neon lights, a floodlight, an electric eye, and a burglar alarm that rang in the police station." Some burglars did not feel the same respect for the way this store was protected, however. Using a large drill to cut a hole in the roof, they pushed in the plaster and wood ceiling and dropped down onto the store shelving, where they helped themselves to "some $25,000 in merchandise" that had not been placed in the safe.

The alarm went off at the police station about 2:00 A.M. Ruth later speculated that falling plaster had disturbed the beam of the electric eye; the actual cause will probably remain unknown. In any event, the police responded immediately.

"Two policemen started for the store a second or two after the alarm was received at headquarters. They checked the front and back doors of the building and looked for evidence of a forced entry. All seemed intact, including the well-laden shelves." When the police were satisfied there was no evidence of intruders within the premises—at least, none visible at street level—they concluded it had been a false alarm and sounded the all clear at 2:10 A.M.

Unfortunately, these policemen did not realize that after ten minutes the alarm system (which had recently been changed to ring only at police headquarters) would stop signaling and would not reset itself. The alarm would be completely out of service until someone entered the premises and reset it.

Not knowing this, the policemen saw no reason to disturb Ruth's sleep to report a false alarm. Her old standby, the ring-till-reset outside bell, had recently been disconnected because it made too much noise. Even if police had noted this, however, they probably would not have attached any significance to its absence.

From the evidence—a battered but resistant safe, stripped showcases, empty Coke bottles and cookie boxes (and the $25,000 loss)—one may assume that once the police had left the scene, the burglars took their time completing the job.

It's intermission time, time for anyone relying on a police-connected alarm system to ponder a while. Is it possible that you face similar problems tonight? Can a situation like this be corrected? How would you establish effective security procedures in conjunction with a police-connected alarm?

RESPONSIBILITY FOR ELECTRIC PROTECTION

With due respect for the fine work of law enforcement agencies everywhere during an era of rising crime, one must consider a basic fact: The front-line responsibility for the supervision of burglar alarm systems, the response to alarm signals, the comprehension of the theory of electric protection, and the repair and restoration of alarm circuitry is not an accepted or integral function of a law enforcement agency. Neither the FBI, the Secret Service, nor any other federal law enforcement units supervise or respond to alarm signals, except those from their own security centers. Almost all state police agencies refuse to permit alarm systems to be connected within their stations, as do police in most major cities including New York, Chicago, Philadelphia, Detroit, Los Angeles, and San Francisco, as well as hundreds more.

Many police departments are now pondering what their rightful role is to be in this specialized security field. The eventual alternatives are either extending this service to the entire community—both residential and business occupancies—or disengaging entirely from providing a service that may more properly be the responsibility of the private business sector.

ORIGIN OF POLICE CONNECTS

Such police alarm services are limited to suburban and rural areas. Police intervention there developed after World War II out of necessity (because of the absence of alarm company facilities) and grew rapidly. Today, alarm system equipment in police stations is usually a hodgepodge of connections with a variety of bells, buzzers, and switches reflecting the individual equipment used by alarm companies installing systems in that area and the local policy as to which classes of business may be served. Some municipalities, for example, limit alarm supervision to banking institutions and jewelers. Further, police personnel are not trained to comprehend the basic principles of burglar alarm systems or the idiosyncrasies of the individual alarms under their supervision. Indeed, only a handful of police departments across the nation have developed internal programs on the effective use and technical aspects of alarm systems in burglary attack detection and loss prevention.

Suburban and rural police departments entered into the alarm business to protect local banks and merchants in the absence of central station alarm company service for remote supervision of burglar alarm systems. At the outset, police agencies did not charge a penny to supervise an alarm system or to respond to an alarm. However, as the workload increases, this concept of free service for the privileged few is rapidly changing. In some municipalities these services now cost the merchant $5 to $25 per month, in addition to the basic connection charges made when the alarm system is placed in service and the monthly charges for the leased telephone circuit.

PROBLEMS INTEGRAL TO POLICE CONNECTS

Let's now discuss the basic problems of police-connected alarm systems. In order of importance these are as follows:

1. Even though the police accept the direct connection of an alarm system, they seldom if ever possess (or accept) keys to the merchant's premises. Thus, they are limited to making a superficial investigation of any alarm signal—a visual check of the building exterior at the ground floor only and of that section of the interior that can be seen from outside. Time after time, crime reports indicate that roof entries go unnoticed, as do hide-ins; entry by "loiding," lock-picking, and duplicate keys; and breaking in through interior walls from adjacent occupancies. Thus, in order to prevent serious losses due to prolonged concealed attack effectively, provision must be made for the prompt notification of responsible key-holding individuals. These representatives of management must be able to respond quickly at all times to admit police into the premises for a thorough search for intruders or hidden evidence of forced entry. In addition, the key-holding representative must be promptly available and able to take charge of the premises when forced entry has occurred.

2. Police are not always available to respond quickly. Higher priorities are necessarily given to other police duties during storms, civil disturbances, and other serious emergencies. In some cities, the load of crimes of violence

absorbs the entire police force. There are often long periods when no officers are available to respond to burglary alarms, which have a much lower priority than calls indicating a risk of life.

Alternate sources of response are necessary, and some assurance should be given that one or more key holders will be available on a standby basis during any closed period, including Sundays and holidays. Further, some form of local annunciation—a loud bell, a siren, or a flashing light—should be installed to upset psychologically the burglar at work. While some skilled burglars have ways to defeat these local annunciators, the less-skilled common thug is likely to flee empty handed or almost. (The combination of Klaxons and strobe lights inside a premises has driven burglars out through plate-glass windows, in their panic to escape.)

3. Police are not electronic technicians. They do not understand the differences in function from one alarm system to another, and they should not be expected to do so. While efforts should be made to furnish simple written instructions as to how the specific alarm system functions and the steps required to reset the alarm, this cannot be considered a satisfactory alternative to having the businessman take charge of his own premises when notified by police that an alarm condition exists.

4. Police cannot be expected to detect the cause of telephone circuit troubles or false alarms or to restore service. The key holder responding, usually an employee of the concern, should be responsible for restoring the alarm system temporarily (if possible) until an alarm company maintenance expert can check out the cause of the alarm or for seeing that the premises are occupied until the alarm can be restored. Obviously, care must be taken to select an alarm contractor who provides 24-hour service 7 days a week.

ALTERNATIVES AND SUPPORTING PROCEDURES

We can close this chapter on a positive note: Alarm companies everywhere are expanding to meet the rising crime market, and it is worthwhile for you to renew your search for more effective alarm service facilities. Where it is not possible to obtain the services of experienced alarm specialists, then make every effort to get police to the premises promptly and to coordinate key holders' arrivals to meet them. You should assist police by identifying for them vital security areas requiring careful search, as well as structural weaknesses (skylights, weak party walls, and other likely points of entry), the location of alarm control units and of hidden alarm devices (installed on the interior doors, infrared beams, and so forth). These measures, plus sound security practices and procedures, will permit the police to function in a more efficient manner under unavoidably difficult circumstances.

12

Corner Cutting in Security

Short Circuits in Security I

CORNER CUTTING

Anyone with a smattering of experience in engineering alarm systems knows that protection layouts and installation techniques are largely determined by almost any factor except security. The prospective customer tempers his layman's specifications to his desires for economy and for convenience in the operation of the system.

The alarm contractor's sales representative (whose income is derived from sales, not the prevention of losses) naturally adjusts his proposal, too. Working within a broad range of company policy and insurance underwriters' standards, he seeks a happy blend of signed contract, sales commissions, and customer security—in about that order.

The shortcuts taken by the customer and the sales representative result in "short circuits" in security that can be—and all too often are—exploited by alert, innovative burglars. Following are some classic examples of penny-wise, pound-foolish security system shortcuts.

EXPOSED ALARM CONTACT TERMINALS

Obviously, alarm-triggering devices such as magnetic or mechanical switch contacts should always be installed within the protected area—on the interior side of doors or windows. The reasoning is obvious: to prevent the attacker from tampering with, and possibly defeating, the protective device *before* opening or forcing a door or window. These same alarm devices must be turned off (that is, disconnected from the central station or other remote supervisory circuit) during the open-for-business period. This leads to the question: Can one of these switches (magnetic or mechanical) be defeated during the open-for-business period so that, when the alarm system is turned on at the close of business, a given door or window will no longer be protected? The answer is yes.

In one such instance, the contact on a rarely used door leading from an office area into a hotel mezzanine hallway was defeated, and an undetected intruder perpetrated a $75,000 burglary. In a similar instance, a fire tower door leading to the seldom visited roof of a suburban department store provided the entry point for a $250,000 haul. In 1982, similar compromises of perimeter doors were key factors that preceded two major bank vault burglary attacks.

Such attempts occur frequently, and in some instances the disconnected or otherwise neutralized alarm device is not detected, even in the subsequent burglary investigation. In such cases the reason for the failure of the alarm system remains a mystery, and the entry point remains unprotected. Occasionally, the cutout (as a disconnect is called by the trade) is used for undetected entry to set up an early-morning ambush robbery attack against opening personnel.

Precautions Against Cutouts

In order to reduce one's vulnerability to this method of attack, certain steps are essential. First, the type of alarm device used in the system should not be susceptible to simple shorting of the wires connected to the device; this can be prevented in installation provided the alarm device permits it. Further, the device's terminals should be concealed within protective covers, which would make a shorting attempt during the open-for-business period both time consuming and conspicuous. In addition, tamper resistant fasteners should be used to mount switches and magnets to deter criminals from detaching these devices from a door or window and related frames.

Despite these precautions, alarm devices installed on doors and other openings in unsupervised and rarely visited areas such as basements, stairwells, and roof towers still present an opportunity to jump out alarm devices that the professional criminal may capitalize on. For this reason, not only should proper identification be required of any person seeking access to these areas during the open-for-business period, but also the visitor should be accompanied by an employee who can supervise the individual's activities sufficiently to be certain that they do not include "extracurricular" work on alarm circuits or devices.

Second, probably the most common exposed weakness of contact alarm devices occurs in retail locations where these are installed above glass entrance doors whose glass is not protected by an alarm circuit. A knowledgeable criminal can successfully defeat the alarm contact device, even during the alarm-on period, simply by breaking the unprotected glass and reaching through this opening to tamper with and defeat the contact on the entrance door.

EXPOSED CONTROL INSTRUMENTS

Frequently several separate alarm systems (each with its own control unit) must be installed in warehouses, commercial office areas, manufacturing facilities, and multi-floor retail premises in order to overcome electrical, security, and operational problems. Since a second or third alarm system involves higher service and alarm supervisory costs (and, often, additional installation charges), contractor salesmen under competitive fire may make every effort to combine as much protection on one alarm circuit or system as is possible. In fact, in his effort to make the sale, the salesman may stretch the possible to the impossible.

When this happens, it is not unusual to find an alarm control instrument into which are connected alarm devices on different floors or in different areas of the premises for the customer's convenience or to meet operational requirements involving different open-for-business hours in different areas. In such a case, the control instrument and, sometimes, the wiring leading to the control instrument are located outside the protected area—vulnerable to defeat by criminals with even limited electronic skills.

Precautions for Alarm Control Instruments

The solution to this problem is simple. Alarm control units and related wiring should always be installed within the area under protection. Compromising this principle can destroy the integrity of the alarm system and lead to substantial losses. Similarly, alarm control units may also be vulnerable to tampering and defeat during the open period in a manner that will not be detected when the alarm is set at the close of business. To reduce this possibility, the cover of the control unit should be electrically protected on a 24-hour circuit, and management should restrict access to the unit. One must reiterate that regardless of the alarm circuit capabilities, it is the user's responsibility for protecting the system from unauthorized access and tampering during the open-for-business period.

Where UL-certified Complete safe or vault alarm systems are concerned, the standard requires that the housing into which the alarm controls are built be electrically lined or laced in addition to the installation of a tamper switch to protect the cover. The user should require the alarm contractor to verify that the alarm instrument installed in conjunction with such systems does, in fact, meet those UL standards.

WALK-TEST CIRCUITS

Most alarm contractors have recognized the importance of providing the customer with a means for testing the operability and range of coverage provided by motion-detection devices at their premises. As a matter of fact, such walk-test capability is a requirement of UL-certified systems. This test should be done each day at the close of business, prior to setting the alarm system for the night.

Such tests perform important security tasks. First, the customer determines if the basic motion-detection system is operating correctly before he leaves the premises. This check reduces the likelihood of the alarm contractor and the police having to respond to unnecessary alarms triggered by faulty motion-detection devices during the closed period.

Second, since the protective coverage provided by motion-detection devices may vary from one time to another and since such changes cannot be determined by tests at a remote central office or police station, the use of on-premises walk-test circuits places the responsibility for checking the operability of the motion-detection systems—and notification of the alarm company—on the user/customer. In fact, many alarm contracts now include a clause establishing this responsibility as that of the customer. Under these circumstances, the failure of a motion-detection system to detect the entry of an intruder into an area supposedly covered by motion detection would be the responsibility of the customer unless he had previously notified the alarm contractor that the unit was not operating correctly.

A walk-test circuit usually consists of meters and/or indicator lights by which the customer can see, by the response to his movements about the premises, the motion-detection coverage being provided by his system. The test devices are installed close to the alarm control unit for convenience and as a reminder to test the system at the close of business each night.

RISK OF ON TEST CIRCUITS

Unfortunately, in some instances the test lights and the motion-detection devices are always operative, even during the open-for-business period. This may be due to limitations of the basic motion-detection equipment, installation shortcuts, or the inexperience of the alarm contractor. Whatever the reason, when indicating circuits are operable during the open period, customers, employees, and anyone else with access to the premises can readily determine the areas of the premises lacking motion-detection coverage. Needless to say, unscrupulous individuals can capitalize on this knowledge to make an undetected entry through an unprotected wall or ceiling into an area where they know motion-detection coverage is missing.

This weakness is inherent in the design of some self-contained mini-motion-detection devices because the walk-test lights are built into the face of the units, which are wired in the operable mode during both open and closed periods. These devices have a limited motion-detection range (10 to 15 feet, approximately), and these limitations can be readily determined by an individual posing as a customer visiting the retail floor. In fact, there is evidence that, in some burglary attacks in shopping centers and malls, entry has been carefully plotted to be just beyond the range of the premises' motion-detection device.

Regardless of the type of motion-detection system employed, walk-test lights and meters should have separate control switches to permit deactivation of the test function during the open period. They should be turned on only when the area has been cleared of all unauthorized personnel and supervisors are performing motion-detection tests. The cost of control switching of the test circuit should be slight in relation to the cost of the total motion-detection system installation and infinitesimal compared to the loss that can result if a criminal is able to exploit this weakness.

13

Attack Against Telephone Alarm Lines

The Cut-the-Cable Caper

Scene: The Mod Corner, a fashionable clothing store for teenagers, located in a one-story shopping center serving a long-established residential community.

Time: 4:30 A.M. any rainy Sunday morning.

Cast: (1) The proprietor, Joe, a tired man who works 6 days a week, 10 to 12 hours a day, to earn his living dealing with affluent and fussy young people who would shop at another store at the drop of a style change and (2) an eager but inexperienced alarm company guard-serviceman whose lack of seniority gets him the "graveyard shift"—the wee hours of the night—as a tour of duty on weekends.

Supporting Players: Police responding to the alarm company's request for assistance and the local telephone company's repair service supervisor.

THE NIGHT EVERY ALARM CAME IN

It was a wild and woolly night in Wettown, U.S.A. High winds were blowing heavy rains from the northeast, and the alarm company switchboard was lit up like a Christmas tree. In response to driving wind, leaky window frames, and other dampness conditions, many alarm systems were in trouble. At 4:30 A.M., when an alarm signal was received from the Mod Corner premises, the central office supervisor was already knee-deep in a backlog of storm-triggered false alarms. The local police department, its own trouble multiplied by the fact that the same situation prevailed at every central station in Wettown, was also very busy. It wasn't a fit night out for beast or burglar—unless the burglar planned on this.

Response by the Book

Miraculously enough, the alarm signal received from the Mod Corner was handled promptly despite weather conditions. An alarm company guard-serviceman, inexperienced but strategically located in a mobile unit not far from the Mod Corner, was dispatched to the scene by radio. At the same time, the alarm condition was reported to police headquarters, where it was quickly radioed to a patrol car in that area.

Within 15 minutes the alarm company agent, equipped with the key to the premises and accompanied by two police patrolmen, opened the entrance door for a careful search of the interior. No intruder was found, and there was no evidence of forced entry through doors, windows, walls, or the ceiling.

As the patrolmen departed, the alarm company serviceman began a test of the alarm circuit to determine the cause of the alarm so that he could repair the defect and restore service. The serviceman quickly determined by the use of test equipment that the telephone circuit connection between the alarm system on the premises and the central office was out of operation. Eureka! This, then, was the cause of the alarm—just another telephone line failure.

Unrestorable Alarm

Unable to communicate with the central office over the alarm telephone circuit or by the store's business phone—that was out of order, too—the guard used his mobile unit's radio to advise his supervisor of the nature of the trouble. The guard was instructed to re-enter the premises and to remain there for half an hour while the central office supervisor endeavored to contact the customer to tell him of the telephone circuit trouble, that the alarm was inoperative, and that he should go to the premises to protect his property. (The supervisor would also contact the telephone company repair service, reporting a break in the telephone circuits serving the Mod Corner and requesting prompt repair.)

So far so good. Only 20 minutes had elapsed from the moment the Mod Corner alarm signal had hit the central station switchboard. But now trouble began.

Responsibility Passes to the Subscriber

At 5:00 A.M. our sleeping proprietor, Joe, was rudely awakened by the call from the harassed central supervisor. He told the sleepy Joe (in no uncertain terms) that the alarm system was out, that the trouble was due to the blinkety-blank telephone company, and that Joe had better get down to the Mod Corner fast to protect his property.

Joe's stupor rapidly changed to irritation and frustration. He told the central station supervisor that it was the alarm company's responsibility to provide service at night, that he (Joe) had already worked 80 hours that week, and that they had blank-blank better keep their guard on the premises because Joe wouldn't go down to the store tonight if his life depended on it! This scene ended with Joe and the supervisor simultaneously slamming telephones into their cradles.

Telephone Repair Not Available

The telephone call to the telephone company repair service was equally unproductive. The repair supervisor said calmly that, due to a recently negotiated labor contract, weekend telephone repair services had been "cut to the bone," and that included the Mod Corner. The central station supervisor angrily reminded him that alarm system circuits were supposed to get emergency service, and so on. Two more telephones "bit the dust."

When the guard again reported to the central office supervisor a little later, "Lock 'er up and leave it!" was the angry order. By 5:13 A.M. the premises was physically secured, with the alarm system left out of order. Tired Joe tossed and turned in his sleep, while our other characters continued their uphill fight against criminals and the weather.

Enter the Hardy Burglars, Unsurprised

At 5:22, two seasoned criminals equipped with complete foul-weather gear, crowbars, torches, and other burglary tools, emerged from their carefully concealed sedan, from which they had followed the first two acts of this play. Indeed, they had created the action since they had cut the telephone lines leading to the building, thus causing the alarm condition.

They knew the likely course of events as well as if they had written the play. Why? Because it was a technique that had worked successfully before. The telephone alarm lines outside the premises were readily accessible, and since they were clearly identified as serving the Mod Corner, cutting the right line had required little skill or technical knowledge.

The burglars knew not only that cutting the alarm telephone circuit would result in an alarm signal but also that under the existing weather conditions, neither the alarm company nor the police would have manpower available to watch the store until the telephone service could be restored.

They also knew that an inexperienced alarm company agent (the most likely to be on duty on a weekend) would not be likely to check the exterior telephone cable leading from the building even if the telephone terminal box housing both alarm and commercial telephone circuits in the courtyard behind the shop had been physically accessible.

The criminals were also reasonably certain that under the circumstances—a hard 6-day work week, a foul night, and "just" telephone line problems—Joe wouldn't consider coming to the store and remaining on watch until sometime Sunday—or even Monday—waiting for the repair of the lines.

All the burglars had to do was wait. When everyone had left, they simply forced entry through the no longer alarm-protected door, torched open the fire-resistant safe, and calmly pocketed Joe's receipts for Friday and Saturday.

THE MORAL AND THE FINE PRINT

The moral: Telephone line attack is a tried-and-true technique that works well because it is based on the predictable attitude of the victims. The solution is simple: If you, the user of central station or police-connected alarm services, are notified at any time (day or night, including holidays) that your alarm system is not operative because of telephone circuit failures, you must recognize that you are without alarm protection. Your stock and other valuables will be vulnerable to forced-entry attack at any time preceding the restoration of alarm service. There is no alternative so someone must take charge of your premises and remain present and on guard until service can be restored. You can't afford to "bet" that the trouble is an act of God.

FAILURE TO ACT CAN VOID INSURANCE

You may also learn, if you read the small print in your insurance policy, that you are not insured under these circumstances unless you take diligent measures to protect your assets. The diligent alternatives available to a tired Joe are admittedly limited.

He may be able to persuade the alarm company supervisor to keep a guard posted on the premises until service is restored, though this may (rightfully) entail additional alarm company charges. Failing this, the proprietor may be able to engage the services of a local guard service organization who will promptly (?) send a man to the premises to maintain the vigil. Other measures might include the performance of hourly patrols by off-duty law enforcement or private security agents. Failing these alternatives, the proprietor may have to take charge of the premises himself.

This last step is the least desirable, however necessary it might be, because the proprietor is not a trained, licensed, or experienced security agent. The frustrated criminals, tired of waiting for the premises to be vacated, might, under certain circumstances, make an armed attack. For these reasons, if it is necessary for the proprietor to take charge of his own premises under these or similar circumstances, he should endeavor to (1) obtain the assistance of an experienced, security-oriented individual; (2) arrange for the alarm company and the police patrols to check on him periodically; and (3) arrange for frequent visits (remember, the phone service is out) by business associates or members of the family to check on his well-being. The use of walkie-talkies and mobile radio units may enhance the defense afforded by these procedures and the safety of the individuals, particularly if the radio equipment permits communications with one individual who is on duty at a safe place away from the premises. If these solutions appear less than satisfactory, it is because they are.

ALARM LINE PRECAUTIONS

In some localities it is possible to obtain a custom-engineered telephone cable installation wherein the alarm telephone circuit is brought into the premises from a different route or direction than that followed by the conventional telephone cable circuits and in some instances via an underground conduit. This work is recommended where high-risk situations exist. However, such work, when possible, usually entails a substantial telephone company cable engineering and installation charge.

In any case, some action is necessary. Substantial case experience indicates a significant number of burglaries are being perpetrated by this technique. Don't take a chance! Think like a thief—act positive.

14

First U.S. Defeat of Central Station-Connected System

Brinksmanship

Most people associate "the Great Brink's" with the robbery of Brink's Boston office on January 17, 1950, when an 11-man gang in Halloween masks made off with $1,219,000, setting off one of the longest manhunts in U.S. history. Unfortunately, Brink's also had another first as the first U.S. victim of successful sophisticated burglary attack by electronic "specialists," when a defeat (compromise) of a high-grade central station direct-connect burglar alarm system made possible a daring and unusual attack against a Gibraltar-like vault.

This attack occurred in Syracuse, New York, on October 24, 1965. In many ways the techniques and equipment used—the modus operandi—were very similar to those employed in a thwarted attack against the Brink's Quebec City office earlier that year.[1] According to the reconstruction by security investigators, a gang of four or five experienced burglars commenced its attack against the security vault of this leading armored car carrier service some time after the close of business on Saturday, October 23.

UNALARMED ACCESS

The gang apparently drove up to the building's truck entrance in a small panel truck or station wagon. They made an undetected entry at the loading dock through an unalarmed pilot door (a man-sized door in a larger overhead loading door), which could be undetectably opened using a celluloid strip or plastic bank calendar card. Once in, they raised the unwired overhead door of the truck receiving entrance, drove in, and closed the door behind

[1] The Quebec City attack was thwarted accidentally. The intruders had waited for the test performed every four hours by the central station and then attached their bypass equipment. Unfortunately for them, the alarm station operator who had made the test became ill, and the tests were repeated by his relief to make sure that they had not been omitted. The gang heard the police dispatched and fled, leaving all their equipment behind.

them. Inside the premises and safe from discovery, they forced open an unprotected interior door and, using sophisticated electrical equipment, succeeded in temporarily compromising the central station burglar alarm system protecting the vault.

It was never determined whether the gang had entered the premises after business hours at times preceding the attack to pretest their ability to defeat the alarm system. However, considering the absence of perimeter burglar alarm protection at this location and the fact that the gang demonstrated knowledge and skill in entering through locks, the opportunity to inspect the premises without detection in advance of the attack was there for them. Perhaps essential to the successful attack was the building location and environmental conditions in the area.

NOISE A CONTRIBUTING FACTOR

The Brink's office was located north of the central city, in an area where light industry and residential dwellings were interspersed. A number of persons, some residing within 200 feet of the building, were at home during the period of the attack. However, the building was near a commercial airport and adjacent to a major highway. Low-flying planes and heavy truck transports at times produced high transient noise levels. Also, the local weather forecast on the night of the attack was for thunderstorms.

Now to the burglary attack: Once inside the premises and under cover, the defeat of the vault alarm system was rapidly followed by the attack on the vault itself, which included the use of a 20-millimeter antitank cannon that police believe was stolen from a railway express office in Plattsburg, New York, during the preceding April.[2] (A similar cannon had been left behind in the Quebec City attack a month earlier.)

CUTTING TORCHES AND CANNON

First, the thieves used oxyacetylene torches to cut away the tempered steel encasing the vault. They then wheeled the mounted cannon into place and, at point-blank range, fired armor-piercing shells at the exposed reinforced concrete wall. The resistance of the vault was indicated by 31 shell casings found at the scene. Although the gang used a mattress to protect against the effects of flying fragments in the confined area just outside the vault, they apparently made no effort to muffle the sound of the cannon fire.

---

[2] Federal authorities had had the cannon under surveillance as it was moved to the delivery point in Plattsburg. Undercover agents were on hand each day, awaiting the man who would come to claim it. The gentleman avoided formalities by breaking into the express office during the night.

THUNDER, PLANES, AND GARBAGE PAILS

It is interesting to note the comments of residents in the vicinity on the Monday following the attack. One man awoke about 3:00 A.M. to what he thought was the thunder that had been forecast on the late TV news. A woman had heard noises that sounded "like cats kicking over garbage pails." A third man, who also identified the sound as thunder, said he "kept a weather eye" on the Brink's installation, and he was at a loss to explain how the vehicle arriving at the building entrance the preceding night could have escaped his observation. Another woman, who returned from her employment as a waitress about 2:15 A.M. Sunday, noticed nothing unusual. Others commented that the noise of approaching planes commonly drowned out other noises. Still another man said he would have heard the sounds of cannon fire if the wind had been blowing from the right direction. One can only speculate whether planning for this attack had anticipated that the sound of cannon fire would be obscured by the environmental conditions.

The gang succeeded in punching a hole approximately 20 by 18 inches through the 12-inch reinforced concrete wall. The oxyacetylene torch was used to remove the reinforcing rods remaining, and one of the gang crawled through to open the vault door from the interior. (The gang left behind a supply of nitroglycerin apparently intended as a last resort if the cannon failed them.)

Once inside the vault, the gang loaded some $500,000 in currency and checks into their vehicle. Final estimates indicated the currency loss was approximately $100,000.

Judging from the amount of equipment left behind, the sound of a police patrol car or ambulance siren on the highway a block away probably frightened the gang into thinking an alarm had been received at the central station office despite their precautions. Investigators found an array of heavy-duty equipment including gas masks, welders' masks, the cannon mount, and the electrical equipment used to defeat the alarm system. Approximately $100,000 in coin was also left behind.

LACK OF PHYSICAL BARRIERS AND SPACE PROTECTION

The moral to this story is quite clear. The installation of highly tamper-resistant deadlocks (locks whose bolts cannot be forced back into the lock when in a locked condition) with pick-resistant cylinders would have made entry more difficult, while a premises alarm system with motion-detection equipment might have detected the gang's entry and the approach to the vulnerable telephone terminal box within the building.

In the absence of interior protection (and in view of the fact that, at this time, there were no commercially available alarm line security systems, due to a lack of demand), only the physical strength of the vault structure stood between the gang and a successful attack. One could not fault Brink's vault security standards because thousands of vault structures protecting similar risks do not afford as much resistance.

This incident marked a turning point in the state of the art of central burglar alarm systems, forcing high risks everywhere to reassess the physical security afforded by their safes and vaults, and the extent to which their alarm systems could protect not only their assets but also the telephone alarm line circuits now proved vulnerable to criminal attack.

15

Defeat of Police-Connected Alarm Systems

Pole Vaulting

Palm trees swayed gently in the early evening breeze, their graceful shapes silhouetted by the setting sun. Whitecaps specked the deep blue water of the bay that lapped softly against the white sands landscaping this modern banking institution only a stone's throw from the water. As the sun slid slowly below the horizon, for a few moments this splendid architectural creation stood stark and magnificent against the orange glow of sky and mirroring water—a photographer's dream, a depositor's fairyland. What a choice site for a banking location, away from busy streets, isolated from brassy competitors who might lure depositors away with service gimmicks and bold signs advertising free gifts for deposit dollars.

As the first stars appeared in the sky, the remaining bank personnel locked the vaults, set the police-connected alarm system, turned off most of the interior lights, locked all exits, and departed. The stage was deserted, left to nature. The illuminated facade of the bank shone brightly in the moonless night. However, had the last departing supervisor made a more than casual surveillance of the area surrounding the bank, he would have observed through the twilight a lone lineman at the crossbar of a telephone pole between the bank and the busy highway a few blocks away. To the occasional passersby this worker in service garb would be as invisible as the hidden face in a puzzle.

A few minutes later the scene was completely deserted. The "telephone repairman," his task completed, had disappeared.

ENTER A "CLEANING VAN"

Soon a panel van like those used by cleaners moved quietly "on stage." It stopped briefly in front of the bank, where one occupant alighted and strode briskly toward the door. The van then swung around the building and disappeared from view, its presence shielded by the L-shaped two-story section of the building.

The man at the front door appeared to have trouble opening the lock; perhaps he was a new cleaner, or the keys did not fit well. But in this deserted setting there were no critics. Even a pelican perched atop a nearby utility pole was too sleepy to complain at the rasp of a sawblade slowly cutting through a soft metal lockbolt. Apparently the late worker had lost his keys but not his determination.

THE BELL THAT DIDN'T RING

One may wonder why, when the door was opened, no alarm sounded. Perhaps the alarm on this entrance door was connected to an exposed electrical shunt switch installed to permit janitorial service people to enter the building during the closed period—a common practice in many banking institutions. Perhaps this branch had no perimeter alarm system protecting entrance doors, windows, roof hatches, and so on. This, too, is quite common in bank installations. Perhaps the "telephone lineman" working outside had "inadvertently" disabled the alarm system. If this were the case, though, would not the police have noted that the alarm system was in trouble? When telephone circuit breaks occur, conventional police-connected alarm circuits usually register a trouble signal at the police station.

And why, if the alarm system was working, was the alarm bell not heard resounding into the still night? There may have been no alarm bell at this location. After all, as remote as this bank was, an air raid siren would hardly have reached the ears of people several blocks away, inside cars, homes, and stores. Under such conditions alarm installers quite often omit a local bell on the grounds it would be useless. Then, too, as previously noted (Chapter 10), many law enforcement officers prefer the omission of the local bell, arguing that a silent alarm is more effective. In any event, the vault was surely completely protected by an alarm system. The depositors' assets supposedly were safe in any case.

THE ATTACK BEGINS

Once inside the premises, the cleaner wedged the door shut, bounded up the stairs to the second floor, walked swiftly down the corridor—he couldn't have been a new man; he knew the premises like the back of his hand!—and climbed an iron ladder leading to a roof hatch. Unfastening the nonkeyed snaplock mechanism, he raised the hatch, strode to the rear of the roof, and whistled softly for action from the darkened van. A rope ladder and a rope dropped to the ground, and a strange array of "cleaning equipment" was hoisted silently and quickly to the roof above.

The Well-Equipped Burglar

The "cleaning equipment" included a hydraulic jack, a 9-foot 4-by-4 wood beam, several lengths of steel rod (looking much like the burning bar described in Chapter 22), two large tanks of oxygen, one flint igniter, a 50-foot length of garden hose, a knotted rope, ten grain sacks, an electric fan, and a wide assortment of electric drills, pinch bars, crowbars, drill bits, sledgehammers, and metal punches. One rope shipment moved more slowly to the roof; this contained sticks of dynamite and blasting caps. Last, the roof attendant hoisted up a homemade heat shield.

The van doors were closed, and while three of the van's occupants ascended the rope ladder to the roof, the lone driver drove the van quietly off the lot, down the street, and into the darkness. The four "cleaners" proceeded to move their tools through the hatch, down the ladder, and next to the wall of a second-floor storage and records vault located directly above the main banking vault. As the roof hatch closed and latched behind the last man, the action was hidden from all but those in the bank.

Records Vault Easily Entered

First, the cleaners forced a man-sized opening in the nonreinforced cinder block records storage vault wall, using the hydraulic jack and the 4-by-4 beam. One man entered through the hole, released the combination lock, and opened the vault door. The equipment was moved in through the vault door and clustered about the center of the vault.

A series of 1-inch holes were drilled into the concrete floor, which of course was the ceiling of the money vault below. Dynamite was placed in the drilled holes, blasting cap detonators wired to the sticks of dynamite, an electrical cord run to an outlet outside the vault, and—fingers in ears—the diligent workers blew a man-sized hole into the ceiling of the money vault.

Blasting and Burning

Once the dust and smoke settled, burning bars were used to cut away the steel reinforcing rods lacing the gaping hole in the concrete. The knotted rope was used to lower the necessary tools into the money vault. At this point, the real cleanup began. Tellers' lockers and dozens of safe deposit boxes were forced open by knocking off and punching out the locks.

Once the loot was bundled up for ready removal from the premises, exit from the money vault was accomplished by disabling the time locks on the interior of the vault door and retracting the bolts. These crooks were lucky because some vault door bolts cannot be retracted until the combination is dialed to release the bolt work.

One may speculate as to the length of time it took these cleaners to complete their task. Certainly when one is engaged in such rewarding work, little notice is taken of time.

Whether this weekend attack was accomplished in one night or two, the intruders must have departed in the black of night through the entrance door (all of the "cleaning tools" were left behind, simplifying exit problems) and into the waiting van whose magical reappearance at just the right time was actually the result of two-way radio communication.

VULNERABILITIES OF THE BANK

The main money vault was protected by a conventional Complete police-connected local bank vault alarm system meeting UL standards for the electric protection of a bank vault. There is only circumstantial evidence that the system was defeated with electronic wizardry. The police department received an alarm signal in the early morning hours of the second day, and officers responding discovered the unbolted entrance door, the open vault, and the messy work of the weekend "cleaners." The receipt of an alarm signal at that time indicates the probability that the telephone lineman returned and, having removed his temporary circuitry and restored the alarm telephone circuit, had permitted an alarm signal to register the fact that the vault door was open.

In analyzing this attack, only a few points need further clarification. Of course, the garden hose supplied water from the utility room to keep things cool, and the fan provided adequate ventilation within the confined vault area. The identity of the "cleaners" may never be known, but the vulnerabilities that permitted this attack to succeed are identified in the following sections.

Need for Line Security

While the vault had more-than-adequate alarm sensing devices, conventional police-connected bank vault systems are no longer adequate against attack by sophisticated criminals having extensive knowledge of alarm systems and telephone circuits. Additional protection is needed to make it more difficult to nullify the alarm system's telephone link with the remote supervisory station. Actually, such sophisticated line security systems (see Chapter 16) are now available for use with most bank vault alarm systems commonly connected to police supervisory panels.

There is no such thing as a defeat-proof alarm system. However, police-connected vault alarm systems that have been equipped with sophisticated (and UL-approved) high line security equipment have not yet suffered a defeat.

Isolation Requires Better Physical Protection

When a banking location (or any facility housing high-value securities, currency, or products) is located in an isolated area away from traffic and frequent police patrols, additional care must be taken in regard to the physical structure itself. Where high values are held in such locations, it may be necessary to double vault construction specifications to present attackers with a more difficult penetration task. While such a measure will not make an attack impossible, criminals are sufficiently lazy to prefer easier targets, of which they have an ample supply.

Additional Alarm Circuits and Local Annunciators

The possibility of defeat of an alarm system, even one with line security, is everpresent. However, additional alarm circuits will further complicate the attackers' task and may unnerve the attackers when they find they cannot deactivate the system completely. For example, loud UL-approved alarm bells in difficult-to-reach locations outside the building, sirens (where permitted), and flashing lights wired to nearby utility poles may create sufficient noise and disturbance to assist them in a decision to depart hurriedly. These devices, properly installed, can usually provide an initial signal that the attackers cannot immediately silence.

The use of secondary alarm systems should be considered as well. If access to the premises is properly controlled during the open-for-business period (and essential information is restricted, as it should be), criminals casing the premises may not learn of the presence of local alarm systems, telephone-dialing devices, and so forth and may be surprised by the presence of these secondary alarm-signaling systems.

Perimeter and Space Alarm Protection

The additional effectiveness of perimeter alarm systems and interior motion detection should not be underestimated. In the absence of these systems, the criminal has ample opportunity to enter the premises during the closed period (using duplicate keys or picking the lock) in order to case the target, assess the tool requirements to penetrate the vault, plan entry and escape routes, and so forth. In addition, if the vault and the premises alarm systems are connected to separate telephone alarm circuits, the electronics "expert" will be presented with the task of defeating two alarm systems rather than one, which is significantly more difficult.

Exterior Private Patrol Service

The use of exterior private patrol services could have been a deterrent to the planning of the type of attack described in this chapter. Such services would have minimized the problem of the isolation of this bank.

LEARNING FROM EXPERIENCE

It is understandable that banking customers with uninsured safe deposit box contents had cause for alarm and displeasure with the previously superb banking facilities. However, no fault should be found with a financial institution suffering a first-time loss through new attack techniques. At the time of the case discussed here, bank vault alarm system defeats and the use of the burning bar were relatively new approaches. As a matter of fact, some ten other banking institutions located in the same geographical area suffered similar burglary attacks during a 6-month period. As a result, many banking institutions in that area moved rapidly to have sophisticated high line security added to their alarm systems, a measure that concluded this crime chapter in that section of the country.

EPILOGUE

Almost two years to the day later, the following headline appeared in a newspaper published many hundreds of miles from the scene of our story:

THE IMPOSSIBLE CRIME: IT WAS DONE WITH EASE
Planning Key to Success of County Bank Burglary

The five-ton steel vault door at the Bank was closed and locked sometime after 6:00 P.M. on Friday, March . When it finally swung open again 70 hours later, horrified bank officials were confronted with a four-foot high pile of smashed safe deposit boxes and a jumbled mess of personal papers, stock certificates, jewelry, coins, wills, and even an urn that contained the cremated remains of a relative of one of their customers.

Bank officials called it "an impossible crime." "It had never been done before," said one—"at least, that's what we thought at the time."

It now appears that there have been other such crimes elsewhere, although they were never publicly acknowledged. Vaults in other banks throughout the nation have been cracked, they say. The Federal Bureau of Investigation refuses to comment.

> The key to the crime, officers say, was the planning that went into it. In the first place, the bank branch was probably selected for its remoteness.

It is interesting to note that the list given of "cleaning materials" and tools left behind at this location was virtually identical to that found at the scene of our story—right down to the electric fan and the garden hose.

Perhaps there is another moral to this story. In addition to planning skills, the underworld seems to have a better communication and training system than some law enforcement agencies, let alone the management of businesses with valuable inventories to protect.

16

Alarm Line Security

What's That Line . . . Security?

Throughout this book, frequent reference is made to the *defeat, compromise,* or *nullification* of an electrical alarm system for the purpose of burglarizing a premises, safe, or vault. While the potential also exists that holdup alarm signal circuits could be similarly defeated, no cases of this kind have been reported. Security considerations preclude detailed technical description of the methods employed to compromise alarm systems, but a general explanation is desirable so that readers may better understand both the problem and the steps that reduce vulnerability to this kind of attack.

In this discussion, compromise of the alarm system will not include the "jump-out," rewiring, or mechanical nullification of alarm sensors. This simpler kind of attack occurs because the criminal has been permitted access to the premises and the sensors during the open-for-business period. Hence, sensor nullification can be largely prevented by access control and sound security procedures by a premises' management personnel.

ALARM SYSTEM DEFINED BY COMPONENTS

To avoid misunderstanding of the meaning of *alarm system compromise* as it is used here, we will review briefly the components essential to a complete electrical alarm system. The first segment of an alarm system consists of the actuating sensors or detection devices wherever they are installed—on doors, windows, walls, skylights, safes, or vaults. Sensors include door and window contact switches; electrical foil; lacing (applied conductive wiring to detect penetration through the body of a door or through a wall or ceiling); floor traps; photoelectric beams; space alarms such as ultrasonic, passive infrared or microwave; vibration sensors; and those sensors—audio, air pressure, proximity, vibration, and so on—associated with safe and vault protection.

The second essential of the system is the electrical circuit wiring that links each device to the third essential, the alarm system control unit by which the system is turned on or off and tested. The control unit identifies the emergency and "does its thing," whether ringing a nearby bell, triggering a whooping siren, or calling the police or alarm company—or all three or more.

Whatever the number or type of actuating device, the total effect is a circuit having a certain fixed electrical resistance. When a DC voltage is applied, a specific electrical current flows in the electrical circuit wiring.

When the alarm system is on and an alarm device is actuated, the electrical resistance of the circuit changes, creating a corresponding change in the amount of current flowing through the circuit. This change triggers a relay in the control unit. This relay sounds the alarm by activating a local annunciator (for example, an alarm bell) and/or by changing the current flow in the telephone alarm line circuit that transmits the signal to a remote supervisory point.

ROLE OF REMOTE MONITORING

In order to prevent loss, someone must monitor this circuit, read the alarm condition, and promptly dispatch guards and police to the premises to capture or otherwise stop the intruder. This someone might be in the central station, police monitoring station, or telephone-answering company monitoring service. An ordinary telephone circuit (without dial tone) is used to carry the electrical alarm signal between the premises and the supervisory station. This alarm telephone circuit is the point at which the compromising of the alarm system has occurred. To clarify how an alarm system can be compromised by attacking this connecting link, let's review remote monitoring.

In its simplest form, the central station or police monitoring equipment remotely supervises an on-the-premises alarm system control unit that when on, reacts to significant change in the amount of current flowing through the circuit and reports this change as an alarm condition. The central (or police) station electrical control circuit in turn reacts to the alarm condition signal by actuating bells or buzzers or code printers that in turn alert a supervisor to take responsive action.

METHODS OF EVADING ALARM CONDITION

Obviously, if the criminal can correctly introduce a dummy electrical circuit component equal in resistance to the normal, non-alarm-state resistance of the premises alarm system in the telephone line link between the control unit and the remote monitoring station, the central station or police monitoring equipment may not detect the difference. The true alarm system resistance (or voltage characteristics) and the resistance produced by the substituted component—the dummy alarm circuit—produce the same amount of current flow in the telephone alarm line circuit. When this match is achieved, the attacker can disconnect the premises alarm system from the telephone alarm line, and the alarm system is compromised.

Because the telephone alarm line must necessarily run outside the protection afforded by the premises' alarm system, the alarm telephone circuit is understandably considered the weak link in alarm security. There are also unnecessary or less necessary instances in which the telephone alarm line is accessible and unprotected within the premises or within the building in which the premises are located.

Point of Attack

While the point of compromise attack is invariably near or on the protected premises, the exact location depends on various conditions. If, for instance, the accessible perimeter (doors, windows, or other openings) is not alarm protected, a burglar may undetectably enter the premises to compromise the telephone alarm circuit at a point within the premises.

In cases where alarm telephone circuits are overhead (as distinguished from underground cabling), compromises have occurred at the utility pole nearest the premises. Where telephone terminal boxes are located in unprotected building hall corridors or basement service areas (a notoriously poor security area), the compromise attempt may be made at this point since the area affords cover for the criminal.

Line Identification

All too frequently these alarm telephone circuits are identified by tags attached to the terminals that indicate not only that they are alarm circuits but even which portion of the premises alarm system such telephone circuit serves. These tags are attached because they eliminate error or facilitate work by telephone installers and repairmen. (The inexperienced telephone installer may disconnect a toneless line.) Unfortunately, this practice is equally (or more) helpful to the burglar searching for the correct alarm telephone circuit.

Even when tags are not used, the line may be identified as an alarm circuit by red insulator sleeves, or covers, over the terminals. Where there is only one alarm system connected through the telephone terminal box, the single set of sleeves is enough information for the attacker to identify his target. Even when there are several such sleeves, the attacker still benefits.

Once the criminal has successfully attached the substitute (dummy alarm) components or circuit and has disconnected the wires linking the alarm system with the alarm telephone circuit, the communicating circuit now flows from the remote supervisory station through the alarm telephone circuit to the dummy alarm and back to the remote point. At this point, the sensors on the premises are ineffective. The opening of a door or window, passing through a trap, or burning a safe or vault cannot signal the remote station. While an intrusion may still ring a bell, sound a siren, or flash a light located at the premises, less skill and expertise are required to compromise or physically destroy local annunciating devices.

THE POLICE CONNECT AND COMPROMISE

The degree of sophistication required to defeat the alarm telephone circuit connection to a police or telephone-answering company monitoring system is at least theoretically lower than that required for the defeat of a central station system. This is due in part to the fact that police departments have neither the time nor the technical manpower required to test and supervise the more sophisticated alarm monitoring systems employed by private central station alarm companies. This is a realistic limitation, of course. The police crime prevention function is primarily geared to the protection of life, the investigation of crimes, and the apprehension of criminals.

CENTRAL STATION ALARMS: DIRECT WIRE AND McCULLOH

Direct wire (also referred to as "direct line") is where a separate alarm telephone circuit is used to connect the premises alarm to an individual, unshared supervisory monitoring position at the central station. Where alarm telephone circuit rental costs or long-line wire resistance characteristics are a factor, such as in outlying areas at long distances from the central station offices, code transmitters on a shared alarm telephone circuit are sometimes employed.

This system, which is referred to as a McCulloh, or party-line, circuit, permits several premises alarm systems to be connected in series through the same alarm telephone circuit loop to the central station. The code transmitter on the premises identifies the premises signaling and the type of signal—fire, burglary, holdup, for example. These series-loop-wired party-line alarm telephone circuits are necessarily more vulnerable to defeat than direct-wire or parallel-configured multiplex circuits since they yield to less-sophisticated compromise techniques.

Compromise and the Direct-Wire Connect

One major advantage of direct-wire alarm telephone circuits is that the central station can (by remote control) simulate an attack against specific sensors in the premises' alarm circuit when the alarm system is on. The responding sensors upset the electrical balance of the alarm circuit, and the change in the amount of current flowing in the circuit is signaled back to the central station as an alarm condition, thus confirming that the true alarm devices are still able to communicate to the remote supervisory point.

It is a matter of record that these tests (which are exclusive to the direct-wire telephone alarm line circuit configuration) have been effective in detecting compromise equipment in use. Thus the frequency of the tests of these circuits during the on period and the ability of the attacker to simulate a correct test response (using additional compromise equipment) are key factors in the probability of success in a direct-wire alarm telephone circuit compromise attempt.

U.S. ALARM LINE DEFEATS

Before we explore the effectiveness of the addition of line security in preventing or deterring direct-wire alarm telephone circuit attacks, let's review the history of such compromise attacks. There were no known compromises of direct-wire alarm telephone circuits in the United States prior to 1965, although it is possible that some unexplained successful attacks may have occurred by this means. U.S. alarm companies, police, and businessmen were then unaware of this technique and may have overlooked prior cases. This form of attack was successfully employed in the United Kingdom and in Canada early in the 1960s (if not before), and by 1965 one major worldwide insurance company had begun to require certain security measures against compromise attack.

In the United States, line compromise attacks apparently began in 1965. For 6 years the incidence of compromise attacks steadily increased in frequency and in success, with the majority of attacks being directed against banks, the jewelry industry, and pawnbrokers.

Throughout the country there have been several hundred successful compromise attacks against premises protected by central station alarm systems. Central station systems bore the brunt of the attacks, obviously because they protect most high risks.

ANALYSIS OF SUCCESSFUL COMPROMISE ATTACKS

In-depth analysis of these attacks by police, FBI, insurance, and private crime prevention and alarm company agents has produced certain basic facts. The following sections discuss these facts.

Prior Access Indicated

In almost every case, there was clear evidence that each step of the operation had been thoroughly planned. The criminals' knowledge of the location of alarm devices, control units, and alarm telephone circuit terminal boxes was apparent, strongly suggesting that a member of the gang had had access to the premises at least once prior to the burglary.

Unalarmed, Poorly Secured Perimeter

In most cases, there was no alarm system protecting doors, windows, and other easily accessible openings. Further, door locks were not highly resistant to lock-picking devices; in some cases criminals could enter the premises using celluloid strips. Without physical and electrical perimeter protection, the attackers were free to case the premises without leaving evidence of their visit or visits. In those few cases where premises alarm devices were actuated prior to the successful compromise, the cause was invariably recorded as unknown. Just another false alarm!

Safe or Vault Relatively Weak

In almost every case, the safe, vault, or physical structure protecting the target was insecure against modern tools and attack techniques. Updating the security of these items is clearly a needed step in reducing the occurrence of a compromise attack.

Alternate Escape Routes

There was always an effective escape route. This factor must have weighed heavily in the selection of the target. Indications are that elevators, stairways, fire escapes, and roof departure points were carefully noted. The criminals had identified not only a preferred point of entry but also several means of exit.

Nights and Weekends Preferred

Almost all of the compromise attacks occurred at night, and most took place on weekends. For major risks, the most vulnerable periods were three-day holiday weekends that provided extra time for the physical attack on the safe or vault structure. There was no geographical limitation: the attacks occurred from Maine to California, from north to south. However, when a gang achieved notable success against a specific alarm system, there was a tendency to attack other subscribers who had the same alarm system equipment. There also were instances of alarm company control equipment being stolen from another location for use as a direct substitute—the necessary dummy alarm.

LINE SECURITY SYSTEMS

Early in 1966 certain central station alarm companies and alarm system equipment manufacturers recognized the seriousness of this situation—a direct threat to the survival of the alarm business. Thus began the intensive research and development that has resulted in the development of equipment that, when added to a conventional alarm system, provides additional protection against telephone alarm line compromise attacks.

These devices are called *line security* systems. In essence, these systems produce, on the alarm telephone circuit, additional or more complicated electrical circuit characteristics requiring greater electronic skills and more sophisticated measuring equipment for compromise. While a few successful compromise attacks against systems with line security have occurred, in nearly all cases the attacks fail. The alarm industry has succeeded in separating the amateur electronic burglar from the rare professional.

While defeats of line-security-protected systems have been few and far between, the number of attempts cannot be accurately estimated. It is probable that many attempts cause false alarm conditions reported as "alarm—cause unknown." Because most attempts occur outside the protected premises, there is no attempt to force entry (and, hence, no visible evidence) until the attackers are satisfied their compromise efforts are ready. Where perimeter protection is inadequate or nonexistent, entry by celluloid or lock picking goes undetected. Whether attacking or casing a premises, the criminals use police radio monitor receivers and are ready to flee in the event of any alarm. When reconnoitering, professionals are careful to avoid leaving any evidence of their presence on the premises, responding police and alarm company guards naturally assume just another false alarm.

Line security devices or systems range from a simple fixed-frequency AC tone-generating device, through intricate interalarm circuit connections, to even more sophisticated pseudorandom direct-wire and multiplex interrogate and response circuits.

Line security systems have been defeated in a few instances. However, an analysis indicates that most of these defeats have occurred where only tone-generating systems were in use. This may be due in part to the fact that criminals have been able to steal alarm control units containing these tone-generating devices in order to substitute them in the defeated telephone alarm line circuits. Two successful compromises of alarm systems employing two different types of line security operating in conjunction—the dual line security concept—have been reported.

Multiplex Signal Transmission

Soon after the alarm industry began to experience compromise defeats of McCulloh and direct-wire alarm telephone transmission circuits, a new multiplex form of signal transmission was commercially introduced by segments of the central station alarm industry. Like the McCulloh system, multiplex alarm telephone circuit transmission afforded the advantages of sharing the cost of alarm telephone leased circuits over many subscribers. However, multiplexing as a concept includes the provision for the high-speed interrogation of each alarm control system connected in parallel to the telephone circuit (some systems scan each instrument once each second). This interrogation, in effect, triggers a specially coded transmitter installed in each protected alarm control instrument. The central station receiving equipment analyzes each distinct incoming coded signal and translates a failure to receive a transmitted code signal within a specific time frame into an alarm condition requiring investigative response.

While in theory compromise by substitution is possible, the time frame during which this might be accomplished is so limited that no successes have been reported to date and UL has accorded the Grade AA high line security listing to many of the multiplex transmission systems presently in use. The author is unaware of any defeats of multiplex interrogate and response systems although attempts have been reported.

UL standards for multiplex systems do limit the number of alarm control units and related transmitters that may be operated over a single transmission circuit serving UL-certified customers. These limitations vary by type of equipment and are designed to maintain the short interval interrogation cycle.

To date, there have been a few defeats of pseudorandom direct-wire systems that were central station or police monitored. These defeats involved digital programs that were relatively short in duration or conditions wherein the program returns to the beginning point each time the alarm system is reset.

Cost Factors

The reader may question why, in view of the record to date, dual systems or digital systems are not commonly in use. The reason is economic; the addition of line security systems may mean considerable additional expense to the user.

For a dual line security system, the user must have at least two separate direct-wire alarm telephone circuits. This entails the cost for a second direct-wire alarm telephone circuit (which can be expensive when the distance—premises to central station—is great) and the additional service cost for central station supervision and operation of the second alarm circuit. While the pseudorandom direct-wire line security systems do not require two telephone alarm lines, equipment requirements entail a substantial installation and purchase expense for the user. Multiplex line security is an inherent part of that concept of signal transmission and is the more economical form of line security, which accounts for its increasing use over the entire range of alarm subscribers.

UL AND LINE SECURITY

Most line security systems have been promptly submitted to UL for analysis, for rating as to their purpose, and for approval or listing.[1] Today, most central station alarm companies, as well as installers and suppliers furnishing alarm systems, have the capability of furnishing UL-rated line security systems. Unfortunately, alarm companies—perhaps for security and legal reasons—are reluctant to report compromise attacks. As a result, UL has received only limited information documenting criminal skills. Their ratings must necessarily be based on the theoretical effectiveness of these line security systems.

Some central station or local alarm companies and equipment manufacturers have not, for one reason or another, sought the approval of their line security components or systems. That this has not been done may be due to a lack of expertise, to incompatibility of line security systems with alarm control units and central station–police supervisory equipment, or to other reasons unknown.

After a decade of experience in evaluating the effectiveness of tone- and interalarm-type line security systems, UL concluded in 1978 that these systems were no longer satisfactory as deterrents, and accordingly, the standards for Grades AA, BB, or CC certifications were modified. The new standard excluded those forms of line security from Grades AA, BB, or CC certification. However, alarm contractors were permitted to retain tone or interalarm certificates in force until September 1980. After that date, only listed pseudorandom direct-wire and multiplex line security systems met the AA, BB, or CC certification standards. Some alarm contractors, as a matter of policy, adopted the higher standards at their inception in 1978 as applicable to new system installations, and by notification to existing certificate holders, they recommended upgrading to the higher line security systems.

Unfortunately, to meet the competition of UL-listed line security, substandard unlisted systems are being marketed under nomenclature that implies that these systems afford line security protection equivalent to that provided by UL-approved components. These substandard devices may have labels such as *line control* and *pulsed security,* but they do not afford equivalent protection against compromise attempt. For this reason, the reader is urged to determine the actual UL rating and practical effectiveness of such systems before incorporating them in his protective circuits.

[1] UL listing is a prerequisite to inclusion in certified alarm systems. See Chapter 5.

In some instances there is a requirement for line security to be applied to a system that, for other reasons, is not UL certified. In those instances, the user should require that the supplier warrant in writing that his line security system will perform to, and in all other respects meet, Grade AA UL certification standards—that is, to standards for a Grade A certificate plus approved line security, Grade AA in UL terms.

Line Security and Grade A Local Alarms

There is no such UL designation as a "Grade AA Local Alarm" system, even where the system is directly connected to another remote monitoring location other than a police or central alarm station. Here again, though, the user may obtain from his alarm contractor the installation of an otherwise UL-approved line security system and require written confirmation from the contractor that the Grade AA rating would otherwise apply.

LINE SECURITY AND THE POLICE CONNECT

The need for the addition of line security devices or systems to alarm systems directly connected to police stations is evidenced by the increasing number of attacks against high-risk targets with this type of alarm supervision. In part, this increase is probably due to the fact that high risks with direct-connect central station service have often added listed line security protection, and this has caused burglars to direct their attention to the non-central-station-supervised alarm systems.

Adding line security to police connects, however, may be easier said than done. While all three listed forms of line security can be added to police-connected systems, most police departments have regulations against more than one alarm telephone circuit per location as well as against the installation in the police station of "foreign" monitoring equipment. The latter restriction is of particular concern in the utilization of pseudorandom line security systems, which require the addition of a considerable amount of monitoring components at the police station.

UL has established a separate standard for pseudorandom direct-wire police-connect alarm systems that permits the alarm contractor who installs line security devices that meet that standard to issue Grade AA police-connect certification. However, we note in some instances, where police regulations require the line security receiving equipment to be located at a point away from the direct supervision of the dispatcher, some alarm contractors are reluctant to issue the Grade AA certification. Their reasoning is that the link between the line security receiver and the annunciator in the dispatch area is not afforded the same line security protection. When this occurs, the user is advised to determine whether a serious weakness exists, in addition to obtaining the letter of equivalence from the alarm contractor.

Sometimes departmental rules would prevent the addition of line security. In this event, the user should discuss directly with police department officers his particular high-risk target, the history of defeats of police-connected alarm systems, and the rise in frequency of such attacks in recent years.

LINE SECURITY FOR McCULLOH-TYPE CENTRAL STATION SYSTEMS

While line security devices or systems providing a high degree of protection are feasible for telephone alarm line circuits serving transmitter or McCulloh central station systems, at this time only two alarm companies provide line security equipment and services for McCulloh systems that are approved for UL Grade AA certification. In part, the reluctance of the alarm industry to provide line security to these party-line connects stems from the costs involved in modifying party-line circuit control instruments to achieve compatibility with line security devices and the additional capital expense for modifying the central station equipment. Further, McCulloh line security devices are effective against sophisticated attack only where the alarm sensors, associated circuit wiring, and control and apparatus boxes are mounted within or on a physically secure vault structure.

THE FUTURE IN LINE SECURITY

It is realistic to predict that central station systems employing the present forms of listed line security will eventually suffer defeats, even though such defeats may be rare in proportion to the number of attempts made. The growing skill of the underworld should not be underestimated, however. Remember, it is essential to think like a thief. If the potential gain is great enough—and it is—criminal efforts will continue to attempt to compromise sophisticated line security systems.

It would logically follow, then, that computerized central station and police monitoring equipment, which tests alarm telephone circuits at microsecond intervals, is the direction in which the development of line security systems must go. Further, pseudorandom direct-wire line security systems should be engineered to provide longer random programming to discourage recording attempts and to increase the difficulty of analysis by an intruder, should that tempt the burglar with "hacker's" talents. The wireless transmission of alarm system signals via protected microwave circuits may offer some additional benefits as far as compromise attack is concerned.

SECURITY PROCEDURES AGAINST COMPROMISE

In the interim, the following steps, in addition to the upgrading of alarm circuits (from local, through police-connected, to direct-wire and multiplex central station systems equipped with approved line security) are recommended.

Check Lines for Identification

Determine if your telephone alarm line(s) are marked by tags or sleeves identifying them as alarm circuits. If so, require the alarm contractor and/or the utility company to remove all identification, and make periodic checks to be sure that such identification is not re-installed.

Check for Tampering after False Alarms

If you are advised of a false alarm from your alarm system, there is no indication of forced entry, and the cause is unknown, request the alarm company and the telephone company security personnel to carefully examine the telephone alarm circuit for evidence of tampering. For example, check for foreign electrical equipment, extra wires, scratches on terminal posts, or the absence of dust on alarm circuit terminals.

Improve Exterior Locks

Install highly pick-resistant locks. Wherever permitted by safety codes, provide for key-locking deadbolts that are operated from either exterior or interior solely by key. These will reduce the criminal's opportunity to gain entry by "pick-lock" in order to case the premises in preparation for a compromise attack and will reduce or restrict escape routes.

Protect the Perimeter

If your present alarm system does not include protection on all accessible openings, consider adding these to the alarm system. This is an important step in avoiding compromise.

Add Space Protection for High Risks

Even though you may have a complete perimeter alarm system in addition to safe or vault protection, if you are a high-risk target you should consider the addition of space alarms—that is, motion- or sound-detection systems designed to detect the presence of an intruder within the premises. This provides additional protection for alarm controls, line security devices, wiring, and alarm telephone circuits.

Re-evaluate Safe or Vault Security

Re-evaluate the physical security afforded by your safe or vault structure (see Chapters 23, 24, and 27). If these are inadequate to resist known attack techniques with the alarm system disabled, defeated, or out of service, consider the reinforcement or replacement of these structures to deter or dissuade the professional from his planned attacks. (Reinforcement is discussed in Chapter 26.)

Reduce Escape Possibilities

Re-examine your building premises and, thinking like a thief, consider his escape routes in the event that an alarm signal is registered during an attempted line compromise attack. Can nighttime grille gates, chain sets, or other physical devices retard or restrict his escape from other than normal means of entry? These safeguards can be valuable in deterring the professional from an attack.

Consider Local Alarm or Dual Alarm

Consider the addition of a local alarm annunciator that, when properly safeguarded, may provide just the element of surprise necessary to thwart the electronic burglar. For very high risks, consider the possible use of a second alarm company, using different approved line security equipment, to confront the electronic burglar with the necessity of defeating not one but two line security systems.

A two-company security arrangement will also result in more random testing of the alarm circuits, making it more difficult for the attacker to intercept the closed-period central station tests, even if he should develop compromise equipment for both systems. (Two-company alarm systems are discussed in Chapter 19.)

WIDER USE OF COMPROMISE INDICATED

As the reader assesses his individual exposure to this form of attack, he should bear in mind that, in recent months, criminals have expanded compromise attacks to a wider range of alarm systems including drugs, tobacco, cameras, and high-value warehousing operations. Think like a thief!

17

Advances in Hard-Wired Sensing Systems

New Technologies for the Installation, Service, and Supervision of Alarm Sensing Devices

ADVANCES IN ALARM CONTROL EQUIPMENT

Early in the 1980s, the development of more efficient microprocessors led to the application of this technology to control instruments supervising burglary, fire, and industrial process sensing devices installed in both commercial and residence locations. Microprocessor-based alarm control units permitted the development of keyless controls (digital pads), multiple zone local annunciation, and built-in duress circuits. Some also provide day annunciator supervision of points of protection like emergency exits that require 24-hour security and the transmission of burglary, fire, holdup, water flow, and industrial process signals over a single alarm transmission circuit. Most of these control units are approved by UL and the Factory Mutual Engineering Division.

CONVENTIONAL SENSOR CIRCUITS REVIEWED

However, until 1983, the groups of alarm sensing devices installed in a given segment of a premises were connected to one or more zones of a control unit via a series loop. With this configuration, the control unit could be used only to identify an alarm or trouble signal from some portion of each loop. To determine the precise source of trouble or intrusion, a technician had to troubleshoot the loop and eventually isolate the specific sensor or wiring segment that caused the signal. In this concept, motion-detection sensors requiring special power supplies were necessarily connected to AC outlets installed at or near each such sensor and were interfaced to the sensor utilizing a transformer.

MULTIPLEX AS A MEDIUM FOR SENSOR CIRCUITRY

In 1983, one alarm company applied multiplex technology to interface each sensing device to a control unit so as to supervise each point of protection at the control unit during both open-period and closed-period alarm system operation. This is accomplished by the addition of a coded transmitter or transponder to each sensor. Control units with a capacity to supervise as many as 200 individual sensors usually are sufficient to address the needs of all but the most extensive commercial installations.

In 1984, while other alarm companies evaluated this concept, two industry equipment manufacturers introduced similar equipment that also affords the user and installer advantages in cost of installation, maintenance, and supervision of the premises alarm systems, although the capacity of these control units is less than the aforementioned system because it requires the grouping of sensors into zones when used to supervise extensive alarm systems. While this technology is more efficiently applied to new installations and certain types of existing sensors are not compatible with this technology, some of the equipment offered is adaptable to fundamental sensors such as door or window contacts at nominal costs.

MULTIPLEX CIRCUITRY APPLIED TO THE PREMISES INSTALLATION

The following comments are applicable to the multiplex premises sensing system first introduced and now used extensively in most domestic markets as a standard of installation for the alarm company that pioneered the concept. As stated, the availability of the microprocessor-type alarm control unit and its capacity for user-friendly up-front management of information permit the design of alarm systems within a given premises utilizing a single two- or four-conductor signal transmission line that is extended throughout the building. Each detection sensor is interfaced through its individual transmitter or transponder via a parallel circuit connection that carries two-way information from the sensor to the control processor. This parallel-wiring concept, in effect, requires the complete rewiring of an existing alarm system and changes in certain types of sensing devices.

IDENTIFY THE CULPRIT

Multiplex application permits both visual and audible annunciation of any trouble or alarm condition at the control unit, identifying the specific sensor or sensors causing a trouble or alarm signal. The advantage is significant; it pinpoints a defective sensor or a specific point of intrusion and permits the user to determine the cause of a trouble at closing time. Given this information, the user can correct and clear most troubles without the assistance of an alarm company technician. Thus, alarm company service costs are reduced. It also eliminates the point of friction that develops when an alarm user is forced to wait what he perceives to be an interminable period for an alarm technician to respond to the premises to clear a closing time trouble condition.

Similarly, when an alarm user is more able to determine the source of a closing trouble or a defective sensor, there is a real advantage for the immediate reduction of alarms created by a careless subscriber—further cost savings for both the alarm company and the user. It also permits a serviceman to identify and correct intermittent malfunctioning sensors on the first response rather than suffering through a series of repetitive false alarms, which in conventional systems is often a necessary part of the process required to isolate an intermittent component of the alarm system. Again, both parties achieve labor cost savings, and charges made by police agencies responding to unnecessary alarms are reduced or eliminated.

IMPROVED TESTING

The system also provides a test mode that permits the alarm user to perform individual sensor tests during the open-for-business period. This substantially improves the user's ability to walk-test each motion-sensing device properly and permits the periodic audit of the entire system. In a conventional loop-type system, verification of each point of protection by the user would, at the least, be cumbersome and, in most cases, would require the assistance of an alarm company technician.

ONE POWER SUPPLY

Equally important, from both a cost and a performance standpoint, is the fact that all sensing devices are powered by the control unit, thereby eliminating the need for low-voltage transformers and a 110 AC outlet at the location of most motion-sensing devices. Thus, motion-sensing devices can be manufactured without standby circuitry and batteries for use with this system. Further, a single standby power supply required to maintain system continuity at the control unit can be provided to permit the user the option of a 24-, 50-, or 100-hour standby power supply pack capable of maintaining the entire premises system.

DAY ANNUNCIATION

This multiplex technology also permits the user to supervise certain protected points using the microprocessor as a day annunciator control. This provision extends to fire exits and other door or window alarm contact devices that are not normally opened during business hours, as well as designated fixed protection such as window foil, skylight wiring, wall wiring, and ventilation screens. Should these points of protection malfunction or suffer damage during business hours, the trouble is immediately pinpointed, and user notification to the alarm company will permit orderly repairs prior to the close of business that day. However, defects in individual sensing devices, like door contacts, will not normally be detected until closing time unless the user performs a special test of these devices prior to the close of business. Of importance, the sensitivity level of motion-sensing devices that are impeded by malfunction or changes in the environment still can only be detected by conventional walk- or motion-tests performed by management supervisors on a frequent basis.

LINE SECURITY

The premises multiplex circuit is also afforded line security comparable to the levels provided by multiplex signal transmission from the premises to the central station since the control unit performs a continuous polling and each transponder reports its status at short time intervals, 24 hours a day. The control unit in this system includes an interrogation feature that permits the elimination of momentary alarm or trouble conditions of 15 seconds' duration or less.

BYPASS CIRCUITRY

A bypass, or shunting, capability is also included whereby an authorized individual must first enter his master code level at the digital pad and then can shunt out, or bypass, one point of protection for the alarm-closed period. When a point of protection is bypassed, the central station will receive a signal indicating only that such action has been taken. The specific point of protection bypassed is visually displayed only at the premises control unit, and this display is automatically erased at the next opening time or when an alarm condition occurs after a closing. Thus, it is important to recognize that there is a requirement for alarm user supervisors to communicate system troubles properly when one supervisor may be responsible for closing the premises and a different supervisor is responsible for opening the premises. If the alarm system is not serviced to correct the defect, a bypassed point of protection will present itself again as a trouble condition at the time the alarm system is next closed.

SYSTEM LOGISTICS

The system is designed to include the concept of backup sensors and may be programmed to treat an alarm or trouble signal from the first of a logistical sensing team as a warning-only signal, not subject to normal alarm response. On receipt of an alarm signal from the second sensor, the control unit would automatically change the status of both signals to one requiring normal alarm response. This feature, coupled with the design of logistical protection layouts, is in theory worthy of consideration to further reduce false alarms caused by equipment or circuit defects.

However, the logistics concept requires considerable expertise on the part of alarm company sales engineers and user management if effective levels of protection against intrusion are to be maintained. If, for example, the logistics concept involved the installation of an alarm contact switch on an overhead door or doors in a dock area and the backup protection device were a beam or motion-detection sensor installed at the point where the receiving or shipping dock joined a warehouse or factory area, the concept of delaying response to a signal from an overhead door contact would be acceptable only when effective procedures prevented the closed-period storage of valuable materials in vehicles or on the platform between the overhead door and the backup beam or motion-sensing device. At this writing, an alternate concept using fully redundant sensing devices such as dual contact switches or motion-sensing devices affords a higher level of protection, albeit a slightly more costly one.

COSTS AND AVAILABILITY

In 1984, the alarm contractor offered multiplex technology nationwide. The company estimates its installation and annual service costs for such systems are somewhat lower than current guide prices for the installation of a conventionally hard-wired system providing the same general level of protection. However, where this technology is offered to replace older existing alarm systems, the user should evaluate improvements in security in relation to installation costs and revised annual service charges. The user facing an extensive additional cost to replace all or part of an obsolescent alarm system should also entertain quotations for comparable services from other alarm contractors.

TRANSMISSION SYSTEM METHODS AND STANDARDS

While multiplex is the method of signal transmission between sensors and the premises control unit, the output of this control may, in turn, be interfaced to a central station utilizing a companion multiplex alarm circuit transmission link, a direct-wire alarm telephone circuit, McCulloh party-line circuits, or digital communicator transmission methods. The multiplex form of signal transmission is designed for interface to two telephone circuits, if desired, to provide a redundancy feature in the event one multiplex alarm telephone circuit was for any reason inoperative.

Of the various options available, only direct-wire circuits equipped with a UL-listed high line security module or multiplex alarm circuit telephone transmission links would qualify the alarm system for UL-certified Grade AA, BB, or CC service. In addition, while the premises-based control unit displays the specific point of protection that caused the alarm signal, the central station receiving equipment at present is limited in capability to register only the existence of an alarm or trouble signal and the zone or circuit from which it emanated.

Fire alarm signals are accorded transmission priority over all other types of signals; however, burglar alarm signals which occur simultaneously are reported immediately after the transmission of the fire alarm signal.

METHODS OF PROGRAMMING

The control unit permits on-site programming of instructions to a central station computer. There are two or three levels of programming dependent upon the specific control unit in use. Each has a basic level that permits the registration of those user employees who are given the authority to open the premises at authorized times and to respond to alarm signals on notification. Individual code numbers are assigned to each individual and programmed into the control unit in a fashion that permits the rejection of improper use and notification of such unauthorized use at central station level. The intermediate level of authority permits individuals so authorized to change alarm opening and closing schedules and to bypass a single point of protection.

SUPERVISING OPENINGS AND CLOSINGS

This alarm company offers intermediate- and full-capacity control units. The intermediate control unit has a capacity to provide for the supervision of a maximum of two alarm circuits for which specific opening and closing times are designated. Thus, if a user at present had separately established alarm circuit opening and closing times applicable to three or more systems, it would be necessary to add a second control unit to maintain this level of protection. If a specific user had five or more such system supervisory requirements, it would then probably be cost efficient to upgrade to the larger-capacity control unit.

Full-capacity control units permit authorized individuals to use a master code level that includes all of the foregoing and a capability for bypassing multiple points of protection. The use of these programming features permits transmission of such changes to the central station computer without any independent corroborating document. Thus, the need for letters changing instructions, over authorized signature, or telephone-coded schedule changes, are eliminated. In high-risk situations, this advantage may not be desirable, and a conservative management may forego the intermediate and master-code-programming features in favor of the conventional use of letter of instruction or central station visit to effect changes in schedules, special openings, and changes in personnel authorized under the lower code level. It is understood that software may be modified to permit the specific programming that is required of a high-risk system. Master codes may be programmed to restrict their use during normally closed periods.

Note: Where intermediate or master code arrangements are permitted, changes effected by authorized individuals cannot be positively audited unless specific instructions to the alarm contractor require that printed verification records of all openings, closings, changes, and so on be provided to the subscriber. Under such conditions, the user must remember that information will be furnished retroactively at weekly or monthly intervals.

OPTIONAL FEATURES

The intermediate- and full-capacity control units allow the optional application of remote digital pads to permit the arming or disarming of the entire system or to permit a momentary bypass of points of protection necessary to access or depart individual zones of protection. In addition, visual status-only display panels may be remoted to building lobbies or entry foyers to permit individuals responding to alarm conditions the opportunity to evaluate the potential danger and the circumstances that may exist within the premises.

The full-capacity control unit is also designed to permit the optional addition of a graphic display panel that enables the user to identify visually the geographical location and status of each point of protection (an aid to day annunciation supervision and closing troubles and tests) and a clear language printer that has the capacity to provide an on-site record of all openings and closings, troubles, and alarm conditions.

MULTIPLEX CENTRAL STATION SUPERVISORY COSTS

Since the system described, in effect, provides the user with an in-house computer or front end that does much of the work normally required at the central station by manual or by computerized means, significant labor savings obviously are achieved using the multiplex alarm transmission interface in conjunction with the premises multiplex installation. Transmission of multiple types of alarm signals over a single leased transmission link, bypass and delayed response features, and automated programming are more efficient to the central station operation. In addition, when a single leased telephone circuit can be used for the transmission of multiple services (for example, fire, burglary, or industrial process), there are significant savings in the cost of that transmission link when compared with the conventional requirement to lease separate circuits for each class of service. The latter may represent a major cost savings that the user had best carefully analyze as it relates to his present costs and the new concept.

For example, consider an alarm user located 5 to 10 miles from a central station who presently incurs the expense of separate direct-wire alarm transmission circuits for several burglar alarm systems, sprinkler supervision, and industrial process circuits. The aggregate cost of these existing leased circuits, compared to a single shared party-line multiplex direct-wire telephone transmission circuit, represents a significant dollar difference that is presently included in the total annual service fee charged by an alarm contractor. When considering conversion to the new technology, that annual cost should be precisely determined and, for the purpose of negotiation, separated from the basic cost of central-station-monitoring services.

CONCLUSION

The alarm company pioneering this multiplex installation technology has spent millions of dollars to convert existing central stations and subscriber systems to the multiplex sensing and signal receiving concept. Obviously, they are firm in their belief of this technology for the future. The author notes that others in the alarm industry have moved rapidly to explore and/or engineer similar designs. However, the alarm user should carefully evaluate the benefits of this technology as they apply to his specific requirements and should determine whether or not the equipment considered meets the listing approvals of both UL and the fire safety agencies and should consult with other users in his area as to their experience in the use and supervision of these alarm systems.

Since multiplex technology does, for the most part, require a major reinstallation, users converting from existing conventional systems should negotiate to provide for the installation and testing of the new system over a reasonable time frame while retaining their existing alarm system online. Normally, a 10-to-14-day test period should be adequate to eliminate any bugs in the new installation, and redundant costs for that period should be limited to the monthly supervisory and alarm telephone circuit charges. The alarm user should also seek reasonable assurances to the effect that his investment in the multiplex and computer technology in the 1980s is adaptable to expansion and refinement at reasonable additional costs to take care of his needs into the 1990s.

18

Business Skills in Criminal Attack

"Corporate" Planning

Fact: The apprehended criminal is usually of low average intelligence and from an economically and socially deprived background.

Fact: Very few criminals are apprehended.

Conclusion: With few exceptions, only stupid criminals of limited background are apprehended.

Perhaps a more logical conclusion would be that just as the successful businessman does, the more successful criminals succeed by application—by careful planning, long hours of work, and the application of logic to problem solving. Like the businessman, the criminal does not always succeed, but he seldom performs so poorly as to "lose his job" although he may suffer a temporary reduction in earnings. In the following cases, we note the broad range of qualities that enables the criminal to succeed.

THE INSIDER

Everyone recognizes that boldness is sometimes the key to major financial success, but one must understand the "market's" technical aspects such as the difference between liquid assets and nonnegotiable instruments. In this case, banking officials and police were confounded when, on responding to a fire alarm signal, they discovered that unknown attackers had compromised the sophisticated central station burglary alarm system (line security and all) and had then drilled a single hand hole through the almost 2 feet of reinforced concrete forming the vault wall. Even then it would still have been necessary to burn through stacked safe deposit boxes at the point of attack.

Imagine their surprise when they finally realized the attackers' target: the contents of a single large safe deposit box in which a large insurance company kept millions of dollars in negotiable securities. The point of attack was squarely in the center of the rear of the box. Only the heat from the core drill, which ignited the securities and produced the sprinkler supervisory alarm signal, "saved the day." Poor planning?

THE OPPORTUNIST

A major diamond manufacturer and dealer employed virtually every form of alarm security, including the use of two separate alarm companies to supervise the protection of his safes and vaults. Even the elevator doors opening on the manufacturer's reception lobby were protected by alarm devices. No sensible criminal would have attempted to defeat this alarm system.

However, the conversion of the building elevators from manual to automatic operation involved the installation of new elevator doors, during which time the alarm protection of those points was temporarily disconnected. It took a good building maintenance engineer to discover that the attackers had capitalized on this temporary weakness in the security system.

THE STRATEGIST

Although the switchboards of the Bank Alarm Company central office were lit up like Christmas, there was little goodwill and giving connected with the incident. What alarm company supervisors first thought to be the accidental destruction of the telephone cable linking the central station to the nearest telephone exchange was not due to some absent-minded bulldozer operator but to a very sharp axe, which the attackers used to sever the alarm company's vital communications link.

Needless to say, the strategy paid off. While the alarm company, telephone company, and police officer labored with the monumental problem of restoring alarm service and notifying hundreds of customers that they were temporarily without protection, the strategist struck one single valuable target, netting several hundred thousand dollars.

THE WELL INFORMED

To succeed in business, one must keep his ear to the ground and develop good communications with those able to provide valuable information that enables the planner to take bold initiatives. Consider the case of the police station that moved to new headquarters. Alarm systems supervised by police headquarters were temporarily disconnected for a matter of hours during the weekend in which the move took place. The planner with the right sources of information knew when to make his move. The result: one substantial haul.

THE INVENTIVE

As is indicated in Chapter 22, the burning bar, or thermic lance, has never achieved its full potential in the hands of the underworld. One of the limitations is its fuel and material requirements. To penetrate substantial steel or reinforced concrete structures, one must bring along a significant number of oxygen tanks and enough pipe to plumb a property. This material cannot always be inconspicuously delivered.

One enterprising scientist in another country, however, found a solution. He selected a flexible metal conduit through which oxygen could be fed from a remote point. The bulky materials no longer had to be delivered to the point of attack. He could retain these at a remote and inconspicuous point, feeding only the flexible burning bar into the attack area. Let's hope these five "corporate" planners do not join together to form any new syndicates.

19

Dual Central Station Protection

How Alarmed Can You Get?

In over a century of protective service, the central station burglar alarm industry has established an enviable record for preventing loss (UL statistics indicate better than 90 percent effectiveness), devotion to security, courage (where else would one find civilians searching buildings for guerrillas equipped with tire irons, crowbars, shotguns, and revolvers?), and efficiency (compare the costs of burglar alarm services to the cost of a watchman working 120 hours per week). The pennies per hour cost for central station alarm services is still a bargain.

CENTRAL STATIONS EFFECTIVE, NOT INFALLIBLE

Of course, alarm service companies—management and employees—are subject to human failure. Despite security procedures that have been tried and tested by years of running battles with burglars, careless subscribers, and more unusual hazards, errors committed by security personnel sometimes offer the professional criminal the opportunity to execute a successful burglary.

Early in the 1960s, a series of burglaries outside the United States received considerable attention. It was alleged that employees of a central station alarm company worked in collusion with criminals to burglarize a number of high-risk premises (jewelers, banks, furriers). The burglars operated in the confidence that though the burglar alarm devices would detect their presence, the central station alarm response would be delayed or omitted.

TWO ALARM COMPANIES FOR ONE RISK

Following this exposé, some insurance underwriters required that their high-risk insureds obtain dual central station services—that is, use two separate alarm companies, each installing one or more central station alarm systems on the same premises.

The insurers reasoned that, with two reliable central station companies protecting the same premises, the chances for employee collusion, errors in the handling of the alarm response, delays in response due to bad weather, the failure of alarm equipment, or total telephone circuit outages would be substantially reduced, if not eliminated. From trial and error, several methods have evolved for utilizing dual alarm service for high risks.

Different Sensors on Each System

One approach requires two separate alarm systems within a single vault. In this approach, one alarm company may install a sound-vibration detection system, while the second company provides an audio detection system. Or one company may substitute ultrasonic or microwave equipment for either.

Similarly, dual safe protection may be achieved by a proximity system, electrical wiring of the safe on the inside, or a safe cabinet to protect the safe while at the same time another alarm company's system floods the area around the safe with motion-detection waves. In some layouts where all vault walls are located completely within the premises (no wall of the vault being a party wall with other tenancies or a hall) and the floors and ceiling are reinforced concrete one foot or more thick, some underwriters require a separate intruder motion-detection system covering the areas surrounding the vault, in addition to the vault alarm system connected into a second central station.

Finally, some variations of dual alarm systems provide for safe or vault protection by one company and the protection of the entire premises (a No. 2 or No. 3 UL-certified system) by another company. Occasionally, one encounters an insurance company that requires for a safe within a vault Complete alarm system protection of each by separate alarm companies.

In theory, the application of dual detection principles would seem to eliminate the possibility of human error. In practice, so far as is known, there have been only three successful burglary attacks against dual systems. The number of such systems in use continues to grow but still represents only a small percentage of the total central station alarm service, and—at this time—these are almost exclusively concentrated within the jewelry industry.

Problems of Service Coordination

Let's examine the practical problems affecting the alarm company asked to provide central station alarm services in concert with a competitor.

1. The management of the alarm companies must meet together to develop a coordinated procedure for guard response to alarm signals from the premises, for telephone circuit failures, for police notification, and for emergency provisions covering blackouts, earthquakes, hurricanes, and other unusual circumstances.

2. If both companies' standard procedures require the notification of police in the event of the receipt of an alarm signal, then the company receiving an alarm signal must necessarily telephone a supervisor at the second central station to determine if they also received an alarm signal. After that is done, these decisions must be made: Which company will notify police? What information will be transmitted to the police (guards from two companies responding, two different alarm conditions, and so on)?

Obviously, police departments will not easily accept or understand the basis for two separate alarm companies reporting a single attack. In addition, if one alarm company normally sends its own agent or agents to investigate alarms and does not notify police until this investigation discloses clear evidence of crime (forced entry, for example), then its procedures must be reviewed in relation to those of the second company and a coordinated procedure developed.

3. Dual protection requires that two separate alarm companies each dispatches one or more armed guards to the same premises to investigate an alarm. Precautions and coordination are necessary to reduce the possibility that, in a darkened premises, one guard may mistake the other for the criminal. Alarm company supervisors have usually solved this problem by planning a rendezvous of the guards, who wait for each other outside the premises and enter together to investigate. In some instances, this could delay response long enough to enable the burglars to escape and could permit a successful hit-and-run attack.

4. Unnecessary alarms from one or the other alarm system will result in the multiplication of unnecessary visits to the premises and of administrative efforts in coordination. These will increase each alarm company's cost of service and may, in time, result in an industry practice of billing special charges for response to alarms emanating from another company's system.

Problems Inherent in Dual Response

Dual alarm systems present other practical security considerations.

1. During bad weather the central station false alarm workload often results in delays up to several hours in responding to burglar alarms. Under these conditions, when the supervisors of two independent alarm companies consider the priority to be given to an alarm received from a dual subscriber, each company's supervisor may accord the dual subscriber a low priority on the theory of "Let George do it."

2. Consider the probable difference in time responses due to the unequal distance to the subscriber's premises of one company's guard station as compared to the other's. When one company is within a block of the subscriber's location and the other central station company must send guards a distance of several miles, the guards walking a single block will probably be required to wait outside the premises a considerable length of time. Also, both companies' guards may wait outside until the police arrive.[1]

3. Some dual central station alarm subscribers (all of whom are in the high-risk category) furnish keys to the premises to the alarm companies. Consider these problems: Should the subscriber furnish both alarm companies with keys? Will he remember to replace alarm company keys whenever he changes a lock cylinder? Which company's guard will break the key envelope seals to use his company's set of keys to gain entry?[2]

4. Another problem can arise when the dual subscriber enters his premises during a normally closed period. Experience teaches us that a subscriber should limit his open periods to the exact hours when he or a responsible employee will be in physical charge of the premises. Good security practice is to precede special openings during closed periods by written notice to the alarm company or by the subscriber's coming to the central station to sign a written authorization. The dual subscriber, of course, must provide dual written authorization.

5. To maintain an alarm system certificate in effect may require special permission from UL for each alarm company.

6. Some alarm company procedures provide for receipt of a signal from the subscriber when an alarm system is opened; others do not. If both systems do not offer the same measure of security, the effective level of security is that of the lower of the two systems.

7. UL standards provide for the alarm contractor to notify the subscriber's authorized representative of telephone circuit outages, delays, and so forth. At present there is no procedure defining this responsibility under a dual alarm system contract. For example, if company A makes a practice of keeping their guard at the premises until the subscriber is notified of a telephone circuit outage and comes to take charge, should company B be relieved of this responsibility, should they share the load, or should both companies retain guards on the premises? While such a duplication may seem ludicrous in some respects, nevertheless, if dual alarm protection is a necessity for these risks, isn't the possibility of criminal attack during periods of alarm outages sufficient to justify the redundancy?

---

[1] In most instances, the police would reach the exterior of the premises promptly. However, without keys they must await the arrival of guards from both companies before beginning a search.

[2] The use of seals on key envelopes is part of the standard practice followed by most central station alarm companies to ensure recording the times and periods during which the keys have been in use by alarm company personnel.

8. For most high risks required to have dual alarm company services, insurance underwriters also require line security against skilled compromise attacks (see Chapter 16). Here, too, dual systems create serious problems, but these, for security reasons, cannot be detailed here. One warning can be given: In the absence of appropriate precautions, persons posing as alarm maintenance men from one alarm company may be afforded the opportunity to compromise the line security of the other company.

9. Problems may also arise when one alarm company provides services superior in speed of response as well as quality. For example, an alarm company with several central stations in the same city (and, probably, a large installation force) might be able to bring in reserves during storm emergency conditions. A smaller alarm company would have considerable difficulty matching the first company's manpower per alarm, and this could effectively delay—or even prevent—the needed two-company response to a dual system subscriber's premises.

10. As far as vault protection is concerned, UL standards require that conventional sound or vibration vault intrusion-detection systems provide for the test and repair of equipment failure within the vault by service performed outside the vault or, at the least, that partial protection of the vault can be maintained until the subscriber takes charge of the premises. This standard assures the insurer (and the subscriber) that some protection still exists or can be established without requiring the subscriber to open the vault for middle-of-the-night service. (Of course, when time locks are in use, the subscriber would not be able to do so even if he had the necessary dedication and fortitude.) However, when insurance underwriters require the additional installation of ultrasonic, audio, or microwave detection systems as the basis for dual alarm system protection within a vault, they often fail to recognize that such systems

- Cannot be properly tested from the central office,
- Are subjected to a high rate of equipment failure,
- Cannot be so easily restored without entering the vault.

The end result may be to render each system inoperative until the other's fault is corrected.

11. In practice, the speed and quality of the response of each alarm company serving a dual system will be gaited to the other company. This raises questions as to liability and responsibility. No cases have tested this question; however, there is legal opinion to the effect that where one company is found guilty of an error of omission or commission, the extent of its liability would be limited to the level or responsibility of the other.[3]

---

[3] For example, the liability of one company in the case of a burglary, occurring as a result of that company's error, against a safe for which that company provides Complete protection would be limited to the liability of the other alarm service company, perhaps providing only a No. 3 Premises alarm service and protecting only open stock.

12. Finally, two-company alarm service is not well suited to existing central station company operating procedures. Necessarily, dual alarm response must significantly increase each company's cost of rendering service. The rapid growth of such arrangements could result in substantial increases in charges for such services. Ultimately, alarm companies might conclude that their security standards have been weakened, that their legal liability has increased, and that continuation of dual central station services is undesirable to them.

ALTERNATIVES

The final evaluation of dual alarm system security is yet to be made. Several alternatives exist, but whether they will prove more or less desirable remains to be seen. Whether you are a user, subscriber, central station operator, or insurance underwriter, however, these possibilities deserve your consideration:

1. A few central station companies have more than one central office in the same city. Where this situation exists, a subscriber can arrange for the connection of separate alarm systems into separate central offices of the same alarm service company. While this move reduces the potential for errors of commission or omission, the guards responding may be dispatched from a common point. Where this is the case, the effectiveness of the one-company, two-office arrangement is lessened.

2. Some protective benefit is derived from the addition of a local alarm system that activates a loud bell, horn, siren, strobe light, and/or direct telephone circuit to a police station. Police station connections are not available in most major cities, but a bell, siren, or flashing light at the premises will harass the burglar and provides reserve protection in the event of delay in alarm company response.

3. A surveillance camera or closed-circuit television system with videotape recorder activated by alarm devices may not prevent burglary, but it can record the attack, identify the criminals, and document the performance of responding central station alarm company agents.

4. The security provided by a single central station company can be improved if the user contracts for additional security services. For example, while UL standards require only one remote central station test of an alarm system for each 8-hour closed period, some alarm companies are willing, for additional fees, to test at more frequent intervals (such as hourly).

5. High risks dealing in currency, jewelry, and securities may satisfy an underwriter asking for additional central station security by agreeing to place a larger amount of the insured value in the safe deposit vault of a nearby bank each night. However, this may be a Catch 22 solution since

the transport of such valuables to and from the bank each day presents a significant exposure to armed robbery attack.

CONCLUSION

This chapter explored dual central station security for the high risk. At this time, dual central station alarm service or its alternatives are primarily required for jewelers, furriers, banking institutions, check cashers, and pawnbrokers. In the long term, the solution should be the expanding role of the central station alarm company as total security contractor. All is not lost when an alarm system fails or is defeated if the safe or vault structure will withstand attack. Further, the total security engineering role, including closed-circuit television, better locks and lighting, and improved intrusion-detection systems, is rightfully as much an alarm contractor's responsibility as is the reduction of errors of omission or commission, the development of alarm system operation that cannot be circumvented, and the close supervision of the performance of alarm company employees.

If the alarm system contractor does embrace the total security concept to create higher standards for alarm systems, for physical protection, and for security procedures, he may at some future date resolve the insurance industry's dilemma by "taking on the risk" himself—insuring against specific loss.

20

Update on Burglary Attack Techniques

Why the Millions Went

In recent years, as burglar alarm systems have been upgraded to include line security circuits to protect the alarm telephone transmission circuit, sophisticated burglaries involving black box electronic burglaries have declined in frequency. However, burglars have made millions of dollars in opportunistic burglary attacks involving subscriber and/or alarm company negligence. This chapter presents many examples of such attacks.

WEAKNESSES IN ALARM RESPONSE PROCEDURES

During a weekend period burglars cut the alarm telephone circuit cables providing a McCulloh burglar alarm system, including line security, that served a major warehouse facility. Even though the central station supervisor could positively identify this high risk as being cut off from central station supervision, the inexperienced employee simply notified the telephone company of the McCulloh loop outage. He took no action to dispatch the police or his guards or to notify the subscriber. Extent of loss: $500,000.

His reason for not taking action was that ordinary McCulloh circuit outages are common and are traditionally handled this way. The supervisor apparently did not comprehend the need for special handling when McCulloh circuit line security was a requirement of a specific subscriber. Then, too, the central station supervisor may not have had any understanding as to the values at hand in the warehouse because few central station monitoring personnel ever visit a subscriber's premises.

Note: Less than a month later this gang struck again, attacking a jewelry distribution center in the same industrial park, using the same MO. This time the supervisor of the alarm company providing service to this account followed the instructions and dispatched police and personnel to the exterior of the premises. He also called the director of security for that company and advised him about the alarm condition. The latter acknowledged the call but failed to respond to the premises. (Fortunately, this alarm company records all its telephone communications and was able to prove that contact and proper notice of the alarm signal had been communicated to the subscriber's director of security.)

Police and alarm company personnel left after a brief surveillance of the perimeter that, at that moment, had not been penetrated. Subsequently, the burglars broke into the warehouse. Loss: $1,500,000.

In yet another instance hundreds of miles away, subscriber representatives did respond promptly to alarm company notification. However, when advised by alarm company personnel that there were numerous incidents of telephone cable vandalism in the area that weekend, the subscriber's representative decided it was unnecessary to guard the premises. Subsequently, the burglars cracked several safes. Loss: over $2,000,000.

Sometimes a little thing is the cause of a large loss. In this case, the alarm company central station and the subscriber's telephone exchanges were originally listed within the same area code. However, as the market grew, the telephone company found it necessary to assign new area codes to part of the region. You guessed it! When the alarm occurred as burglars penetrated the premises, alarm company personnel diligently dialed the right numbers but in the wrong area code of all of the subscriber's representatives. Their continued dialing was fruitless, and for some reason telephone company "incorrect dialing" intercept messages were not in place. Loss: $200,000.

A European jewelry company, whose practice was to leave high value merchandise overnight in show windows protected with burglary-resistant glazing material, decided when constructing its U.S. branch to install a solid steel curtain grille across the entire front entrance to the store in lieu of the more expensive burglary-resistant glazing material. However, burglars found their way into the premises through adjacent buildings and made their way out via the same route with more than $1,000,000 in merchandise. Of course, the alarm functioned and police and alarm company personnel stood helplessly outside the premises, able to hear but not able to see the action or to reach the burglars' escape routes.

Note: The alarm company had not been given keys to the locks securing the grille work in place. The store manager's refusal to go to the premises compounded the error.

BURGLARS' SKILLS ARE IMPROVING

In recent burglaries committed in the eastern and southern regions of the United States, one or more burglary gangs have demonstrated their ability to compromise certain forms of high line security circuits applied to direct-wire central station alarm transmission circuits and have scored heavily in a few instances. Authorities and alarm companies cannot ascertain the number of failed attempts that may have preceded these successful attacks since the burglars concentrate on telephone transmission lines and terminal points outside the protected premises and do not enter until they believe their efforts to compromise are successful.

However, there is a common denominator in most of these cases: While these alarm systems had previously operated trouble free, false alarms and closing troubles occurred several times during the weeks preceding the burglary. Given these experiences, it would seem that alarm companies providing service to high-risk subscribers should re-examine their procedures for investigation of unusual alarm or closing troubles and re-evaluate the effectiveness of that form of line security. In the cases reported, there were no instances where alarm services were provided by two alarm companies or separate monitoring central stations. Subscribers should give further consideration to that security measure.

SOMETIMES IT'S THE CHALLENGE

On occasion, a specific merchant, selected as a burglary target, finds his premises is subject to repeated attempts by the same frustrated burglars. In one series of attacks, the merchant continued to improve alarm systems by addition of alarm companies, line security, and redundant systems. His supervisory personnel were trained to respond properly and successfully coped with numerous compromise attempts and cable cuts. Unfortunately, floor load weight restrictions applicable to the building in which his premises was located inhibited the merchant's ability to use burglary-resistant safes or vaults. Thus, when a major blackout struck, the persistent burglars swiftly gathered and exploited the weakness, knowing it would be some hours before the alarm company could cope with the hundreds of alarms created by the power failure and that subscribers notified of alarms would be unable to respond promptly during blackout conditions.

Now some readers will say first-class alarm systems should include standby battery power supplies to carry them over periods when a power failure exists. True. However, some vintage age premises and vault sensing devices that preceded the solid-state age cannot be economically equipped with standby power supplies. In this instance, had the alarm company management and the subscriber evaluated this weakness in relation to the persistent burglary attacks, they could have effected the replacement of certain sensing equipment that, while effective in detecting intrusion, could no longer be categorized as a fully dependable system component. Examples of such devices may include postwar ultrasonic and photoelectric sensing equipment. And, while these components may not seem vital to the detection of attacks against safes or vaults, when they are combined with safe or vault sensors in one alarm circuit, their failure due to loss of power, in effect, masks the alarm signals created by the actual burglary attack on the safe or vault. In this case, central station supervisors assumed the cause of the alarm signal was limited to the sensor lacking a standby power supply.

In a classic example, a burglary gang spent three consecutive Easter weekends, in all kinds of weather, intent on a successful attack against a single target. The first year, their elaborate plans were thwarted when heavy rain grounded the compromise cables they had spliced into the telephone terminal box on a pole outside the target premises.

In the year following the burglary attempt, the alarm subscriber, reacting to this near catastrophe, added a police connect alarm transmission link to the output of his vault McCulloh circuit central station alarm system. He did not, however, add line security to either system. He believed running the telephone link serving the police connect circuit out of the building via a different cable route than the one the burglars had first attacked would be sufficient to his cause. Oh, yes, he also installed a burglary-resistant dead bolt and cylinder on the rear factory door the burglars had pried open to establish an escape route.

Sure enough, on the Easter weekend one year later, the burglars returned to their efforts. This time they were successful in compromising the central station McCulloh circuits but did, in fact, miss the new backup police connect alarm circuit. When they forced their entry through the rear factory door by removing the unsecured hinge pins, the alarm signal reached the police station, and once again the Easter egg hunt was called off.

Recovering from the shock of the second near catastrophe, the subscriber listened more carefully to expert advice. He did add line security to the central station vault alarm circuit and also added another alarm system provided by a second alarm company that consisted solely of ultrasonic sensors installed in the area over and around the vault, also monitored at the police station. Prudently, but not without anguishing over the cost, he also replaced the fire-only-rated vault door with a 3½-inch bank-type vault door.

On the next Easter weekend, the burglars returned—prepared for anything. They weren't concerned about the rain this time. They brought along canvas tents, pitched one on the roof, attacked the original telephone cable as it entered the roof from the pole, ran an extension of the central station alarm system telephone circuits to an adjacent unprotected factory building, and set up their command post under cover where they compromised the central station system. Next, they entered the premises by chopping a hole in the roof and dropping directly into the telephone panel equipment room, where they identified the police connect circuit originally installed as a backup system and compromised this circuit as well. At this point, feeling secure, the gang proceeded toward the vault. This precipitated the transmission of an alarm signal caused by their disturbance of the ultrasonic sensors near the vault. Of course, their failure to anticipate and identify still a third alarm telephone transmission link foiled this third attempt. They also were dismayed to see the new vault door in the few seconds they had before their lookout, using a walkie-talkie, announced that police were being dispatched to the premises.

The gang again fled the scene, but this time waited in the wooded area at the rear of the plant. Quickly, a police patrol car appeared on the scene. The officer entered the yard area, having been furnished keys to the entry gate, and searched the perimeter of the building. There were no signs of intrusion. He failed to spot the foreign telephone cables that had been snaked down the poorly lit east side of the building where it ran through the brush to the adjacent plant. He radioed back his findings. The dispatcher in the police station contacted the sleepy subscriber and gave him the following facts:

- Alarm from the ultrasonic system you recently installed—the one that has been nothing but false alarm troubles from the day it was installed,
- No alarm on our vault police connect circuit,
- No call from the central station concerning any alarm or disturbance on their circuits.

Given these facts, but failing to realize it was again the Easter holiday, the subscriber concluded the police were right: just another false alarm. He thanked them for their trouble, told them to pull the switch on the troublesome ultrasonic circuit, and asked them to patrol the premises and watch the alarm circuits. He went back to sleep.

At this stage, the good news/bad news burglars returned to the scene of their crime. The good news, of course, was that they now had the remainder of the weekend free to assault the vault. The bad news was that they were not prepared for a bank-vault-type door attack. Making the best of a bad situation and reflecting that there aren't many thermic lance supply depots open on Easter Sunday, the burglars borrowed acetylene cutting equipment from the adjacent plant and fell to, attempting to cut the combination lock and bolt work mechanism out of the solid steel door. On and on through the night they worked, and by 5:00 A.M. on Monday morning they were close to success when, much to their dismay, an employee assigned to open the adjacent premises blundered into their command post. On frightened feet, he escaped the burglars and called the police. By this time the dispatcher was sensitive to the plea and, although neither understood what they had discovered, the police sergeant reckoned it was time to call out the troops. Three cars were dispatched to block the getaway routes, and the subscriber was summoned to the scene. The net result: Four burglars caught in the trap and one subscriber breathing one more sigh of relief, hoping these criminals would not be free next Easter weekend.

Indeed, this was still another close call, one that emphasizes the necessity for optimum burglar alarm system defenses in every case, but particularly in those instances where prior attacks have occurred. Certainly, the false alarm trouble, which existed from the day the ultrasonic system was installed, should have been corrected. Failure to do so created a lack of confidence on the part of the police and the subscriber. In addition, no search can be considered adequate unless you can see the entire six sides of the protected premises. When a roof area is inaccessible for search or there is any possibility that a tunnel might be constructed under the floor of the premises, the subscriber must go to see the premises and admit law enforcement and alarm company agents to facilitate a proper search of the entire premises. In many cases where one or more segments of a vault structure are not accessible to permit an exterior search, the vault must be entered to check. If time locks secure the vault against entry, provisions must be made for closed-circuit TV and light inside the vault to provide that surveillance.

Finally, on completion of the search, if no indication of burglary exists, the alarm systems must be reset and one or more sensors in each circuit tested to be sure that the central station control circuits are monitoring the sensors in the premises instead of a dummy alarm circuit operated by the burglars from a remote point outside the premises.

In one other classic case, the burglars were thwarted only when an alert alarm company agent radioed from outside the premises, after securing it, to inquire if the central station had received the alarm signal created when he and the subscriber exited through the protected entry door. Only then did the central station detect, in the absence of that signal, the fact that the burglars were continuing to monitor the circuit using their compromise black boxes and had, in fact, simulated the alarm circuit conditions the central station anticipated when the police and alarm company personnel entered the premises but failed to do so precisely as they departed.

WHAT-IF SITUATIONS

Truly, major burglary attacks and encores present what-if situations. An alarm subscriber potentially vulnerable to similar attacks should explore all the possible conditions that might exist if police, alarm company personnel, and his own employees fail to perform their related security functions precisely as required to maintain the optimum level of defense. As you perceive those errors that might permit the attack to succeed, the fail-safe measures necessary to correct the error should be drafted into the response plan, and all parties should be trained in their execution. Dry runs are useful in testing these defenses. Certainly, the response procedures should never be assigned to anyone who is either inexperienced or insufficiently skilled to handle these complex situations. Most certainly, digital paging services would serve to strengthen such situations by always involving the most experienced company supervisors in each alarm response situation (see Chapter 21).

21

Digital Paging and Effective Alarm Response

You Must Go!

SCENE ONE

Place

A one-story cinder block office/factory building tucked into the commercial zone of a bedroom community that had seen better days. The office faced the now deserted highway, while factory walls looked out at row-type residence properties and, at the rear, the too small company parking lot. At one time such an environment afforded an additional measure of security against crime. These days, neighbors in this area had little civic commitment to the factory. They just wished employees would "stop parking their damned cars blocking their driveways." Of interest to the reader, the 15-foot factory roof was readily accessible via a shed appended to the rear of the building to store hazardous materials, and the electric power and telephone cables entered the building from a pole set at the curb line a few feet from the factory employee entrance.

Time

Six P.M. on a wintry Saturday in January. High winds and freezing sleet, which started falling shortly before dark, were playing havoc with people's pleasures and, coincidentally, burglar alarm systems. Guards and servicemen working for area central stations were skidding slowly from one alarm to another, trying to cope with the usual backlog of false alarms such weather generates. Police, dealing with accidents and stuck traffic lights, were faring no better.

Cast

First, there were Pete the Pro and his band of burglars. True, they swore a lot as they clawed their way from the top of the shed onto the factory roof, and Pete's profanity, as he described the giant who spaced the spikes on the telephone pole, was something better omitted from this account. Nevertheless, he managed to climb the pole and deftly cut the telephone cable that ran from the pole terminal pouch, via a short messenger line, into the building. Cut ends of the cable wire were taped to the steel messenger line to stop them from blowing in the wind, and Pete's job was done. He scurried down the pole and then up onto the roof, joining his buddies who together huddled under a piece of canvas. Their "play" had begun.

At Central Station Able, the high line security vault alarm circuit monitor instantly registered the cut line as an alarm signal. An alert supervisor, recognizing the priority required for a vault circuit alarm, took proper action. He notified the police dispatcher, advising the dispatcher that his company's guard and a representative from the factory would be alerted. He also advised the police that the alarm signal came from a vault alarm system and that the premises was, in fact, protected by the ZZZ Alarm Company that would also be alerted. Hanging up, he used the mobile radio unit to dispatch a guard who he reckoned would arrive at the premises in less than 10 minutes.

Next, he telephoned the residence of Wilson, the factory supervisor listed first on his emergency call records. On the third ring, a young boy answered the telephone. Mom and Dad were at a cocktail party, he said, and would be late coming home. The supervisor started to tell the boy about the factory alarm and then, realizing that this was only a child, excused himself and hung up.

The second call, to the home of the "next on the list," took longer. The phone rang and rang and finally was answered by an irritated company president who resented the interruption while entertaining dinner guests. Gruffly he asked, "Didn't you call Wilson?" When the alarm company supervisor started to explain that call, he was cut short: The prez said, "You left a message there, don't bother me," and with that, slammed down the phone.

Six minutes later our undaunted central station supervisor finally reached the dispatcher at the ZZZ Central Station. He reported the signal from the vault alarm system and advised that police, a company guard, and maybe the subscriber were on the way to the premises. This would require that they—the friendly competitors—would have to dispatch their guard since their premises alarm system would be opened to search the premises and restore the vault alarm system. The dispatcher at ZZZ tersely acknowledged the call and said he would take care of it. He hung up without informing the other supervisor of an alarm signal received from the premises circuit—perhaps because his workload backlog would delay dispatch of his guard for an hour or more.

Meanwhile, at the premises, police officers in Sector Car #3 and the Able Company guard arrived at virtually the same instant. They quickly checked the perimeter of the building but found no breaks or unlocked doors or windows. Then they waited for someone with the keys. After 30 minutes, the police were called away to deal with a major accident. The alarm company guard radioed his boss. "Where the hell is the subscriber?" he asked. The supervisor, recognizing that any prompt response by either of the subscriber's representatives was unlikely, told the guard to wait up to 1 hour and then move on to his next assignment. The conscientious supervisor went back to his records and tried telephoning the last two supervisors on the list, but no one answered. (What do you expect on a Saturday night?) Finally, he tried the first residence again. By now the little boy was scared because his folks were not back from the party. The supervisor gave up.

Now back to Pete and his friends. The soon-to-be frostbitten burglars were gleeful as they watched the taillights of the receding police car and then the alarm company patrol unit. They slithered off the roof and gathered near the rear door leading to the parking lot while Pete made his way stealthily to the employee factory entrance door, which had been modified (to permit access control identification) by the insertion of a 6-inch square ordinary glass viewing port in an otherwise sturdy wooden door. Pete quickly smashed the glass, reached in, and released the snap latch securing the door. He entered, used the same latch to relock the door and then moved swiftly to admit the rest of the boys through the overhead door opening to the parking lot. By now, their van had also been moved into position near this shipping door to load the loot. They were all set—cozy and warm again, escape route available to them. Now on to the vault.

The vault, a later addition to the building, was actually an 8-inch thick cinder block structure with reinforcing rods installed vertically only through the cores. It was equipped with only a fire-resistant vault door—not much of a challenge for someone like Pete. Under his direction, a sledgehammer was used to knock out a hand hole between reinforcing rods at a point adjacent to the vault door. He then reached in and turned the bolt release handle. Presto, the door was open without force and without need for knowledge of the combination. Now it was "Miller time"!

SCENE TWO

Enter Our Hero

Approximately one and one-half hours after receipt of their alarm, the harried guard from the ZZZ Alarm Company pulled up outside the employee entrance. Tool box and key envelope in hand, he glanced neither left nor right, up nor down. Removing the keys from the sealed envelope in the teeth of the storm and opening the relocked door apparently required his complete attention. He took no notice of the broken viewing port or the glass on the floor inside the entrance but concentrated on banging his tool box about and waving a flashlight. This awoke Pete's now drowsy lookout who, without further ado, ran toward the rear door and shouted "The cops are coming," alerting the gang to the danger. Of course, no cops were coming because the ZZZ Alarm Company had failed to contact the police and had not attempted to notify the subscriber. Perhaps they wished to avoid explaining their delayed response. In any event, to Pete's gang escape had the number 1 priority. They fled the scene, abandoning the stolen van and the loot, and were last seen slipping and sliding down a hill at the rear of the parking lot—never to return again.

Meanwhile, the ZZZ guard entered the premises and walked directly to his alarm control instrument, which was actually only 25 unobstructed viewing feet from the hole in the vault wall. The guard attached his meter to the instrument panel and determined that his alarm trouble was due to an open in the alarm telephone circuit. Flashlight in one hand, pencil in the other, he scrawled "telco trouble" on the subscriber's copy of his alarm ticket, pasted it to the instrument cover, departed as he had entered, radioed the central station, reported the trouble, and was off to the next port of call. If only he had noticed the broken glass, the hole in the vault, the open rear door, or the loaded van, he would truly have been labeled "hero" rather than "clown."

Meanwhile, Back at the Subscriber's Ranch

A now sober but shaken company supervisor had been having a scary skidding adventure on ice. When he arrived home and awakened his son, the sleepy boy told him that the alarm company man had called twice. By now, this otherwise dedicated company man had had it. His answer to tonight's problem was, "Let the boss handle it, I'm always called out and there's too many false alarms. If he'd only pay to upgrade the alarm system, things would be better."

SCENE THREE

Place and Time: The Same Old Factory
7:00 A.M. Monday

The sun was shining outside, but not in the factory! Pandemonium reigned. True, the loss to burglary was probably minimal since neither burglars nor neighbors had revisited the scene. However, with the telephone lines out, there were no customer orders coming in and no immediate way to notify employees to stay home until stock was returned to vault shelves and repairs effected. The boss was furious about the loss of business and the lost production time and the fact he had failed to heed his broker's advice to purchase business interruption insurance.

It's intermission time. In keeping with our honor system, let's stop for a moment. List the human errors that contributed to what might have been an economic disaster.

PROLOGUE: THE CRITIC'S CORNER

Technically, the buck rested with the boss, who reacted very poorly. As the chief executive officer, he had the primary responsibility for the protection of the business assets, and given the circumstances, he should have gone promptly to the premises to admit the police and the Able Alarm Company guard to enter and search, whereupon they would have determined that the alarm system monitoring circuit was inoperative and would have recommended guarding the premises until telephone alarm circuits were restored: end of burglary attempt!

However, our first-on-the-list company supervisor also muffed his chance to save the day. He was placed first on the list because he was experienced in responding and delegated that responsibility for security. Despite his harrowing evening on ice, he should have realized the need to contact both alarm companies to determine the status of the systems at the premises, which would have led to his taking charge, discovering the boss's mistake, and recovering the loot. Perhaps those actions would have merited a raise.

In addition, while we're sympathetic to the Able Alarm Company supervisor, this experienced individual should have realized that two phone calls to a small boy, one to a diffident company prez, and two no answers did not equal effective response. He should have bitten the bullet, recalled the boss, and bluntly informed him that his company assets were without protection until someone took charge of the premises. He should also have persisted in further contact with his counterpart at ZZZ who would have reluctantly confirmed the receipt of an alarm signal and the guard response delay. This information also would have reinforced his effort to persuade the company president to go to the premises.

The ZZZ company supervisor shirked his responsibilities in failing to dispatch police, calling the subscriber's representatives, requiring effective search procedures by the guard, and notifying the subscriber, following the guard visit, that the alarm service was out and/or interrupted. Of course, if the police patrolling the area had returned following their accident investigation to check the perimeter for a possible break and entry, they would have discovered the loot-loaded van and earned the "saved-the-day" award.

Structural security weaknesses also contributed to the vulnerability to such an attack. If, for example, the employee entrance door had been equipped with a double dead bolt lock for closed period use, Pete and his boys would have had to use greater force to gain entry, and perhaps, a door pried off its hinges would not have escaped the attention of the second guard. Similarly, if the vault structure had been reinforced (see Chapter 27) and a bank-type vault door installed, the probability is that burglars would not have attempted the job.

Of course, Pete's boys aren't exactly blameless. If a lookout had been on the roof and alert, he would have advised Pete of a lone, unarmed guard entering the premises, thereby permitting an orderly retreat with loot—or even a temporary withdrawal until the ZZZ guard "split." But then, had Pete done his homework, he would have anticipated the eventual response by the ZZZ Alarm Company and would have delayed the attack until that guard arrived and departed.

STRENGTHENING ALARM RESPONSE

In Chapter 13 we discussed a similar cable cut burglary attack and established the principles that must be followed to prevent loss in such circumstances. This second look at the problem illustrates the probabilities of human nature leading to human error under such circumstances and the need to introduce a nearly fail-safe response procedure that will reduce the chances of human failure. In considering ways and means to strengthen the effectiveness of response to alarms by company supervisors, various approaches have been tried.

Provide Keys to the Premises

Providing both alarm companies with keys to the premises slightly improves the chances of an effective search and discovery of forced entry or cut cables. The argument against this approach, however, includes the danger to individual alarm company guards responding at slightly different times to the premises; one might mistake the other for a burglar.

Add a Third Central Station

Adding a third central station to the alarm-monitoring arrangement only slightly reduces the chances of human error. From the experience of others (some do use three alarm-monitoring stations), we note the arrangement is cumbersome because it complicates alarm opening and closing procedures, causing closing troubles and increasing the numbers of false alarms unless special installation and service techniques are employed in the design of such systems.

Establish Duty Rosters

Others have sought to improve the probability of response by company supervisors by establishing a duty roster wherein daily or weekly schedules are assigned to supervisors who are expected to be available throughout the closed period at a telephone number known to the alarm company. This concept requires the preparation of schedules and imparts a discipline on supervisors that is often difficult to maintain. Illnesses, promotions, terminations, retirements, transfers, family conflicts, and personal priorities all tend to reduce the reliability of a duty roster concept.

Increasing the number of employees assigned to the emergency list usually results in the addition of individuals who are inexperienced in security. There is a proven danger that inexperienced individuals will be influenced by the illusions (for example, "it's only a telephone company trouble") and will not effectively protect the property. Further, the expansion of an emergency call list usually exhausts the number of available supervisors and leads to the addition of nonsupervisory employees such as maintenance personnel and, sometimes, office employees. Such individuals responding to an actual crime face real danger and may encounter difficulty in effecting full police and alarm company efforts since, in the eyes of those agencies, they appear to lack authority and security experience.

THE DIGITAL PAGER

With experience, many businessmen have realized ineffective response to alarms is the Achilles' heel in their security program. They have also recognized equal need for management response to other emergencies that may relate to fire, flood, explosion, earthquake, blackout, and so on. They have correctly evaluated the need—namely, to select and fully train a dedicated security-responsible supervisor who will always be available to respond directly or to supervise indirectly the security of the premises under such conditions. Having established the principle, the trick is to provide a communication device that will enable alarm company and law enforcement agencies to contact that supervisor 24 hours a day, 7 days a week.

Radio paging services have been available for many years and, in fact, are commonly used by physicians and other professionals whose services require they be on-call at all times. The application of paging services to alarm response by company supervisors is equally effective.

The Way It Works

Operating on special frequencies allocated by the Federal Communications Commission (FCC), paging service companies offer their subscribers an individual telephone number. When dialed, the call is fed through a computer and then interfaced through a transmitter to the receiver, or beeper, carried by the subscriber, who then need only contact the person or company who has been given this number for emergency use to receive the message. In alarm response application, the security supervisor would recognize the beeper as a signal to contact the alarm company.

While the range of transmission varies, depending upon terrain and transmitter location, in most geographical areas a 50-mile range is possible. Paging service charges approximate $20 per month.

Tone and Voice

While a tone-only paging service is satisfactory when only one alarm company is given the number, a combination tone and brief (5–10 seconds) voice message is necessary if police, additional alarm companies, or other company supervisors are given instructions to dial the paging number for emergency communication.

With this arrangement, a calling party is provided with the subscriber's special paging telephone number and instructed to dial the number and then, at the tone, deliver a message not to exceed a certain number of seconds. Such instructions may be furnished to business associates, alarm companies, and fire and police departments without compromising the supervisor's personal security since neither home address nor personal residence telephone number need be provided to anyone other than the alarm company.

Tone and voice monthly service rates are approximately $25 to $30 per month when such service is provided. Transmission range may be slightly less than that available with tone-only service.

ADVANCES IN TECHNOLOGY

As we enter the expanding age of communications technology, significant improvements in the quality and range of digital paging service are expected. Already, some equipment used to provide paging service includes the capability to combine tone-only service with a Light Emitting Diode (LED) display of up to three telephone numbers, permitting the party being paged to expand the use of this device. For example, the supervisor paged would know instantly whether to call the alarm company, another company supervisor, or any third party to whom he wishes to provide the paging service number. Other advances in cellular radio technology will provide paging services over a nationwide network, thereby assuring that the most experienced security supervisor may be reached no matter where he is.

In preparing an emergency call list for distribution to alarm companies or law enforcement agencies, the incorporation of digital paging service will normally result in the security-responsible supervisor's residence phone being listed first with subsequent instruction to the caller to dial the paging number if there is no answer to the residence phone number. In the event the paging effort does not result in a return telephone response from that supervisor within 3 to 5 minutes, the caller will continue to contact other supervisors on the emergency call list.

In some applications, several of the supervisors assigned to the emergency call list are provided with the paging device to increase the probability of prompt contact with one of the supervisors. While this may be a practical application, care must be taken to establish internal procedures that do not result in unnecessary dual response to the premises or in decisions like "let Joe do it" on the part of one or more supervisors.

There may be some resistance to the digital paging concept by a supervisor who does not clearly understand he is delegated the direct operating security responsibility for the company. In those instances, and particularly where a specific alarm system is false alarm prone, there may be a need to relieve the supervisor from the constant middle-of-the-night response conditions. However, when this is the case, the principle remains the same. By placing the paging device in the hands of the experienced supervisor, management is assured that the alarm company will reach the right person to report the initial alarm. That supervisor may, in turn, elect to call another supervisor on the emergency response roster to delegate the actual response to that person while instructing him to report back via telephone on arrival at the premises so that the circumstances encountered can be properly diagnosed and the effective remedies executed promptly. This arrangement tends to strengthen the alarm response performance of all supervisors.

The use of digital paging also reduces the risk of an error on the part of an alarm company supervisor who might dial an incorrect residence number or, as in one major loss, use the wrong area code in an attempt to reach a supervisor. It most certainly eliminates excuses like "the line was busy" or "there was no answer" when an alarm company delays or fails to effect prompt notification for one reason or another.

In summary, ineffective alarm response is the major cause of significant burglary losses, and while the alarm user can do much to improve alarm response procedural efforts on the part of the alarm company and law enforcement agencies, it is clearly the user's responsibility to take those actions that will prevent the burglar from success once an alarm signal occurs. To that objective, the use of digital paging service adds that touch of professionalism to the company's security program that leads to special effort on the part of the responding agency.

22

The Thermic Lance

Lance a Lot?

Well, actually, not a lot. The thermic lance, known in the United States as "the burning bar," really hasn't lived up to its advance publicity. For the reasons behind this decline "from fuse to fizzle," let's explore the origin and design details of this destructive supertorch.

DEMOLITION TOOL

Experts tell us that the thermic lance was a European development designed for use in structural demolition. Whether you call it lance or bar, the device consists of a ⅜-inch to ½-inch (inside diameter) steel tube or pipe approximately 10 feet long, into which are packed as many as a dozen smaller ferrous alloy rods. While one manufacturer states he uses eleven different alloys to maximize burning temperatures and minimize smoke, an amateur could procure the raw materials and assemble the lance with less trouble than if he wanted to produce an explosive device.

The "cool end" of the burning bar is threaded and, when ready for use, is coupled to an oxygen tank by means of a flexible hose. To ignite the bar, one must use an acetylene torch (a portable blowtorch will do) or a burning ember of wood or coal.

Pure oxygen feeds through the ferrous "pack," burning—bar and all—at temperatures ranging between 4,500 and 10,000 degrees F. This is more than enough to boil the toughest steel safe or vault alloys. It is also hot enough to melt concrete.

In one attack, it is reported that, instead of ferrous rods, iron dust was fed in, hopper style, together with the oxygen supply. This method may have provided greater efficiency or extended the burning life of each bar. Perhaps this was a cheaper method: cost reduction is popular in any business endeavor today!

When the lance is used under laboratory conditions, the only accessory equipment needed are welder's antiglare goggles (a mask is preferable), a laboratory apron, and industrial gloves. Under burglary attack conditions, however, one needs barriers to prevent passersby from seeing the glow; a method of protecting against stray sparks igniting papers, rugs, and other flammables; and a means of quenching the burning bar "nub ends." Thus, canvas to shield the glare and water buckets to protect against fire are added to the shopping list.

TEST REPORTS DIFFER

During the period 1968–1969, there was substantial fear that the thermic lance might be used in conjunction with the underworld's newfound ability to defeat or compromise conventional high security (direct-wire) central station alarm systems. Leading safe and vault manufacturers, alarm service contractors, and law enforcement agencies conducted various tests and demonstrations to determine the pros and cons of this new underworld toy. Reports flowing back from such demonstrations included statements to the effect that (1) the lance cuts through steel like a hot knife through butter; (2) it is smokeless (antipollution leaders take heart); (3) there are limited vibrations; (4) it works well underwater (we need two burglars for Noah's next expedition); and (5) it's noisy—"it pops."

While the reports varied, the most important consensus was that the thermic lance, when used against steel alone, is a very effective, rapid cutting tool. The other significant area of agreement was that the lance produces little in the way of vibration effects, thus circumventing the standard vault protection vibration detectors.

Noise and Smoke Levels Vary

Noise and smoke levels varied with the materials consumed and the skill of the operator. Testers concluded that, under ideal conditions, it would be unlikely that either smoke generation or noise levels would be sufficient to activate the conventional smoke detectors or sound pickup devices employed in vault protection systems.

Heat Spread Limited

Further, in the event the lance were used to attack a large safe or a vault door, there was some question about the probable effectiveness of heat detectors, normally installed on the interior wall above the safe or vault door or threshold for the purpose of detecting conventional torch attack. This doubt arose because the lance's high temperatures result in so rapid a burning or cutting process that the heat does not have time to spread through the body of the safe or vault door as it does when conventional burning devices are used. For example, in one experiment a burn through a 3-inch steel plate was accomplished so rapidly that a person could safely put his hand on the surface 6 inches above the burn line as soon as the lance was removed.

UL ran extensive tests on the lance under laboratory conditions. UL concluded that, while UL-approved sound- and vibration-detection systems would afford some measure of protection against this form of attack where steel alone is involved, a combustion-detection system was to be recommended as additional protection.[1]

Attack Against Reinforced Concrete

Under laboratory conditions, the lance melts reinforced concrete and can burn a hole 1½ to 2 inches in diameter through 12 inches of reinforced concrete in approximately 5 minutes. This is less serious than it appears because, unlike drilling, the lance burn tends to wander through concrete, usually piercing the inner wall some distance off center from the outside point of entry. Further, the lance cannot be used to burn laterally like the proverbial hot knife through butter. In applying the thermic lance to concrete, the recommended procedure is to burn a series of individual holes an inch or so apart, one hopes without one burned hole wandering into an adjacent hole since it is virtually impossible to correct the resulting irregularity in hole separation. If everything goes well, a skilled attack could—at least in theory—burn a 16-inch square pattern of approximately 20 holes through a 12-inch reinforced concrete wall in less than 2 hours. In the process, however, the attacker would necessarily consume several tanks of oxygen and as many as two dozen 6-foot-long burning bars. This presents, in military terms, a serious supply and logistics problem, including the undetected delivery of so much equipment at the site of the attack.

Once the lance attack has produced the necessary pattern of 20 to 24 holes, a battering ram must break loose the remaining webbing of concrete and knock out the manhole-sized concrete block. Assuming that line security has preserved the integrity of the alarm system up to this point, this process should activate a sound- or vibration-detection alarm device.

At this point, however, the vault entry is a fait accompli. The attackers are already through the physical defenses of the vault, and the alarm starts a race against time: Will the police or alarm company guards arrive more rapidly than the thieves can depart with enough loot to make their efforts profitable? Or how much loose loot can loose looters liberate before "the guys in the white hats" arrive to do their thing?

Of course, all this also assumes that there is "only" a 12-inch reinforced vault with some steel inside and out. This is equivalent to an R-rated vault,

[1] Conventional smoke-detection systems are based on smoke obscuring a measured light; combustion detectors discern the charged ions that are the precursors of smoke.

one built to the standards of the Bank Protection Act. A vault lighter in construction (and many are) would be easier to defeat. Vaults that were built in penny-wise days may now be pound foolish.

Now we come to the real issue. Even assuming that saving on safe or vault construction cost is done with the best advice of architects and, therefore, those making such a choice know the risks involved, what of the vault door? Recently established UL standards applicable to burglary-resistant vault doors indicate that doors that are constructed of special alloys afford considerably more resistance to burning bar attacks than just steel-constructed doors (see Chapter 27).

PROTECTION FROM THERMIC LANCES

Exterior Combustion Detectors for Early Alarm

The lance has been used successfully against tough steel vault doors up to 7 inches thick to burn a hand hole large enough to permit the attacker to reach in to release the door-locking mechanism. Also, we have not been able to gauge reliably the ability of conventional vault door rate-of-rise heat detectors to detect a lance attack against the lower vault door section; UL tests are inconclusive on the subject. However, in view of the UL position that "an ionization and combustion detection device is recommended," we may conclude that UL's engineers are concerned.

A combustion-detection device within the vault will certainly react quickly to a lance attack but only after the lance has penetrated to the interior of the vault. If a criminal burned through the vault wall directly into the interior of a cashier's chest secured to the vault wall, it is unlikely that a combustion detector would register the attack.

Further, while the addition of vault combustion-detection systems may save the assets within the vault from lance attack, these units cannot sound the alert until after the vault has suffered considerable physical damage. It would therefore appear advisable to install combustion-detection devices immediately outside vault walls exposed within the premises to detect attack well before penetration. (Of course, if one or more vault walls are also building exterior or party walls, this problem cannot be completely solved in this manner.)

Separate Alarm Circuits

At this writing the combining, or "duplexing," on a single alarm circuit of combustion-detection devices to a UL-approved vault alarm system might violate the UL certification so important for insurance purposes. Thus, the combustion-detection devices should be connected to a separate alarm circuit.

There are technical considerations as well. For example, if combustion-detection devices installed inside the vault were duplexed to the vault alarm circuit, a malfunction of this device would make it difficult to maintain operation of the basic alarm system without entering the vault during the closed period—an impossibility where time locks are employed.

Line Security and Telephone Circuit Protection

Since the lance, rods, oxygen tanks, and so forth are cumbersome, and far more than is needed to penetrate most U.S.-manufactured safes, it may logically be concluded that the lance will be reserved for vault attacks, particularly vault doors and substandard vault wall construction. But safes or vaults, no matter how well protected, may succumb to the fast burn unless the central station alarm system is equipped with adequate high line security devices and some intruder motion-detection equipment is utilized to protect the areas outside the vault and around the vital telephone circuit wiring.

23

Safe Choice and Considerations

How Safe?

BURGLARS RANSACK SAFE—NET $200,000

"Police call the burglary the most skillful operation in years. After disabling the burglar alarm, the safe was overturned and cut open 'like a tin can.' "

THIEVES USE TORCH TO OPEN STORE SAFE—LOSS PLACED AT $77,000

"Investigators report that, while the safe was new, the store had no burglar alarm system."

CROOKS KNOCK DIAL OFF SAFE—GET AWAY WITH $40,000

"Burglars avoided the perimeter alarm system to loot display cases and the store safe. Detectives said the safecrackers' equipment was hoisted into the store by means of a ladder belonging to the firm."

COPS SEEK ROBBERS IN DEPARTMENT STORE HEIST

"Police continue investigation into $240,000 burglary by team of safecrackers. Investigators report two safes were burned open with welding torches, and a third safe (located in the store's money room) was "punched." How the thieves bypassed the alarm system protecting the safes remains a mystery. All three safes were alarmed, according to police."

PROS LOOT BANK SAFE

"Over the past weekend, professional safecrackers bypassed sophisticated alarm systems and drilled almost a dozen neat holes in the three-inch steel door of a Center City bank safe. The burglars escaped with $235,000 in currency, police report."

Cutting, ripping, peeling, prying, punching, drilling, burning, attacking with explosives, and manipulation—even X-ray—are techniques used by hundreds of professional and semipro safecrackers in attacks against the thousands of substandard safes, large and small, in use by businesses from Maine to California. Of the so-called safes in use today, 95 percent are not safe from the modern-day safecracker armed with efficient cutting and burning tools.

WHEN IS A SAFE UNSAFE?

A brief discussion of "the nature of the beast" will explain the safe problem, which has become critical since certain skilled criminals have found ways and means to defeat sophisticated (as well as unsophisticated) alarm systems. The safe in the form we recognize today was first produced about 1850. Since safes are principally iron or steel and not subject to a great deal of wear, they last forever—or until they are attacked. Many safes over a century old are still in use today, although the protection afforded by the old-style safe is minimal, if not technically nonexistent.

Since alarm systems were considered absolute protection for safes until recently, little or no reason had existed to develop safes that afforded substantial physical resistance to burglary attack; instead, the prime consideration has been the safe's ability to protect its contents from heat in the event of fire.

FIRE-RESISTIVE SAFES AND THEIR CLASSIFICATIONS

UL classifies as "fire-resistive" those safes that are a steel shell containing fire-resistive insulation and having a combination-locked door or doors. Such fire-resistive safes generally have less than 1-inch total thickness of steel in the body and less than 1½ inches of steel in the door. The volume of insulating material determines the safe's UL rating.

By definition (and test), a Class A safe will protect its contents despite external temperatures up to 2,000 degrees F for a period of 4 hours. A Class B safe can protect against a 2-hour exposure of 1,850 degrees F and a Class C safe for 1 hour at 1,700 degrees F. Fire-resistive safes are further tested for their resistance to building collapse in a fire.

UL does not rate Class A, B, or C fire-resistive safes as affording any protection against burglary attack. It is a matter of record that criminals with modern metal-cutting and burning tools can open these fire-resistive safes within a span of 30 seconds to a few minutes.

Fire-resistive safes can be, and almost all new ones are, equipped with "relocking" devices that deadlock bolts in place in the event of a common type of attack against the safe door. However, such devices cannot provide any resistance to attacks against the body of the safe and offer little or no protection against oxyacetylene torch or burning bar attacks against the door.

BURGLARY-RESISTIVE SAFES AND THEIR CLASSIFICATIONS

As classified by UL, burglary-resistive safes must be constructed of open hearth (tempered) steel (or other material affording equivalent strength) at least 1 inch thick and have doors made of steel at least 1½ inches thick. These safes must also have the following features:

- A UL-listed combination lock,
- A UL-listed relocking device,
- Cast or welded plate bodies,
- Door(s) of special metal alloys that resist carbide drills.

In addition, burglary-resistive safes weighing less than 750 pounds should be equipped with anchors to secure them inside larger safes or in concrete blocks or to attach them to a building structure, as the case may be.

Since burglary-resistive safes usually do not contain any fire-resistive insulating material—and, indeed, conduct heat to the interior due to their construction—for protection of the contents against destruction by fire, such safes should be installed inside larger fire-resistive safes or inside fire-resistive vaults or enclosed in properly applied concrete. The user of a burglary-resistive safe must make certain that the fire protection afforded by the safe or by its location within a fire-resistive structure is adequate to meet fire insurance requirements.

Burglary-resistive mercantile safes are classified by the Insurance Services Office[1] in their *Manual of Burglary Insurance,* the standard of the insurance industry. Most of these classifications utilize the listings of UL, as follows:

- E: A 1-inch steel body with a 1½-inch steel door;
- ER: A safe bearing the UL label "Tool Resisting Safe TL-15 Burglary"—that is, tested to resist tool attack for 15 minutes;
- F[2] : A safe bearing one of the following UL labels:
  "Tool Resisting Safe TL-30 Burglary,"[3]
  "Torch Resisting Safe TR-30 Burglary,"
  "Explosive Resisting Safe with Relocking Device X-60 Burglary,"

---

[1] The Insurance Services Office, 160 Water Street, New York, is the successor organization to the Insurance Rating Board. *Note:* UL has recently established a tool-and-torch-resistant safe classification, #TRTL-15X-6. Testing standards apply to all six sides of this safe. It is not known whether this is considered by the Insurance Services Office in the ER or the F category.

[2] The same labels qualify a safe for a "G" classification under "Bank Safes" in the *Manual of Burglary Insurance.*

[3] *See* page 158.

- H: A safe bearing one of the following UL labels:
  "Torch and Explosive Resisting Safe TX-60 Burglary,"
  "Torch Resisting Safe TR-60 Burglary,"
  "Torch and Tool Resisting Safe TRTL-30 Burglary";[3]
- I: A safe bearing one of the following UL labels:
  "Torch and Tool Resisting Safe TRTL-60 Burglary,"
  "Torch, Explosive, and Tool Resisting Safe TXTL-60 Burglary."

The SMNA (Safe Manufacturers National Association) label usually designates the manufacturer's code or model number. When rated relocking devices are used in the door, this is shown by a separate label.

LET THE BUYER BEWARE

Safes manufactured prior to World War II may not be labeled. Also, used safes are generally repainted prior to resale, often obliterating the labels. In such instances it is imperative for insurance purposes that the user obtain a written classification warranty from the seller stating the manufacturer of the safe, its classification or rating, and the construction of the safe, whether fire or burglary resistive. Conversely, the seller's warranty cannot establish the degree of physical protection the used safe actually offers, should the seller be mistaken, or if a fire safe has been previously exposed to fire. It should also be noted that the UL tests for the burglary-resistive qualities of any safe do not include the use of sophisticated attack devices such as diamond core drills and the burning bar (see Chapter 22).

CONSIDERATIONS IN PURCHASING A SAFE

While a safe may represent a major investment, experience has demonstrated it can be adequate for decades. Thus, the cost difference between a safe offering minimal resistance to burglary attack and the best available, measured over the probable length of service, is only pennies a day. Indeed, with certain capital equipment investment tax credits, one may even save money (from a profit-and-loss statement standpoint) by a larger expenditure for the best possible safe protection.

The final decision in safe choice must couple the safe's physical vulnerability factor with the protection afforded by the best possible alarm system. (The latter is discussed in Chapter 25.) The following additional factors should be included in safe-purchasing decisions:

---

[3] Recent UL standards additions also provide for the listing of such safes as tested on all six sides. When this standard is met, the designation X-6 follows the foregoing classification.

1. A number of major safe manufacturers offer burglary-resistive UL-rated "money chests." Generally, these should be chosen when a safe must meet insurance company requirements. If the safe under consideration is not UL listed, written approval should be obtained from the insurance underwriter before the purchase is final. Of course, if a switch is later made to another insurance company, difficulty could develop in obtaining the new underwriter's approval of a nonrated safe.
2. There are many good buys in used safes. However, the safe rating must be clearly warranted in writing, and one must look for rating violations (for example, a hole drilled in a safe door or the body of the safe may void the rating). Also, the fire-resistive insulation may have deteriorated with age.
3. If the safe selected is not fire resistive, how will fire insurance requirements (or self-insurance standards) be satisfied? This can be done by encasing the safe in concrete, by anchoring it securely within a fire-resistive safe, or by placing it in a fire-resistive vault.
4. Will the safe be large enough to meet future inventory storage needs? Not only may a larger safe satisfy future needs, but also the small additional initial investment may save hours of labor in time required for daily loading and removing of the safe contents.
5. Is the interior of the safe designed to accommodate the kind of inventory, including cartons, cases, and so on, that will be housed in the safe?
6. Is there a need for individually locked interior compartments for customer goods, employees' assigned stock, materials that should not be mixed with others, additional security, and so on?
7. Does the safe include an approved relocking device? If not, can one be economically added?
8. Will the safe accommodate the addition of a time lock at a later date?
9. Is the combination lock protected against X-ray analysis?
10. Is the combination lock "antispy"—that is, is it designed so that numbers are plainly visible only to the person operating the combination?
11. Will the weight of the safe preclude, or increase beyond acceptable limits, the cost of delivering and installing the safe at the desired location within the premises (for example, will you need to use a crane to move the safe in through the window of a high-rise building)?
12. Is a range of suitable compartments, shelves, and drawers available on an open-stock basis to meet possible future needs?
13. Have you considered and analyzed the cost of constructing a vault, easy of access and large enough for future needs, as compared with the cost and the operational aspects of one, two, or more safes?
14. Since some safes weigh 3,000 pounds or more, the building structure and permissible floor loading should be checked to be sure that the safe can be installed without violation of safety codes or after adequate floor reinforcement is completed.

COST VS. RISK

The burglary-resistive qualities provided by a safe relate directly to the cost of the product. Since a safe represents a major capital investment for most businessmen, an evaluation of the total security risk is essential in the determination of individual safe requirements.

The factors involved in risk assessment include the extent of the value to be protected, the availability and cost of an alarm system appropriate to the risk, and the feasibility of adequate security procedures to safeguard the combination and the operation of the alarm system.

A thousand dollars in cash taken from a weak safe represents good—and tax-free—pay for a few minutes' work to a skilled safecracker. To a large firm such a loss would be likely to be uninsured; it would fall within the firm's insurance deductible. The uninsured firm would also lose the full amount.

It would seem practical, in any event, to consider seriously the investment necessary for a safe and an alarm system capable of making an attack less likely, more difficult, and less worth the effort. When a much higher range of values is at risk, the total investment can reasonably be substantially higher since the loss and its effect on a firm's insurability (and insurance costs) are of proportionately greater consequence. In practice, accomplishing the level of security that should be attained to safeguard a given risk will require all the skills and imagination of the user, safe suppliers, alarm contractors, insurance underwriter, and security consultant.

METHODS OF PHYSICAL ATTACK

Perhaps we can gain a better perspective on the need for improved safes if we examine the experience of others whose safes have been defeated. For the moment, let's concern ourselves with the physical defeat of the safe, assuming either that the safe is not protected by an electric alarm system or that the alarm system has already been defeated. The following sections describe some of the techniques used to crack safes.

Peeling

Safe doors as well as safe bodies are frequently constructed of thin steel plates (⅛ to ¼ inch in thickness) laminated or riveted together to form the required total thickness of steel. These plates may enclose fire-insulating material. The burglar attacks the seams or joints of these plates, peels back the layers of steel, chops out any fire-resistive material, breaks through the thin steel inner liner to reach the bolt mechanism release, opens the safe door, and removes the contents. When the attacker is unable to open the door in this fashion due to relocking devices, he enlarges the hole in the body or door and removes the valuables through his point of attack.

Ripping

Ripping is a similar method of attack frequently aimed at fire-resistive safes having only an outer plate of ⅛-inch steel and fire-resistive insulation retained by a 1/32-inch or 1/16-inch inner wall. Ripping attacks are usually made against the body of a fire-resistive safe since the door is stronger.

While peeling and ripping methods of attack lack finesse and are messy as well as noisy, a practiced hand can peel or rip most fire-resistive safes in less than ten minutes. In the absence of a working alarm system, of course, the attackers can take much more time if they need to. There are actually super "can openers" that are designed, using leverage principles, literally to cut through thin steel plates, much as one opens a canned goods container.

Note: In some cases, burglars avoid exposure to patrols and pedestrians by attacking through a weak party wall against which the rear of the safe is placed. For this reason, care should be taken to avoid locating safes against vulnerable walls.

Drilling or Punching

As professional safecrackers well know, too many safe door-locking mechanisms can be defeated by knocking off the combination dial or by drilling a small hole in the door to expose the locking mechanism. Barring adequate relocking devices, the attackers can then punch the locking mechanism, releasing the bolts for operation by simply turning the safe door handle. This method, in a fire-resistive safe, may take a skilled attacker as little as 30 seconds.

Burning

In the slang of the underworld and law enforcement, to "burn" a safe (or vault door) is to cut (or to puncture) with high-temperature oxyacetylene torches or burning bars. The attack on the door or body of a safe may be done to release the bolt mechanism or to create an opening large enough to remove the contents. While oxyacetylene torch attack is the more common method, the burning bar operates at far higher temperatures (6,000 to 10,000 degrees F) and melts concrete as well as steel (see Chapter 22).

Power Tools

The use of power-driven rotary and hydraulic tools for spreading or cutting attacks against safes has increased in recent years. In one area of the United States, attackers have successfully opened round-door burglary-resistant money chests using hydraulic tools, while power drills have been used nationwide.

Explosives

The use of explosives as a means of safe attack has decreased greatly since the advent of improved drills and burning equipment. Not only is less skill required by the new tools, but also there is less danger of the attackers' being done in by their own means. (The effective use of nitroglycerine also requires at least a working knowledge of the construction of the specific safe being attacked.) However, increased familiarity with plastic charges, which is developing from the use of these explosives by terrorists, suggests we may one day see a return to this method of attack.

X-ray

Use of X-ray is hardly a common technique since it requires both X-ray equipment and special skill in its use. Even so, X-ray examination of the combination is a definite threat wherever high values are held in safes whose doors lack shielding materials to protect the combination from the X-ray eye.

MANIPULATION AND THEFT OF THE COMBINATION

Safe burglary by manipulation of the combination dial is another rarity requiring unusual skills. There are, however, frequent instances where safes are opened when the combination dial is "feathered" (rocked or vibrated) back to the last number of the combination. This technique is effective against safes with worn tumblers when the user fails to "scramble" the combination properly (spin the dial several times in each direction) when locking the safe.

Theft of the combination due to careless security practices probably accounts for as many successful safe burglaries as all the aforementioned techniques. From case experience we know burglars have found safe combinations written on the wall near the safe, on the back of wall calendars, on the underside of desk blotters, on desk flyleaves, or filed under "C" for combination, "S" for safe, or under the name of the safe manufacturer. In other instances, combinations have been "stolen" by using binoculars and telephoto cameras to observe authorized personnel operating the safe combination. In one well-known case, the safe had been located in the front of the store for security reasons: passersby could observe a physical attack. Instead, the burglars stole the combination by observation.

LIMITATIONS OF SAFES

In analyzing the burglary-resistive qualities of the variously classified safes in the light of modern attack skills and equipment, it is obvious that no safe is impenetrable. In general, fire-resistive safes are inadequate to protect valuables in excess of $5,000. And, as the values to be protected increase, one may conclude that many safes leave something to be desired. In recent years, safes manufactured in Europe, Israel, Japan, and Australia have increased in popularity, even though a safe (by weight or bulk) is an expensive commodity to transport 3,000 miles or more. (For further information concerning the advantages of these "tough" imported and domestic safes, see Chapter 24.)

PROBLEMS OF SAFE CHOICE

In some instances, the need to improve the present degree of safe security presents special problems. For example, while fire-resistive safes are inadequate against burglary attack, valuable contents usually require fire as well as burglary protection. For this reason, the use of a burglary-resistive safe that lacks fire-resistive ratings requires that the safe be located within a fire-resistive vault.

Burglary-resistive safes may take the form of money chests with round doors (generally more difficult to defeat) and as such are unsuitable for storing quantities of bulky valuables. Round-door safes are suitable for currency, gem stones, and small quantities of securities or jewelry but are too small to hold the extensive stocks of watches, gold bracelets, and so on typical of a jeweler's inventory. Square-door burglary-resistive safes that are now available up to sizes providing 30 cubic foot capacity are adequate for housing the average jeweler's or pawnbroker's valuable stocks in a single unit.

METHODS FOR IMPROVING SAFE SECURITY

Though fire-resistive safes are inadequate for burglary protection, some users will, for one reason or another (usually cost factors), elect to stick with the weak link. If this is the decision taken, following are some suggestions for reducing one's vulnerability to various forms of attack.

Encasing a fire-resistive safe in concrete or other burglary-resistive material will make it less vulnerable to peeling or ripping. If the safe is light in weight (less than 750 pounds by most standards), the possibility that the safe may be physically removed from the premises can be reduced by securely anchoring it to the building structure. In no case should wheels be left on safes.

While these measures are not all-protective, safe security is largely a matter of making one safe more difficult to attack than another. Relocking devices may be added to existing safes to reduce vulnerability to drill or punch attack techniques.

Security procedures that will reduce your vulnerability to a simple no-force attack by burglars and, for that matter, to internal theft are practical and simple to institute. Safe combinations should not be written anywhere (including slips of paper in wallets) unless a carefully guarded code is developed. This code should not be based on reversal of sequence of digits, sequence transposition, or substitution of letters for numbers since the pro needs little time to try the few combinations such a code presents. Better than any code and more secure is committing the combination to memory.

Further, safe combinations should be changed periodically (every 6 months or year) as well as simultaneously with the departure of anyone entrusted with the combination (for any reason, including retirement) or whenever you suspect the security of the combination may have been compromised.[4]

With proper instruction provided by a safe technician, the user can learn the steps necessary to change a safe or vault combination. This will permit a more efficient practice for achieving necessary changes promptly. However, certain precautions are necessary if this policy is established. First, when a combination is changed, the locking and combination mechanism should be tested using the new combination numbers with the door open to assure that the change has been correctly made. Second, when the design of the combination lock requires the use of a combination-changing key to effect the change in numbers, that key should be safeguarded to reduce vulnerability to an internal theft.

Further, individuals who lock the safe at the close of business should be instructed to be sure that the combination dial is spun to move it away from significant numbers. Also, double combination locks or key locks additional to the combination can often help to reduce potential vulnerability to attack.

Other steps that can be taken to reduce vulnerability to various known

---

[4] A classic case concerns a nightclub, where the manager was forced by robbers to telephone the owner for the safe's combination. The next night the thieves returned—and used the combination.

methods of attack include locating and illuminating the safe so it is in full view of passersby and police patrols. One ingenious proprietor located his safe near the entrance door and adorned it with "art"—a hard-to-miss statue of a nude woman. If the safe is to be visible, precautions must be taken to ensure against spying when the combination is used. Further, the safe must be securely anchored if it is located near an exit or show window and thus more vulnerable to removal in toto.

The use of two or more safes reduces vulnerability by reducing the value of the loot obtainable by penetrating a single safe. Two or more safes also substantially increase the length of time required for a "clean sweep." Here again, the security advantage is comparative; that is, a firm employing two safes would be a less attractive target for attack than a firm that holds approximately equal values in a single safe. The attackers of twin safes also are confronted with a dilemma: Which safe contains the top value?

CONCLUSION

Alarm devices, alarm systems, and security procedures appropriate to safe protection are discussed in detail in Chapter 25. No safe is secure without an alarm system, just as no alarm system can always remedy deficiencies in the safe structure.

Total safe security combines the best possible safe structure consistent with the risk and a separate supervised safe alarm system affording a high degree of resistance to tampering, weaknesses in operational procedure, and skilled attack against the alarm telephone circuits.

24

Imported Tough Safes

Important Safes

Most conventional safes in use today, even burglary-resistant, afford only minimal resistance to attack with modern tools and weapons. The physical security these safes offer is inadequate for the protection of valuables and must be buttressed by electronic security—alarm systems and related security procedures.

In the event of the defeat or compromise of the alarm system or of related security procedures, permitting unhurried physical attack, these safes are virtually defenseless. Clearly, this has been a classic example of the need for a better security "mousetrap."

Better mousetraps are being built. In recent years, safe manufacturers worldwide have led the way in the development of high-security square-door safes with features and construction not previously available in conventional U.S.-manufactured fire-resistant safes and burglary-resistant chests. These tough import safes owe their development to the fate of older models that failed to repel high-speed diamond core drills, new applications of explosives, and the thermic lance, or burning bar (see Chapter 22).

SPECIAL FEATURES

New Drill and Torch Resistance

Special features include tough drill- and torch-resistant nonferrous metal alloys and, in some cases, special concrete. One manufacturer casts these special alloys in a continuous mold that eliminates any seam or joint, a weakness common to standard safes.

The safe doors, constructed of similar materials, are recessed into the body of the safe, reducing the vulnerability of door edges to peeling, cutting, and burning. Other steps reduce hinge vulnerability. In some models the safe casting design provides additional defenses against special explosives for penetrating armor plate.

One manufacturer also points to the addition of special chemicals to the alloys. When the safe is attacked by torch, these chemicals produce dense, oily smoke similar to smokescreens used during World War II. Without gas masks and a means of ventilating the thick chemical smoke away from the point of attack, the "torch artist" cannot continue.

Multiple Relocking

To foil attempts to drill, punch, or apply explosive charges to the combination locking mechanism, special "traps"—multiple relocking devices—function independently of each other to jam the bolt mechanism in the locked position. In order to defeat the locking mechanism, the attacker would have to drill or burn through these special alloy plates at as many as five specific locations on the safe door. In practice, this would be a futile attempt unless the attacker had knowledge of the precise location of each of the relocking devices.

Added Key Locking

Door-locking features may also include double-bitted, highly pick-resistant key locks used in conjunction with a five-tumbler combination lock. Separately keyed "covers" to prevent manipulation of the combination dial are another feature.

The U.S.-made combination locks permit the customer to change the combination at will. This feature increases security by limiting knowledge of the combination to a greater extent than has been possible and permitting more frequent changes.

Combination dials are partially enclosed to prevent the detection of the combination by spying—watching as the combination is operated. Key locks may be added to the combination lock as an extra precaution. Of course time locks may also be added to ensure that the safe cannot be opened before a scheduled time of day and day of the week.

These safe manufacturers do not claim their safes are impervious to attack; no structure is impenetrable. Adequate alarm systems and sound security procedures will remain an integral part of any total security concept for the protection of safe contents. As discussed in Chapter 23, such a security program must include strict control and secrecy as to combinations and authorized use of keys.

SIZES AVAILABLE

The import safes are manufactured in various sizes and provide interior storage capacity ranging from 3 to 20 or more cubic feet. Weights range from 2,000 to 6,000 pounds, and the floor load factor will vary between 400 and 600 pounds per square foot on the average. Provisions are usually incorporated for bolting the safe to a concrete floor. The absence of wheels also hampers criminals with ideas of carting the safe away to a remote location that would allow unlimited, uninterrupted time for the penetration attempt.

In some locations, building elevator weight-load limitations may be less than the weight of the safe. In such cases it is sometimes possible to remove the safe door, thereby reducing the weight load to elevator capacity limits, or to use an industrial crane to convey the safe up the exterior of the building and in through a window or other opening.

When all of these new safes' anti-intrusion features are compared with conventional fire-resistant safes or money chests, the reader and the criminal may well conclude that the import safe is most difficult to penetrate. It will deter attack.

UL LISTINGS

In the early years of introduction of the import safe into the U.S. market, international manufacturers did not, for one reason or another, submit their products to UL for standards tests and subsequent rating. This resulted in some unanswered questions as to the real levels of security such safes afforded, and in the absence of any UL label, some insurance companies were reluctant to accept those models as qualification for user insurance credits. However, as competition increased and insurers toughened their stance, most international manufacturers of burglary-resistant safes have, since 1980, submitted their current models for UL test and listing.

As a result, the buyer now has a broad choice of UL-listed burglary-resistant safes. For example, in the TRTL-30X-6 category, a most popular safe for high risks, some ten safe manufacturers now offer this equipment. In addition, a new listing category, a lower-cost TRTL-15X-6 is now available through eight safe manufacturers.

These recent years of progress in the development of stronger burglary-resistant safes have been invaluable in the prevention of loss. In the United States, successful burglary attacks against safes meeting these new listing standards have been rare. Contrast this with the Jewelers' Security Alliance report of the increase in the successful burglary of safes bearing lower ratings that in recent years occur in the jewelry industry once every 5 days.

SAFE DEFENSES

Let's explore one other security aspect. The defenses of these tough safes are designed to prevent, delay, and increase the effort required to make a hand-hole-sized opening. Since highly valuable contents can be removed through a small opening, the user of one of these strong safes may wish to reduce the potential for loss further by compartmentalizing the safe interior, limiting the value reachable through any one hand-hole penetration.

In addition to problems of insurability, weight, and installation, these tough safes present a challenge to the installer who must attach alarm devices to its drill-resistant surface. Since damage to the safe through faulty alarm installation may be difficult and expensive to repair, the user will want to assure himself that his alarm contractor has the capability to do the job correctly before any agreement is entered into for alarm system installation.

Similarly, the care and use of this safe are equally important. For example, the labor required by a locksmith to open and to repair a jammed safe door is likely to be lengthy and expensive.

FIRE RESISTANCE NOT RATED BY UL

One last word of caution: It should be noted that UL has not provided any fire-resistance rating for safes listed in the TRTL-15X-6 and TRTL-30X-6 burglary-resistance listings. Anyone whose valuable goods may be destroyed or devalued by extreme heat or fire should obtain warranties that the safe will meet his fire insurance underwriter's requirements and that uninsured merchandise will be adequately protected against fire or heat loss and destruction. Alternately, the problem can be resolved by placing the burglary-resistant safe inside an adequate rated fire-resistant vault.

THE PROBABLE FUTURE

The new tough safes range in price from approximately $2,500 to $15,000 including delivery and installation. While a UL-labeled domestic fire-resistant safe or burglary-resistant money chest of comparable size costs less, there is clear evidence that anything less than a tough safe is no longer adequate for the high risk. As the jeweler, banker, moneylender, and other prime targets upgrade their physical safe security, criminals will necessarily turn their attention to safes protecting currency, coin, stamps, and so on as tomorrow's target for attack.

It is important to know that the new tough safes cost more because the construction of all six sides of the safe must stand up to UL testing. When a manufacturer submits a safe for listing in the TL-15 or TRTL-30 categories, UL burglary-resistance ratings applicable to those safes are based on a specified but limited standard for the body (which is accepted without tests), and actual tests are performed on the safe door and frame only. The bodies of such safes are more vulnerable to attack unless they are encased in reinforced concrete or other material that adds resistance to equal that of the door and frame.

25

Capacitance Alarm Safe Protection

Close Proximity

SAFE VS. CASH PICKUP

Ira Pinchpenny settled back in the comfortable lounge, toyed with his second extra-dry martini, and paid scant attention as his host, the sales engineer for the Do-It-Right Alarm Company, continued his pitch to provide alarm protection for Ira's new safe. Ira, a soft-goods buyer recently promoted to controller for the fast-growing Suburban Discount Department Store chain, was privately congratulating himself both on his recent promotion and on his prompt "executive decision" to purchase a new safe to secure store receipts (cash and checks) for the main store operation. The savings realized by elimination of the twice-daily (three times on Saturdays) cash pickups by armored car would be (Ira was certain) recognized by his boss—another feather in the cap on Ira's rapidly swelling head.

Of course, Ira also recognized that an alarm system would be necessary for the security of the safe's contents since receipts could exceed a quarter of a million dollars on weekends and during the holiday season.

As the sales engineer droned on, Ira smiled inwardly. He had no intention of obtaining service from the Do-It-Right Company. After all, similar service could be obtained from several alarm contractors, and Ira reasoned shrewdly that some would be willing to discount their bid below Do-It-Right's for the prestige and advertising value of being able to say "We protect Suburban."

PROXIMITY ALARM PLUS

Do-It-Right had argued that proximity, or capacitance, alarms were undeniably the most sophisticated electronic protection for safes. The salesman spelled out his arguments: proximity alarms took up no additional space, detected intruder movement within 4 feet or less of the safe, and could be, if installed on a separate alarm circuit, covered by a UL certificate.[1] The salesman explained, of course, that for such a high risk it would be prudent to add line security to the system; this would upgrade the UL certificate to a Grade AA and substantially increase security while decreasing insurance premiums. The luncheon concluded with Ira thanking his host for his hospitality, shaking hands, and saying, "Don't call me; I'll call you."

Next day Ira interviewed eager sales engineers from two other alarm companies. From behind his imposing desk, an imposing Ira cut both men short with, "Never mind the sales pitch—we know all about alarm systems. We want a proximity alarm with a UL certificate. And if you want our business, we expect your lowest price."

UNREAD SPECIFICATIONS

Within an hour Ira had evaluated the two alarm contract proposals and issued a purchase order for a system that would cost Suburban 50 percent less on installation as well as a similar savings in annual service charges. Ira had not bothered to obtain a written proposal from Do-It-Right and did not "waste time" reading the specifications that accompanied the contract submitted by the low bidder. His final coup was extracting a promise that the new alarm installation would be completed within 48 hours!

GROUNDED SAFE

When the low bidder's installers arrived several days later, Ira was sorely annoyed over the delay in starting the job. These off-on-the-wrong-foot relations weren't improved when the installers asked to have the safe raised off the floor in order to install insulating blocks. (Most proximity alarm systems must be isolated from ground electrical conditions, which can be accomplished only by insulating the metal safe from the floor.) "Do it yourself," Ira snapped. The installer explained that raising the safe required a safe man, at a cost of an additional $150. Ira said, "Forget it!"

Next the installers realized that the safe was located against a flimsy partition separating the office from the 24-hour computer operations room. They suggested that the safe be relocated to a more isolated location to

[1] Some alarm companies will issue a UL certificate covering Complete Safe or Vault alarm systems combined with premises alarm systems, both being supervised over one alarm telephone circuit. UL does not restrict this practice. However, there are generally two reasons for the alarm contractor's approach. First, and most important, by separating the safe or vault protection these high-risk areas can be secured at the earliest possible moment. Second, there is a question of additional service revenues involved in the supervision of a separate alarm circuit.

avoid problems. This idea was—naturally—rejected; after all, Ira knew the secret of cost control: "Head 'em off at the pass!"

NO TIME FOR EXPLANATIONS—NO SEPARATE CIRCUIT

On completion of the installation, the alarm contractor attempted to explain to Ira how the system functions—that it reacts to the electrical body capacitance (which affects the balance of the alarm circuit) introduced when an intruder passes in close proximity to or actually touches the safe. Ira was far too busy for these technical explanations.

He was also adamantly opposed to the contractor's suggestion that the safe protection should be on an alarm circuit separate from the premises sensors. The alarm company recommendation was based on their knowledge that the store's perimeter alarm system was frequently not set until cleaners and computer operators finished their shifts, late at night. In fact, when computer operations were running around the clock, the store perimeter alarm sometimes was not activated at all.

Ira's violent opposition was of course due to the fact that a separate alarm circuit would have increased Suburban's annual service charge to a level higher than that quoted for similar service by Do-It-Right. No one was going to cut down *that* feather in Ira's cap; here was another "threat" to his astute "savings."

CAME THE DAWN THE NEXT NIGHT

At 6:00 the following evening the proceeds from the day's sales were placed in the safe, the doors closed and locked, and the proximity alarm turned on. Of course, nothing could happen until the computer operation shut down and that department manager set the perimeter alarm system. Then the central station supervision of all the store's alarm devices would be activated.

CLEANERS ON PREMISES

Being Saturday, the computer operation closed at 6:00 P.M. (rather than its usual 10:00 P.M.), and cleaners were locked in the premises with the alarm system turned on. This was a standard Saturday night practice of the Suburban Discount Department Store to which the alarm company had fruitlessly objected. The cleaners were expected to complete their work at 11:00 P.M., at which time they would telephone the alarm company for a special opening and closing of the alarm system to allow them to exit from the store. However, an alarm signal was received at 8:00 P.M. With the safe protection combined with the perimeter alarm, the alarm company could not pinpoint the cause of the alarm. Cleaner personnel could be passing merchandise out the door, so they were forced to notify police and dispatch guards to the premises. Arriving guards and police searched the building and found neither intruders nor evidence of forced entry—though their sudden appearance scared the pants off the cleaners.

REDUCED SENSITIVITY

The following Saturday the same condition occurred. This time the alarm company guards and police found the cleaners sweeping near the safe. Obviously, they felt, the cleaners had created the false alarm by passing near to, or coming into contact with, the safe. A service representative of the low-bidder alarm company "corrected" the situation the following Monday by reducing the sensitivity of the proximity alarm system. Now someone would have to come within a very few inches or actually touch the safe to create an alarm condition.

Within two weeks, however, guards and police were again responding to an alarm. This time they found that a lone computer operator, left in the premises with the alarm on, had set off the proximity system by walking close to the partition that separated the computer room from the safe in the controller's office. To prevent future alarms from this cause, the alarm company service representative *again* reduced the sensitivity, this time to its lowest point, and placed a metal shield between the rear of the safe and the wall. These steps eliminated this particular false alarm condition, but it also left the system at the lowest possible sensitivity level.

EVERYBODY UP!

A few weeks later, Ira—last on the calling list but the only one available at the time—was rudely awakened from his warm bed at 3:00 A.M. to travel icy roads to the premises. There were two reasons for notifying Ira and insisting upon his presence at the store: First, the alarm company and the police could not locate an intruder (indeed, it is difficult to search for "hide-in" intruders in a large department store served by a single alarm system). Second, they were genuinely irked at the frequency of false alarms since the addition of the proximity alarm system to the circuit and thought the inconvenience would motivate Ira to do something constructive.

The cause of the false alarm was not determined that night or on several similar occasions in the following weeks. Finally, the alarm company service representative discovered that there were substantial fluctuations in the voltage of the power supply during the early hours of the morning that were caused by the utility company's adjustment to load conditions. These fluctuations, coupled with the improper installation of the proximity alarm system, caused the intermittent false alarms. The problem was eventually solved (at the alarm company's expense, of course) by raising the safe and installing under it the insulating blocks that should have been provided at the time of installation.

NO FURTHER ALARMS—OF ANY KIND

Following this unpleasant series of incidents, which naturally earned for Ira the disrespect of both police and the alarm company guards, no further false alarms were received. As a matter of fact, office workers occasionally and jovially questioned whether the system was still working. Their doubts were apparently confirmed on Monday, "Comeuppance Day." Ira entered his office and was about to slide into his comfortable executive chair when, out of the corner of his eye, he noticed something wrong: the safe doors were open.

Quickly Ira went to the safe and stared into nothing. The entire weekend's receipts were gone. Recovering from his initial shock, Ira called the police, the alarm company, and his boss, in that order—with the last call being an extremely painful one.

On arrival, law enforcement agents duly confirmed that the safe was empty. As usual, there were no usable fingerprints. Worse, there was no evidence of force having been used against the safe, and the alarm company was quite emphatically sure they had received no alarms from the premises alarm circuit (and, hence, none from the safe itself). "How in the world," asked an irate Ira, "could the safe door be opened without your receiving an alarm signal?" The alarm company had several possible explanations, none of which satisfied either Ira, the insurance company, or Ira's boss.

What do you think explains the absence of an alarm and the success of the theft? Was it possible someone had learned the combination and had entered Ira's office after the safe was locked but before the perimeter alarm was turned on? Yes, this was possible.

As it turned out, police interrogation revealed the following. Ira had left early on Saturday to play golf and had delegated locking the safe to his assistant. The assistant forgot to close (let alone lock) the safe. A cleaner found the safe doors open, succumbed to all that green stuff, and promptly left for Las Vegas with it. By Monday morning the store's cash was really gone, and there was only his guilty conscience left to show for it. How is it possible for an alarm system to be tested and set while the safe door is open?

NO CONTACTS ON SAFE DOORS

Again, there was an unbelievably simple answer. There were no alarm contacts on the safe doors. Why? The low-bidder alarm company installers (less experienced than Do-It-Right's personnel) did not realize that door contacts were necessary to the proper protection of the safe. Yes, it was technically possible to set the proximity system whether the safe doors were open or closed. And since the alarm contractor had adjusted the sensitivity of the proximity system to the level that required direct body contact to create an alarm condition, the intruder wearing insulated gloves did not actuate the alarm sensing circuit.

NO RECOVERY

When the dust settled, Ira was behind an assistant buyer's desk at the Podunk branch of the Suburban Discount Department Store, while the corporation's legal department, the insurance underwriter, and the alarm contractor fired legal missiles back and forth. Yes, the alarm system had been improperly installed. Yes, the UL certificate issued by the alarm company (acting as an agent of UL) to warrant that a Complete Grade A safe protection system had been installed was issued in violation of UL standards.

The insurance company "got out" of the claim because the department store had not fulfilled its obligations to see that the safe was properly closed and locked. In a subsequent civil suit, the low-bidder alarm company was found negligent but had neither the insurance nor sufficient resources to satisfy the judgment. And the cleaner, poor soul, having repented his sins, received a brief but suspended sentence and was soon employed elsewhere. Oh, the justice of it all!

One sometimes learned best from one's defeats. Not so the Suburban Discount Department Store—today the new controller is Ira's former assistant soft-goods buyer. He, of course, doesn't realize that the "correction" of the fatal alarm system defect has left the store still vulnerable.

The low-bidder alarm contractor no longer provides "protection" at this location, of course, but neither does Do-It-Right; another contractor offered to reinstall the system at a lower price. The installer for Low Bidder No. 2 did install an alarm contact on the operating door of the safe, the one with the combination lock and handle, but there is none on the second door. The reasoning of the Low Bidder No. 2 company was that no one can open the unalarmed door without first opening the alarmed operating door—that is, not when both doors are properly closed. One wonders what will happen the night another harried assistant closes and locks the combination-equipped door, leaving the other door free.

PROXIMITY ALARMS STILL THE BEST—BUT

These incidents actually happened. Nevertheless, proximity alarm systems are, by and large, a most effective means for providing complete alarm protection.[2] If the proper (and simple) installation precautions are followed, Ira's problems (and those of his successor) cannot occur. However, while proximity alarms sense the introduction of body capacitance into the protected area, successful attacks have been made by individuals who had the combination and used insulated gloves to manipulate the dial and handle. For this reason, among many others, the combinations to safes, even those protected by capacitance systems, must be carefully safeguarded.

If desired, the safe electrical protection system can provide for an alarm-connected attachment to the combination. Such an attachment requires that, before the alarm system can be set, the combination must be properly "scrambled" (away from the last digit). Once the alarm is set, any manipulation of the combination will cause an alarm.

OTHER METHODS FOR PROTECTING SAFES

Sophisticated Vibration-Detection Systems

At least one equipment manufacturer has developed a vibration-detection system suitable for the complete protection of safes (as well as vaults) and it may be UL certified for Complete Safe protection provided that the safe door(s) is also equipped with an approved alarm contact switch. The number of vibration-sensing devices required to protect a safe is dependent on the size of the safe. If desired, more than one safe, located in close proximity to each other, may be protected using a single vibration-detection system master control unit. Combination guards or attachment devices can also be combined with this system.

Wiring

An old method is to install electrical wiring on all interior surfaces of the safe (including the interior of the door or doors). This method is no longer popular, particularly since the labor required is far more expensive than that required by proximity or vibration detection alarm system installations. In addition, this wiring must be protected by insulated panels in order to prevent damage due to normal wear and tear as valuables are placed in or removed from the safe. Wiring also requires removing shelves, cutting

[2] This is true not only for safes but also for metal filing cabinets. Banks of files filled with proprietary information can be protected by a single capacitance alarm system.

them to reduced size, and in some cases, removing money chests bolted or welded in place.

To top it off, when a safe is wired on the inside, there is no alarm signal until the interior safe walls have been penetrated. At the least, this means the expense of repairing a heavily damaged safe, and in some instances (like drilling the combination), the intruder may have sufficient time to remove valuable contents and make his escape since the alarm is only received "after the hard work is done."

Some safe manufacturers offer prewired safes. However, this prewiring is usually limited to the safe door, leaving the body of the safe vulnerable to attack.

Safe Cabinets

Another method that has been used to protect safes is a "safe cabinet," a wooden enclosure built around the safe and having electrical wiring on the interior of the cabinet. While this system is effective, it is dying out because the skills required to construct custom-made cabinets are disappearing, and labor costs reflect this.

COMPLETE PROTECTION ESSENTIAL FOR SAFES

So much for Complete electrical alarm protection of the safe itself. Needless to say, in view of the fact that 95 percent of the safes in use today do not offer any substantial physical protection against modern methods of attack (see Chapters 23 and 24), the author does not feel that anything less than Complete electric protection can be considered adequate.

PARTIAL PROTECTION

Alarm contractors sometimes provide safe protection that consists simply of alarm contacts on the door or doors of the safe. In fact, some insurance underwriters will recognize this partial protection with insurance premium discounts, even though it is seldom effective against skilled attack unless the body of the safe is encased in burglary-resistant (reinforced) concrete or similar materials and the doors of the safe are tool- and torch-resistant.

This form of partial safe protection is sometimes supplemented by the installation of heat detectors and/or mechanical vibration-detection devices inside the safe. The theory is that the heat detector will register an alarm condition when oxyacetylene torches are employed to attack the safe, while the vibration detectors will alarm when someone attacks with drills or a pickaxe, chisel, or sledgehammer.

While some supplemental protection may be provided by these additions, it is significant that neither—heat detector nor mechanical vibration-detection device—is inherently fail-safe in design nor is either sensor (or the combination of them) recognized by UL or insurance underwriters for certification.

Continuing in the order of descending effectiveness, electrical "traps" are sometimes used to provide safe protection.[3] (In one application, the trap conductor was simply wrapped around the safe at the close of the business day!) Needless to say, floor traps do not constitute satisfactory safe protection, particularly against dishonest employees.

Some firms do not provide direct electrical protection of any kind to the safe. Instead, they rely upon motion-detection devices (such as infrared beams or ultrasonic units installed near the safe). These, too, can only be considered supplementary protection at best and are inadequate to provide the total security required to protect valuable safe contents.

SEPARATE SAFE ALARM CIRCUITS AND ROBBERY

The combining, or duplexing, of safe alarm systems into premises alarm circuits is poor practice. In most business operations, cleaners, computer personnel, store security guards, and other employees working overtime delay the closing of the premises alarm system hours beyond the time when safe assets can (and should) be alarm secured.

It is not sensible to sacrifice the safe alarm system protection for the small dollar savings realized by combining the two alarm systems into one. It is much more effective, particularly to prevent internal theft and to provide management with adequate supervisory controls, to separate the safe protective alarm system. When the systems are separated, not only can the safe protection be set at the earliest possible moment but also the alarm system protecting the safe can be left on (during the opening period) until the majority of the store personnel is on hand. This action measurably reduces one's vulnerability to armed robbery aimed at the contents of the safe; almost half of all major armed robberies are timed for the early opening period or the period just before closing, when only skeleton forces are on hand.

SUPERVISED SEPARATE REMOTE ALARM RECEPTION

Some "sadder-but-wiser" insurance companies do not recognize even Complete safe alarm systems for insurance premium discounts unless they are

[3] Electrical traps are current-conducting trip wires strategically located across interior walkways at the close of business to trap the intruder who has entered through an unprotected point.

connected to a remote central station or a police station by a separate alarm circuit. Further, tying the system to a central station alarm circuit permits the use (and increases the effectiveness) of sophisticated alarm applications such as line security and early-morning ambush signaling units. The independent monitoring provided by the central station in these cases also allows security practices and procedures to be established and (more important) maintained at a higher security level.

26

Burglary of Mercantile Vaults

Crunnnch

Shortly before 5:00 P.M., the Quick and Dirty cleaning van rolled slowly through the crowded Center City streets and pulled up to a curb in the busy light manufacturing and warehousing hub of the commercial metropolis. Five men casually emerged from the van; removed cleaning buckets, mops, brooms, and other tools of their trade; and with deliberate purpose, locked the van and set the vehicle burglar alarm.

Then, strangely—but unnoticed by the crowd of busy workers headed for home and evening relaxation—the five men ambled single file through the crowds to the corner, where they turned. Two blocks north they entered an ancient multi-story loft building typical in layout (and in lack of building security) of such structures in most major cities.

TURN-OF-THE-CENTURY CONSTRUCTION

The building entrance had been modernized. It presented a facade of marble, chrome, and shatter-resistant glass entrance doors. Behind this dazzling entrance, however, one found typical turn-of-the-century construction. Passenger elevators had only recently been converted to automatic operation (to reduce labor costs, of course), while a bank of freight elevators opened onto a receiving hall and exited adjacent to and separate from the building entrance.

In addition to the elevators, there were two enclosed stairwells running from the basement to the roof as prescribed by law. On the rear of the building, two fire escapes terminated in the alley behind the building. Beside the building (perpendicular to the building front) ran another passageway, this one from the rear yard, creating a third exit to the street.

Building tenants were various commercial firms whose products ranged from millinery to camera supplies to men's clothing to jewelry manufacturing. Naturally, many firms with operations in the high-risk category used sophisticated central station alarm systems and, in some cases, kept their stock in safes and vaults.

By 5:34 P.M. all five cleaners had filed into the building, but no cleaning was in progress. At precisely 6:48 the five men assembled in the dingy, poorly lit stairwell on the fifth floor. Somehow they had "lost" their cleaning equipment and now carried two large sledgehammers, several crowbars, three huge burlap bags, a wire cutter, a section of steel chain, a padlock—and some toothpicks.

By now the building was virtually deserted. The building watchman, having satisfied himself that the superintendent was gone for the night, settled down to read and relax in his "private office," the boiler room in the depths of the building. Machinery noise drowned all other sounds, but the watchman was used to that; this was his home-away-from-home. The five men waited in silence for the last stragglers to leave their offices. Finally, at 8:32 P.M. they "moved out."

THE ACTION

Two men proceeded quietly down the stairwell to the street level and the now-locked building entrance door. While one watched, the other carefully inserted toothpicks in the keyways of the lock cylinders. Quickly they melted back into the stairwell to avoid attracting the attention of the homeward-bound stragglers still passing by on the street.

Two others took the second stairwell to the interior of the freight entrance lobby and proceeded to chain and padlock the unlocked (someone forgot) freight entrance doors. Now, except for the fire escapes, the building entrances were sealed.

Meanwhile, the fifth man had gone to the elevator control box. Cutting here, removing a wire there, he effectively disabled the automatic control equipment for the four passenger elevators. He then proceeded to ascend by the freight elevator to the seventh floor. The elevator opened onto the unprotected hall of a Hong Kong gift goods distributor. The fifth man propped the door open; now the freight elevator too was out of service.

By 9:05 all five men had assembled at the seventh floor. It seemed likely they were about to collect giftware, but they climbed the stairs to the eighth floor, where a German import camera distributor's warehouse was located. Since the premises and the vault were protected by a central station alarm system, one might wonder whether they were about to commit an error. After all, the alarm company central station was only two blocks away. Forcing entry without defeating the alarm system would bring alarm company guards and police to the scene in a few minutes.

CRUNNNCH!

At 9:17 P.M. the two sledgehammers moved in unison against the unprotected wall separating the premises from the stairwell. The gypsum block and plaster wall crumbled away under the brief onslaught. The opening into the premises was large enough for the men to enter easily.

A lookout opened the unprotected window overlooking the street and the building entrance. A second man opened a window adjacent to the fire escape at the rear of the floor (an alternate escape route). In just another moment, the muscle men began to swing their murderous sledgehammers against the vault wall. Constructed of gypsum block and covered with sheet rock, the wall disappeared as if by magic. In 30 seconds a man-sized hole had been made into the vault.

TO THE RESCUE—MORE OR LESS

As three of the men began to stuff cameras and petty cash from the vault into burlap bags, the lookouts tensed. They knew that the moment the sledgehammers penetrated the vault an alarm signal would register at the nearby central station. Three minutes later a police car stopped at the building entrance, but responding officers waited for the alarm company guard with the keys to the building.

Three minutes after their arrival, an experienced middle-aged alarm company guard arrived at the scene. As the officers left their vehicle, the guard tried to insert his key in the building entrance lock cylinder. Lo and behold, it would not fit. After shaking the door and trying the key several times, the guard began to try the other keys he carried on behalf of the camera distributor. Of course, none fit the building entrance lock. The guard swore loudly about landlords and customers who changed building entrance door locks and forgot to provide new keys for the alarm company. The police tried the freight entrance doors, knowing they were seldom locked. They found them locked by the chain, which held the doors securely in place. By now ten minutes had elapsed, and the burlap bags were nearly full.

After further debate, the guard and the police decided to force entry through the freight entrance doors rather than risk the wrath of building management by breaking in through the main building entrance doors. Using a heavy-duty crowbar, door spreader, and bolt cutter (relics of other burglary cases), the "law" was on the inside shortly—but not at the scene of the attack. To their dismay, they found all the elevators unavailable or inoperable.

As they began their ascent of the seven long flights by one stairwell, the lookout left the street window and signaled the retreat. Leaving their sledgehammers and crowbars behind, the five men quickly made their way down the other stairwell to the sixth floor where they exited to the fire escape, descending the rest of the way on the outside of the building. As they had moved down the stairwell, they had heard the responding police and the alarm company guard moving up. Reaching ground level, the gang found cover in the maze typical of such seldom-used commercial cul-de-sacs.

At the eighth floor stairwell landing, the guard found that his key would not function there either. One of the policemen descended to the street and retrieved his crowbar, and a few puffing and panting minutes later the trio emerged into the premises. If they had used the rear stairwell, they could have entered through the hole in the wall, of course. However, the alarm company had been assigned premises keys only to the passenger elevator lobby door and the door by the front stairwell; using the rear stairwell was not logical.

TOO LATE

The sequence of events that followed included a search of the premises (which of course revealed no one), a trip through the hole in the vault wall to survey the nearly empty stockroom, and a glance at the street from the lookout's vantage point. As soon as the guard had notified his supervisor that a burglary had occurred, the police called the precinct to request that detectives be sent to the scene. At 10:03 P.M., as several additional police, a precinct detective, and the two principals of the firm sorted through the debris, it was discovered that a window next to the fire escape was unlocked. Police descended the fire escape to ground level and searched the immediate vicinity. Of course, they found no one.

At 10:58 P.M., an alarm company guard had been assigned to watch the premises for the rest of the night. The building watchman, having been questioned ("I didn't hear anything!"), returned to his underground castle, and the police, the subscriber, and the principals of his firm departed the building. Once more, all was quiet.

At 11:47 P.M. five men casually emerged from the passageway beside the building and proceeded back to the parked van. As they entered the van and drove away from the curb, the leader of the gang said, "Score Number 36." Another promptly retorted, "You're wrong, this job was the thirty-eighth." By police records, this attack was the gang's fortieth in a two-year period. The value of their loot is estimated to have been approximately $2 million.

CAUSES

This "success story" raises several questions. What weaknesses guaranteed the success of this crude yet effective, unskilled but successful, form of attack?

No Building Security

To begin with, the Center City industrial-warehousing complex is at fault. In light of present-day crime levels, there is no excuse for building management to operate an unsecured, unwatched, or unpatrolled building. The damages to elevator control equipment and building structures alone exceeded $50,000, not to mention the "hidden" costs: tenants were unable to receive and ship goods until the restoration of elevator service. Unfortunately, restoration took weeks.

Of course, in addition to the landlord's cost of repairs, tenants spent thousands of dollars repairing and reinforcing vault walls and adding additional alarm protection.

If such buildings were properly secured and patrolled, this type of attack would fail. True, the gang members would have been able to enter the building during open-for-business hours to case their victim and to select escape routes. They would not, however, have had unrestricted freedom to roam stairwells, building basements, service entrances, and so forth.

Lightweight Vault

Those tenants with stocks valuable enough to warrant the use of a vault should have realized that a vault structure must be strong enough either to deter attack or to delay penetration long enough to permit effective response by alarm company guards and police. Although mercantile vaults are often constructed of lightweight material, these structures can be reinforced with steel or waffle plate or other forms of steel mesh, steel strip, or boiler plate, even plywood, to provide sufficient time delay capabilities to deter this type of attack.

Unprotected Walls

Further, high-risk tenants should consider the installation of intruder motion-detection equipment to back up unprotected premises walls and signal penetration at the earliest possible moment. In some cases, detection devices installed on walls adjacent to stairwells and unprotected corridors might also be effective.

Lack of Authority to Alarm Company

The tenants should have authorized the alarm company to force entry through inoperative building doors without delay on receipt of alarm signals from safes or vaults. Safe or vault alarms do not ordinarily have a significant false alarm rate.

Lack of Effective Central Police Investigation

Finally, once a pattern of attack has developed, merchants should act—individually and through their associations—to obtain more effective police services. In this particular instance, although some forty crimes had been committed, the jobs were scattered through various police precinct areas. In no precinct had sufficient knowledge and experience been accumulated to enable the detective force to develop strategy against this operation. This gang could have been apprehended sooner if a police central intelligence unit had been assigned to the case in its early stages.

EPILOGUE

As the gang in the Quick and Dirty cleaning van approached the intersection a scant block from its parking place, plainclothes policemen converged on them, halted the van, and took them into custody. The apprehension was made by special police investigation forces operating independently of the local precinct. These detectives, who had been on stakeout in the general area, awaiting such an attack, had been notified of the alarm signal caused when the gang burst through the vault wall. They had immediately proceeded to the vicinity and remained concealed until the alarm company guards, the principals of the business firm, and the local precinct police left the scene. They then observed the gang members leave the building, followed them to the van, and closed in.

If the strategy required to accomplish this apprehension was so simple, why had it not occurred earlier? Actually, members of this gang had been apprehended on two prior occasions during their two years of activity. In each case they were almost immediately released on bail and were free to continue their attack, secure in the knowledge that the backlog in the courts would delay any trial for months or years. Clearly, this is a cost paid by the commercial sector for the slow, ineffective forms of justice prevailing in some cities.

27

Vault Construction and Protection

Deter and Detect

A vault is a complete enclosure constructed of materials that resist fire, heat, explosion, and flood. A vault is used to store for protection valuable records, jewelry, currency, art, stocks, and so forth. A vault differs from a portable safe in that it is much larger and is permanently affixed or integral to the building structure. In theory, a vault should be stronger than a safe since it will likely contain many times more value than the average safe.

OLD VAULTS MASSIVE

Prior to the invention of the electric burglar alarm system, bankers and others with high values to protect against both burglary and fire constructed massive vaults with walls, floors, and ceilings 2 to 3 feet thick and having doors of 8 to 12 inches or more of tough steel. These vaults virtually defied attack, but they were very expensive to build even in those days.

ALARM SUCCESS BROUGHT INSECURE VAULTS

As a consequence, once electric burglar alarm protection proved itself, businessmen began reducing their specifications for vault wall and door thickness, as well as using substitute materials (hollow clay tile, gypsum block, and so on). While these new materials had little or no burglary-resistive qualities, they would resist fire and water. Insurance companies, then enjoying a profitable return from their vault contents burglary underwriting, accepted these economies.

For many years these alarm-protected, featherweight vaults went without loss (more accurately, the vault alarm system was not defeated), and many other violations of vault construction standards came to be accepted by insurance underwriters and businessmen. These violations included the use of substandard hall and party walls as one or more sides of a vault and the introduction of man-sized ductwork to air condition or ventilate the vault. These substandard walls or openings, however, though protected with alarm devices, were (and are) vulnerable to hit-and-run attacks. Similarly, fire-resistive vault doors armored with only ⅛-inch-thick steel plate were accepted as being burglary-resistive.

However, times have changed. Ancient scholars thought the world was flat, fifteenth-century navigators proved it was round, but today some believe the world is crooked.

CRIMINAL SUCCESS

Burglars equipped with core drills, oxyacetylene torches, the thermic lance (burning bar), hydraulic jacks, and X-ray and electronic devices have proved themselves capable of defeating burglar alarm systems and of forcing entry into vaults (and safes) that are merely or mostly fire-resistive structures. Many businessmen are faced with the necessity of constructing vaults or improving existing structures and doors. The reasons are several:

- Existing fire-resistive safes are very frequently defeated.
- Safe storage capacity is inadequate for expanding inventories.
- Open stock (cameras, watches, coins, stamps, guns, gold bracelets, and so on) can no longer be left out in showcases overnight; burglars are entering through flimsy premises walls and ceilings to avoid alarm devices or to complete successful hit-and-run burglaries.
- Burglary insurance premiums applicable to vault contents are lower than open stock rates.
- Hit-and-run gangs have clearly demonstrated their ability to force entry into a substandard vault and to escape with high values before responding alarm company guards and police can stop them.

VAULT RATINGS

Retailers, manufacturers, and wholesalers with high-value merchandise should know the basic burglary-resistive specifications for vault doors and vault construction as long established by the Insurance Services Office (ISO). For classification of mercantile vaults, ISO has two ratings:

- E: Steel door at least 1½ inches thick; vault of at least ½ inches of steel, 9 inches of reinforced concrete or stone, or 12 inches of nonreinforced concrete or stone;
- G: One or more steel doors (one in front of the other, each at least

1½ inches thick) aggregating at least 3 inches; vault of at least ½ inch steel or 12 inches of reinforced concrete or stone or 18 inches of nonreinforced concrete or stone.

ISO has much higher standards for bank vault classification (pages 206–207 of the *Burglary Manual*), but these differ from the vault standards promulgated under the Bank Protection Act. A bank coming under the provisions of the act should consult its federal supervisory agency in regard to that agency's application of Regulation P (Section 216) and Appendix A as currently revised.

UL LISTINGS FOR VAULT CONSTRUCTION

As crime loss experience revolutionized the UL role in testing burglary-resistive safes, so did similar attacks against conventional vaults cause insurers and UL to expand their testing and listing of material used for the design and construction of vault doors, vault panels, vault walls, and vault floors and ceilings. The new UL standards are discussed in the following sections.

Vault Doors

Class 1

Doors and frames equipped with combination locks or time locks have been subject to expert burglary attack using cutting torches, fluxing rods, portable electric power tools, and common hand tools and have withstood attack penetration for one-half hour. A successful attack is defined as one that achieves a "manhole" (96 square inches) or opens the door within 30 minutes by any of the described attack techniques.

Class 2

Doors achieving listing in this category defied the same attack techniques for 1 hour or more.

Class 3

Doors in Class 3 resisted successful entry for 2 or more hours.

Materials used to manufacture the vault doors in various categories include exotic metals, steel, ceramics, and special concrete. Thickness of the doors also varied. It should be noted, however, that conventional steel alone may not be satisfactory. For example, in a controlled attack test, a 100-square-inch hole was cut through a 1-inch thick plate of mild steel in less than 3 minutes.

Similarly, earlier acceptance of doors containing 1½ inches of steel or less, such as fire-resistive doors rated as B (2 hours), A (4 hours), AA (6 hours), with interior steel day gates and UL-approved relocking devices, does not measure up to the lowest UL vault door listing.

Despite their acceptance, fire-resistive vault doors have neither burglary-resistive ratings nor qualities. Thus, adequate steps must be taken to provide suitable and effective alarm systems that will signal tool, torch, or explosive attack against the body of such doors.

The UL-approved relocking device defends against hit-and-run attacks by torching, punching, or drilling techniques. Without the relocking device, an intruder torching a fire-resistive door would be entering the vault when the alarm company receives the alarm signal.

Vault Panels

Since vault walls, floors, and ceilings must afford attack resistance equivalent to that provided by a burglary-resistive vault door, in 1982 UL began to test and list materials that might be used in vault construction. The three categories of resistance were established to coincide with the vault door listings—namely, Classes 1, 2, and 3.

The attack tools established as fair game for testing vault materials included common hand tools, picking tools, mechanical or portable electric tools, grinding points, carbide drills, pressure-applying devices or mechanisms, abrasive cutting wheels, power saws, coring tools, impact tools, fluxing rods, and oxy-fuel gas cutting torches. As a result, ten vault manufacturers have, at this writing, achieved listing for Class 1, 2, or 3 vault panels. However, it is noted that most of the listings are for Class 2, or 1-hour, ratings.

Materials used to construct panels included ceramics, special concretes, exotic metals, and plywood. Bonding or laminating different materials to each other proved to provide resistance to attack equal to or exceeding conventional reinforced concrete, although the laminated panels were thinner and weighed considerably less.

The ISO, the American Insurance Association, and the American Bankers Association, together with UL, are to be congratulated for their recognition of the problem and the action taken to provide standards by which vault construction may be accurately evaluated for strength and weakness.

Prior to 1983, insurance underwriters providing Mercantile Insurance coverage were less informed and more flexible than they are now in regard to vault and vault door requirements. As a result, the following forms of vault and vault door constructions were accepted in practice.

Vault Walls

Nine inches of reinforced[1] concrete or 8-inch-thick concrete blocks with cores filled with special concrete and reinforced[2] were required.

Vault Floors

Six inches of reinforced concrete were required.

Vault Ceilings

Eight inches of reinforced concrete were required. When one reviews the 1982 UL tests against reinforced concrete samples, wherein a 9-inch-thick test sample failed the Class 1, or 30-minute, listing, a 12-inch-thick sample lasted just over 30 minutes, and an 18-inch sample just over 1 hour, it is clear that prior requirements are inadequate against today's attack arsenal.

LIGHTING

Electricity run into the vault should be in rigid conduit, and the space around the conduit (a hole penetrating the vault wall or ceiling) should be completely filled with cement grouting. The light switch receptacle should be surface mounted, whether inside or outside the vault wall, requiring no hole into or through the vault wall.

VENTILATION

No ventilation ducts or pipes should enter through any part of the vault structure. Ventilation should be through the vault door only. If air conditioning or heating is necessary, this should be accomplished using movable ducts that can be positioned to deliver air through the vault door when it is open.

It is noted that UL has listed vault-ventilating ports, defined as devices intended for installation in a vault wall to provide a means for introducing warm or cool air when the vault is open. These devices are designed to

---

[1] Requires special concrete reinforced by steel rods ½ inch or more in diameter running vertically and horizontally on 4-inch centers.

[2] Requires special concrete and steel rods ½ inch or more in diameter, run vertically through core holes and horizontally between cores of block.

close the ventilation opening automatically in conjunction with the closing of the vault door and are tested using the same standards applied to vault doors and classified for ½-, 1-, and 2-hour listings as well. Several manufacturers have listed devices in one or more of these categories. However, it is noted that the devices are designed to be installed in reinforced concrete walls or ceilings 18 inches or more in thickness and are approved for listing only when installed in accordance with the manufacturer's instructions for mounting. In the closed position, these devices do not reduce the burglary resistance of the wall significantly.

EMERGENCY AIR DEVICES

The door-locking mechanism should enable a person locked inside the vault to unlock the door from the inside. The door release can be a risk in a substandard vault structure. Attackers may quickly gain access by making a hand hole in the vault wall adjacent to the door, reach in, and actuate the door release. This possibility can be eliminated by removing the interior door handle and storing actuating tools or devices within the vault for use by persons trapped inside. Most times locks are also equipped with release devices that can be operated by someone inside the vault.

However, some times locks are located inside a locked cover, and therefore, it is necessary to secrete a duplicate of that key inside the vault. In addition, some vault door combination locks are so configured that the locking mechanism cannot be released from the inside unless the correct numbers have first been dialed on the outside. In any event, a precise analysis should be made of each specific vault as to escape requirements, and individuals who could possibly be trapped inside a vault (accidentally or by attackers) should be properly instructed as to release procedures.

BURGLARY ATTACK

The structure of the vault and the door, the existence of a relocking device, and the extent of alarm devices are all considered by the burglar planning an attack. From this information he determines the tools and equipment he will need.

The common methods of burglary attack against safes also apply to vault doors and to vaults constructed solely of steel and "soft" fire-resistive materials (for example, gypsum block). However, since fire-resistive (and, hence, heat-resistant) vault doors present exposures over a wider surface area, the use of a single interior heat detector mounted above the vault door will not be sufficient for reliable detection of a torch attack.

Dial Manipulation

Contrary to popular belief, few criminals can open a safe or vault door combination lock by manipulation. However, many criminals can and do take advantage of the careless businessman who fails to scramble the combination at the close of the business day.

Businessmen and their employees often have the bad habit of setting the combination dial only a few numbers from the last digit in the combination sequence so that the dial need only be moved to that digit at opening time. Safe burglars are just as lazy, and in many cases need never open their tool box—they simply think like a businessman. And when the safe is opened without force, as in these instances, it also opens a Pandora's Box: Was it an inside job? Is there a valid insurance claim?

This problem can be solved simply by a firm policy of turning the safe or vault dial several revolutions clockwise and counterclockwise after the safe has been closed. An alarm device attached to the combination dial can be added to ensure that the dial is scrambled.

Safeguarding Combinations

As has been pointed out, combinations should not be written down and filed anywhere—on the wall, on the back of desk calendars, on desk flyleaves, in the file under C or S or the name of the manufacturer, inside the safe, in a wallet, at home, or anywhere else. The supplier or locksmith should also destroy any record of any combination that he establishes. A feature of the newest safes permits a businessman to change his own combination, a real security improvement (see Chapter 23).

Whenever anyone who knows the combination leaves your employ—for any reason—the combination should be changed. It is also a sound practice to change the combination periodically to thwart the combination holder you don't know.

In view of the much higher values safeguarded by vaults, the prudent businessman may decide to take extra precautions. These can include:

- The installation of a key-locked inner door or gate. Should the attacker succeed in opening the outer vault door, the inner door presents a delay barrier that slows the attack, permitting alarm company guards and police to arrive before a major loss has occurred. Properly constructed and positioned, the interior door or gate will also thwart the attacker seeking to make a hand hole to release the vault door from the inside.
- The use of two combination locks.
- The use of time locks. These devices, which can be added to existing vault doors, prevent the operation of the combination lock during pre-

programmed closed periods. Time locks can be set to operate for periods as long as 144 hours, more than enough for the 3-day weekends so attractive for vault attacks.

Some time locks can also be programmed to provide additional protection against robbery during open-for-business hours. One application would relock the vault door for 20 to 30 minutes to thwart an early-morning ambush robbery attack. It is important that time locks not be confused with relocking devices, which defend against physical attack. A time lock simply makes it impossible to operate the combination during the controlled time period.

VAULT ALARM SYSTEMS

Choice in burglar alarm systems for the protection of vaults must consider the construction of the vault and the vault door. Vaults structured of reinforced poured concrete or reinforced concrete block may be protected by the following:

- Alarm cables embedded in poured concrete while the vault is under construction;
- Alarm wiring applied to all interior surfaces of the vault—walls, floor, and ceiling (alarm wiring often used to be applied to an exterior cabinet that completely enclosed the vault; however, this is now obsolete for practical reasons);
- Alarm systems consisting of approved sensitive sound or vibration detection devices. This method is often the most efficient method of protection.

Vault structures that are only fire-resistive may be protected by the following:

- Alarm wiring applied to all interior surfaces of the vault;
- Audio alarm devices that truly register the sounds of the intruder penetrating the vault as distinguished from sound/vibration-detection devices (sound/vibration detectors register the vibration of tools attacking vault structure).

Other System Considerations

When *alarm wiring* is applied to the interior of the vault, the wiring must be physically protected by covering material such as masonite or plywood.

Intruder motion-detection devices (microwave, ultrasonic, passive infrared, and so forth) are not suitable for vault protection. They may not detect an attack in which the intruder removes valuables without actually entering the vault.

Electromechanical vibration devices and shock sensors (sometimes used for show windows and party walls) are not as responsive as seismic/microphone (sound/vibration) detection devices and are neither approved nor suitable as primary vault protection.

VAULT DOOR ALARM PROTECTION

If constructed of 1½ inches or more of steel, vault doors may be protected with approved heat or reverberant sound detectors (to detect torch attack) and contacts to register an alarm if the door is opened more than 2 inches at the handle end.

Additional alarm contacts are recommended for the bolt mechanism to register an alarm if the bolts are retracted. In this application, the bolts must be thrown before the alarm is set, another security advantage.

The total visible thickness of the vault door should not be considered as being solid steel or laminated steel plates. The amount of steel in almost every fire-resistive vault door is less than ½ inch—the balance of the door thickness is fire-resistive gypsum.

If a vault door contains less than 1½ inches of steel, the body of the door should be protected by electrical linings (lacings) coupled to the alarm circuit.

An alarm device attached directly to the combination tumblers ensures that the bolts must be extended and the combination scrambled before the alarm system can be set.

UL STANDARDS

Vault alarm systems may be classified as Partial or Complete. Partial certificates may be issued for vault door alarm contacts alone. Under certain circumstances (such as massive vault walls), protecting only the vault door might be practical. However, unless the vault door contains many inches of steel, lining the body of the door is to be strongly recommended over the employment of heat detectors for this purpose. A Complete vault alarm system includes electrical protection of all vault surfaces and the door, using systems and devices described for Partial systems.

HOLDUP ALARM DEVICES

Careful consideration should be given to the placement of an emergency signal device in the vault. In the event someone is accidentally or deliberately locked inside, it offers a more reliable means of summoning aid than a telephone extension (or even a special telephone line). In addition, an early-morning ambush alarm device can be installed to signal the opening of the vault door while a robbery attack is going on.

REINFORCING SUBSTANDARD VAULTS

Recent experience and analysis of hit-and-run burglary attacks against vaults resistive only to fire indicate that heavy-duty steel mesh, strip steel, or steel plate secured to the interior vault walls can delay the intruders' entry long enough to permit police and alarm company guards to respond while the loss can still be prevented or minimized. However, this method of reinforcing fire-resistive vaults is neither adequate for defense against compromise of the alarm system nor invulnerable to attacks while the alarm is out of service or where police response can or may be long delayed.

The recently introduced vault wall panels, which are lighter in weight than reinforced concrete, also may be prefabricated to specific dimensions and, when properly installed on the inner or exterior sides of an existing fire-only structure, may serve to strengthen it to a burglary-resistive level.

28

Shopping Center Burglary

J.B. and the Joneses

Less than 5 percent of all U.S. burglaries are as sophisticated, well-organized, and skilled as was the case detailed in Chapter 3. Not many burglary attacks require "permission" from organized crime. Smaller, less-sophisticated gangs plan and execute hundreds of thousands of burglaries throughout the United States each year.

One of the most costly types of "nonlicensed" burglary attack is directed against high-risk retailers. These include retail jewelers, furriers, men's and women's clothing stores, camera shops, coin and stamp dealers, and liquor stores. The potential for the burglars includes both cash on hand and highly attractive merchandise that is easily resold at relatively high prices.

CASING THE TARGET

This burglar's game plan is uncomplicated (let's call him J.B.). He visits the store and "shops" his target to locate vulnerabilities in the physical structure and any perceptible weaknesses in the alarm systems and security procedures. He also estimates the amount of "profit" (tax-free, of course) he may anticipate. By casing the interior as well as the exterior of the premises, J.B. also makes sure that he will have a sure escape route under any foreseeable situation.

While J.B. relishes attacks against premises without alarms (electrical protective devices, to use the technical term), he recognizes that the most worthwhile targets in retail business today have learned their lesson (some of them the hard way). They do employ basic security devices and procedures, and successful circumvention of this security requires a specialty attack. For one favorite method, aptly dubbed "the chop-and-hack attack," J.B. usually has one or two muscular accomplices to facilitate entry, attack, and escape.

From experience, J.B. recognizes that almost all retailers in the high-risk category have been required by insurers to install burglary alarm systems that detect intruder entries through doors, windows, skylights, and other movable openings and that some have been required to alarm ordinary plate glass show windows. Seldom do insurers require alarm protection against entry through walls, floors, or ceilings.

THE SUBURBAN RISK

To locate his target, J.B. travels many miles from his home base. He is looking for a bright, sparkling, well-stocked retail establishment, preferably one located in one of the shopping centers and mall extravaganzas so typical of Suburbia, U.S.A.

Unfortunately, many retailers located in suburban shopping centers do little and know less about making J.B.'s attack against their new location more difficult. Oddly enough, many of these store owners are seasoned veterans of retailing, having experienced burglaries and holdups at the old family store in the central city, where they were located in solid masonry structures in well-patrolled downtown or city neighborhood shopping areas. Over the years, these retailers had taken the security precautions necessary to reduce the success of burglary attacks in that environment. But the old family store is gone; the movement of the population to suburbia, combined with urban crime and commotion, has attracted the retailers (whom we will call the Joneses) to new locations in suburbia and, they hope, to future success.

Lightweight Construction

Unfortunately, though, these Joneses have not realized that modern design and the high cost of new construction have led to building with fashionable but lightweight materials at a real sacrifice in physical security. J.B. knows this, however, and recognizes that entry into such premises through an adjoining wall, the floor, or the ceiling is practically "duck soup." He knows that modern mall shopping center construction consists of continuous lightweight steel-truss roofing with (at best) prefabricated fire- (not burglary-) resistive partitions separating tenants. Roof height is usually 1½ to 2 stories. Conveniently for J.B., retail area ceilings are dropped to conventional levels, and heating and air conditioning ducts, as well as electrical and telephone cables, pass above the ceiling through usually unimpeded overhead space. The careful intruder can often move from mall end to mall end through this area. Although fire walls should be extended upward to provide physical barriers in this ceiling-to-roof space, well recognized as an acute hazard in the spread of fire, fire walls can be penetrated without difficulty. Even motion-detection alarm devices within a store will seldom detect movements above the dropped ceiling.

The usual solid-appearing partitions separating retail tenants can be penetrated by as little as a knife, screwdriver, small chisel, or other lightweight carpenter's tools. Nevertheless, a perfectionist like J.B. may prefer entry through the overhead to going through the partition wall, since the thoughtful, careful burglar can remove ceiling tiles, enter a premises, remove merchandise, and leave by the same route—after having replaced the tiles from above—without evidence of entry into the premises. Once this route is established, the burglar can return from time to time for repeat performances, which the puzzled retailer will think are due to employees, shoplifters, maintenance services—even employees of the shopping center management.

Entry through a wall partition is unmistakable and usually alarms the retailer into increasing his protection against a similar attack. Nevertheless, the need to remove heavy merchandise, as well as the wall entry's attraction as a faster escape route, may weight the burglar's decision in favor of this point of entry.

Other Vulnerabilities

Meanwhile, back at the mall, the retailing Joneses are unaware of other physical security weaknesses that did not exist in the city. Utility and service areas offer the burglar opportunities for making his forced entry while screened from view by an exterior wall. There are also those convenient easy-off roof ventilators that, when removed, present a man-sized opening suitable for all except the tubby burglar. And, because of slower police response, stock left in showcases overnight is far more vulnerable than it was back in the city.

There's also a little matter of lock cylinders. It's likely that the lowest bidder of door locks and related hardware did the best he could, wrestling with the specifications, his successful low bid, and his security standards, by furnishing easily master-keyed lock cylinders that are, unfortunately, more easily picked. After all, he reasons, the specifications spelled out the lack of security desired—and someone else would have been low bidder if he had not "gone along."

ALARMS AND THE SUBURBS

When the Joneses move to their new premises, they contract (or try to contract) for a complete Grade A No. 3 premises burglar alarm system, and if the insurance company has its way, the system will be connected by a telephone company alarm line to the central station of an approved alarm company. However, some locations may be so distant from the city-based central station that they may have to settle for the alarm system signaling the local police station or, worse yet, an unsupervised alarm system relying entirely on a gong or bell mounted on an exterior wall.

If the Joneses have recently moved to these premises, they no doubt were also required (or were sufficiently knowledgeable) to install certain interior alarm traps to detect the movements of any burglar who might evade the perimeter devices or manage to hide in the premises prior to the close of business. Usually, these interior trap devices are photoelectric beams (perhaps infrared), current-carrying trip wire floor traps[1] (black, to be less noticeable), or pressure-sensitive electric mats that silently alarm when stepped on.

Contrary to their prior alarm service experience in the city, the Joneses are not likely to find an alarm company or police department willing to accept the keys to the premises. They are also likely to have trouble finding someone to take the related responsibility for entering the closed premises in response to an alarm condition, to safeguard the merchandise, to capture an intruder, or—more important—to locate the cause for the alarm and reset the system so it can "do its thing" another time.

MALL GUARDS

This rather unsatisfactory situation often leads to the suggestion by shopping plaza management that an economical and suitable substitute for key-carrying police or alarm servicemen would be to subsidize (by a shared increase in the monthly rental) the employment of a guard to patrol the shopping center area during the closed period to save us all from crime. Unfortunately, this one man cannot be everywhere at once, and though the keys are now available in theory, in practice the mall security guard often cannot admit police or alarm company agents to the premises under attack in time to prevent a loss. Too, the interior design of most retail stores is such that the stockrooms (where the action is likely to be) are partitioned off from the selling floor so they won't distract from the store's esthetics. Even a conscientious scrutiny through the plate glass entrance may not reveal activity by the burglars. Even when the alarm is signaling, our mall guard will, we hope, remember his instructions: Wait for backup; never enter alone. So he waits—and waits—while the burglars work on or exit over the roofs or through the ceiling crawlspace.

PLANNING THE SUBURBAN STORE ATTACK

With the suburban retail environment in mind, let's put ourselves in J.B.'s shoes and imagine how he might do this job. Of course, he's been in and out of these premises so often he can navigate with his eyes closed. He has carefully noted a shop selling paperback books and gift cards neatly

[1] Less-sophisticated string trip wire traps are too easily compromised.

sandwiched between a retail jeweler and a fine men's clothing store. Thus, J.B. has an excellent choice—once in, he can attack to his left or right. His entry from the roof into the stockroom of the book shop won't be detected since nobody "burgles" paperbacks and greeting cards and that proprietor has no need for a burglar alarm system.

J.B. has spotted the exact path of the photoelectric beam through the jewelry store and has grudgingly recognized a thinking alarm installer—the beam's location is such as to make attack at the door of the safe difficult. However, J.B. has noted that the safe is not protected by alarm devices, is not bolted or otherwise firmly secured to the building structure, and is a Class A fire-resistant safe, easily drilled and opened once it is safely away from the photoelectric beam path. J.B. has gratefully noted that the rear of the valuable watch showcases (conveniently shielded from view from the storefront) is not similarly hampered by a photoelectric beam. Possibly a recommendation for a second beam fell victim to economy, or the possibility of using a mirror to create additional beam paths had been overlooked. The small wafer-type locks on the showcases present no problems, and a night visit has confirmed that the Joneses' procedures at closing time do not include tucking the watches in the safe. J.B. also knew that police, alarm company, and shopping center security forces are at their lowest work strength from Sunday afternoon to Monday morning.

THE HIT

With checklist and D-Day-minus-One critique finished, J.B. and his husky cronies agreed on the jewelry store and on Sunday night for their attack. They chopped through the building roof into the paperback bookstore and then made a neat man-sized entry hole through the partition separating the stationer from the employees' work area of the jewelry store, a point well concealed from view from the mall.

Skillfully avoiding the almost invisible infrared-filtered beam, they first rifled the watch showcases, gathered up cash receipts that hadn't been put into the safe, and bundled up a number of solid silver items found in the rear storeroom. They then made their way to the safe, being careful to avoid the photoelectric beam (sometimes J.B. ran a clothesline parallel to the beam path to alert his friends to its "alarming" danger), and managed to maneuver the safe 90 degrees out of position. They now had access to the door of the safe and were still conveniently out of sight. They drilled the combination, released the locking arm, and opened the safe. J.B. made a mental note that the safe was heavier than he had estimated it would be—good thing no one had thought to remove its wheels!

Monday was a sad day for the Joneses. The insurance company was mourning, but the Joneses found they couldn't replace the lost stock in time for the Christmas business, and they were short of cash in a tight money situation. Christmas sales suffered, employee bonuses disappeared, and customer relations were irreparably damaged.

J.B. selected jewelry as his prime target. He prefers jewelry because gems are small, lightweight, easy to fence, easy to transport, and fetch "high dollars" on the illicit market. But when the Joneses take steps to reduce their vulnerability to another attack, J.B. will be happy to try on sports jackets in the men's store on the other side of his "entrance." This is his profession; "beating" security is his full-time job. How much time do you spend reducing your vulnerability level?

LOCKING THE BARN

What steps would you take if you were in the Joneses' shoes? Now that some of the structural weaknesses have been made obvious, we assume that Jones will consult with his alarm contractor and his insurance company to identify other weak points in the structure and that he will take steps to improve his security.

First, he will probably recognize that the only near-certain path to prevention of another major loss will be the acquisition of a burglary-resistant safe, one large enough to accommodate his most valuable stock, plus a complete burglar alarm system custom engineered to include special protection for the safe, with (if possible) central station supervision and line security. Having established his first line of defense, Jones will see that the new safe is firmly secured to the building structure—J.B. and his cronies can also mount hit-and-run attacks, breaking in and dragging the safe away faster than police or alarm company agents can respond.

Further, Jones learned a lesson from the loss of many regular customers who couldn't wait for post-Christmas delivery. He now recognizes the need to protect the balance of his stock, which cannot be conveniently placed in the safe at night. He will reduce this risk by installing motion-detection alarm devices that will signal the presence of intruders as soon as they penetrate into his premises. Whether the intruder-detection system selected is ultrasonic, microwave, passive infrared, or audio will depend upon the heating and air conditioning systems in use, the materials used in constructing the roof, and other technical considerations. Jones need not solve these problems, but he must satisfy himself that his security contractor knows the answers, will install the chosen equipment properly, and will maintain it to ensure a high level of security.

Jones will now keep his store well illuminated during closed hours and will downgrade the priority formerly given window displays to provide the mall guard with an unobstructed view into the premises. In order to protect the areas the guard can't see, Jones will make sure the intruder-detection system covers backroom areas as well as the retail floor. This system not only will detect the burglar working in the rear of the store but also will protect Jones from a hide-in robber waiting for him to open the premises for business in the morning.

CONTINUING SECURITY

Jones will consider reducing the size of the target he offers by reducing his inventory to the lowest level compatible with good business, backing the lower inventory level with suppliers pledged to improve delivery schedules and meet rush orders. If this can be done, Jones will be a less-inviting prospect for J.B.'s professional study in the future.

Given good advice, Jones will insist on a method of periodically testing the motion-detection alarm devices to make sure they are still functioning properly and have not been accidentally tuned down or reduced in effectiveness by changes in the store displays or partitions. Jones may want to consider the installation of supplementary vibration-detection alarm devices at vulnerable points on partition walls. However, Jones must keep in mind that such devices necessarily contribute a considerably higher rate of false alarms if adjoining premises are open for business during his closed periods and heavy movement occurs in those tenancies. An alarm system having a high number of unnecessary alarms is like the boy who cried wolf—the more alarms received, the less seriously they are regarded and, probably, the slower the response by both police and alarm agents. Keeping this in mind, Jones will also make sure that his personnel operate the alarm system correctly, to avoid customer-error false alarms.

Even with a telephone alarm line connection to a central station or police department, Jones may want to consider including a loud alarm-activated bell or flashing lights at the premises to alert the guard and unnerve J.B. Finally, Jones—sadder but wiser—may spend more time in the company of alarm contractors, insurance personnel, and law enforcement agents, learning the latest in crime techniques that could affect his livelihood and peace of mind in suburbia tomorrow.

29

Hit-and-Run Attacks Against Glass

Smaaaash!

BASIC BURGLARY TECHNIQUES

We perceive there are actually four basic burglary techniques in high-risk attacks. One involves the defeat or compromise of the alarm system (see Chapter 3); a second avoids alarm devices by entry through unprotected points (see Chapter 28); and a third capitalizes on weakness in security procedures (see Chapters 12, 33, and 34).

The fourth is based on structural weaknesses, which is the basis for this chapter. Given such a weakness, the smash-and-grab professionals are unconcerned if alarms sound (even silently) because they know the response of police and alarm company guards will be too late to prevent their SMAAAASHing success.

DISCOUNT STORE CAMERA DEPARTMENT

The action takes place at a typical suburban discount store or mart late on any one of its six open evenings. One of the most popular and heavily trafficked areas is the camera department, located near the mart's main entrance so that more people will pass through the department. This night is no exception. People jostle each other to reach the camera display counters. Customers wait while salesmen attend to other purchasers.

Suddenly, several young men walking through the department remove short lengths of lead pipe from under their jackets and bring them down in a loud concerted SMAAAASH! Three glass showcase tops disappear in a rubble of shattered glass. Helping themselves to a dozen of the most expensive cameras, the youths literally walk out the exit and disappear into the parking lot.

MENSWEAR STORE

The place is the same shopping center; the time is early Sunday morning, one of the few periods during which retailers in this suburban shopping center rest. Today there are no parked cars, no shopkeepers in their premises. A few service employees are seen emptying wastebaskets and sweeping mall entrances to clear away last night's debris.

A car drives through the deserted lot and parks near a men's clothing store featuring expensive imported Italian suits, the one-of-a-kind that sells at a high profit. This store is Sunday's target for attack.

SMAAAASH—this time it's a glass entrance door struck by a pipe wrench. Almost as fast as words can describe it, three youths are inside piling fine suits over their arms, running for the door, into the waiting car, and driving away.

This time, of course, the entrance door is electrically protected, and an alarm system is activated. In the central offices of the alarm company, a supervisor records an alarm, and the police are notified almost instantaneously. Officers Jones and Schwartz, manning a church crossing a couple of miles away, respond posthaste to the scene of the crime.

Lights flashing and sirens wailing, the officers arrive within three minutes of the alarm. Alas, they too are late—these hit-and-run burglars know they must finish in two minutes because this is "their thing," and they do it very well.

These burglars score repeatedly in different shopping centers on different Sundays. Different merchants—clothiers, jewelers, camera suppliers, small appliances stores, furriers—all fall victim. Wherever glass is all that stands between the criminals and the merchandise, these burglars enjoy a SMAAAASHing success.

JEWELRY STORE

It's 4:00 A.M. and the city street is quiet. This is New York, Fashion Row: fine clothes, expensive jewels, perfumes, good restaurants. Millions of dollars change hands on this street during the day.

Now, there's a strange sight—two men in workmen's clothes with a lantern, a big chain, and a sledgehammer. What on earth are they doing at this hour? Probably called out to fix something. They've stopped in front of that jewelry store. Hey, he swung that big hammer at the show window and it bounced right off—must be some new kind of glass. Wait a minute, he's swinging again. And again. He's made a small hole in the window! The other man's reaching in. They've dropped the tools, they're running away, around the corner, into an alley, it looks like. And here come the police—that was quick! Shame it wasn't quick enough!

ANOTHER JEWELRY STORE

It's 4:00 A.M. in another big city. Here is a branch store of the same jewelry company burglarized by sledgehammer in New York. Two young fellows are getting out of a sports car that just pulled up across the street. One's carrying a sledgehammer, like in New York, but it's a smaller hammer, and they're jaywalking right toward the jewelry store window. He's hit that glass with the hammer and it broke. He swung that hammer just once and the glass broke.

There they go, back across the street, getting in the car. Too late—they're gone. You don't suppose, do you, that they read about that burglary in New York?

CRITIQUE, ALL SCENES

Every scene was a smashing success, but there really wasn't much of a plot. All of the characters in this real-life drama used the same simple ploy—break down the inadequate physical barrier, grab what you can, and run as fast as you can. In each case the criminal's actions immediately alerted either the alarm company central station, the police, or store management, and police response was generally quick. Nevertheless, the thieves all got away with the loot they wanted.

The message is clear: When a well-rehearsed smash-and-grab professional selects the script, no one is likely to catch his act or prevent his exit. He may occasionally be forced to abandon some of his loot to assure his getaway, but usually these techniques are completely successful.

Inadequate Physical Barriers

These crimes were successful because physical barriers were inadequate to delay the entry of the thieves. For example, the camera display cases were ordinary plate glass, as were the entrance doors. These attacks could have been deterred, and probably prevented, if burglary-resistant glass had been installed. If budget limitations ruled out burglary-resistant glass in the entrance door, an appropriate alternative would have been the installation of a metal grille secured on the inside of the door frame (or across the width of the store, inside) to delay entry in the event the glass was shattered.

For display cases, a less-costly method would have been the use of plastic materials able to withstand heavy blows. True, these burglary-resistant plastics do scratch if cleaned with abrasives (some material less than others), and for that reason in particular, these materials are not considered practical for exterior show windows. However, showcases can be cleaned with soft cloths and occasionally rebuffed to remove light scratches, so the plastics do provide a practical alternative deterrent to showcase-smashing attacks and consequently are more commonly used to protect high-value showcases.

The two attacks on the fashionable jeweler's branches offer a case for considering the effect of newspaper publicity on the criminal opportunist. True, the first show window was protected with UL-approved burglary-resistant glazing material, but given time and muscle, an attacker can penetrate the material, create a hand hole, and make off with individual pieces of jewelry and watches. This type of glazing material is more effective in protecting valuable displays during the open-for-business period when store personnel, alerted by the sound of the attack, can take quick action to prevent a loss. If displays must be protected during the closed period, heavy-duty UL-approved bullet-resistant glass must be used.[1] Further, display cases or windows constructed of burglary- or bullet-resistant glazing material and equipped with appropriate sensors and a loud siren or bell-type annunciator are more effective in reducing losses to closed-period or daytime attacks.

---

[1] A famous risk adds, on the exterior side of the bullet-resistant glass, a layer of plastic glazing material to ensure that casual or clumsy attacks do not scar the far more expensive glass.

30

Residential Alarm Systems

Burglary in Bestport

(From the *Bestport Gazette*)

Monday, February , 19 : The Arthur A. Adamses, of 212 Tinkers Lane, returned last night from a winter cruise to find their 22-room home ransacked, apparently by burglars. Mrs. Adams, wife of the head of a local advertising agency, told police that two full-length mink coats, a chinchilla wrap, forty of Mr. Adams's suits, valuable family silver, costume jewelry, and an undisclosed amount of cash were missing from the home designed by this city's foremost architect.

It is reported that the thieves would have had a bigger haul except for the fact Mrs. Adams's jewelry had been placed in a bank before the couple's trip. The burglars may have been seeking these jewelry pieces, which were usually kept in a safe at the home, police said.

Entry was apparently gained by breaking a large rear window concealed from neighbors by a privacy fence. Sgt. Tracy of the burglary squad said several leads are under investigation.

Thursday, February , 19 : Mr. B. Baker, Jr., today called police to report the daytime theft of a grand piano. The burglary occurred sometime between 9:00 A.M. and noon while the Bakers were attending funeral services for B. Baker, Sr., well-known retired engineer of this city's Water and Utility Department. The Bakers' next-door neighbors were also absent because of the funeral. Other residents of the neighborhood noted nothing suspicious.

The burglars apparently entered through the garage, where the kitchen door was forced. A large screwdriver was found at the scene. Besides the grand piano, a combination color TV and stereo unit was taken, as well as silver and jewelry. Police theorize the thieves may have driven a truck into the garage.

Sunday, February , 19 : A Saturday night burglary at the Charles C. Caution residence has resulted in the loss of a rare coin collection worth more than $25,000, city police report. The theft was discovered Sunday morning. Mr. and Mrs. Caution spent Saturday evening with friends and saw no evidence of the burglary upon their return. The family maid, also away Saturday evening, told police that all the doors of the residence had been locked when she left.

No evidence of forced entry was found, and a duplicate key may have

> been used, police said. Detectives theorize the burglars had "inside information" regarding the coin collection's hiding place.
>
> The family's pet dog, a large Irish setter, was unharmed.
>
> Mr. Caution said the loss was insured but that some of the coins were irreplaceable. Detectives said the collection would probably be melted down unless the thieves knew the real value of the rare coins.

And so went another week in affluent Bestport, U.S.A. True, burglary losses are more spectacular in well-to-do Bestport, but the methods are typical of thousands of residential burglaries occurring daily throughout the United States. Vacations, funerals, and Saturday night out are common to all walks of American life. The only unusual aspect of the three instances reported is that each must have involved experienced burglars. A more complete review of the *Bestport Gazette* would no doubt have revealed many more (and less-professional) residential burglaries involving addicts and juveniles looking for cash or jewelry and quite willing to take guns, furs, TV sets, and stereo equipment.

EXPERIENCE VS. SKILL

While these jobs were successful and were accomplished by experienced burglars, it does not follow that these criminals were particularly skilled. Anyone of average intelligence and willing to chance getting caught could probably have been just as successful because residences offer easy targets for burglary, amateur as well as experienced.

We've all heard the familiar "We never used to lock our doors, until . . ." This simple phrase, which is repeated thousands of times, emphasizes that "only yesterday" the American family home was a symbolic castle requiring neither moat nor drawbridge. Then, too, our American prefers a windowed castle with easy access in and out—two, three, or more doors open from the home.

Locks have been simplified for convenience: a turn of the key both unlocks the cylinder and unlatches the door. Snap latches make it unnecessary to relock the door by key once inside. A single key opens every door, and duplicate keys were given to the wife, the children, relatives, servants, and friends. No padlocks or iron bars on doors or windows for us! No, sir!

FAMILIAR RULES NO CERTAIN PROTECTION

But the times they are a-changing, as the song says. Today the travel editor runs articles on "foiling the burglar while you're away." Utility companies kill two birds with one stone; they advertise "light up and lock out the burglar." Even the village locksmith offers booklets titled "101 Tips on the Prevention of Residence Burglary" principally having to do with locks.

We all are familiar with the standard instructions by now: Use timing devices to turn interior lights on and off at night while you are away; stop milk, mail, and newspaper deliveries before leaving; avoid "advance mention" in the society columns; lock doors and windows; keep valuables in safe deposit boxes; notify the police of your absence; floodlight the grounds; cut down shrubs close to windows (good cover for the criminal); get friends to watch the house while you are on vacation; and so on.

While each tip has merit, the plain fact is that they cannot prevent residence burglary. Probably the single most effective suggestion in these rules would be keeping someone in the house, but this is seldom practical. Private guards, or even patrol services, are expensive, and the best of friends cannot always be available at the right time or be expected to maintain 24-hour vigils.

ROLE OF RESIDENTIAL CONSTRUCTION

Unfortunately, the village locksmith can contribute little to deterring house burglary. Better lock cylinders, locks, and related hardware can and do substantially reduce the vulnerability of apartment dwellers to forced entry burglary, particularly where only the door is accessible. But burglary at the cliff dwellers' is a different cup of tea, as is explained in Chapter 31.

The reason why locks are of limited value in residence protection is simple: our twentieth-century castle is virtually a house of glass. While improved locks and bolts on doors and windows can make it less easy for the burglar to enter through the lock or at the latch, standard glass windows, hollow doors, and lightweight door frames will not withstand the slightest determination backed by a crowbar—or even a brick. And most homeowners strongly resist the recommendation to install steel bars and grille gates over every accessible opening.

The most effective answer to the need for preventing residence burglary losses or, more to the point, deterring residence burglary, lies in the effective application of an alarm system that incorporates a local bell or siren to harass the criminal and remote supervision of the alarm system for prompt dispatch of police or guards to the scene.

THE WOES OF RESIDENTIAL ALARM SELECTION

When Charlie Caution read that he was the third Bestport burglary victim in a single week, he realized that more than one burglar was probably operating in Bestport. One of them might reason that the Cautions had other valuables just as available. This was not really the case because Charlie had recognized the risk of burglary. His wife's jewelry and the best of the family silver were indeed in the bank safe deposit box, and cash was not kept at the house.

However, Charlie's work did keep him at the office several nights each week, and there was that occasional poker game and the once-in-a-while overnight trip out of town. Charlie was concerned that burglars might strike while his wife was home alone or that she might surprise them on her return. He reasoned that the primary use of an alarm system should be the family's personal safety and its secondary purpose the prevention of loss of personal property.

Vendor Choice

On reaching his office on Monday morning, Charlie's first action was to open the classified section of the telephone directory to B for burglary. He was surprised and puzzled to find 16 different advertisements for alarm systems installers. The advertisers ran the gamut from the local locksmith to the big-city alarm company whose insignia Charlie had seen on the door of his local bank.

Charlie first chose to contact a large local electrical contracting firm because their ad for "residence alarms of all types" was the most prominent. A reassuring salesman told Charlie his worries were over. They had just received some of the latest space-age electronic devices manufactured by that big, well-known aerospace company, and a salesman would be right over to see Charlie at his office. When Mr. Caution indicated he thought it would be more realistic to have a survey made of the Caution residence, the salesman said that was unnecessary—the equipment protected "all of the house" and Charlie could install it himself.

Before calling the big-city alarm contractor, Charlie made a call to a friend, the manager of a banking branch. Asked about the service provided by the big-city company, the friend answered, "We've never suffered a loss." Charlie's subsequent toll call to the big-city alarm company office was referred to the sales department, where a man said a representative would visit Charlie's home the next morning to make a "survey." Told that Mrs. Caution worked during the day and that in any event Mr. Caution wanted to be present when the representative came, the voice on the other end of the line suggested Charlie take the day off. It developed that the big-city alarm company's salesmen rarely worked evenings or Saturdays; if Charlie insisted on such an appointment, it would be a couple of weeks before they could "get to him."

Charlie's third telephone call was to a local telephone number for a small alarm company—they apparently couldn't afford more than a mere listing in the Yellow Pages. Charlie found that the alarm company was actually in the big city but that they had local telephone service in several nearby suburban communities. This firm agreed to have a sales representative make an evening visit to the Caution residence within a week.

The Alarm "Survey"

The salesman, who arrived only an hour late, presented his business card and asked, "Where'd the burglars break in?" When Charlie told him no one knew how or where the thieves entered, the salesman declared, "This was the work of a mastermind. You'll have to put in an elaborate alarm system." (If the salesman had examined the snap latches on the doors, he might have seen that anyone with a plastic bank calendar could have entered any door.) Mr. Caution counted slowly to ten and then counted again.

The Dick Tracy of the private security field next proceeded to "survey" the residence. First, he went outside and trampled through the shrubbery, circling the residence several times "to determine which doors and windows the burglar would use." He then went from basement to attic several times to determine what alarm system should be used and how it could be wired.

When the salesman found that his suggestion for "foiling the windows" would not meet with Mrs. Caution's approval and that Mr. Caution would not budge from his position that all the wiring had to be concealed, the salesman abandoned the idea of protecting the residence as one would a commercial premises. He offered an alternate suggestion—the "latest" in ultrasonic motion detection. When the salesman answered Charlie's question as to whether the dog moving about at night would not cause false alarms, with "Of course, you'll have to get rid of the dog," Charlie asked the man to leave.

The "Professional" Approach

The next day, "hat in hand," Charlie again called the big-city alarm company. He agreed to take the next day off and to wait patiently at home until the sales representative arrived, "sometime tomorrow." ("You know he has other calls to make, too, sir.") The sales representative would "survey" his home.

Late the next afternoon a seasoned veteran of the commercial burglary alarm wars appeared at Charlie's home. Armed with the newspaper clipping on Charlie's burglary, a visit to the local police station, and a refreshing stop at a nearby tavern, our "expert" told Charlie that the crime had no doubt been the work of a friend of the maid. He knew just how the premises should be protected. Fortunately, he was experienced in selling residence protection and quickly agreed there was no need to foil the windows and that his company was "experienced in concealing all the wiring." ("However, it costs more that way, you know.")

Today's "expert" didn't bother to trample down shrubbery or wear out the carpeting. Quicker than one can snatch a coin collection, he announced that the way to go was to put alarm contacts on all doors and to install an "eye." This, he explained, was a photoelectric beam that would cross the downstairs center hall. The pet problem would be solved by installing the beam about chest high (on Charlie). Unless the dog jumped a lot, the beam would be out of the dog's reach. The "expert" brought out a contract form, filled in a few figures that added up to a large dollar total and said, "Sign here." After a few questions, Charlie found out he was signing a contract to pay for the installation and lease of a burglar alarm system that would have a local bell installed in the attic ("loud enough to wake the dead") and a connection to the local police station. Charlie would not own the system but would pay the big-city alarm company about $400 a year for service. In addition to a substantial installation charge there would be $100 for the connection into the police station and about $4 a month for the telephone line connecting the alarm to the police station. Charlie was "lucky," he was told. "In some towns around here, the police charge $10 a month" service charge for the alarm system connection.

After Signing the Contract

Unfortunately, there were several things Charlie didn't find out until the contract had been signed. In the first place, the big-city alarm company was very busy so the alarm wouldn't be installed for about three months. Also, the special keyswitch that would permit the Cautions to turn the alarm on or off when leaving or entering the premises would be outside the front door. When Charlie meekly asked how they could enter the kitchen through the door from the garage without causing an alarm, he was told, "You can't. Just put your car away and then walk around to the front door and come in that way." Considering Charlie's first concern was his family's safety, this news was not encouraging.

Some other things Charlie didn't discover until the system was installed four months later were the following: The bell might wake the dead, but it would disturb the neighbors only if they happened to be in the attic at the time. The big black box (very suitable for a factory wall) that was the "guts" of the alarm system was to go on the wall in the hall. As a special concession, if the Cautions would clean out part of the coat closet, it might be installed there. Later, Charlie learned that some alarm contractors offered "user-easy" high-style control units with finishes to match the decor. When Charlie's wife was to be home alone, there was no way for her to set the alarm system before going to bed. The photoelectric beam was located between the control unit and the bedroom.

If the account of Charlie's negotiations with the alarm companies appears to border on the satirical and if the reader has the impression that

Charlie bordered on hysterics, that is correct. These and similar incidents occur all too frequently in the residential alarm field, but there is a reason for it.

PROBLEMS OF THE RESIDENTIAL ALARM FIELD

Until recently, residence burglar alarm systems had only a limited market of the most affluent residences, homes where both valuables and family members could be the target for criminal attack. In addition, alarm companies have traditionally attempted to meet the need for residential alarm systems by adapting alarm devices and control equipment designed primarily for commercial or industrial applications. These systems were not designed for residential installation and thus lack the flexibility residence application requires.

To meet the growing demand for appropriate residence burglar alarm systems at a price "within range" for the middle-income family, equipment manufacturers and alarm companies are developing equipment and installation techniques that offer the homeowner an alarm system that will neither significantly affect his family lifestyle nor dramatically alter the appearance of his home. However, it is still necessary for Charlie Cautions everywhere to select their alarm contractor carefully, to know what they are getting, and to make certain the system contracted for will be appropriate to the different living conditions of all the seasons of the year.

SIGNIFICANT CONSIDERATIONS IN RESIDENTIAL ALARM CHOICE

No single standard detailed specifications could provide suitable and effective security for every individual residential burglar alarm system application. Actual on-site or building plan analysis of the residence, the family, and their lifestyle is necessary to determine the points of potential vulnerability and to make effective security recommendations. The same need for individualized consideration is true of the "operation" of a residential burglar alarm system and the related choice of effective lock cylinders, locks, and door hardware to provide total security for the homeowner.

Following, however, are some of the significant considerations for the selection of residential burglary alarm systems. The alarm system should allow entrance and exit through any door commonly used by family members. Included would be the main entrance door, doors leading from the garage to the interior, service and garden doors, and so on. Each alarm keyswitch at each point of entry should be keyed alike. (The keyswitch is the means by which the alarm is turned on from the door by which the individual is leaving.)

Special UL-approved time delay shunt control devices, operated either by digital pad combination or key-controlled locks, are available that provide the capability to locate this device within the protected residence. In this type of system the individual simply presses a button (or turns a key) to activate the system and promptly departs through a protected door within a reasonable period of time, like 30 seconds. On entering, the resident uses his standard door key and enters to deactivate the alarm device within the same time period. If this is not done within the time limit, an alarm signal will be transmitted. A small audible annunciator and an indicator light are usually installed on the interior alarm control switch to alert the resident of the status of the alarm system and to remind him of the activation or deactivation procedures he must follow.

Once instructed in the proper use of these systems, all the occupants of the residence, including young teenagers, can readily use the system without weakening the security or causing false alarms. The intruder, however, lacking the special key or the combination, would not be able to deactivate the alarm within the time limit.

Cutouts for Interior

Where photoelectric beams or motion-detection devices are essential to detect intrusion through otherwise unprotected window glass or other openings, then the location of these devices in relationship to sleeping quarters, kitchen, and so forth should be carefully considered and cutout switches installed at strategic points within the residence. These switches permit the resident both to set the beams and/or motion-detection devices on retiring and to maintain perimeter protection while temporarily deactivating those sensors that would be triggered by movement within the house in the event it is necessary to move back and forth during the night. Of course, the previously described entry control switches also turn the beams and motion-detection devices on and off.

Noisemakers

Loud bells, sirens, flashing lights, or other types of annunciators intended to alert neighbors, passersby, and cruising police units must be within hearing range of these individuals if annunciation is to be effective. A bell or siren installed inside the residence is not usually effective enough to accomplish this. It may be practical to install these units under eaves, protected from the weather. If the house construction does not allow this, a weatherproof housing permits the installation of the annunciation units without regard for weather. Some form of annunciation should also be installed in the master bedroom to awaken the sleeping resident.

Fire Protection

When a burglar alarm system is considered, the addition of smoke and fire detection devices should have a high priority. The margin of safety provided by correctly placed fire sensors saves lives. If fire sensors are combined with intrusion devices, however, a separate and distinctive annunciator must be installed so the hearer can immediately determine whether the alarm is of intrusion or of fire.

Auxiliary Protection

Alarm sensors can also monitor heating and air conditioning systems, sump pumps, freezers, and so forth. A small additional investment allows the prompt detection of equipment failures that could otherwise result in extensive damage.

"Panic buttons"—emergency signaling devices—should also be installed, both in the master bedroom and at entrance doors. The housewife alone at home can signal police and/or neighbors when suspicious sounds are heard outside or if someone is attempting to force entry. Such devices are also available in wireless form. The signal unit, approximately the size of a cigarette package, can be carried on the person and may be used to initiate an alarm from anywhere inside the residence or from the exterior area immediately adjacent to the home.

Existing AC power is normally used to operate photoelectric beams and motion-detection devices. The alarm system installation naturally should include standby battery power to maintain protection during power outages and to prevent false alarms due to momentary power failures.

Telephone Dialers

Telephone-dialing devices are commonly suggested by alarm contractors for the alarm-reporting connection from residence burglar alarm systems to the remote supervision point. When an alarm device is activated, these dialers utilize the existing residence telephone line (or a second, unlisted line) to send a prerecorded voice message to the police or a digital code message to a private central station equipped to monitor digitally coded signal transmissions on a round-the-clock basis and to take action to assure prompt police response to the premises.

In some areas, however, police departments have developed regulations controlling the use of dialers. Before accepting an alarm system proposal incorporating a dialer, the homeowner would be well advised to contact his police department to determine if the unit selected is approved for contacting that department. If the police are not fully informed of the arrangement to transmit a recorded message or if they oppose the use of certain alarm equipment because of previous false alarm experiences, their response to alarm condition reports may be unsatisfactory, even if the prerecorded message goes to a security service or answering exchange rather than directly to the police station.

Wireless Alarm Systems

Some residential alarm system installers use short-range radio, or wireless, transmitters with alarm sensors that are more usually connected to control units by conventional low-voltage wiring. Wireless systems avoid the costly labor of installing (and concealing) wire in residential installation. Earlier generation wireless alarm systems were not fail-safe in operation; if the transmitter at a sensor was without power (normally battery power), no alarm was signaled, but the alarm system could be set with the affected sensor or sensors powerless to signal intrusion at that point. Further, if a window or door was left open at the time the alarm was set (turned on), the equipment was incapable of transmitting an alarm signal, and that opening remained unprotected until the condition was seen by the resident or a burglar!

Newly introduced wireless sensing devices include interrogation and other fail-safe features (see Chapter 32) that greatly enhance the performance of the system. Users operating wireless alarm systems without fail-safe provisions are well advised to consider upgrading their protection.

Service

Not only should the alarm contractor contract to provide 24-hour service 7 days a week, but also the police should be able to instruct the alarm contractor to restore the alarm system when the homeowner is away, if necessary. The homeowner may also need to provide the police with the names, addresses, and telephone numbers of friends or other family members who can be called to the premises to facilitate a search for intruders and/or repairs of the alarm system.

Similarly, the homeowner should consult with the alarm contractor and the police to develop effective procedures for the exterior search of the property, to establish key interior search points, and to familiarize individuals responding to alarm signals with the home's alarm devices and other conditions that might be encountered in a search when the family is away.

In any event, the alarm contractor should be selected with care. The contractor's ability to provide both periodic maintenance service and emergency service when required should be proven before a contract is signed. One method for determining this "reliability factor" is to obtain from the prospective alarm contractor a list of his residential alarm system users in the vicinity, together with their telephone numbers. By contacting several of these homeowners, the prospective buyer can obtain a realistic assessment of the quality of installation, comparative costs, and the user's experience of the contractor's ability not only to provide an effective intrusion security system but also to maintain it and provide service over a period of time.

Leasing or Purchase?

The general practice of the alarm industry in regard to commercial burglar alarm systems has been to lease rather than to sell them to users. This practice developed from the fact that most commercial burglar alarm system users are tenants rather than building owners. Also, commercial premises are frequently altered because of expansion or changes in methods of operation. In the residential field, however, these conditions rarely apply.

There are advantages to the homeowner in the outright purchase of the alarm system. First, the cost of purchase of a system and the continuing maintenance service for it are less than the homeowner would pay on a lease basis over a period of 5 years or more. Second, having title to the burglar alarm system may enable the homeowner to finance the purchase of the system under a home improvement loan. Finally, the intrusion and fire alarm system can be considered a capital improvement, a property improvement that can be added to the selling price when the homeowner wishes to dispose of the property and one that usually appreciates in value at the same inflationary rate as the home.

INSTALLATION STANDARDS

As far as the technical aspects of the alarm system installation are concerned, the homeowner would do well to require the alarm contractor to install the system in accordance with UL's voluntary Standard of Safety for Household Burglar-Alarm System Units (UL 1023-ANSI SE 2.4-1972) and their standards for certification of installations. Copies of these standards may be obtained by writing to Underwriters' Laboratories, Inc., 333 Pfingsten Road, Northbrook, IL 60062. The National Fire Protection Association has similarly established standards for residential fire- and smoke-detection systems. Copies of these fire system standards can be obtained from the National Fire Protection Association, Batterymarch Park, Quincy, Massachusetts 02269.

INSURANCE PREMIUM DISCOUNTS

As standards for residential burglary and fire alarm systems evolved and the residential crime rate increased, insurers offering homeowner's and other forms of residence insurance began to offer reductions in insurance premiums where bona fide alarm systems are installed. While the percentage of premium discount is still relatively small, additional credits (up to 10 to 15 percent) are offered where both burglary and fire systems are monitored by 24-hour central stations. Since properly installed and maintained residence alarm systems do discourage burglary and reduce burglary and fire losses, one must assume that the premium discounts will increase as the insurers reflect on improved loss ratios in their alarm-protected homeowner portfolios.

31

Apartment Burglary

Sex and the Single Burglar

At precisely 9:30 A.M., a handsome well-dressed man in his thirties entered a fashionable high-rise apartment building in one of Bigtown's prime cliff-dwelling residential areas. A raincoat was draped over one arm and he carried an attaché case.

Nodding casually to the doorman as he passed, he proceeded to the building reception area. Without hesitation he pressed the button for Apartment F on the ninth floor. Within a few seconds he heard the door's electric strike[1] released by the tenant, enabling him to enter to reach the passenger elevators.

IN AND OUT

The salesman (or so he appeared) entered the elevator and pressed the button for the twenty-second floor, the top floor in the building, rather than the ninth. At that hour of the morning, the elevator was empty.

Our friend (we'll call him Ron Rapid) left the elevator at the twenty-second floor, glanced up and down the corridor, spotted a red "Exit" sign to his right, and proceeded down the hallway to the last apartment by the exit stairwell. He did not push the doorbell, however, but drew from his attaché case a supply of advertising flyers for a "fabulous" seasonal sale being conducted by the Zitz Furniture Company, located across the river in an adjoining community. Moving quietly and efficiently, Ron Rapid slid the single sheets under each of the six apartment doors closest to the stairwell. Approximately half the sheet was under the door; the other half remained clearly visible in the building corridor.

Next, Ron walked down the exit stairwell to the twenty-first floor where he inserted flyers in another six to eight apartment door entrances. He repeated this process again on the twentieth and the nineteenth floors before descending by elevator to the lobby. Here he walked casually out, muttering

[1] An electrical release of the lock is remotely actuated within each apartment and commonly used to control access through apartment lobby entrance doors.

as he passed the doorman about "people who postpone appointments." Reaching the sidewalk, Ron disappeared into the pedestrian traffic moving toward nearby offices.

AND BACK AGAIN

When Ron Rapid again approached the apartment building at 11:15 A.M., it was almost as if he were a tenant. He and the doorman again exchanged brief glances, and Ron repeated his buzzer routine, this time pushing an eighth-floor tenant's button. When his first try brought no quick response, he casually pushed another button and—sure enough—the door to the elevator lobby was opened for him. Ron may well have been grateful that building management had not yet seen fit to install a closed-circuit television system that would enable tenants to see persons seeking entrance.

Ron again ascended to the twenty-second floor. He stepped off the elevator, smiled at a woman entering the elevator with her market cart, and paused until the woman was on her way down. Ron then walked quietly toward the exit stairwell. He noted that flyers were gone from two apartment doors, but because he had met the woman at the elevator, he entered the stairwell and walked down to the twenty-first floor. Here he saw flyers still exposed at the doors of the three apartments nearest the stairwell. Two or three other flyers were missing, indicating that someone had been home and had removed them to read all about the big sale.

Ron Rapid moved to the apartment door nearest the emergency stairwell, placed his briefcase on the floor to his left, and moved his London Fog raincoat to his left shoulder. He drew from a jacket pocket two slim metal instruments, inserted these in the keyway of the door's lock, moved one in several deft motions, and within 15 seconds, turned the lock cylinder as if it had been opened with a key. Ron quickly tucked his special tools under the edge of the hall carpeting, picked up his attaché case, and quietly opened the door.

PREDICTABLE TENANTS

He was not surprised to be greeted by silence. After all, his efforts had been intended to determine which apartments were still occupied. While there was some risk of encounter, Ron knew his trade. The tenants of these apartments could be counted on, by and large, to be engaged in their business or social day by 11:30 in the morning. This apartment building was not likely to be occupied by retired people or by late sleepers.

Once inside, Ron closed the door and inserted the straightened end of a paperclip into the lock keyway. If the tenant returned to the apartment while Ron was still there, his key would not operate the cylinder. After several attempts (which would be audible to Ron), the tenant would logically head for the elevator and the building superintendent's office. After all, most superintendents have duplicate or master keys to all apartments, and a malfunctioning lock would be the superintendent's problem. Of course, the tenant's departure would provide Ron with plenty of time to exit from the apartment, reset the lock cylinder, and leave the floor by the stairwell.

On this day no one returned in the brief time Ron was inside the apartment. Unlike similar scenes on television and in Hollywood scenarios, great pains were taken not to disturb anything. Ron moved quickly to the bedroom and opened the wife's chest of drawers, searching for money, bankbooks, and expensive jewelry. In the upper right-hand corner of the top drawer he found, as he had expected, several trays of jewelry and one small silver jewelry box. His quick eye appraised the jewelry in the trays as being moderate in value. He opened the unlocked jewelry box, found a single dinner ring worth about $500, but did not remove it.

His gloved hand closed one drawer and opened the next. This drawer contained a wide selection of lingerie. Carefully he felt through the lingerie—taking care not to disturb the orderly folds—until he felt an oblong object sandwiched between silk at the rear of the drawer. He removed the hidden wallet with several hundred dollars in it (saved from housekeeping funds, Ron guessed). Transferring the money to his own wallet, Ron replaced the housewife's wallet exactly as he had found it.

A similar search of the next two drawers and the husband's clothing closet revealed nothing. The desk in the foyer, on the other hand, yielded checks for several checking accounts, the key to a safe deposit box, and a bankbook showing active deposits and withdrawals. If the savings account had been inactive, Ron might have considered a modest withdrawal, but under the circumstances, Ron concluded that his visit had been as productive as it could be. Quickly his experienced eye surveyed the apartment to be sure everything was in order and to "file away" the layout for future reference.

GRACEFUL EXIT

Ron moved to the door, listened for sounds in the corridor, opened the door, and stepped out backward, saying in a casual but audible tone, "Thank you for the opportunity to discuss our program with you. I am sure you will find it a worthwhile investment." As he completed his statement, he pulled the door shut. No one was in the hallway, so Ron quickly retrieved his lockpicks, and in 1 second relocked the door.

Having gone down the stairwell to the twentieth floor, he repeated his performance in another apartment, this one two or three doors away from the safety of the stairwell. His "score" in the second apartment was another $200 in cash.

THE BURGLAR SURPRISED

Flushed with success, Ron decided to make it two winners on the same floor. He tackled the next apartment from which the "gala sale" flyer still protruded.

Since all the apartment locks were of the same manufacture, Ron's skills were improving with experience—the third door opened in something less than 7 seconds. This time, however, as Ron moved away from the paperclip-secured lock, he was confronted by a sleepy housewife emerging from the bedroom, a little frightened but not yet able to comprehend either the stranger or the odd sounds she had just heard. Without the slightest hesitation, Ron displayed a key of the type that would fit this lock, smiled broadly, and said, "Hiya, baby—here I am. Dottie—you know, on the ninth floor—said you're looking for company and gave me your key."

"Surely," he hesitated for a moment, then continued, "You're Mabel, aren't you?" The housewife's look confirmed that she wasn't Mabel.

"Don't tell me I've got the wrong apartment! And you're such a pretty gal; we could've really had a ball. Well, gee, ma'am, I'm terribly sorry about this. Funny her apartment key opens your door; you ought to talk to your husband or the superintendent about that. Gee, I'm sorry; I'll get out of your way right away." Displaying his widest smile and still talking, Ron stepped back to the door, palmed the paperclip, and closed the door with a "So long." Ron made his way without further ado down the stairwell to the next floor and the elevator.

Fifteen minutes later and some 3 miles from the scene of the unexpected confrontation (and the loss of a set of lockpicks he would have to replace), Ron decided there was no reason to work any more that day. Better to start fresh the following morning on the other side of town.

LITTLE RISK OF DISCOVERY

The reader may wonder if this apartment building was now "off limits" to Ron. On the contrary, the chances of his being suspected of the theft of money from the other apartments was near zero. Ron had taken pains to avoid any apartment on the floor where he had been seen by the shopping housewife at the elevator. Too, he had taken only untraceable cash. There was no way he could have been charged with the burglary of the two apartments. As a matter of fact, since the housewives' rainy-day funds were probably a well-kept secret, there was a good chance that, even when each loss was discovered, it might not be reported.

Finally we come to the sleepy housewife who did not conform to the norm, by Ron's calculations. One may wonder what transpired after Ron left the apartment. It is certainly likely that the housewife spent some time trying to recall the name of the tenant who had "given" Ron the key and whether she could ever have intimated (even subconsciously!) any such desire to a woman friend. Also, she would have to determine the merits of discussing the incident with her husband.

KEYING WEAKNESSES

While the reader may wonder at this method of burglary, the conditions given are typical of apartment buildings everywhere. Apartment door locks are commonly master keyed for the convenience of building management.[2] The superintendent can open all apartment doors with but one or two masters, and in the event individual keys are lost or misplaced, service is simpler than if picking the lock were to be necessary. While the initial cost is a little higher, a mastered system represents a far lower operational cost for the landlord.

Other Door Hardware Problems

Sometimes keying weaknesses are complemented by weaknesses in the choice of a lock (usually a latch), by the door frame itself, and by the mounting of the lock and its strike. Spring-loaded self-locking latches are common, and many latches of this type can be opened by inserting a piece of plastic such as a bank calendar between the door and frame.[3]

A latch may also be overcome by prying, even if it is a dead latch, particularly if the "throw" (length) of the latch bolt itself is short (½ to ⅝ inch), unless the door and door frame are reinforced or otherwise constructed to resist prying. However, prying leaves evidence of forced entry that can be matched to the tool used. Further, the size of tool needed is difficult to conceal, thus increasing the chance of apprehension for the possession of burglary tools. To the professional, entering by picking the lock is understandably preferable.

The economical key-in-the-knob lock used in hotels, motels, and offices, as well as in residences, may be defeated by extra pressure on the knob. The knowledgeable burglar can do this without leaving marks. This disables the locking mechanism, thereby opening the door, but the burglar can restore the lock to an apparently normal condition that continues to accommodate the tenant's key, though the lock is still disabled. The experienced burglar using this technique establishes—for himself or anyone else who tries the locked door—a quick and certain means of entry at any future time.

---

[2] Master keying makes lock picking easier because the multi-segmented pins used for mastering need only be raised to any division of the pins.

[3] Adequate latchlocks currently manufactured have a dead latching feature that prevents this kind of attack, except in cases of tampering or malfunction.

IS ANYONE HOME?

In apartments where handbills are frowned upon, burglars use other techniques to determine if someone is home. Posing as a salesman, Ron may simply ring the doorbell or knock at the apartment door. There is the possibility, of course, that although the tenant may not be at home, neighbors may hear the knock or ring and, feeling curious or helpful, may open their doors to see who the caller is. However, since Ron is ready with a sales pitch tailormade for such an encounter, this does not present a serious risk.

Ron's preference for apartments near the stairwell is, of course, based on the advantage of a convenient exit that avoids any chance of meeting persons entering or exiting at the passenger elevator. His choice of the upper floors is also well considered; Ron knows his rental economics: the higher the floor, the higher the rent, the higher the income of the tenant.

BURGLARY IS PREVENTABLE

Protecting an apartment against burglary or holdup attack is relatively easy in comparison to the protection problems of a detached residence with its many accessible openings. Apartment security is also more economical in terms of the cost of appropriate alarm devices, systems, and service. Indeed, 98 percent of all cliff dwellers could eliminate criminal attack against or within their apartments simply by taking positive action to protect themselves properly.

Preventing apartment burglary can be accomplished easily and usually at modest cost. Use of pick-resistant UL-approved lock cylinders, dead locking latches, and supporting break-resistant lock hardware would prevent both forced entry and entry by lock picking. Other precautions appropriate in high-risk apartment buildings include the use of security hinges on doors to prevent the burglar's opening the door from the hinge side. Where these simple precautions are taken, apartment burglaries immediately decline. The following sections present other ways to protect apartments from burglars.

Closed-Circuit Television

An important aid to tenant security is a closed-circuit TV system that permits tenants to see and speak to a visitor before releasing the electric strike controlling the building entrance door. In itself, however, an unattended closed-circuit TV system is not a sufficient deterrent because many tenants will admit anyone. The building entrance door is not the only problem; in most high-rise apartments there are unalarmed, unattended service entrances and fire exit doors that offer the skilled picklock all the opportunity he needs.

Alarmed Locks

Where the exposure is great, further deterrents to this form of burglary include alarmed lock devices that, in addition to being difficult to pick, register an alarm signal if anything other than the correct key is inserted into the lock cylinder or if an attempt is made to open the door against the secured chain set. These alarmed locks may be wired to a local annunciator (which usually can be heard in the hallway but perhaps not in the adjoining apartment) or connected directly to a remotely supervised alarm register in the building lobby, a central station, and so on.

Alarmed Windows

Windows and sliding doors may be accessible from terraces or other building offsets often found in penthouse apartments and garden apartment complexes. When these exposures exist in high-risk occupancies, alarm devices should be installed on accessible windows and doors and connected to a burglar alarm system supervised by a central station or other remote 24-hour-manned facility. Effective locks exist for sliding doors and for windows, but these are never (or very rarely) installed except to order.

A cat burglar can use a rope ladder to make his way from the roof of the apartment to the tenant's window (or balcony) and enter at that point. One West Coast burglar specialized in this method of entry, going from floor to floor by rope ladder from balcony to balcony. While this aerial method of attack is rare, it does happen when the stakes are high. Of course, alarm devices on windows, sliding doors, and fixed glass will signal such an intrusion.

To Call for Help

In addition to better locks and burglar alarm devices, the tenant should also consider installation of "panic" signal devices. These push buttons can be installed in conjunction with the burglar alarm system and provide the tenant with a means of silently signaling for help in the event of an intruder. These emergency signal devices should be located at the bedside (usually the master bedroom is the strategic location) and on the interior wall at the apartment's entrances.

Wireless radio-signaling emergency alarm devices are also available. These short-range units are carried on the person and can be used to signal silently for help if the individual is accosted near his apartment, such as in the building corridors, the garage, or the laundry room.

Avoiding the Unwanted Visitor

Wide-vision peephole units and heavy-duty chain locks give the tenant an alternative to opening the door to the "salesman." The landlord can also improve building security by replacing the doorman with a capable trained security guard, particularly if the guard contacts the tenant before passing the visitor, a measure proven to be highly effective.

The landlord can further improve building security by installing alarms on building service entrances and other points through which a burglar might gain entry unobserved. Protecting these alternate entrances forces the attacker to enter through the building lobby where he can be challenged by the security guard.

As for the Ron Rapids—the professional pick-lock burglars—their job life expectancy is quite good. Experienced law enforcement officers tell us that this type of criminal is able to carry on for years, seldom being caught in the act and hardly ever serving time. Unlike other professionals, Ron faces neither mandatory retirement nor income tax. Ron Rapid himself says, "Putting it all together, I enjoy my work and earn a good living from it."

32

Advances in Low-Power Wireless Sensing Systems

Residence Alarm System Application

IN THE BEGINNING

The battery-operated low-power limited range wireless RF transmitter married the garage door operator early in the postwar housing boom. The newlyweds' experiences were both frivolous and frustrating. Stripped gears and dented fenders occurred, but the most frequent complaints related to the wireless transmission system. Users seldom remembered to replace the battery in the transmitter until it failed. They didn't appreciate the magic of electronics when a neighbor's transmitter, coincidentally operating on the same frequency—one of only ten channels permitted by FCC rules—opened their garage door. When ghostly garage door dances occurred, users also were not satisfied with explanations such as lightning, diathermy equipment, mobile radio signals, and other external sources of interference.

ENTER THE WIRELESS EMERGENCY SIGNAL DEVICE

Within a decade, the same generation of wireless transmitters and receivers was adapted to holdup alarm signal circuits used by financial institutions and other high-risk businesses that were subject to robbery attack (see Chapter 39). This wireless signal technique afforded two major advantages over fixed location, hard-wired holdup signal devices. These advantages are described in the following sections.

Economy

Installation of hard-wired, fixed location emergency signal devices entailed special problems in running connecting wires into counters, cash drawers, and display showcases. The need to protect against false alarms caused by damaged wiring further complicated and increased the cost of such installations. Usually the installation of conduit, floor channel, or other labor-intensive measures was necessary to protect the wiring. Use of wireless signal transmitters eliminated substantial portions of these installation costs, which were in excess of the cost of wireless equipment.

Security

Hard-wired, fixed location holdup alarm signal devices required an individual to move some part of the body in order to make contact with and to actuate the device—a dangerous undertaking in the face of a gun. However, a wireless transmitter with built-in trigger could be clipped to the employee's belt or carried in a pocket and might be actuated by "body language."

BRING ON THE FALSE ALARMS

However, there were problems inherent in the design of a wireless emergency transmitter. Features such as requiring two fingers to operate or recessed triggers, implicit in an emergency signal device, were ignored. Another problem was that this trigger-happy unit did not include a lock-in feature. Thus, when a false signal was transmitted, there was no way to determine whether it was the result of careless or malicious use by an employee, a mechanical malfunction, or the result of spurious RF signals or electrical noise generated within range of a receiver.

Initially, only 40 wireless channel frequency codes were permitted under FCC regulations. Sometimes careless planning or the close proximity of retailers and banking branches resulted in the installation of wireless systems in adjacent premises that were operating on the same frequencies. Clearly, police responding to false signals and customers experiencing police drawn-gun response were upset. Small wonder many alarm contractors shied away from wireless signal system applications.

Further, since these wireless signal devices were passive, many went unused and untested for long periods. These factors led to dead battery failure and further loss of user confidence in this technology.

THE GROWTH PERIOD

Nevertheless, the advantage of wireless emergency signaling devices in terms of installation cost savings was significant, and when such systems were carefully installed and properly maintained, they proved to be a major deterrent to robbery and sneak theft. The criminal, casing his targets prior to attack, could visually identify the receiving units and sometimes spot the wireless transmission devices and conclude he would not be able to control the stickup scenario. Given this risk of apprehension, smarter criminals abandoned such targets. The deterrent factor was strengthened in recent years by design innovations that included the production of emergency signal transmitters in the shape of pendants, belt buckles, key chains, and other items that could be worn and readily activated by both male and female employees.

The Medical Alert Application

During this period, wireless signal devices were also adapted for use by disabled or ill people whose condition at times required emergency medical response. The principle was the same. When an emergency developed, the medical alert transmitter was triggered, and utilizing a digital communicator interfaced to the individual's telephone, the emergency signal was transmitted to a 24-hour monitoring station that in turn notified a physician, ambulance unit, or others who were designated to provide the emergency aid required.

The Residence Market

During the 1960s and 1970s, as neighborhood crime increased, the market for residential burglary, panic, and fire alarm systems expanded. Alarm contractors soon found that the labor costs and the aesthetic requirements for hard wiring a residence were significantly different than in commercial installations. This led to the adaptation of the wireless signal transmitter to the magnetic contact switch. An installer could attach the transmitter switch and magnet to a door or window in much less time and with less skill than that required to conceal conductor cables in walls, door frames, and ceilings.

However, since a penlight battery used with the transmitter also provided the power to the alarm sensing device, this application was limited to low-power consumption-type devices such as contact switches, smoke detectors, and emergency signal buttons. Motion-detection devices, which then consumed greater power, were not adaptable to the wireless transmission concept. Further, this unsupervised wireless signal transmitter was not fail-safe since the sensor depended entirely on the user's performance in ascertaining that doors and windows were closed prior to setting the alarm system and to the user's test of each battery-operated transmission device at frequent intervals to detect and replace dead or dying batteries or to detect a malfunctioning transmitter.

The RF method of wireless signal transmission was also suspect since, in theory, alarm signals could be masked or interfered with by the generation of a similar RF from an area adjacent to the residence. In addition, while alternate methods of wireless signal transmission, such as the use of infrared energy or ultrasonic sound waves, which are more or less immune to external interference, were available, the disadvantages of these methods (line-of-sight transmission required) then precluded their ready acceptance.

In the absence of fail-safe circuitry and a lack of experience relevant to the resistance of wireless systems to attacks or compromises by skilled burglars, wireless was limited in its acceptability for application in other than the residence market.

RF WIRELESS SYSTEMS COME OF AGE

Late in 1981, changes in FCC regulations permitted manufacturers to increase the number of channel codes for alarm-signaling use from 40 to 256. This provided the manufacturers of wireless transmission equipment the opportunity to design a product that is significantly less susceptible to false alarms created by external RF signal transmission and other interference. A second change in FCC regulations now permits the operation of such equipment to include frequent automatic transmission of test signals, at very low power, between transmitting and receiving units.

Coincidentally, the development of user-friendly microprocessors provided manufacturers the opportunity to improve their techniques to incorporate heretofore missing fail-safe features in wireless transmission circuits. Wireless transmitters have been designed to send status signals at hourly intervals. In addition, any change in status such as opened protection, low battery supply, or an alarm condition, are reported immediately. This development permits an individual operating the system to close a protected door or window or replace a weak transmitter battery before turning the alarm system on. Such systems provide fail-safe features wherein any change in status, including intrusion, will be received as an alarm signal.

IMPROVEMENTS IN SENSORS

Utilizing solid-state technology, manufacturers are now producing intruder motion-sensing devices that operate on very low battery power as available from wireless transmission devices to expand the protection coverage to provide an all-wireless burglar alarm system. Indeed, passive infrared devices using power supplied by a wireless transmitter eliminate the need for interfacing that motion-sensing device to an electrical outlet near the sensor. Wireless transmitters may now also be interfaced to shock sensor circuits and may be used to monitor the AC outlet supplying power to a computer terminal, typewriter, television receiver, or other valuable electrical appliance that might be disconnected by an intruder.

With the introduction of smaller, compact magnetic contact switches and transmitters, which can be concealed within the core of a door and frame, an aesthetically pleasing residence burglar alarm installation is feasible. Other wireless detection-transmission devices including holdup or medical emergency signal units and smoke and heat detectors now enable the residential installer to offer complete burglary, fire alarm, and emergency signal systems that are cost effective and easier to install than wired residence alarm systems.

ADVANTAGES OF CONTROLLERS

Following the advances in wireless sensing and signal transmission circuits within the premises, the need to interface the control and supervision of the sensing system was filled by the application of microprocessor-based alarm control units suitable for application to both wireless and hard-wired residence alarm systems. A microprocessor-based control unit includes many features that enhance a residence alarm system. These include the following:

- A digital key pad that permits activation of the alarm system and control of time delay entry or exit circuits by insertion of a simple code, thereby eliminating the need for keys. This code permits full use of the system by each adult member of the household and reduces the incidence of false alarms that might otherwise occur.
- A multiple number of zones for both individual and remote monitoring of the system.

  For example, an eight-zone control may include (1) the aforementioned time delay entry/exit circuit, permitting the user to enter or depart the alarm-protected premises through one or more designated points; (2) a zone to supervise signal transmission applicable to the entire intruder-detection circuits, including both perimeter and interior sensing devices; (3) a separate zone to permit the user to shunt out interior sensing device circuits while utilizing the perimeter circuit when occupants are in residence; and additional individual zones (4) to annunciate fire- and smoke-detection devices, (5) individual emergency signal transmitters, (6) medical alert devices, and (7) industrial process circuits that may signal faults in heating, air conditioning, and water or gas leaks. The control unit has the capacity to transmit distinct digitally coded alarm signals from any of these zones to a remote central station where monitoring personnel are able to take the appropriate action required by the type of signal received. Still another zone may be utilized (8) to enhance the deterrent value of the burglar alarm system by interfacing to outdoor-indoor lighting circuits and/or activation of bells or sirens. The control unit also provides local annunciation to alert the user to other conditions that may affect the total performance of the system. These include monitoring the power supplied to the control unit and the status of the telephone line used to transmit signals to a remote monitoring station.

Remote Central Station Monitoring

A wireless alarm system interfaced to a microprocessor-based control unit may be linked to remote monitoring stations that are equipped with compatible receivers that receive signals transmitted over an ordinary commercial telephone circuit or by the installation of dedicated multiplex signal transmission and receiving equipment, the latter system affording a high degree of security against telephone alarm transmission circuit attack. In either form, such wireless systems and their interfaces are suitable for residence and certain low-to-moderate-risk commercial applications.

Other Applications

Since wireless sensors can be installed quickly and require fewer installation skills, they are adaptable to temporary installations where time is of the essence. Such installations might include an unprotected portion of a premises where valuable merchandise must be stored on short notice or when premises renovations (for example, changing store fronts and show windows) require a modification or addition to conventional alarm sensors.

Wireless sensors are also installed temporarily on short notice as "traps." For instance, these traps would address the disappearance of petty cash or records from an area that otherwise requires no protection.

Wireless devices are also utilized to protect vehicles parked against or near a commercial facility when the vehicle cargo must necessarily be left in the vehicle during a closed period. In this application, whether temporary or permanent use is intended, a wireless device eliminates the need for installation of connectors running from the vehicle to the premises alarm circuit—a major maintenance headache.

Wireless systems might also supplement primary conventional alarm circuits in high-risk premises applications. Thus, a form of redundancy might be added to an existing hard-wired alarm circuit.

IN THE FUTURE

While some observers predict advanced wireless sensing techniques will permit application to, and gain acceptance in, the commercial burglar and fire alarm system market, it is noted the alarm industry has limited experience with the integrity of such circuits since they may be affected by the deliberate introduction of externally generated RF signals designed to compromise individual points of protection. Also, interference problems that may develop in close-quarter multiple system applications, as found in shopping malls and residential developments, are not fully known. Some manufacturers are addressing both the compromise and the interference problem by the addition of RF signal detectors that will alert the user and/or the monitoring station to the presence of external RF signals.

It is anticipated that low-power signal transmission limits, proper placement of receivers, spacing of channel codes, and use of system codes will eliminate the garage-door-operator syndrome. Nevertheless, the fact remains: Burglar, fire, and emergency systems are, in fact, life support systems requiring a high degree of reliability at all times. Accordingly, the alarm industry, while showing great interest in the newest wireless technology, is moving slowly toward the use of such equipment.

Similarly, despite the ease of installation afforded, manufacturers of wireless signal equipment are cautious in their development of a do-it-yourself market. However, as the demand for residence alarm systems is great, it is likely that wireless systems will account for an increasingly large share of this market and that the experience gained by this venture will provide the basis for application in commercial markets, as well as further improvement in the technology. For example, designers of ultrasonic transmission systems have recently added low-cost repeater-type receivers and have interfaced both AC line carrier and hard-wired techniques to extend the application of ultrasonic transmission beyond the line-of-sight range.

33

Procedural Weaknesses in Security

Short Circuits in Security II

For our purposes, security may be defined as the total defense against the possibility of criminal attack. Its elements are resistance, detection and response, and security procedures.

Under *resistance* come the deterrent and delaying values of physical security devices such as pick-resistant deadlocks, burglary-resistant glass, and safe and vault structure. Such devices would also include all other physical barriers that provide a measure of delay against physical attack.

Under *detection and response* fall the supervisory values of central station and police-connected alarm systems. These register the presence of an intruder or attacker on the premises by means of an alarm signal received at a remote station equipped to dispatch central station guards and law enforcement officers promptly and accurately, thus reducing the possibility or extent of loss.

Finally, *security procedures* are those measures the owner or manager of the premises employs to ensure that doors are locked, the security of keys maintained, and alarm systems properly closed when the premises is locked for the day, as well as the necessary coordination between control of the premises by store personnel during the day by remote alarm supervision during closed periods. A breach in any of these three elements of security can result in a defeat or impairment of the security defense.

WEAK LINKS IN SECURITY PROCEDURES

Breaches or weaknesses in security procedures can undermine and destroy the effectiveness of the finest physical barriers and electronic alarm systems. Following are some illustrative case histories, followed by the measures that could have prevented loss. In each case, the victims had several things in common:

- Each employed "classic" central station alarm systems, including UL-approved Complete[1] safe and vault protection, intruder motion-detection alarm equipment in the areas surrounding safes and vaults, and the best available line security protecting the link between the subscriber and the central station.
- Each had adequate physical security as far as safe and vault structures were concerned, as well as pick-resistant lock cylinders in adequate doors.
- Last but hardly least, each of these high-risk businessmen had permitted one or more procedural weaknesses to creep into his security program.

Despite all the other factors, the last step proved "fatal."

Poor Memory

Albert enjoyed a prosperous, rapidly expanding jewelry manufacturing business. He had come into his own as a skillful creator of high-style jewelry for fine retail jewelry stores everywhere. But Albert was a bit forgetful. One day he wrote the safe combination on the back of his wall calendar, and it soon became the most expensive pinup in the world.

Time and time again investigators report that significant burglaries occur where victims have jotted down safe combination numbers on the underside of desk blotters, in address books, in the file under "C" for "combination," within the safe, and believe it or not, on an exterior wall of the vault. Professional burglars search diligently for these security giveaways before starting a drill or torch attack. Where their efforts are rewarded, as they often are, not only do the burglars save a great deal of time and effort, but also these "aids" sometimes open a vault or safe door that would have defied their tool or torch capabilities.

Couldn't Be Bothered

Ben had a keen memory for details such as numbers and combinations, but he just couldn't remember (or was it that he couldn't be bothered?) to set the alarm system at night—particularly when he was in a hurry to get somewhere. Ben's lapses of memory were so frequent that it is not surprising that one or more of his employees overheard heated telephone conversations between Ben and the frustrated, irate manager of his central station, who was "sick and tired" of dispatching an agent to Ben's premises to set the alarm Ben had ignored—again.

Sooner or later some astute listener realized that the period of time

[1] In this context, *Complete* is a technical term meaning all surfaces of the safe or vault are electrically protected to detect attack by all known means.

elapsing between Ben's careless departure and the arrival of irritated central station alarm company agents to close the alarm system had grown to be quite sufficient to clean out the open stock. Since the listener was close to the operation, he could pick his time to hit—a day when a substantial shipment was packed, ready for pickup, and left outside the vault area. He didn't even have to find the handle on the vault!

The Free Spirit

Carlo was a furrier, an extraordinarily creative man happy in his work. He had only one little hangup: Carlo disliked being "boxed in" by security procedures. Despite the advice and warnings of his alarm contractor, Carlo insisted that he should enjoy access to his own premises 7 days (and nights) a week if he felt like it, even though the business normally operated on a Monday-through-Friday basis. Carlo couldn't and wouldn't believe that, if someone learned his alarm code signal and gained possession of a key or two, this someone could enter the premises on a Saturday or Sunday, properly open the alarm system, and take his time stealing stock. (Oh, yes—being an insider had other advantages; the thief knew stock levels rose to meet holiday needs and attacked on a Saturday in September to take the fullest advantage of the season.)

If the thief had used this technique to steal small quantities of stock, he could have struck repeatedly, the losses might not have been detected until inventory time, and the method could have remained a mystery even then. Thus, a weekly report of alarm system opening and closing times to Carlo from the alarm contractor could have reduced the vulnerability inherent in Carlo's thoughtless security procedures by making it possible for him to detect unauthorized openings. But would Carlo have bothered to look at the report?

The Lone Wolf

Dave was a clothing manufacturer. He ran an exceptionally tight ship and seldom made business or security mistakes. However, being an individualist, Dave made all the decisions, rarely consulting others, and made it clear that he shared responsibility with no one.

When his union employees won a shorter work day with a later starting time, Dave overlooked advising the alarm company of the change. The alarm system opening time should now be 7:30 A.M. instead of 7:00. As is possible in any business, there was one small bad apple in Dave's clothing barrel who was satisfied with neither the union contract nor his employer's regard for his ability. This bad apple was sharp enough to realize that, under the new work schedule, there was a 30-minute gap between the "OK to open" of the alarm company and the arrival of the plant supervisor at the premises.

One morning our bad apple arrived promptly at 7:00, used his assigned key, and reading from a careless aid-to-memory scribbled on the wall, sent the correct code signal to the central station. In the next 20 minutes or so, he proceeded to shift enough fine menswear from the shipping area to his station wagon to enable him to open his own retail outlet. Dave couldn't believe it—he hadn't realized how little time it takes to load a station wagon when it isn't really loading time!

Alarm company personnel are not mind readers, and they expect a responsible businessman to take charge of his own premises at opening time. In fact, some alarm companies do not offer to receive opening signals—they simply "pull" the central office supervisory switches (turning off the supervision of the alarm) at the time appointed by the subscriber. Under this method of operation, it is doubly important that supervisory personnel arrive at the proper opening time to take control of their own property. Failure to do so is the same as giving someone control of the premises for the intervening period of time.

Odd Hours

Ed learned from others' mistakes and avoided the common security pitfalls. But he did have an Achilles' heel: Ed expected his salesmen to make their quotas, no matter the time and effort required. He didn't recognize the security problems created when a weary but successful salesman straggled in late on Friday night with a valuable sample line. Ed simply arranged for the alarm company to accept as authorization a special code signal given by the salesman by telephone to the central station any time between 7:00 and 9:00 on Friday nights, signifying the return of the hero and providing him with the opportunity to put the line in the vault rather than endanger his family over the weekend.

Unfortunately, salesmen with valuable lines do not go unnoticed. It did not take long for one clever character to make a careful appraisal of this procedure, solve the telephone code identification system in use, and achieve his own special 7:00 Friday night opening. At least our clever character did not know the combination since he had to use a torch to enter the vault.

Fortunately for the salesman, the clever character was in the vault and out the door before the star salesman arrived on the scene, perceived that something was amiss, and dutifully notified his employer that, while his line was safe, the vault was empty.

A Trusting Nature

Frank ran a frantic business, and alarm systems really bugged him. He would never have suffered the security system had it not been for his insurance company. To "simplify" operation of the alarm system, he instructed the alarm company to accept openings at any time of the day or night, 7 days a week. Frank then furnished several of his employees with the code signal and went merrily about the business of making a buck. Unfortunately, some of the employees realized they could make an even faster buck by opening on Sunday and making their own shipments.

The Nervous Type

George was usually careful to heed the advice of his insurer and the alarm contractor to maintain strict security and to limit the number of persons authorized to operate the alarm system. On occasion, however, George rebelled. For example, after a pleasant Sunday evening cocktail party, when he drove a valued customer to the shop to arrange an impulse sale, George first had to stop at the central station to arrange for a special opening. Sometimes he felt certain he had been followed from the alarm company to his premises. George finally decided it would be safer to arrange special openings by telephone identification procedures.

For several months George followed this new routine, secure in the feeling that he wouldn't be coshed on his way to the sale. But an eavesdropper found it all too easy to imitate George's voice and the identification procedures (which the alarm company had warned were not sound security) in order to arrange his own "special opening sale."

MORAL

Alarm systems and physical security barriers are only as effective as the security procedures employed. Sooner or later, shortcuts in security procedures will result in a short-circuit loss.

34

Oversights in Security

Short Circuits in Security III

ECONOMY OVER ALL

Charlie's shop was chockablock with valuable merchandise, particularly at holiday time. The local police had suggested that he needed more than a simple perimeter burglar alarm system protecting only doors and windows, but his insurance company had made no such demands. Under those circumstances, Charlie naturally saw no reason to spend more for protection.

Besides, Charlie had tenants who would be sure to report any unusual noises coming from the store. As a matter of fact, just the week before Charlie had been delighted to fill his vacant second-floor apartment with just the right kind of tenant—a well-dressed, "obviously successful" real estate salesman. The new tenant not only paid two months' rent in advance but also paid Charlie to change the lock so that only the tenant would have a key. Our well-dressed realtor was proud of his hand-tailored suits and didn't want anyone stealing them.

You can imagine Charlie's consternation (and, later, his chagrin) when he opened his store the next Monday morning and saw the glint of sunlight through a hole in the store ceiling. Not only was the second-floor apartment empty, but so were Charlie's shelves. One of Charlie's tenants on the third floor had heard someone sawing on Sunday morning, but she thought the new tenant was making bookcases for his apartment.

THE OBVIOUS CAN LEAD TO OBLIVION

Exposed Labeled Keys

It's rare for local police to be willing to hold keys to business premises protected by burglar alarm systems connected into their police station. However, the friendly and willing police of Helpersburg did so. They were determined to deter crime, and they recognized the fact that you can't catch burglars if you can't get where the action is—inside the premises.

So if you visited the Helpersburg police station you would see the keys, row on row, neatly identified with tags listing store names and addresses—that is, you would have seen these keys if you had visited the police station yesterday. Last night four youths brought to the police station saw the possibilities offered by the keys and took off with several sets when they were released from custody. The youths headed straight for the store with the most to offer and fled with the loot, helpfully leaving the keys so the police could hang them back on their hooks. Today Helpersburg police returned all the keys to the merchants.

Fast Safe Closings

The way most safes are designed, when the last digit in the combination sequence is in line with the combination indicator, the locking mechanism is released, the bolts may be retracted, and the door opened. However, bookkeepers and others responsible for opening and closing safes sooner or later learn that spinning the combination dial when the safe door is open, the procedure they are advised to follow, locks the bolts in the thrust position, requiring the entire combination operation to release the bolts for closing and locking the safe at night.

Many thousands of people responsible for opening and closing safes regard this locked-open rule as a nuisance, especially when one is trying to catch the 5:10. They have a simple solution: After opening the safe in the morning, leave the combination on the last digit! Comes closing time, slam the door, spin the combination, and they're ready to catch the 5:10. However, if you're observant, you may have identified the last digit of the combination.

At best, there are only two more numbers to find. At worst—as many burglars and crooks can tell you—when some older safes are locked for the night, if the combination dial is not turned more than 30 or 40 digits in either direction, the thief does not need to know the first two digits. He need only move the combination dial slowly, digit by digit, through this series of positions to find the lucky number, and open Sesame!

SOUND SECURITY PROCEDURES ESSENTIAL

Is there a moral to these stories? Yes: Successful security is procedural security.

Tenants may make fine "watchdogs," but if you expect that of them, investigate their background, consider the hours they are likely to be on the premises, and inform them that you expect them to report unusual noises or suspicious persons in the premises. While you're at it, tell them to whom they should report this information. But don't persuade yourself—or your insurance company—that you have "live-in watchmen."

If you are a keeper of the keys, establish security procedures and controls limiting access to the keys. In addition, keep identification (as to location, for example) separate from the keys, and establish careful records of key use.

Finally, having invested a large sum of money in a safe, and having represented to your insurance company that the safe is used to protect your valuables (thereby establishing your eligibility for a premium discount), make sure the safe is properly used and the combination carefully guarded. And then, just in case, change the combination frequently.

35

Attacks on Out-of-Order Alarms

"Lightning Never Strikes Twice"

FIRST ATTACK

During the very early hours of a Saturday, burglars smashed an unalarmed glass side wall adjacent to the entrance door of a retail premises, climbed through the opening created, walked to a display case about 10 feet inside the store, and rifled it of valuable stock. Though the store had an ultrasonic motion-detection system, no alarm was heard. A patrol service spotted the break before dawn, and the alarm company was duly notified that the police-connected (with local bell) alarm system was defective.

The alarm company advised the proprietor but also reminded him of the terms of his alarm contract: "Service within 24 hours on the next business day." That would be the coming Monday!

SECOND ATTACK

The burglars' next work day, however, was Sunday—early Sunday. This time they broke in through the entrance door, avoiding the plywood temporarily installed over Saturday's point of entrance, and cleaned out the next display case.

As far as the still-defunct alarm system was concerned, it is doubtful the burglars even knew it existed—after all, there was no foil on the plate glass or an alarm contact on the entrance door, the usual evidence of an alarm system. Bright and early on Monday, the defective ultrasonic unit was identified and replaced, and several additional units were ordered to be added to the system—just in case there might be some "dead spots" in the existing motion-detection coverage.

THREE STRIKES AND OUT!

Nevertheless, late Monday night the overtime burglars struck again. Were they surprised when, on this occasion, a local alarm bell sounded?

Perhaps they were, but they were hardly deterred. After all, there were no physical barriers to delay their entrance or their exit. The thieves emptied the third display case—perhaps a little more hurriedly than before—and were gone well before police arrived.

Thus ends our short tale. There haven't been any more attacks, but wasn't the proprietor lucky this wasn't a three-day weekend? Certainly these repetitive attacks illustrate the need for prompt corrective action once alarm system defects or the need for additional protection becomes known.

36

Amateur Alarm Systems

Dawggone!

SELF-SERVICE SECURITY

The Browns operated a "Ma and Pa" retail jewelry business in a small but busy shopping center in a prosperous resort community. Mr. Brown was an artist who fashioned unusual and moderately high-priced jewelry for sale in the shop.

As is generally the case in small business, the Browns were without expert security advice and formed their own opinions on security. This process led them to the following conclusions:

- Their business was not a serious security risk.
- Burglary insurance rates were unreasonably high.
- In view of the first two conclusions, they could dispense with burglary insurance.
- Man's best friend is the best defense against burglary—in this case, their pet dog.

DOGS AS SECURITY

They did supplement this "local burglar alarm" by installing a microphone in the store. This was connected by a leased telephone line to their home, approximately one mile away.[1] When the dog was on guard in the store and the Browns were at home, they would be alerted by the sound of barking received through the monitor speaker whenever the dog was aroused. When this occurred, Mr. Brown drove to the store to investigate or called the police and asked them to visit the premises.

As a matter of fact, Mr. Brown had investigated such an "alarm" only two weeks before. On that occasion, he discovered that someone had attempted entry through the flimsy wall separating the Browns' store from

[1] A similar system was actually employed to protect a bank. The president of the bank monitored the microphone from his home. (See "Hearings" *in re* the Bank Protection Act of 1968.)

an adjacent and even more unprotected occupancy. And just a week before, another attacker had cut a hole through the roof of the jeweler's premises but, for reasons unknown (the dog's presence?), had not entered.

However, as Mr. Brown found out, lightning does sometimes strike three times. Mr. and Mrs. Brown followed their usual midweek routine: closing, dinner at a local restaurant, then return home for the dog and head back to the store to "install" their "alarm." This time they found the store a shambles—they had suffered a substantial loss of rings and watches from showcases and other display areas. The fact that the safe was untouched indicated the attackers were not really professionals, but then a burglar doesn't have to be an expert when he's dealing with amateurs.

Criminals have also been known to neutralize unaccompanied watchdogs by feeding—sometimes drugging or poisoning—the animals. Dogs have been enticed by the introduction of attractive female dogs; other dogs have been shot or clubbed to death. Thus, such "alarm systems" should clearly be avoided.

37

Pretext and Impersonation in Burglary

Think I

One cannot overemphasize the fact that skilled burglary, holdup, and theft attacks are all "crimes of opportunity" arising from the vulnerability of the victim. The criminal first identifies his potential targets and then evaluates whether there are sufficient areas of vulnerability to assure success. To make this crucial evaluation, the criminal often gains entry to vital security areas by pretext or by impersonation.

PRETEXT

This method involves ploys like visiting a premises under pretexts such as inquiring about employment or pretending to be a messenger searching for another firm, a "lost" delivery boy from a nearby luncheonette, a postman, and so forth. If the business concern has any security at all, pretext visits stop at the reception desk. Even then, the pretext visit may be successful if vital security areas are exposed to view from that point. In most cases, however, the criminal must resort to impersonation.

IMPERSONATION

Unlike the pretext method (where an innocent party may sometimes be employed to make the visit), impersonation is riskier because the visitor may well be asked for identification, and detected impersonation may lead to police reports, if not arrests. Because of this risk, criminals are usually forced to conduct their own impersonation reconnaissance.

Impersonation is often necessary if the criminal is to get beyond the retail area or the reception desk in the outer office to locate and evaluate safes and vaults, locks, alarm systems, and security procedures. Following are just a few of the impersonations reported in recent successful criminal attacks:

- A uniformed "police officer" visited the merchant's premises to "assist" the merchant in protecting himself against burglary. The officer made several recommendations, but before these could be implemented, the merchant had been burglarized.
- An "insurance company inspector" arrived to make a "security survey" of a high-risk retail premises. A trusting office manager admitted the inspector without identification and was most cooperative in answering any and all questions about security procedures, safe combinations, alarms, and so forth.

In the latter case, the impersonation was discovered before an attack occurred. When the inspector began to "case" a second retail branch of the company, a more alert supervisor asked for identification. The inspector beat a hasty retreat. The "only" cost to the company was the considerable cost of changing safe combinations and locks, as well as altering security procedures, since their utility entirely depends on their being held confidential.

In other instances, individuals posing as representatives of security associations and as investigators from security agencies have successfully penetrated into vital security areas and, with the information gained from the impersonation, were able to plan successful major crimes. Security "representatives" should never be admitted to premises, and no security information should be communicated to them until their identity has been cleared by a reliable source (mutual acquaintance, law enforcement official, or insurance underwriter) who can verify the individual's position and qualifications.

Since no employee is able to supervise the activities of telephone company repairmen (or their counterfeits), each visit should be confirmed by checking with the telephone company and with the person ordering the work, in addition to careful scrutiny of the identification the serviceman carries. Following are two examples of how "telephone company personnel" have easily acquired security information:

- A "telephone company repairman" was given access to highly vulnerable telephone equipment rooms. This led to not one but several successful burglary attacks because the criminals had acquired the circuit information they needed to defeat alarm system protection at telephone terminal connections.
- An individual posing as a telephone company installer spent two full days inside a high risk's security area, working on ways and means of defeating the alarm system without arousing suspicion.

It would be impossible to say in how many hundreds of instances apparent electricians, alarm company repairmen, heating and air conditioning servicemen, or other types of service people have been matter-of-factly "given the keys to the castle." These disguised criminals locate alarm devices, alarm control equipment, and vulnerable telephone terminal boxes. They are able to shunt out or disable individual alarm devices protecting doors or windows, thus providing a means of unalarmed entry during the closed period. They examine locks to determine their pick resistance; steal keys left in locks or conveniently tagged and placed on hooks in unlocked key cabinets; determine alarm system opening and closing procedures; look inside open safes and vaults to determine whether relocking devices, tear gas, or other deterrents are installed; and otherwise make their final attack more certain of success.

Impersonation in Attack

This section provides illustrations of how easily and cleverly impersonation has been used to attack.

- A merchant who had just opened his premises and turned off the burglar alarm system was preparing to receive customers. He had followed security precautions in keeping his entrance door locked and a metal grille gate in place while he distributed valuable merchandise from the safe into display cases.

  Two armed men dressed in the uniform of the merchant's burglar alarm central station company appeared outside and rattled the gate to get his attention. When the merchant opened the door, they explained the alarm system must have developed a trouble condition during the night, and they wanted entry to check out the system and locate the "trouble." The merchant opened the gate without requesting further identification. The two thugs overpowered him and completed a successful robbery.
- "Alarm company agents" arrived at the premises in a van with all the special emergency vehicle identification of the "right" alarm company. The merchant admitted them without identification.
- A "telephone repairman" worked for hours on the terminal box on a telephone pole, attempting to defeat the alarm system of a nearby high-risk occupancy. A female resident who saw him working "so hard" in the rain and felt sorry for him, police learned later, had let him into the building.
- In a daring grab for more than a million dollars in gems, two gun-toting stickup men disguised themselves as telephone repairmen. The two men, in khaki work clothes and wearing tool belts with phone sets, called through the well-protected door, "We're telephone repairmen. There's something wrong with your line; we've come to check it." When the jeweler released the electric door lock to admit the "repairmen," they attacked. The jeweler had just turned off the alarm system and opened the vault—coincidence or planning?

- At a busy international airport, two men wearing the white coveralls of airline employees readily approached an airline truck and robbed the driver of a high-value consignment.

Does the criminal worry about being caught while acting as an impersonator? Probably not. He knows from experience that impersonators are seldom detected and, if detected, usually get away uncaught. After all, he is planning to commit a felony, and impersonation is a minor risk to one ready to commit a major crime.

COUNTERMEASURES

Concrete steps exist that can be taken by businesses, large or small, to reduce their vulnerability to these intrusions into the heart of their security systems, as well as to attacks based on pretext and impersonation. Following is a list of such countermeasures:

1. Establish security procedures that permit no one entry beyond the retail or reception area without proper identification by supervisory personnel. An important part of this step is establishing standards for identifying service and maintenance personnel who may visit the premises and training supervisors to acquire identification by those standards.

   Assign to those admitted visitors' badges that are frequently changed as to color, shape, and so on, and recover the badges before the visitors leave the premises. Instruct all employees to be on the alert for strangers within the premises as well as to report suspicious activities.
2. Question (in depth) all unscheduled or seemingly unnecessary visits by "outsiders." Such visitors should be politely but firmly detained in the visitors' reception area and calls placed to their employers to establish positive identification and the reason for the visit. Remind supervisors that an incoming telephone message making an appointment is not identification.
3. For a number of reasons, visitors should be accompanied by well-indoctrinated supervisory personnel when they are to be admitted to vital security areas. One reason is to safeguard the security program against friendly employees inclined toward loose talk.
4. Refrain from discussing vital security procedures with anyone who does not have an urgent need for such information. Many sophisticated criminals are able confidence men. Also, people without need to know may be tempted to boast of their inside information.
5. Never discuss vital security procedures where the conversation may be overheard by strangers, customers, visitors, service personnel of any kind, or uninvolved employees.

6. On doors entering vital security areas, install alarm devices that will sound if there is unauthorized entry or exit during the daytime period. Such devices have a key-controlled bypass for authorized entry. These keys must be carefully controlled and the door closed after each entry or exit.
7. Keep safe and vault doors closed if they are within outsiders' range of observation.
8. Move safe and vault combinations away from the last digit immediately after opening the safe or vault door.
9. Insist that insurance agency, alarm contractor, and telephone company records be maintained under proper security control.

Remember—think like a thief. If you can imagine some way that you, if you were an outsider or an uninvolved employee, could obtain security information vital to the protection of your assets, take steps now to prevent anyone else's discovering and capitalizing on this vulnerability.

38

Impersonation in Robbery

Think II

Early-morning opening hours present the greatest robbery risk for pawnbrokers, coin dealers, and retail jewelers. This is the period when valuable stock is moved from safes and vaults to showcases and show windows. This danger period is repeated in the afternoon, when stock is being returned to safes and vaults for nighttime safekeeping. During these risk periods the burglar alarm systems are off, fewer employees are on duty, safes and vaults are open, and the valuable stock is concentrated in one area, making it possible for the robber to scoop up a major haul in a matter of moments.

At a different time such a robbery requires keeping employees (and possibly customers) under threat of force while the robber or an accomplice moves from showcase to showcase (each of which should be locked), sorting valuable stock from items of less worth.

For these reasons an experienced jeweler will not open his doors to the public until his valuable stock is in showcases and show windows. A prudent manager will also invariably keep his door locked until his staff has arrived and all are ready for duty. Further, a wise manager will, if conditions permit, relock grilles covering the entrance door and show windows after each employee arrival until opening time.

A successful closing operation under proper security conditions is more difficult to manage. There is a natural tendency for most employees and, indeed, proprietors to want to complete their daily chores on time to catch the 5:43 express to Martiniland, to meet that special date at Fifth and Vine, or to get a bite to eat before the Monday night bowling league. Thus, exceptions are occasionally made when a regular customer is still considering a purchase at closing time. After all, one should make a profitable sale; that's the name of the game. Occasionally, other closing-time exceptions are made, and sometimes the exceptions prove fatal.

WHEN IS A CUSTOMER NOT A CUSTOMER?

In the instance we are now to relate, everyone's mistake was failing to remember the old adage, "Appearances are deceiving." Sam owned an established retail jewelry business. While some temporary employees were used during holiday seasons, for the most part Sam and his son staffed the operation alone.

One day Sam and his son were halfway through their closing procedures (behind locked doors, of course) when a lone individual appeared at the entrance door and tapped on the glass. Sam "recognized" the man; he had been in the store earlier that day, looking at a number of high-priced rings. While the stranger often seemed to have made up his mind to make the purchase, each time he had shaken his head and, in the end, had left without making a purchase.

The "customer" at the entrance door mimed what Sam expected—he'd finally made up his mind and was ready to buy. Sam went to the entrance, admitted his "customer," and relocked the entrance door.

WHEN HE'S A ROBBER

Once inside, the "customer" asked to see one of the rings he had previously inspected. Sam walked toward the safe to remove the tray of rings. As he did, the "customer" pulled a small but ugly gun from a paper bag and forced Sam and his son into the rear of the store, out of view of passersby.

Sam and his son were handcuffed and locked in the restroom. The robber returned to the front to admit an accomplice, relocked the entrance door with Sam's keys, and thoughtfully placed a "Closed" sign in the show window.

Together the two robbers systematically began to loot the showcases and windows, having first gathered up the merchandise already placed in the safe. Well dressed, calm, and precise in their movements, the two attackers appeared quite unremarkable to passersby.

ENTER THE POLICE

Meanwhile, back in the "john," Sam or his son managed to reach and activate a silent holdup alarm device installed there—after all, everyone knows the restroom is the place into which people are herded and locked when a robbery takes place. Only a few minutes later Sam heard one robber shout to the other, "Here come the cops!" Sam correctly surmised that the police were responding to his holdup alarm.

By all rights, this story should have had a happy ending. You might imagine that the police spotted the attackers and, with guns drawn, intimidated the criminals into immediate surrender. Unfortunately, both Sam and the police missed the point. They failed to "think like a thief."

Responding to the holdup alarm radioed to their patrol car, the two policemen had raced to the jewelry store. One officer ran through an alley to block escape by the store's rear door, while the other policeman approached the entrance. This officer saw an "employee" calmly removing stock from the showcases. Now it was the officer's turn to tap on the door glass. The "employee" looked up from the showcase, smiled, and cheerfully unlocked the entrance door.

The officer began walking toward the rear of the store, his back to the "employee," inquiring as to the cause of the "false" alarm. Imagine his chagrin when he, too, found himself under the same gun as Sam. You guessed it—the officer joined Sam and his son in the men's room.

While the thieves completed their looting and left the premises by the front door, the second officer faithfully remained at his back-door post, awaiting some action on the part of the other officer. He saw and heard nothing. The newspapers not only reported that the loss might run to $200,000 but also were quick to report all the sordid details of the attack.

LESSONS TO BE LEARNED

This sad tale offers several morals. Two intelligent, normally alert individuals—the jeweler (who had been held up on three prior occasions) and the police officer—were taken in by appearances. Each learned that not every well-dressed, quiet, courteous, calm, and smiling individual is necessarily a customer or storekeeper. The policeman and Sam should have followed security procedures to the letter rather than permitting their preconceptions to override their ordinarily sound judgment.

Except in the largest cities, our police forces are not so numerous that district personnel cannot be expected to familiarize themselves with the names and faces of at least the high-risk businessmen on their assigned "beat." Too, Sam probably had been remiss in failing to seek continuing close relationships with law enforcement people and to encourage them to make periodic visits to his premises, particularly during the high-risk opening, closing, and lunch periods when holdup attack is more probable. Indeed, police departments often send police personnel to visit high-risk establishments on a regular basis. In some financial institutions, police even sign a log recording the time of day at which their daily visit was made.

Throughout the country, police departments report that well over nine out of ten holdup alarms turn out to be false or unnecessary. Nevertheless, this fact does not give police any less obligation to respond to a holdup alarm signal with any thought other than that this call is the one time out of ten when an attack is in progress—any other attitude would be acutely dangerous. At the same time, the person responsible for the security of a business must recognize that if a substantially high number of false holdup alarms are transmitted from that premises to the police, whether through the carelessness of employees or because of defective equipment, the police will come to know their store as "false alarm alley" and will respond to that firm's alarms indifferently and reluctantly.[1]

Finally, insurance does not really cover a high-value robbery loss of this kind. The payment of one such claim—coupled with recognition of the fact that the loss was caused by carelessness—means insurance rates will skyrocket, that the loss will reflect on the insurance rates of others in the same field, and that the insurance company might even consider cancellation of coverage, citing bad judgment as a factor.

---

[1] In many cities holdup alarms are responded to as acute emergencies, at high speed and under siren. In one city, one bystander died, one man was paralyzed for life, and three were seriously injured in an accident that occurred when a speeding police car, responding to a false holdup alarm, was struck while going through an intersection on the red light.

39

Robbery Attack

"We Wuz Robbed"

Robbery is defined as the taking of something "by menaces"—that is, by force or violence or by the implied use of force or violence. The incidence of robbery in the United States has increased more than 212.4 percent in the past decade, a rate of increase exceeding that of any other type of crime with the exception of homicides, rapes, and drug offenses.[1]

Study of robbery attacks reveals that one-half of the attackers are armed with guns or knives, one-half to two-thirds of the attacks involve two or more criminals, and one-half of the robbery attacks were made against lone individuals in business places or in residences. While violence occurred only 10 to 20 percent of the time, the percentage of robbery attacks in which violence occurs is steadily increasing.

Robbery attacks occur in a wide range of circumstances involving confrontations between frightened strangers. The attack, like a poorly rehearsed play, often produces unexpected climaxes. For these reasons, extreme danger lurks in the wings of every act of robbery. Unwilling or unwitting participants are often injured or killed because they did not know what would be best to do during a robbery.

Of course, there is no "script" for what to do when being robbed. There are, however, certain basic rules that can reduce the likelihood of physical harm in the "average" robbery attack. This chapter deals with the deterrents that can reduce the likelihood of robbery attack and the actions that should be followed if a robbery actually occurs.

TOTAL PREVENTION OF ROBBERY

Theoretically, robbery could be prevented if access to and the removal of valuables could be made impossible. For example, armored vehicles are less susceptible to direct attack, and bank tellers behind bullet-resistant drive-in windows are not often targets for robbery.

---

[1] *Crime in the United States*, Uniform Crime Reports 1971, Superintendent of Documents, Stock Number 2701–0009.

Another method to prevent robbery would be to eliminate merchandise or valuables from the business or home. Unfortunately, most businesses cannot function solely on credit card transactions, and customers are not always content to make their purchases from a mail-order catalog. Valuable stock and its medium of exchange—money—must necessarily remain highly accessible to criminal attack.

Increasing the probability that robbers will be apprehended, convicted, and punished could—at least in theory—reduce or prevent robbery attacks. However, though the legal penalty for armed robbery is still relatively heavy, the inability to apprehend and to prosecute and sentence the criminal swiftly greatly reduces the robber's fear of apprehension, conviction, and confinement.

DETERRING ROBBERY

Since these three deterrents are not available, users and suppliers of security services must resort to compromise. They must discourage robbery attack by sound security procedures, by physical barriers, and by appropriate alarm and surveillance systems.

When values on hand can be reduced and access to valuables can be denied by physical and electronic barriers and the application of effective surveillance and/or identification systems, the result does reduce vulnerability to robbery attack. Like any other defense, however, total security against robbery must be constantly practiced. In addition, it must be "advertised" to ensure that outsiders understand that security defenses exist. Statistics show that signs advising of the presence of cameras, closed-circuit TV, emergency signaling systems, unbreakable or bullet-resistant glazing materials, and so on, together with a well-publicized willingness to pay rewards for information leading to the conviction of robbers, contributes significantly to the reduction of vulnerability. Conversely, like idle threats, counterfeit ("beware of the invisible dog") or poorly practiced security procedures not only do not fool the robber but also may increase the danger of violence.

Our discussion of defenses against robbery includes measures especially applicable to financial institutions, commercial or mercantile enterprises (retailers, wholesaling, and manufacturing), and transports and messengers. As always in security, what is particularly applicable to one type of risk has its applications to risks in another category. A current example is the extent to which measures used by banks to deter robbery, to increase the safety of personnel during robbery, and to increase apprehensions are being adopted by other robbery attack targets.

In Financial Institutions

As far as financial institutions are concerned, the Bank Protection Act of 1968 prescribes the physical construction of drive-in tellers' windows and the standards for surveillance systems (photographic cameras or closed-circuit TV) that deter robbery attack. Teller training programs are also obligatory under the act and incorporate what to do in the event of robbery, what to notice (if possible), and what to do immediately following a robbery.

The application of photographic cameras and closed-circuit TV systems is treated in depth in Chapter 41. Other steps banking institutions can employ to reduce vulnerability to robbery are discussed in the following sections.

Physical Barriers

Probably the most significant weakness contributing to bank robbery is the absence of significant physical barriers between tellers' funds and the criminal. Banking institutions that have suffered repeated robberies have eliminated robbery attacks by erecting bullet-resistant physical barriers that separate the tellers' section (and, sometimes, other banking personnel) from the customer area of the banking floor. When well designed, such barriers have been welcomed by the customer and have been extremely effective in eliminating robbery attempts, particularly by lone bandits.

Guards

Other steps employed to reduce robbery vulnerability include the stationing of an armed security guard on or, if feasible, overlooking the banking floor from a less-vulnerable vantage point. However, the guard must be carefully trained, experienced in handling dangerous situations, in good physical condition, and of above-average intelligence. Procedures the guard should follow in suspicious circumstances should be carefully detailed and rehearsed to reduce the danger of armed confrontation. Indeed, some banking institutions hold the theory that an unarmed security agent wearing plain clothes is a better treatment of the security problem than the use of armed guards. Others use the plainclothes approach but add a concealed gun and Mace. In any event, infirm or unalert security guards cannot provide an effective deterrent. "Broadening" the guard's duties to include light housekeeping and directing traffic in the parking lot also is very bad practice.

Robbery-Resistant Enclosures

Another technique successfully employed by banking institutions to reduce their vulnerability to robbery is drawn from the virtually robbery-free experience of the automobile drive-in and sidewalk walk-up tellers' windows. These windows are well accepted by virtually all banking customers.

Many banking institutions have made the teller's position remote from the customer, using closed-circuit TV visual and audio communications and pneumatic tubes for the exchange of funds. This approach has been successful and probably will continue to expand rapidly since it combines improved security with labor savings; during slow to moderate business periods a single teller can often handle several customers efficiently.

The defenses described here equally apply to similar operations such as check-cashing, money-lending, and ticket booths having a substantial accumulation of cash during relatively short periods of time. These and other merchants have also reduced their vulnerability to robbery by the installation of drop-type safes. Employees on duty are required to place deposit accumulations into the one-way safe "throat" at periodic intervals, but they are not given access by key or combination to the safe. Pickup and deposit in banking institutions is accomplished by an armored car service or by a security supervisor who visits the premises and handles the transfer under special security procedures.

Bulletproof partitions with security passthroughs for merchandise and money have also been successfully utilized by robbery-plagued liquor stores, 24-hour convenience stores, and pharmacies in high-crime areas.

In Manufacturing and Wholesaling

Manufacturers and wholesalers, in contrast to banking institutions, do not often offer significant attraction for armed robbery attack. However, specific situations can make them targets for attack.

Cash payrolls, common knowledge to employees and many outsiders, are frequent targets. This problem can be eliminated by payment by check, or alleviated by assigning the cash payroll and check-cashing responsibility to an experienced security contractor. Large amounts of cash collected from C.O.D. customers also increase the risk of armed attack.

Occasionally, manufacturers or wholesalers of lightweight valuable stock such as drugs, jewels, precious metal, cameras, and so on are also the target of robbery attack. This vulnerability can be reduced by firm access control procedures, the use of strong locks with pick-resistant cylinders,[2] strict key control, and by specially constructed security vestibules (a dividing area that denies access) or cages separating vehicle docks and shipping and receiving areas from warehousing or manufacturing supplies and stock. Such measures ensure that only qualified personnel enter the vulnerable area or its perimeter, that drivers are isolated from the shipping area or its docks, and that these areas are isolated from the warehousing and manufacturing areas. Guards placed in protected positions commanding key points are used in addition.

Enterprises responsible for the delivery of valuable stocks like those previously mentioned, but also including liquor, men's and women's clothing, and other highly salable commodities, must concern themselves with defense against hijacking and robbery attacks upon vehicles and drivers.

---

[2] Where the lock protects a restricted area, a lock cylinder which can be picked in a few seconds offers a means of surprise attack.

In Messenger Delivery

Businesses that involve the delivery of money, securities, and jewelry by messenger are common knowledge to the criminal; thus, such messengers are highly vulnerable to attack. As experience has proven time and time again, this is not a safe means for the transport of such valuables—they would better be handled by armored car delivery.

Where messengers are employed, the defenses available are limited. These include special briefcases containing alarm devices, tear gas, and so on and chain and lock sets that secure the case to an individual's arm or body, portable two-way radios, the licensed use of arms for self-protection, travel in taxis and other commercial vehicles, armed escort service, and so forth. None of these measures, unfortunately, is adequate to defend against determined attack. If the use of messengers cannot be abandoned, the user should be certain that he is adequately insured for the values so carried. The Federal Crime Insurance Administration, which insures firms that cannot otherwise get coverage, sets a limit of $5,000 on the amount recoverable from robbery of a messenger unless the messenger was accompanied by an armed bodyguard.

In Retailing

The threat of robbery attack falls most heavily upon retailers. The nature of their business requires that every customer must have access to the areas in which merchandise is displayed and paid for because one can't transact retail business without having personal contact with customers. Retailers can consider certain defenses, however, that need not—and normally do not—affect their business with legitimate customers.

In addition to the use of robbery-signaling alarm devices and photographic camera or closed-circuit TV systems (which serve as a deterrent to robbery attack), the retailer can reduce his vulnerability by providing appropriate access controls and physical barriers and by adequately staffing his premises. For example, some high-risk retailers employ electrically actuated remote-controlled entrance door releases that give them the opportunity to deny or permit access to the store after seeing persons seeking entrance, particularly during periods when staff is at a minimum, during after-dark hours, and so on. These releases may be employed in varying degrees in varying situations and can of course be turned off during peak daytime business hours when the presence of many customers in the retail area is in itself a deterrent. Retailers can also employ a security guard, and the standards for the guard should be little different than those recommended for banking institutions.

Physical barriers can separate the cashier's function from the rest of the retail area and provide those working as cashiers with a defense against robbery attack. The most common is a bullet-resistant glazing material partition at the cashier's counter (full height or the equivalent below eye level) having a small pass-through to accomplish the exchange of currency and checks.

Vulnerability to robbery attack can also be reduced by employing people who are alert and in good physical condition. A small staff, or an elderly female clerk, can attract attack. Keeping cash at low levels will also reduce vulnerability. Frequent visits to a banking location to make deposits may be required to do this. Regardless of frequency, precautions should be taken to protect those traveling to the bank to make deposits. Varying the time of day, the routes taken, cars used, and sending more than one person with the deposit are proven deterrents to en route attack. In no case should after-dark deposits be made unless extra security measures are taken. Police escort can be requested or an armored car pickup service used. Some armored car carriers will pick up deposits from a premises money chest after the close of business. Where armored car service is used, a two-key system is common, the proprietor having no or only one key to the lower section into which the deposit falls. This system reduces the proprietor's vulnerability to robbery and is usually "announced" by a decal stating that the safe cannot be opened except by the armored car company.

HOLDUP ALARMS

Whenever emergency or holdup alarms are employed, close adherence to proper standards of installation and special attention to the quality of the alarm actuators and control equipment are important for two reasons:

1. Police response to emergency or holdup alarm signals is usually swift and anticipates armed conflict. Vehicle accidents and the accidental shooting of customers or employees can result, with serious consequences.
2. The emergency alarm system should be highly reliable since the need may be (and should be) for response to dire emergency—someone may have suffered injuries in an attack and is in need of prompt emergency medical attention, or individuals may have been locked in vaults or stockrooms and be in need of emergency release.

Supervision of Holdup Alarms

Holdup alarm systems may be supervised by a remote central station or by connection directly into a police department. In either event, the holdup alarm should be silent at the premises because a loud bell or siren activated by an alarm device can startle the attacker into violence. A local (unsupervised) holdup alarm system sounding only at the premises not only is virtually useless but also is actually dangerous.

A holdup alarm system may also signal to a telephone answering service or any other location manned on a 24-hour basis. However, when other than professional supervision is involved, great care must be taken to establish—and maintain—the exact procedures to be followed in reporting the emergency signal to the police.

Holdup alarm systems may be connected to the supervisory point by a separate telephone circuit or by combining both burglary and holdup alarm systems on a single telephone circuit. Holdup alarm systems on direct-wire central station alarm circuits are usually combined (or duplexed) with the burglar alarm system, except in financial institutions. When the holdup and intrusion systems are so combined, the user should make certain that the alarm contractor can provide signal-generating equipment that will produce at the central station a holdup alarm signal that is distinctively different from the intrusion alarm signal.

Distinguishing Robbery from Burglary Alarms

When duplexed alarm circuits are connected into a police station, however, a distinctively different signal is seldom possible. In such cases, the determination as to whether the alarm signal is indicating holdup or burglary is based on the time the alarm signal is received. The police compare the proprietor's scheduled open-for-business hours (previously furnished to the police) with the time the signal is received in order to determine whether the premises is open or closed. Under such circumstances, the user must be careful to adhere to the established schedule of business hours and to notify the police promptly of any changes in the schedule. Clearly, an alarm signal from a high-risk proprietor who has remained in the premises after the scheduled closing time is not likely to get a police response that anticipates a holdup in progress. More likely police will assume the signal to be a burglary alarm. Not only will this delay response, but arriving police units may not recognize the proprietor and may even assume he is one of the burglars.

To some extent, a similar problem can arise in central station alarm systems: An identifiable holdup alarm signal transmitted after the burglar alarm system is set may be misconstrued by the central office supervisor as equipment trouble, telephone circuit failure, cleaner error, and so forth. A typical case would be the accidental transmission of a holdup alarm by cleaners working in a banking location after the safe or vault burglar alarm system has been turned on. This problem of misconstrued signals can arise in high-risk business operations with one or more burglar alarm systems if personnel with authority to change alarm procedures or knowledge of the combinations to safes or vaults work alone or with skeleton forces outside the normal business hours. In such cases the alarm company must be instructed to treat all holdup alarm signals as such, even when they occur in normally closed periods.

TESTING THE SYSTEMS

McCulloh or Party-Line Alarms

Where holdup alarm systems are connected to a remote central station by a McCulloh party-line alarm telephone circuit, special problems develop due to two reasons:

1. Since other customers may be transmitting alarm opening or closing signals at the same time as the transmission of a holdup alarm, the signals may "clash," or print on top of each other, producing a confused or unintelligible alarm transmission. This can delay or even prevent effective police response.
2. Holdup alarm-actuating devices are not often used (in comparison with burglar alarm control units and devices that are tested daily at least in part). For this reason, holdup-signaling devices should be tested periodically by preannounced activation of the device and resulting transmission of the signal to the remote central station.

When a direct-wire central station system is involved, this prearranged test (preferably conducted after business hours) can be performed between supervisors at the premises and at the central office, with the supervisors at the premises activating each holdup alarm signal device, while the supervisor at the central station receives each alarm transmission and facilitates the reset of the alarm circuit to receive the next test.

However, when a transmitter (McCulloh) circuit is involved, the restoration cycle for the alarm system usually requires approximately one minute for each signal device tested. Testing at a location having ten or more alarm devices becomes a laborious task under these circumstances and is discouraged by alarm contractors. Nevertheless, even if the holdup alarm circuit is of the McCulloh or transmitter type, careful procedures for periodic testing should be established because there is no other way of determining whether the individual alarm devices will function when needed. This can be accomplished by modifying the signal-sending transmitter to shorten only the test cycle or by a practice of testing one button each week.

Testing holdup alarm devices connected to multiplex control instruments is not as difficult. However, it is preferable to arrange this testing with the central station at times other than the busy opening or closing periods.

The Police Connect

This limitation on testing also applies to police connects because in many communities police do not have the manpower for frequent alarm tests. In view of the fact that police direct-connect services are generally provided free of charge, their users may have to "compromise" as to the extent and frequency of holdup alarm device tests. Again, the procedure might be to test a single device each week in rotation.

Test Precautions

Regardless of the type of supervision and the nature or frequency of the testing, the following criteria are important to any test procedure:

1. A telephone line should be kept open between the premises and the supervisory point to permit the voice transmission of an alarm if a holdup attack occurs during the test.
2. Employees who would normally be actuating a holdup alarm device should be permitted, under supervision, to perform the test of the specific device they would be operating. This familiarizes the employee with the location and method of activation of the device.
3. The employee should be indoctrinated as to the circumstances in which he should transmit a holdup alarm signal and what happens when the signal device is actuated—for instance, that the alarm is silent, that police are immediately notified, that they will normally reach the premises within 2 to 5 minutes, and that they will enter through certain specific entrances.

If alarm devices are equipped to "lock in" (a feature considered a must by most), the restoration key should always be held by supervisory personnel, even though employees are permitted to operate the buttons on test occasions. The purpose of the lock-in feature is twofold: (1) it determines that the transmission of an accidental alarm was indeed due to activation rather than an equipment failure, and (2) it pinpoints the source of the alarm signal and enables management to identify careless employees.

SELECTION AND PLACEMENT OF ALARMS

Certain criteria for design and location of holdup alarm devices should also be met. For example, the holdup alarm-triggering device normally concealed behind tellers' counters, cash registers, and so forth should be of the single-finger trigger or push design, preferably recessed to permit actuation of the device without groping while still maintaining a fairly high degree of protection against accidental actuation. As previously stated, all alarm holdup devices should be equipped with a lock-in feature that requires a special supervisor-operated restore key.

In high-risk applications involving money, special alarm-actuating devices may be used. These include money clips that are installed in a cash drawer and are automatically actuated when the teller or a bandit removes the money in the clip, closing the alarm circuit. Pressure pads are similar in nature and application to the money clip. When tellers' cash drawers are removable for storage in the vault, holdup alarm devices such as money clips or pressure pads must necessarily be of the plug-in type. Therefore, the design of the circuit should be fail-safe—that is, a trouble signal should be registered if, when the teller's drawer is placed in position, the alarm device circuit is not properly restored to a ready state.

In locations where the hand actions of the teller, checker, or cashier are visible to the robber, foot rails are used. These, too, should have the lock-in feature requiring special key restoration. Where these foot-actuated devices are used, the treadle should be far enough above floor level to prevent accidental activation by toe tappers or by cleaners' brooms or mops and should be protected by a secure cover to eliminate common mechanical and electrical problems. In addition, cleaners should be instructed as to the care required in cleaning near foot rails.

Wireless holdup alarm devices are coming into greater use in both premises and approach-to-premises applications. These small units permit the transmission of alarm signals from any nearby point without any noticeable evidence that a device has been actuated. They may be used by floor security guards, platform officers in banking locations, proprietors and other supervisory personnel. Devices designed to be worn on a belt, carried in a pocket, attached to a neck chain, hidden behind a belt buckle, or attached to keys are available. These "user-easy" features are intended to convey to a would-be robber the potential dilemma: Has a signal been sent or not? This dilemma significantly enhances the deterrent value of such systems.

When wireless alarm-signaling devices are contemplated, the equipment selected should be relatively false-alarm-free (not affected by various radio transmissions from taxis, trucks, aircraft, and so forth) and must operate within a transmission range of usually no more than 150 feet. Battery power supplies for wireless alarm transmitting devices must be replaced at frequent intervals. These devices should be tested at more frequent intervals than the hard-wire holdup-signaling devices.

On occasion, one encounters emergency alarm systems actuated by ordinary doorbell push buttons. This practice cannot be recommended because the devices are easily activated by accident, there is no lock-in feature to pinpoint the cause of the alarm, and fail-safe features are not as good as those designed into conventional emergency alarm-signaling devices. However, such emergency alarm systems have been successfully used by low-risk retailers in cooperation with adjacent tenants. This arrangement, sometimes referred to as the "buddy-buzzer" system, has proved effective in decreasing holdup attacks at low-risk locations, and a number of holdup suspects have been captured by police as a result of signals from such systems. In a high-risk location, however, the proper use of this simple type of trigger would be as a local annunciator (to alert supervisors on the premises rather than the police) or to activate cameras without signaling an alarm.

Holdup alarm devices are primarily installed at the expected points of attack, while other holdup alarm-triggering devices are installed as backup at points from which the target area is observed or supervised. Thus, we find holdup alarm-signaling devices at tellers' counters, cashiers' positions, and service desks; within vaults, restrooms, and stockrooms; at managerial, supervisory, or reception desks; and at switchboards.

Alarm Annunciation

Whenever a number of holdup alarm-signaling devices are employed in a single premises, it may be important for supervisory personnel to know, prior to the arrival of police, both the fact that an alarm device has been actuated and the specific location of the device triggered. To accomplish this, an annunciator system may be used in conjunction with the holdup alarm devices. Annunciation may be grouped into zones (for example, the tellers' counters might be zone 1; the receptionist, zone 2; and officers' platform, zone 3), or individual stations can be annunciated by a number (jewelry counter, cashiers' cage, cash register, or mezzanine office).

Zone annunciation on a local basis is also applicable to situations where holdup alarm devices are installed in separate areas or on separate floors. In those cases where police response to the premises must be directed to and determined by the particular target area, the division of alarm-actuating devices into separate and identifiable alarm systems is preferable. If this cannot be accomplished efficiently, a somewhat less satisfactory alternative would be to have a supervisor assigned the responsibility for directing the police to the proper area, as designated by the local annunciator signal.

In any event, it is preferable that the annunciator system be visual. If audio annunciation must be used, it should employ low-volume buzzers or chimes that do not alert the robber to the fact that an alarm signal has been transmitted.

Camera Operation

As discussed in Chapter 41, camera systems can be actuated by holdup alarms to provide for an automated two-frames-per-second record of the robbery. It is important that the camera system also be silent in operation.

Preferably a single security contractor should provide both the holdup alarm system and camera system services.

UL Standards

There is usually no insurance credit for holdup alarm systems, though credit is given for protected physical barriers to tellers' areas. There is, however, a voluntary UL standard for holdup alarm system installation and service, and this standard can be required of the alarm contractor. The user is urged to require an emergency alarm system that meets or exceeds these standards, as well as a warranty in writing to this effect, as part of the contractual agreement for alarm services.

WAYS TO AVOID ROBBERY ATTACK

The following factors are also very important in avoiding robbery attacks:

- Written instructions: The procedures for the test, operation, and maintenance of the holdup alarm system should be determined and reduced to writing.
- Physical barriers: Physical barriers to holdup attack—glazing materials, doors, frames, dead bolts, lock cylinders, and other access barriers—should be of the highest quality and maintained in top condition at all times.
- Training: Recently we encountered a supervisor in a critical shipping area who, after 16 years of service, still labored under the misapprehension that activating the emergency alarm signal device would require placing a pencil end in the unit.

This is typical of the lack of training given personnel in what to do in a holdup attack situation. Management fears to come to grips with this subject, believing employees may be frightened of the potential risks involved and leave for safer pastures. There is, admittedly, some risk of this nature. In the long run, however, it is more advantageous for personnel engaged in a target business to be realistically aware of the situation and of the most practical measures to be taken under attack conditions. Human lives are more important than any risk of turnover of personnel. Further, experience shows that most employees engaged in risk situations are already aware of the danger, and their fears are actually decreased by instruction as to the safest course of action in the event of robbery.

WHEN ROBBERY OCCURS

While one cannot predict the events that will occur in a holdup, the following steps, based on the experience of others, are least likely to result in physical harm to employees and customers:

1. Each employee should do exactly what he is commanded to do by the attacker and should not move without instructions. Hands should not be raised until an order to do so is received.
2. Always assume that the criminal is capable of killing; take no risks whatsoever. Do not attempt to grab his gun, to assault the criminal, or to reach for a gun.
3. Do not attempt to actuate an alarm device or to escape from the premises to give the alarm unless you are absolutely certain your actions are beyond the view or hearing of the robber and that the subsequent course of events will not result in violence.
4. Do not speak unless ordered to.
5. Do not go beyond the specific instructions issued by the criminal in handing over money or other valuables.
6. Expect to be forced into a vault, a small stockroom, or the washroom and to be handcuffed or tied to a pipe, post, chair, and so on.
7. Expect strong language. Do not overreact to threats like "Don't move or I'll kill you."
8. Keep cool—set the example. It may save your life as well as others' lives.
9. If ordered to remain in a fixed position ("Lie down and stay on the floor for five minutes"), do so; an accomplice could be waiting outside.

The citizen or businessman taking adequate precautions to deter robbery attack hopes not to become a victim. However, never forget that robbery is an unpredictable form of attack and that robbers exhibit a greater degree of risk-taking. Thus, one should always be alert to the possibility that deterrents may not be enough.

WATCH FOR PREROBBERY PLANNING

Most robberies are planned in advance, and the criminal visits the premises—particularly the open retail area—to plan his attack. Be alert for suspicious persons who spend prolonged periods browsing. Be suspicious of persons who comment on or ask questions about alarm systems, the location of cash registers, the number of people on duty, and so on. If a suspicious incident occurs, seek counsel and assistance from the police.

Last, but not least—think like a thief. If you have a valuable commodity on hand, on your person, in your residence, or in your place of business, think how you would plan an armed attack. If you can think of one or more ways in which such an attack would be feasible, you can be sure the experienced criminal is already several ahead of you. Take prompt action and advice from experienced security contractors and police to reduce your vulnerability.

40

It's Robbery Time

Think III

Every retail or commercial business should establish a safe, regular routine to start the day. Bad habits are noticed and will invite robbery or theft attack. Merchants and bankers agree that armed robbery is more likely to occur during those early morning hours when one or two employees, preferably supervisors, arrive at the premises to prepare for the business day. Their primary functions, including turning on lighting and heating or air conditioning and distributing merchandise in show windows and showcases, should also include security measures involved in entering the premises, deactivating alarm systems, and opening safes or vaults. When these functions are properly addressed, the employees may then prepare other details for the arrival of the work force and later, they hope, steady customer traffic.

The robber anticipates one or two employees can be more easily placed under duress since at break of day fewer people are around to observe or resist his actions. In addition, since he anticipates no customers will interrupt his attack, he enjoys substantially more time to collect loot and get safely away.

Some insurers require openings of premises include two or more employees using a "buddy system" and other deterrents to robbery attack. This procedure requires one member of the opening team to remain a short distance away in a position to observe the partner approach the premises, unlock the door, safely enter, and relock the door. The latter then searches the premises for intruders and, if clear, transmits an all-clear signal to his partner. When the second team member recognizes a change in lighting, the movement of a display sign, or receives a telephone message, that employee then walks to the entrance, is admitted, and the door is again locked until a specific time when the remainder of the work force is permitted to enter the premises. These people in the following case histories forgot these rules, however.

ENTER ADAM WRONG

Adam had recently hired a pretty new assistant who soon was assigned to team with him on the early morning opening of their retail shop located in an enclosed mall. This made early morning opening a pleasure. In his desire to please his new partner, however, Adam mistakenly established a new perk. Each morning, after he and Penny carefully timed the opening of the curtain grille securing the premises entrance during a visit made by the mall security guard, Adam routinely turned off the burglar alarm, unlocked the safe, then reopened the grille gate to dash for coffee and donuts at Fred's fast food booth a short distance from his premises. Of course, Adam was gone just a few minutes (unless there was a line at Freddie's) so why bother to relock the grille gate?

One morning Adam and the patrolling guard failed to notice an individual in maintenance garb sitting by the fountain across from the shop entrance. Adam never had his coffee that morning; he returned with it but was met with a gun and locked in the same restroom with Penny, while the maintenance man and a late-arriving accomplice looted the store.

ANOTHER ADAM?

Eve ran a tight retail ship—perhaps because she realized a woman opening a coin shop alone was a more-vulnerable target to robbery attack than a man was. Once safely inside, she kept entrance doors locked and permitted no customers inside until the staff arrived. But one morning, when a uniformed officer arrived and shouted through the closed door that he must talk to her about her teenage son, Eve quickly unlocked the door and admitted the uniform. She suffered the same fate as Adam and Penny because she failed to identify this pseudo–police officer properly.

Note: The New York Times reported that 279 known impersonations of police officers occurred in New York City during 1980. Thus, merchants and residents should properly identify a police officer who appears on their scene prior to any request for police services. The officer should be asked to provide his ID number and name and to state the purpose of his mission. Then, while the officer remains outside the premises, this identification should be verified by a telephone call to the officer's police precinct or the police dispatch center using the commercially listed numbers found in the telephone directory.

NOW, WHAT'S IN THE BOX?

Eddie was smarter than the other two. He owned his own jewelry manufacturing plant and had a lot of security savvy. In addition to careful opening and closing procedures, his plant entrance included a bullet-resistant double entry foyer, the doors of which could be electrically controlled from the reception position, and a bank-type pass-through for receiving envelopes and packages from messengers and contractors. Monday through Friday, his efficient receptionist stood guard at this entry bastion. She admitted no one who was not first identified, and she forced mailmen, UPS representatives, messengers, and suppliers to do business through the pass-through enclosure. No one but fully identified, authorized individuals put one foot in the inner sanctum while she was on guard.

Sometimes, however, during busy periods, Eddie would work a small group of factory employees on Saturday mornings. He was careful to arrange to have a private security agent available outside the premises to see that he was opening safely, and he required that all employees enter together, at which time the premises entrance was relocked.

But one Saturday someone rang the bell outside the entry foyer and announced over the intercom that there was a special delivery package for Eddie. Eddie personally responded to the bell and told the deliveryman to leave the package inside the outer foyer entrance door. "No," said the messenger, "You have to sign personally for this." So Eddie ignored his own security procedures, blithely opened the inner entrance door, and found a gun under the box still in the hands of the messenger who now took over temporary management of the business and cut himself in on a huge tax-free profit. Eddie should have paid his receptionist overtime, or as a well-known comic once said, "He shoulda stood in bed."

Moral: Early morning is no time to be half asleep at the security switch.

THE SOPHISTICATED RESPONSE TO ROBBERIES IN PROGRESS

For years, experts in security, insurance, and law enforcement have counseled the Adams and Eves of the business world on proper opening, closing, and identification procedures and strongly advocate the installation of silent emergency signal devices to alert police to a robbery in progress. However, it must be clearly stated: A holdup alarm system is primarily a deterrent to robbery. If it does not achieve that purpose, no emergency signal device should be activated while a robbery is in progress if there is even a remote possibility the subsequent response action by police will further endanger the safety of employees, customers, or bystanders.

Where silent holdup alarm systems are installed, police department crime prevention officers should be asked to train each employee having any access to an emergency signal device. Such training will ensure that no employee will activate a device during a robbery in progress, take other actions that might be so construed by the robber as signaling or resistance, or maliciously or vicariously transmit false alarm signals. The officer should also explain how the police will respond to an emergency signal and what actions the employee might safely take to remember the identity and/or mannerisms of the robber(s) so he can later assist the police in their investigation of the crime.

In certain instances where robbers commit unprovoked violent assaults against the victims, police may suggest that employees activate emergency signal devices if the signals can be sent surreptitiously. Their reasoning is that prompt police response will reduce the likelihood of further unprovoked violence. However, law enforcement should also recognize that some modern day robbers carry portable police radio receivers to alert them to the dispatch of police to a robbery scene. Clearly, the time has come when law enforcement agencies must use coded signals or scramblers to conceal the business name and address when dispatching police in response to holdup alarm signals. Further, police responding to holdup alarms should always assume the robbery is still in progress and should avoid sirens, flashing lights, and police officers with drawn guns converging on the premises. Instead, procedures recommended by the FBI for police response to holdup alarm signals involving bank robberies should be adapted for similar response to mercantile premises.

Using these techniques, police vehicles are positioned a "safe distance" from the premises under attack to maintain surveillance and to block escape routes. When vehicles are in position, the police dispatcher then telephones the merchant's premises to report the receipt of a holdup alarm signal and to inquire if a robbery has occurred. If the merchant says "no," he is asked to state his name and then requested to exit the premises and proceed to the location of a police surveillance vehicle where he can properly identify himself and the police may withdraw. In this manner, if there is a robbery in progress, the merchant will not be permitted to comply with the police request and the police will avoid the imminent danger of direct confrontation with robbers within the premises. However, they can remain in position to apprehend the attackers as they flee the premises. At this point, police officers specially trained in negotiating with criminals in robbery-hostage situations may be sent to the scene in an effort to negotiate the surrender of the robbers in the safest way possible. It is noted that these special police negotiation teams have established an enviable success record in dealing with robbery–hostage situations.

41

Surveillance Systems Choice

A Candid Camera Discussion

Any discussion of surveillance systems for the deterrence of robbery and the apprehension of robbers must necessarily begin with the application of cameras in banks, where their utility was first proven. In 1955 Mr. Gerald Van Dorn, an experienced investigator, left the Federal Bureau of Investigation (FBI) to assume the post of chief security officer for the Chase Manhattan Bank.

The events that led to this move were directly related to an infamous holdup attack against a Queens (New York City) branch of the Chase Manhattan Bank. Van Dorn was the FBI agent in charge of this case, which involved the loss of more than $300,000. Brilliant work by Van Dorn led to the apprehension of the criminals responsible and impressed the bank management. The bank and the banking industry lacked the expertise necessary to deter the soaring frequency of criminal attack, and Van Dorn accepted the challenge.

PREVENTION BY DETERRENCE

Van Dorn approached the bank holdup problem logically, concluding that the name of the game was prevention. His analysis of the bank's existing defenses against holdup attack confirmed that holdup alarm systems seldom brought police in time to apprehend bank robbers and prevent losses. He suggested the use of alarm-triggered surveillance cameras as a deterrent. Van Dorn reasoned that the bank robber, professional or amateur, would not care to leave an identification photo behind him.

This reasoning proved correct. After camera systems were installed in all Chase Manhattan banking branches during the period 1956–1960, holdup attacks—both professional and amateur—dropped to near zero. The camera as a deterrent to holdup attack had arrived.

Other major financial institutions recognized the effectiveness of camera systems and added them to their banking facilities. As a result, the major chain banking institutions in metropolitan New York City enjoyed a relatively holdup-free decade, though the rate of such attacks against other financial institutions continued to rise.

In 1968, the year Congress passed the Bank Protection Act, the FBI reported that holdup attacks against financial institutions had reached an annual national rate of one attack for every 10 bank locations. In New York City, however, though other forms of crime continued to set new records, the rate of robbery attack against major chain banking institutions and similarly protected individual banks was less than one robbery for each 15 bank locations. For the Chase Manhattan Bank, however, where camera surveillance had been augmented by other sound security procedures, the holdup rate was one attempt for each 47 bank locations.

ROLE OF THE 1968 BANK PROTECTION ACT

The Bank Protection Act, enacted to counter the escalating rate of crimes against banks, particularly robbery, required financial institutions regulated by one of the four federal bank supervisory agencies[1] to follow security regulations to be developed by their particular supervisory agency.

The agencies cooperated in drafting the regulations. It is widely believed that the agencies originally contemplated having financial institution security officers advised by FBI agents since the bureau had primary jurisdiction for crimes against banks and the most experience in the occurrence and investigation of these crimes. Unfortunately, the FBI lacked the manpower necessary to furnish such services to so many financial institutions. As a result, the final regulations (released on January 13, 1969) required only that the security officer appointed by the bank's board of directors should consult with "law enforcement officers," and then take "appropriate action" to reduce the bank's vulnerability to holdup and burglary attack.

The exact language of Regulation P [Section 216.3(4)] in regard to preventive equipment is "such other devices as the security officer, after seeking the advice of law enforcement officers, shall determine to be appropriate for discouraging robberies, burglaries, and larcenies, and for assisting in the identification and apprehension of persons who commit such acts." To clarify when "such other devices" were to be considered appropriate, the regulations stated, "For the purposes of subparagraph (4) of paragraph (a) of this section, considerations relevant to determining appropriateness include, but are not limited to,

> 1. The incidence of crimes against the particular banking office and/or against financial institutions in the area in which the banking office is or will be located;

---

[1] The four agencies are the Federal Reserve, the Federal Deposit Insurance Corporation, the Controller of the Currency, and the Federal Home Loan Bank.

2. The amount of currency or other valuables exposed to robbery, burglary, or larceny;
3. The distance of the banking office from the nearest responsible law enforcement officers and the time required for such law enforcement officers ordinarily to arrive at the banking office;
4. The cost of the security devices;
5. Other security measures in effect at the banking office; and
6. The physical characteristics of the banking office structure and its surroundings."

Intent of the Rules

If a bank location was in a geographical area that had been free from holdup attacks, it had the option to "stand pat" as far as installation of camera systems or other deterrents were concerned. In order to take such a position, however, the financial institution's security officer was required to obtain board approval and to record this top-level action (or, rather, lack of action) formally in the bank files.

In the main, the Bank Protection Act of 1968 and the bank rules (the subsequent regulations promulgated by the agencies charged with administering the act) were intended to achieve voluntary compliance by the majority of the country's financial institutions. In general, the financial institutions have accepted this responsibility and have taken appropriate steps.

In subsequent years, the regulatory agencies strengthened the policy, noting that "except in extraordinary circumstances, a bank can no longer justify installing security devices after it has been robbed and that the regulatory agency should insist on affirmative action, such as the installation of the necessary number of cameras, in all offices which have experienced one or more robberies."

While the regulations afford considerable leeway as to whether the financial institution shall install camera systems, the regulations do provide that—once "appropriateness" has been established—the equipment installed must meet minimum standards spelled out in Appendix A at the end of this chapter.

SURVEILLANCE SYSTEMS

Photographic Surveillance Systems

Surveillance systems may be photographic or video in concept. The photographic equipment used for security purposes involves two types of cameras.

Continuous Camera Surveillance

The *continuous surveillance camera* (often referred to as an *automatic camera*) is one that will take pictures at preset intervals throughout the entire period the premises is open for business. These cameras are usually turned on and off by clock timers programmed to opening and closing time schedules.

While the primary purpose of a continuous, or automatic, surveillance camera system is as a deterrent to holdup attack, such camera systems are also effective in reducing (and increasing apprehensions in cases of) sneak theft, diamond switch, check fraud, and grab-and-run attacks against high-risk retailers. And while consideration must be given to the weekly replacement of film, film costs, proper developing facilities,[2] and programming the system to span the period of time required, recent reports of substantial reductions in losses from theft may signal a trend toward the dominance of continuous surveillance camera systems in the security marketplace.

Sequence Cameras

The second type of photographic surveillance camera is the *sequence camera,* which takes pictures only when someone pushes an activating button. The button may be a simple push button that activates the camera to take one picture or a few pictures at a time (the "suspicion mode"). If the sequence camera is connected to a holdup alarm system, it will take continuing frames at a fast rate until the alarm device is restored. Of course, if the camera film supply is not sufficient, the picture taking will cease even though the camera may continue to operate.

Video Surveillance

Closed-circuit television does compete with photographic automatic surveillance or sequence camera systems. When closed-circuit TV cameras are used, effectiveness of the system depends upon either continuous on-site physical monitoring of the TV pictures by capable personnel ready to actuate the videotape recorder or video recording of the entire open-for-business period.

Closed-circuit TV picture quality is dependent upon ample fixed lighting conditions or automatic light-compensating aperture control. While videotape recording has the advantages of immediate replay, no cost or delay for processing, longer recording, and the economy of tape re-use, videotape recording equipment represents a $3,000 to $4,000 investment.

Closed-circuit television/videotape recorder problems include picture reproduction quality, equipment costs, videotape storage life, and mainte-

[2] Unless a crime occurs or is suspected, the film is stored undeveloped.

nance. However, solid-state equipment costs and reliability have improved manyfold in recent years, resulting in a substantially broader market for closed-circuit TV in the deterrent and surveillance applications. This space-age equipment is relatively trouble free, but spare components, including a second video recorder, may be necessary to maintain security levels in theft prevention applications.

Videotape recorders are available that can accommodate up to eight closed-circuit TV cameras by time-lapse recording from each in automatic sequence. Additional interface equipment that permits features such as dual monitoring and the use of the system to record intrusion and alarm response conditions is also readily available, thereby increasing the versatility in application of closed-circuit TV systems. If required for holdup protection, the video recorder should be able to hold in the constant on position to function continuously or to record instantaneously when a holdup alarm device is actuated.[3]

It is important to note, also, that closed-circuit TV recordings may not be admissible as evidence in court cases. Indications are that admissibility is increasing, but potential users will wish to clear this point with local prosecutors because laws of evidence (and courtroom practice) vary widely.

Some significant demonstrations have been made of microwave transmission of closed-circuit TV pictures from a risk location to a remote supervisory point. When these locations are within a few miles of each other on a line-of-sight path, remote monitoring, utilizing one microwave channel or frequency assignment, is feasible at costs presently approximating $10,000 per system. This may seem a steep investment at first. However, if more than one location can be supervised by closed-circuit TV at the same remote point by the same security manpower required for a single location, the economics of remote closed-circuit TV monitoring become more practical.

Surveillance Systems Standards

In reviewing Appendix A requirements for surveillance systems, the security officer should consider the following points. Appendix A minimum standards accept either photographic equipment or closed-circuit television as the means of surveillance.

When photographic equipment is used, the cameras must be capable of clear reproductions of persons photographed, providing upon enlargement at least a 1-inch vertical head size. The equipment selected must be reasonably quiet in operation, readily serviced, inspected and maintained, and capable when activated of taking pictures at a rate of at least one frame

[3] Videotape recording requires a startup time from the off position, during which no clear pictures can be obtained.

every 2 seconds for a period of 3 minutes. The minimum film size is specified as 16mm.

Oddly, the regulations do not specify the means by which the surveillance systems, whether cameras or closed-circuit television, are to be activated. In practice, however, almost all photographic systems are electrically connected to holdup alarm-signaling devices that alert police or the central station to holdup attack and simultaneously activate the surveillance cameras.

There is an absolute necessity for holdup alarm-activating devices capable of inconspicuous actuation by bank tellers, secretaries, bank officers, and others in a position to overhear or observe such an attack. Accordingly, and particularly in recent years, security equipment manufacturers have risen to the need, developing emergency alarm-activating devices such as foot rails, money clips, pressure pads, and so forth (see Chapter 39). Even though these devices may be the cause of some false alarms, they afford banking personnel a better opportunity to activate cameras, if not the holdup alarm system. (Some banks utilize emergency alarm devices that are subject to a higher incidence of false alarms solely to activate the camera circuit; more "goof-proof" methods are used to signal the robbery. This arrangement keeps false alarms to police at a minimum.)

A current assessment would still affirm the effectiveness of camera and closed-circuit TV surveillance systems in reducing the incidence of holdup attack. The Bank Act standards for surveillance equipment also have direct applications to retail-mercantile security.

When crimes occur, automatic surveillance camera systems (and sequence camera systems promptly activated by a holdup alarm) record the events in sequence. This photographic record often identifies the attackers and, of equal importance in many cases, provides an indisputable record of the actions of employees and customers. Claims of bodily harm by customers have been readily refuted by camera sequences showing the customers were in no way harmed or intimidated. The camera record also can be used as a training tool to correct dangerous actions made by employees during actual attacks.

Camera Standards and Choices

In recognition of the importance of surveillance/holdup recording to security, in 1970 the UL Burglary Division developed standards for camera equipment. These are voluntary standards, however, and only one or two camera equipment manufacturers have sought UL approval. This is unfortunate, since standards are invaluable to the user who must select, from the myriad of systems and claims advertised, the surveillance equipment that will best suit his special needs.

UL standards and Appendix A of the Bank Protection Act require:

- A 16mm film frame size, as a minimum. The film size can be 35mm, 70mm, or more; the larger frame sizes afford significantly sharper reproductive quality without significant sacrifice in shutter speed.
- A rate of speed, under emergency (holdup) conditions, of at least one frame every 2 seconds and a minimum emergency-period film capacity of 3 minutes. The average holdup attack is over well within that length of time.
- A sufficient number of cameras placed either to photograph anyone transacting business at tellers' positions or to record identifiable images of persons leaving through any normal exit.

Over and above the basic specifications of the bank rules, the bank security officer and the executive responsible for the security of a high-risk retail operation faced with the threat of holdup attack should consider the following performance factors when selecting either continuous or sequence photographic cameras or closed-circuit TV surveillance equipment:

1. Camera units should be nearly silent in operation. Nothing could be more unnerving to a teller, salesman, or robber than the reverberating sound of a camera shutter audibly clicking away.

2. The equipment selected should include a superior optical system, particularly the best lens appropriate. An unfocused picture or one in which the scene is over- or underexposed or where the robbers' movements are not "stopped" by the camera cannot provide the selective identification necessary for apprehension.

3. During a robbery, the frame speed is vitally important. Many banking institutions consider a rate of two frames per second a minimum requirement.

4. Film or videotape capacity should equal or exceed the 3 minutes stipulated in the bank rules. This is particularly important where the same cameras are utilized to photograph suspicious incidents. When cameras are to be used to photograph suspicious characters on a few frames of film as a precaution, procedures should be established to log camera use and the number of film frames expended. This log and the camera's film frame counter should be checked frequently to ensure that at least 3 minutes of unexposed film always remain.

5. The camera should be able to be operated by a low-voltage power supply. If there is no need to wire line power to each camera location, installation costs can be substantially reduced. Naturally, camera power cords must not be exposed to attack—hence, the necessity for permanent electrical wiring rather than a plug-in arrangement if line power is required.

6. It is helpful if the camera is a photographic reflex camera—that is, it will provide an actual view by which you can always see the coverage the system is presently providing without taking and developing test frames.

7. Require the camera equipment contractor to furnish test photographs taken by the camera in proposed positions over a wide range of open hours, including sunny and cloudy days. Allow further for changes in the sun's position and brightness in other seasons.

8. The sequence camera should have nonbinding shutters and takeup reels. Such camera systems may remain inactive for weeks or months so every care must be taken to ensure the system is always capable of operation. Early surveillance camera design failed to allow for idle-time effects on the mechanisms, and users were afflicted with camera failures caused by chemical emulsion deposits on takeup spools and other problems.

9. Camera control equipment should include visible and audible runout indication, alerting personnel to the fact that the entire film roll or film cartridge has been exposed and the camera is now out of service until film is replaced. Visual indication should also be provided of the frames remaining at any time since repeated use of the suspicion mode, which activates the camera but does not signal the central station (or police), will reduce the film reserve below the 3-minute limit without warning.

10. When other factors in automatic surveillance (time-lapse) camera systems are equal, such as effective coverage and cost, an advantage deserving consideration would be the snap-in cassette film cartridges. These cartridges reduce the skill required in removing exposed film and reloading the camera without exposing the film.

11. Care should be taken to select camera equipment that accepts a wide range of available lenses to permit the optimum adaptation of the camera to the layout and to any location in it. The camera's shutter speed, too, is an important factor; upon it depends sharp stop-action photographs of rapid action.

Camera Protection

While camera systems are not frequently the target of direct attack, instances have occurred where attackers have sought to "blind" the camera system before the robbery. For this reason, camera equipment and control units should be in electrically protected ("trapped") cabinets that will signal to on-site security personnel or central station supervision attempts to tamper with the film, directional coverage, or the electrical operating circuit of the camera system. The height (above the floor) and location of each camera should also be considered with a view to the possibility of physical attack against the camera lens.

Pinpointing the Camera Action

When continuous surveillance cameras are used, it is essential to locate a digital clock and a calendar within the camera field. This step provides a ready means of identifying those sections of the filmstrip that contain the pictures of suspects, based on the date and approximate hour when the suspects were within the banking premises.

For camera equipment control units, the following basics are suggested:

1. Control units, whether solid state or relay operated, should be located away from the public area. Operational noise levels of the control unit are frequently higher than those of the camera units.
2. The control unit should have the capacity to operate two or three cameras. Security, compliance with standards, or both may require two or more cameras.
3. The control unit should include a reasonably exact frame-counting device that monitors film usage for each camera connected to the control unit. This device enables security personnel, by a check of the frame counters of the control unit, to determine readily the number of unused frames remaining in each camera unit and to replace the film when the number of frames of unexposed film approaches established minimums.
4. The ideal control unit would be capable of actuating and monitoring either 16mm continuous (time-lapse) surveillance units or 35mm or 70mm sequence cameras, thus providing for both present and possible future needs of the individual risk.

16mm, 35mm, or 70mm?

We now discuss the merits of 16mm automatic surveillance versus 35mm or 70mm sequence camera systems. When 16mm film is employed, approximately 4,000 to 8,000 frames are available, depending upon the size of the camera's film magazine. Standard film rolls are 100 feet and 200 feet, though greater length can be achieved in the same film magazine by the use of thinner film.

Given a 200-foot magazine, the camera can be programmed with timers to photograph at the rate of one frame each 30 seconds. This rate will provide complete coverage of all activities on the retail or banking floor for 2 40-hour business weeks, with film changes at 2-week intervals. Automatic operation does away with the need for camera activation by an employee and provides a stronger deterrent both against the threat of robbery and the activities of the confidence man, whether intent on palming a valuable gem, using a stolen credit card, or employing "the split-check con."

Against this major advantage, one must weigh the disadvantages: The quality of 16mm enlargement is less than that afforded by 35mm or 70mm film systems, while the much more extensive use of film represents a significant additional expense of as much as $25 per camera per month.

Thirty-five and 70mm camera systems should be employed where actuation is only by holdup emergency alarm devices or by "suspicion buttons" controlled by tellers or retail store personnel. Such systems meet the requirements of the bank rules in running time and in rate of operation, while overall film replacement costs are much lower due to their intermittent operation as compared to continuous 16mm automatic surveillance. However, alarm-actuated sequence cameras do place on tellers and clerks the responsibility to activate some device that will in turn actuate the sequence camera. Sixteen millimeter cameras can also be used in a sequence mode, but the savings in equipment and film costs (16mm versus 35mm or 70mm) must be weighed against the worse quality of enlargements.

Logically, 16mm automatic surveillance cameras should be located behind the teller or retail sales location to photograph the faces of individuals transacting business at that position. The better lighting and fixed focus possible with this application permit one to obtain the best possible picture quality from a 16mm camera. In contrast, 35mm and 70mm sequence camera systems are usually located at exits to record the images of persons leaving after an attack when their attention is on the exit and their backs are turned to the teller or clerk.

When sequence (alarm-actuated) camera systems are to be employed, one should consider how long it will take the attacker to move from the point of attack to an exit. If the distance from the teller's counter to the exit is only a few feet, it is unlikely that enough frames will be taken to ensure good identification.

Mounting and Film

The type of camera mount is important. The camera bracket should be firmly mounted to a vibration-free structural surface because vibration during operation can blur the photographs. In high-risk situations, camera brackets should also be electrically "trapped" and tied into the burglar alarm system's 24-hour supervisory circuit to detect tampering to prevent the taking of usable photographs during a later attack.

Film for photographic surveillance systems should be of high quality and capable of operation at the photographic speeds that provide the best picture quality over a wide range of lighting conditions. Significant differences often exist between imported and domestic film. If the former is being considered as an economy measure, photographic tests should first be performed during all actual operating hours and lighting conditions to make certain the film will be adequate under every condition.

Film Lab Criteria

The availability of adequate, local, 24-hour film development facilities should be determined in advance of purchasing a surveillance system. Few film-processing concerns have facilities for developing 16, 35, or 70mm film rolls on a 'round-the-clock, 7-day-week emergency basis. Neither do they anticipate compensating for varying lighting conditions nor know the legal requirements. For example, film presented as evidence must be intact; it cannot be cut. Further, it must be followed through the developing process to establish that the film submitted for developing is the same film offered in evidence. Unfortunately, many "recorded" bank crime films have suffered from inadequate developing facilities or errors in processing.

In many cities, even law enforcement agencies (including the FBI) lack facilities to process these types of films properly. Law enforcement agencies have sometimes resorted to using the film-processing facilities of local TV stations. Of course, this too can result in improper processing of the film. Worse, some TV stations have even cut holdup films in order to get shots of the suspect on their newscasts, quite unaware they have thereby destroyed the value of the film as legal evidence.

When 16mm continuous surveillance camera systems are employed, a photographic laboratory with the following facilities is essential:

- Capability of developing complete rolls of negative films;
- Competent evaluation of periodic test filmstrips for film quality, area of coverage, and equipment performance;
- Storage of film reels or cassettes for 6 months or more. When fraudulent check transactions and sneak thefts occur, the availability of the day's transactions is essential to prosecution.

8mm Surveillance Cameras

In conjunction with the advance of the automatic surveillance camera concept, improvements in 8mm and Super 8 camera equipment enable a mercantile user to procure automatic camera operation for less than $300 per camera.[4] While 8mm reproduction quality is marginal in comparison with 16mm and 35mm systems, when properly installed the equipment serves well as a deterrent to theft and robbery.

When selecting 8mm camera equipment for continuous automatic surveillance applications, some additional factors should be considered:

1. Is the film capacity sufficient to take pictures at 30- or 45-second intervals throughout an entire work week?

[4] 8mm cameras (automatic or sequence) do not meet the standards (primarily covering picture size) of the bank rules and therefore are not suitable for financial institution use. However, these less-expensive cameras might be used to provide supplementary coverage at points in banking locations where compliance is not necessary, such as employee entrances, emergency exits, docks, and work areas where securities and currency are handled.

2. Is the reel of film (or, preferably, the film cartridge) easy for a layman to load?
3. If a holdup alarm is activated, has the camera an override circuit that will operate the camera at a faster speed (one or two frames per second)?
4. Does exterior lighting (strong sunlight or clouds) compromise picture quality? Some cameras using a built-in light meter must be carefully installed to overcome this problem.
5. Is there enough coverage? Since an 8mm camera system cannot (and should not attempt to) cover as much "territory" as a 16-, 35-, or 70mm unit, two or more 8mm units may be required for proper coverage. At this point, the economics of the situation (the cost of one 16mm camera versus two 8mm cameras, plus extra film and service) may dictate the selection of the larger unit.
6. Is the equipment engineered for the more demanding industrial usage?

Motion Pictures vs. Sequence Photography

While it is true that 8mm and 16mm camera systems may be employed to take motion pictures (movies) of an entire attack sequence, this mode of surveillance or photography has not been generally accepted by banking institutions. This is due primarily to the fact that stop-action sequences taken rapidly produce sufficient coverage of the action to identify suspects and actions taken by employees and customers, while complete motion picture coverage requires significant additional film capacity.

LEASE OR PURCHASE

Surveillance camera systems are available on either lease or outright purchase terms. The high capital investment required precludes some central stations and local alarm companies from offering camera equipment on the same lease basis as the holdup and burglary alarm equipment they provide. In such cases, the user is often faced with having to purchase or lease camera equipment from a supplier other than his local or central station burglar alarm contractor. This situation should be avoided, if at all possible; dividing responsibility for the camera system between the alarm contractor (responsible for activation) and the camera supplier (responsible for camera performance) is undesirable.

When there is no alternative to separate arrangements, the user should require written agreements binding both the supplier of security and of the camera surveillance equipment. These agreements should provide for the interconnection of each system and the proper maintenance of the equipment without conflict between the suppliers. In circumstances wherein surveillance cameras are used primarily as a theft deterrent and are not actuated by holdup alarm devices, the user might well consider suppliers specializing in such equipment and outright purchase.

PUBLICIZING CAMERA SYSTEMS

The installation of camera and closed-circuit TV surveillance systems has recently been publicized by some banking institutions to highlight the banks' posture toward crime prevention. Signs and newscopy advertise the existence of camera systems, and one financial institution advertised a "reward" for customers who identified pictures of themselves taken by the bank's camera systems.

While it is unlikely that many users will take such a direct tack, signs on entrance doors and at service counters announcing the presence of the surveillance cameras are vital to the concept of deterrence—the would-be attacker must know he's likely to be identified.

Banking institutions in major cities have displayed photographs of bank robbery suspects in newspaper advertisements and on counter cards, with substantial rewards offered for the identification, apprehension, and conviction of the suspects. A high percentage of bank robbers so "advertised" have been identified, and the practice also serves as a deterrent to future attacks. It is the author's belief that bank robbery could be almost wholly deterred and prevented if continuous automatic cameras or closed-circuit TV systems with recorders were used with access control systems incorporating automatic weapons detection, provided personnel had no control over the equipment and this was known to potential attackers.

In conclusion, camera surveillance equipment and closed-circuit TV are now accepted as useful by most high-risk institutions, and it is the author's opinion that, as the state of the art improves, the effectiveness of such systems in deterring crime and reducing the risk of liability will be of inestimable value. Considering the rapid advancements that have taken place in photographic and closed-circuit TV surveillance systems, users may now be well advised to purchase rather than lease the equipment.

While our "candid camera" discussion has primarily focused on high-risk robbery applications, the increase in crime, the necessity for private enterprise to protect itself (from within and without), and improvements in equipment will be prompting wider use of cameras, closed-circuit TV, and other recording devices, alone and in conjunction with alarm systems, to deter employee theft, to document acts of vandalism and sabotage, and to identify burglars.

Appendix A of the Bank Protection Act

Minimum Standards For Surveillance Systems

(1) *Surveillance systems.* (i) *General.* Surveillance systems should be:

(A) equipment with one or more photographic, recording, monitoring, or like devices capable of reproducing images of persons in the banking office with sufficient clarity to facilitate (through photographs capable of being enlarged to produce a one-inch vertical head-size of persons whose images have been reproduced) the identification and apprehension of robbers or other suspicious persons;

(B) reasonably silent in operation;

(C) so designed and constructed that necessary services, repairs, or inspections can readily be made. Any camera used in such a system should be capable of taking at least one picture every two seconds and, if it uses film, should contain enough unexposed film at all times to be capable of operating for not less than three minutes, and the film should be at least 16mm.

(ii) *Installation, maintenance, and operation of surveillance systems providing surveillance of other than walk-up or drive-in teller's stations or windows.* Surveillance devices for other than walk-up or drive-in windows should be:

(A) located so as to reproduce identifiable images of persons either leaving the banking office or in a position to transact business at each such station or window; and

(B) capable of activation by initiating devices located at each teller's station.

(iii) *Installation, maintenance, and operation of surveillance systems providing surveillance of walk-up or drive-in teller's station or windows.* Surveillance devices for walk-up and drive-in teller's stations or windows should be located in such a manner as to reproduce identifiable images of persons in a position to transact business at each such station or window and areas of such station or window that are vulnerable to robber or larceny. Such devices should be capable of activation by one or more initiating devices located within or in close proximity to such station or window. Such devices could be omitted in the case of walk-up or drive-in teller's station or window in which the teller is effectively protected by a bullet-resistant barrier from persons outside the station or window, but if the teller is vulnerable to larceny or robbery by members of the public who enter the banking office, the teller should have access to a device to activate a surveillance system that covers the area of vulnerability or the exits to the banking office.

The Bank Protection Act of 1968

42

The Diamond Switch

Now You See It; Now You Don't

A sleek out-of-state sportscar curled off the expressway into mid-morning street traffic. A few blocks farther, the car was driven into a self-parking garage in the downtown shopping area. The occupants—a well-dressed man and his attractive female companion—walked purposefully toward the shopping area.

The man was handsome and expensively but tastefully attired. His blonde companion was also well dressed in a conservative manner. She carried a small handbag and wore an expensive diamond ring.

The couple seemed attracted by the fashionable shops that surrounded the department stores. They disappeared into a modern jewelry store but emerged 2 or 3 minutes later. A half-block later, they made an equally brief visit to another fine jewelry establishment. An observer might have concluded that the couple were shopping for jewelry not obtainable in the first two stores. That's correct. Let's watch them as they enter a third store.

On entering, the man led the way toward the fine jewelry counter. He beamed a pleasant good morning at a young salesclerk polishing the countertop and said that he and his wife were interested in purchasing a fine loose diamond; could Miss direct them to someone who could be of assistance? The young lady promptly produced an elderly man who identified himself to the young couple as the person in charge of the diamond jewelry department—he would be most pleased to be of assistance.

INTRODUCTION

The customer explained that they were seeking a fine-cut, flawless, 2- to 3-carat diamond for mounting in a recently acquired family setting. Mr. X indicated that he would be interested in an immediate purchase if the store carried fine-quality diamonds.

The salesman walked to the open safe at the rear and returned with a diamond wallet. He produced for the customer's inspection a folded white tissue envelope that opened to reveal a sparkling 2.46-carat emerald-cut diamond. Mr. X admired the stone but said that only a brilliant cut would be suitable for the setting. This diamond was returned to its nest, the paper carefully folded and returned to the wallet. A second tissue held an equally select stone, brilliant cut, slightly under 2 carats but with unusual brilliance. Mr. X agreed that the stone was fine quality and inquired as to the price, but before the salesman could respond, he dismissed the stone as being too small for their purposes.

With a gleam in his eye and the scent of an extraordinary sale, Mr. Diamond Salesman triumphantly produced, from a third tissue, a full 3-carat diamond that virtually fired the counter area. The salesman's description of the stone as flawless was undeniable, and of course the price he quoted was top of the range for a diamond of this size and quality. Mr. X commented that the price was high and asked to examine the diamond more closely. He handled the stone and the jeweler's loupe with professional ease, commenting on the fine faceting work and the precision and brilliance achieved. If the salesman had paid any attention to the lady, he might have noted a hint of tension. Understandably, however, our salesman's attention was directed exclusively to Mr. X.

OUT . . . AND BACK

The salesman was shocked, to say the least, when Mr. X suddenly removed the diamond and the backdrop cloth and strode toward the entrance. As the salesman, leaning over the diamond case, cried out in some anguish, "Please, sir, wait a moment!", Mr. X moved to within inches of the door, looked again at the diamond in the north light exposure, and turned smiling to the salesman, saying, "Sorry, just wanted to look at this in proper light."

Returning to the counter and the recovering salesman, Mr. X talked about the beauty of the stone and its suitability for their purposes. "However," he said, "my wife and I are vacationing in the area and will look at some other stones this afternoon. After all, this is quite a price, you know." They thanked the salesman for his time and strolled out.

Oddly enough, they did no further shopping but returned to the automobile and left the city. Needless to say, Mr. Diamond Salesman was not feeling overjoyed at this point. But they said they would be back, so there was hope.

THE RETURN

Shortly before noon the next day the young couple again entered the store. Mr. Diamond Salesman, having already consumed his entire day's quota of cigarettes and several cups of black coffee in increasing gloom, suddenly saw a healthy commission in sight. Today was indeed going to be bright. And it was further brightened, he saw, by Mrs. X, today more attractively attired in a brief and revealing sun dress. As the couple approached, the salesman beamed and retreated to the safe to obtain the diamond wallet.

Mr. X, now accorded all the conviviality extended to the store's best customers, was greeted with assurances that he would not regret the forthcoming purchase. Mr. X smiled in return, said he hoped that he and his wife would be pleased, and asked to examine the diamond again. Today the salesman did not flinch even when Mr. X reached for the folded diamond paper and, holding it in the palm of one hand, began to unfold the tissue.

A NEW VIEW

At this point his wife, fumbling through today's far larger handbag and scattering cosmetics on the countertop, sighed and asked the salesman if he had a light for her cigarette. She leaned over the counter, cigarette in lips, revealing even more of an already well-displayed bosom. In view of her entrancing position, it is small wonder that the salesman had trouble with his lighter and even seemed to linger in lighting the cigarette. His efforts were oddly rewarded with a puff of smoke, which blew across the counter into his face, causing him to blink and cough. Mrs. X apologized profusely for her carelessness and began to replace her scattered belongings in her handbag.

SUCCESS

By now Mr. X had apparently made up his mind and had already refolded the paper. He handed it back to the salesman, saying "You have a deal. Please seal this stone and we'll go to the bank for a certified check. We'll be back with it soon after lunch."

Mr. Diamond Salesman was elated. He slipped the folded diamond paper into an envelope, sealed it, wrote Mr. X's name across the envelope flap, assured Mr. X that it would be awaiting his return, and returned the envelope to the safe. Pausing a moment to direct them toward the bank, Mr. Diamond Salesman headed for a well-earned luncheon at the club—with a cocktail or two to celebrate this notable sale.

Not wishing to be late, the salesman returned shortly before 1:30. Learning that the couple had not been back, he began his vigil. At 2:30 he began to smoke more rapidly, and by 3:05, shortly after bank closing time, he discovered that he was actually smoking two at a time. By 3:30 P.M. he was kicking himself for not having learned where his customers were staying.

At 4:00, the now distraught salesman went to the safe, withdrew the diamond wallet, opened the sealed envelope, and took out the diamond paper. By now he was suspicious. Seconds later he was frantic. Nestled in the center of the soft tissue folds, he had found a perfect (in size) 3-carat, brilliant-cut Yag—a synthetic stone.

As the salesman turned to the telephone to call the proprietor, the insurance broker, and the police, let's ask a few questions:

1. *When did Mr. X make the switch?*
2. *Why did the thieves make two visits to the store, when conceivably one might have done?*
3. *What were the telltale signs that should have aroused the salesman's suspicions?*
4. *What fatal mistakes did the salesman make?*
5. *What was the key factor that permitted this charade to succeed—and that also led to the eventual downfall of Mr. and Mrs. X?*

One can answer all of these questions simply by "thinking like a thief." The fact that Mr. X was knowledgeable and experienced in dealing with jewelry and jewelers improved his performance, but it was not the key factor. The technique relied on human nature; once the salesman sensed the kill—a "big ticket" sale—he would overlook basic security procedures.

THREE REASONS FOR TWO VISITS

No, the diamond was not switched when X ran to the door the first day. A store that carried a good stock of fine quality big-carat diamonds would be experienced in the pitfalls of this type of business, and the salesman, despite his warm and courteous behavior, was alert and suspicious up to a point. The "run for the door" was staged to arouse suspicion to a fever point and then to allay the fear, an experience that would gain the salesman's confidence. Indeed, X was counting on the fact that the diamond would be carefully examined when he returned from the doorway.

X also expected the salesman to be alert—at first—to all the diversionary tricks of the trade; the handbag, briefcase on the counter, the raincoat, newspaper, shopping bag—all the gimmicks used to palm or switch a piece of jewelry would be foremost in the salesman's mind until a confidence could be established.

X figured the salesman could be temporarily distracted by an impressive display of feminine charm. The change in costume and character were important bits of timing essential to the successful switch. True, the change from conservative to daring dress should have aroused the salesman's mental warning signal. However, as he explained at the time, his mind was on other things.

X was also a bit of a psychologist. He knew the tensions that would build up in the salesman in anticipation of a major sale and that they would peak during the first moments of their second encounter. He knew, too, that if he timed it right, the salesman would not immediately become suspicious when the diamond paper was returned with the assurance that they were on their way to a bank for a certified check. After all, the salesman would reason, this was the proper way to complete the sale. And then, for the next hour or so, there would be the matter of luncheon to attend to.

Further, X reasoned, if the salesman did become suspicious, he would delay any action until after lunch. Certification of a bank check would take a little longer during the luncheon hour, and a phone inquiry to a bank officer would probably not be returned until after the banker's luncheon hour. Of course, the two-visit ploy enabled the Xes to determine the exact size and approximate weight of the synthetic diamond they would need from their stock of Yags for the next day's switch.

THE BASIC ERROR

The salesman's fatal mistake, of course, was his failure to examine the diamond closely each time it had been in X's possession. Indeed, if he had scrutinized each stone X examined during the first visit, there might have been no return visit.

In addition, the salesman would not have been out of line to have requested, during the first visit, X's name, hometown address, and local vacation address. He could also have asked for some form of identification as being helpful toward establishing X's entree with local banking officers. The salesman might have volunteered to accompany the Xes to the bank, to bank personnel.

But Mr. Diamond Salesman's basic mistake, like that of so many other businessmen, had been a mental lapse. Until this time his security philosophy had been "think like a thief" because the salesman was experienced and knew that diamonds—like money, precious metals, and other highly negotiable loot—are primary targets for professional attack. And while few thieves have all the talent displayed by X, every criminal actively and industriously schemes ways and means of "striking it rich" one way or another.

EPILOGUE

Some crime stories have happy endings, as in this case. Due to the "Flash Bulletin" warnings of the Jewelers' Security Alliance of the United States, Mr. and Mrs. X were apprehended before their scheme was much older. The Jewelers' Security Alliance of the United States is a nonprofit association devoted exclusively to the prevention of crime against the jewelry industry. It is supported by 5,000 members—retailers, wholesalers, and manufacturers—located from coast to coast and has been preventing jewelry losses since 1883, 100 years of outstanding service to the jewelry industry. Once members of the Alliance reported losses due to X's operation, the Alliance quickly circulated descriptions, an MO (modus operandi), and suggestions for prevention of loss. Within a few days of the first bulletin, members' further reports enabled the Alliance to identify the area into which X was moving. Nonmembers as well as members, private security agents, and law enforcement were notified, and as a result, Mr. and Mrs. X were arrested. While this type of service is virtually exclusive to the Jewelers' Security Alliance operation, it could be invaluable applied to other commercial sectors.

43

Internal Theft Through Unprotected Points

The Fishnet Caper

Sherlock Holmes would find today's criminal world a challenging one because, while many crimes are quite commonplace, ample opportunity remains for "mysterious" and successful crime. Because we often fail to "think like a thief," we fail to see vulnerabilities. Opportunities abound for the latter-day Moriarty. This is a sad commentary on our security expertise in comparison with our demonstrated ability in merchandising. It seems a pity to have to "cut in" common thugs for a chunk of bottom-line profit when, with a little foresight and preventive planning, we could retain those hard-earned dollars.

Pity, too, the lot of today's detective, who rarely faces a challenge on a par with Poirot or Holmes. However, rarities do occur, and such a case challenged both business management and private investigators. This case concerned the loss of valuable merchandise, light in weight and virtually unidentifiable when stolen.

THE STOCK THAT WASN'T THERE

To be sure, management knew their products were a prime target for criminal attack, and they had taken what they believed to be every precaution to protect their stock. Nevertheless, this firm lost over $2 million in inventory in the course of a single business year. Management was puzzled and angry. Every conceivable aspect of alarm service and access control was restudied in an effort to determine if some unidentified weakness existed.

This 15-story building had a number of entrances. The guards who protected these entrances during working hours were themselves investigated. Closed-circuit television was installed to supplement the guard surveillance. Controls and searches were instituted, but not a shred of evidence was uncovered.

Management next turned its attention to those police and employees of their alarm company who came to their premises when false alarms occurred during closed hours. Personnel involved in these visits were subjected to intensive investigation, which they passed with flying colors.

And still the losses continued. It appeared that the shortages would remain unsolved and unchecked. Even the company's insurance underwriter agreed that they had properly implemented all the security steps that could be recommended. Of course, that didn't mean the insurance company would recognize any claim for the loss because without evidence of forced entry or proof of the method of theft, there could be no recovery. After all, the insurance was against burglary and theft, not inventory shortages.

A FISHING EXPEDITION

Except for the curiosity and determination of some detectives who saw in this case the opportunity to add their names to the Whodunit Honor Roll, the case would still be a mystery. One detective noted a hotel overlooking the company's premises and took a long chance. He wrote a letter to guests who had stayed in rooms that commanded a view of the fire escapes at the rear of the company's building. In the letter he introduced himself, indicating his understanding that Mr. Smith or Mr. Jones and his wife had occupied a hotel room on that side of that wing during the preceding year. He asked if they had seen any unusual occurrences at the windows or fire escapes across the way.

The detective didn't really expect any replies, but one dear old grandmother answered. During her stay in the big city, she wrote, it had rained for several days. Having nothing to do, she had amused herself by watching the antics across the way. Granny had been particularly entertained by the unique method employed to move stock from the upper to lower floors: simply dropping materials out of a top-floor window down to a fellow stationed on a lower floor fire escape, who deftly caught each item in a big fishnet. Obviously, this was much quicker, as well as less expensive, than any other method of moving merchandise. Granny had been much impressed.

Neither the detective nor management had been aware that the company had such efficient employees. Within a few days, they too were privileged to observe the procedure firsthand, watching as two of the most trusted employees demonstrated the speed with which merchandise could be transported to an unsecured first-floor area and out of the building into the trunk of an automobile.

OPEN-HOURS PERIMETER PROTECTION

Of course they netted some big fish. But did you ever stop to consider that you may have some little fish playing a similar materials-handling game in your operation? Remember, UL burglar alarm standards for the protection of windows and doors are effective only when the premises are closed and the alarm is on. Unless doors and windows are secured, alarmed, or supervised by management during normal business hours, they can be used by anyone having access to secured stock as a means of moving valuable merchandise out of controlled areas without passing secured building exits.

You might consider this vulnerability within your own operation. Perhaps you will see where you should secure windows and doors with locks and/or alarms that annunciate in an office or at a guard post.

Where ventilation presently requires open windows, air conditioning may be advisable. If windows must remain openable, small-mesh attack-resistant screens may be used. These should be secured to the window frames with security fasteners, screws, or throughbolts that can be readily installed but that must be drilled or sheared to remove.

44

Metal Detection and Inspection

A Deterrent to Theft

Magnetic detection equipment, also referred to as magnetometers, has long been used in industrial processing applications to keep nails out of soft drinks, to sort materials, and so forth as well as in prisons to detect weapons concealed in the clothing or personal effects of prisoners and visitors. Today, most people associate metal detection with skyjackers and the equipment in use at airline boarding points to detect weapons on passengers or in carry-on luggage. Indeed, most manufacturers of metal inspection equipment have recently enjoyed a boom in sales to airlines, airports, and law enforcement agencies.

Since guns, knives, and grenades are made of ferrous metals (iron or steel alloys) in most instances, the basic (and most economical) metal inspection equipment signals the presence of ferrous metals. This equipment does not, unfortunately, detect any weapons or other items made only or mostly of nonferrous materials such as nickel, brass, aluminum, lead, or silver.

As a result of careful analysis, the Federal Aviation Administration (FAA) modified its specifications to require that all metal detection equipment purchased have the capability of detecting nonferrous as well as ferrous material. Several companies market such equipment, and while it is somewhat more expensive than the basic magnetometer unit, the difference in equipment cost is negligible as a proportion of the cost of labor necessary to supervise metal inspection posts.

Electronic metal detection equipment has become essential to the prevention of crime or the threat of crime because of its "no-touch-search" capability, detection not being affected by clothing or other noninsulating material. This aspect is of special consequence when there is need to inspect the person and effects of women.

APPLICATIONS OF METAL DETECTORS

While there are limitations as to the application of magnetometers, equipment capable of detecting both ferrous and nonferrous materials has many practical applications. These include the following:

- Detecting contraband weapons and metal-enclosed explosives;
- Detecting missiles, explosive mines, and various sensing devices like bugging equipment;
- Preventing individuals from removing large inventories of base metals necessarily stored in areas where access is difficult to control;
- Detecting narcotic needles;
- Detecting precious metals in small quantities, such as silver, gold, and platinum;
- Detecting magnets that might be used to sabotage computer tapes;
- Detecting attempts to remove magnetic computer tapes;
- Sensing the movement of vehicles for parking control, toll counting, and so on;
- Detecting metals underwater (for example, in the salvage of wrecks).

Industries using metal detection equipment include refiners and smelters, auto and appliance manufacturers, electronic and computer manufacturers, manufacturers and suppliers of guns, jewelry manufacturers, silversmiths, mints, and computer data centers. In addition, many military applications are special in nature.

Metal inspection equipment should be carefully designed, thoroughly field tested, and capable of a wide range of applications. This means it should have a sensitivity range that can be adjusted to detect only large masses such as handguns and knives or set to detect small pieces of precious metals such as gold and silver no larger in mass than a dime.

PRECAUTIONS AT MAXIMUM SENSITIVITY

Some equipment has this range of capability. However, when maximum sensitivity is required (as in detecting small amounts of precious metals), the environment of the equipment, particularly the structural components in the surrounding area, becomes critical to the equipment's proper use. Under these circumstances, the inspection unit should be so located that there is no large moving metal surface within 20 to 25 feet in front of or behind the equipment threshold. Similarly, moving metal surfaces or other magnetic fields produced by additional metal inspection units should be approximately 20 feet away from the adjacent sides of metal inspection units. In contrast, the distance of moving metal surfaces adjacent to the exterior sides of metal detection threshold units is not as critical—usually 3 feet is adequate. One should look for moving metal in elevators, escalators, lightweight interior metal partitions, moving metal doors, overhead conveyors, towmotors, and magnetic fields generated by high-voltage electrical equipment.

ADDITIONAL FEATURES

Other desirable features of metal detection equipment include the following:

1. The equipment should be self-contained and capable of operating either on conventional AC power supplies or on a battery power supply. These features will permit easy relocation of the equipment as necessary.
2. The equipment should include the capability of remote supervision, thus permitting one security guard to monitor systems at two or more locations. Remote monitoring is only practical when searching for large metal masses. Where extreme sensitivity is required, a guard must be present and provision must be made for instructing individuals passing through the equipment field to remove all jewelry and metallic objects from their person. Such items include cigarette packages, fountain pens and pencils, watches, belt buckles, penknives, coins, keys, key rings, and so forth. It is seldom practical to remove undergarments having metal supports.
3. Metal inspection equipment should not affect or damage items sensitive to magnetic fields, such as magnetic tapes, X-ray and photographic film, and so on.
4. Basic walk-through inspection units should be supplemented by handheld scanning devices that allow security personnel to pinpoint the source of a metal detection signal. These devices are used to identify irrelevant metal in undergarments, safety shoes, shoe arches, fillings in teeth, orthopedic devices, and so forth.
5. Walk-through systems should readily fit into a standard door or corridor 36 inches or less in width.
6. The sensitivity adjustment should be accessible but secured to prevent tampering. Access should be by pick-resistant lock cylinder keys controlled by authorized personnel, since in some applications it may be necessary to change sensitivity levels during the course of a day's operations. For example, a firm handling precious metals might wish to inspect visitors for weapons that could be used in a robbery attack. In the same day, the inspection equipment would be used as usual to check individuals leaving the plant to detect any unauthorized attempts to remove precious metal.
7. Equipment that has the capability of detecting low-mass precious metals such as metallic powders, salts, and solutions would be desirable. No existing equipment is foolproof in this application, but while the equipment available will not always detect small quantities of low-mass materials, it sometimes does, deterring the would-be criminal by offering a substantial risk of apprehension for a relatively small potential gain.
8. The equipment must require little or no maintenance since the number

of manufacturers and the extent of their service facilities and replacement part stocks, are extremely limited at present.

Other desirable features include the ability to conceal the equipment under certain conditions to detect large masses of metal being moved from the premises or from storage areas. Of course, the inspection unit must not produce any harmful physical effects on individuals using pacemakers.

For the most part, equipment is available that meets all these requirements. One device, which detects ferrous metal masses only, is concealed in a flashlight.

The cost of equipment ranges from $300 to $500 for portable handheld devices and from $2,000 to $5,000 for more sophisticated door-frame or standard industrial process units. The latter often involve custom engineering to the electromechanical requirements of the specific application.

X-RAY EQUIPMENT

As commercial users of metal detection and inspection systems have gained experience, some have improved their metal detection programs by the installation of manual-feed or conveyorized X-ray systems identical to those used in airports to search luggage and personal effects. Such equipment, which meets government radiation limit standards, simplifies and improves a security officer's ability to detect contraband material secreted in wallets, purses, thermos bottles, lunch pails, shoes, and other containers. As precious metals are of a higher density, such materials placed within other metal containers are readily distinguished by X-ray.

X-ray equipment affords other advantages such as reducing time required to inspect personal items, eliminating most of the negative reaction to removing and touching an employee's personal property, and imparting a level of sophistication that puts a metal inspection program on a higher professional level. In turn, companies using X-ray in their programs report improved employee attitude toward the inspection process and improved performance by the security officers involved.

Costs of X-ray equipment range from $12,000 for manual-feed systems to $35,000 to $40,000 for conveyorized systems capable of handling several hundred parcels or totes per hour. It is noted that, for this application, the user must select a system in which the X-ray tube is mounted to provide for vertical rather than horizontal scanning of personal effects.

WEAKNESSES OF METAL DETECTION SYSTEMS USE

The two most significant weaknesses in the effectiveness of metal inspection systems are:

- Faulty or careless operation by security personnel, often including discriminatory screening;
- Unwillingness on the part of operations management to modify the premises, the work hours, and the points of entry and exit to maximize the utility of the metal detection equipment.

These weaknesses are fortunately compensated for by one simple fact: The ability of the equipment to detect metal may be variable but only within a narrow range—the would-be criminal can never be sure he will be able to pass through without a detection indication and further search. When you think like a thief, uncertainty of success is a strong psychological deterrent.

45

Bomb Threat Planning

Bombs Away

$125,000 FIRE HITS SECOND COAST BANK

Oct. 26 (AP)—Fire that the authorities said had been set by an arsonist badly damaged a branch bank near a University of California campus early today.

"Death to pigs" and other messages were sprayed on the branch's outside wall with black paint.

Fire Marshal Jay Trotter of Orange County said a preliminary investigation indicated that a flammable liquid had been used to start the fire. Damage was estimated at $125,000.

It was the second major fire at a campus branch of the bank this year in California. Last February, demonstrators, saying the bank represented the "establishment," burned down a branch adjacent to another University of California campus.

Other branches of this bank have been targets of fire bombers and window breakers.

The interior of the bank, located south of Los Angeles, was burned out. Nine other businesses in the same two-story concrete building sustained smoke damage. The bank occupies the first floor.

BOMB THREATS ARE SERIOUS

Bomb threats once were idle chatter. Today such phone calls are taken seriously. Financial institutions, major corporations, museums, universities, and governmental installations (federal, state, or local, military or civilian) are common objects of attack. Branches of key U.S. banking institutions have been severely damaged. Operational hubs—the nerve centers of corporate giants—have been repeatedly attacked with significant damage to property and life. Major chemical plants, oil refineries, and aircraft have been bombed.

During 1969 there were 602 major bombings in the United States. In 1972 roughly 2,000 such attacks occurred. In 1969, 12,000 pounds of explosives were sold to civilian users by munitions suppliers across country, and during the first 5 months of 1970 over 18,000 pounds of explosives (military and civilian) fell into "enemy hands."[1]

These attacks against major institutions were hardly symbolic, and their success in damage, disruption, and publicity has attracted many imitators. The conflicts of foreign nations are producing terrorist attacks in uninvolved countries around the world. Every day corporations and public institutions large and small receive domestic and international threats, by telephone and mail, most involving real or hoax extortion or ransom demands.

It has reached the point where some swear to the veracity of the story of the hard-pressed bank security officer who was the recipient of that inevitable phone call just before 2:00 P.M. on a Friday. The voice on the other end growled, "There is a bomb in your building set to go off at 2:00 P.M.—better get everybody out." The stunned security officer looked at his watch and blurted, "Gee, I have a staff meeting at 2:00; couldn't you make it 3:00?"

It is one of the happier American traits that we tend to laugh at ourselves, particularly in a time of crisis, but there is no doubt that bomb threats are not really a joking matter. More and worse terrorism may well lie ahead.

PREPLANNING ESSENTIAL

Thus, another assignment has been added to all the other hats worn by the security officer. Plans must be developed for coping with the threat of bomb attack and for the safety of company employees, customers, and property. In addition, security officers responsible for high-value, high-risk operations must decide whether a bomb threat is due to the company's stature as part of "the establishment" or occurs because a bomb or a bomb threat evacuation would facilitate a burglary or robbery. Ready cash is a necessity for subversive activities, and explosives have been used in aid of robbery for this purpose.

Readers may recall the devastating 1969 bomb attack against the Danbury (Connecticut) police station. While the news media handled it as an attack against a police station and, hence, a blow at law and order, the actual target was the department's alarm supervisory panels, to which were connected burglary and holdup systems for most of Danbury's banks, jewelers, and other high-risk businesses. Immediately after the bombing the attackers proceeded to rob one of Danbury's banks, secure in the knowledge that the police alarm supervisory center was knocked out, no alarm could register, and hence there would be no police response. Clearly, where high

[1] Not all explosives are munitions. For example, the $3 million blast that leveled the mathematics building of the University of Wisconsin was an explosion of a truckload of fertilizer, appropriately treated and triggered.

risk and high values are concerned, the course of action charted by the security officer must be concerned not only with problems of evacuation but also with methods for the protection of assets while the building is evacuated.

EVACUATION

Probably the most difficult decision, and one for which there is no magic formula, is that of whether or not to evacuate the building in the event of a bomb threat. If a definite policy decision can be established that evacuation will take place, this eliminates any calculated risk (guessing whether the bomb threat is real or false) and gives priority to the safety of the people in the building. However, while it may be a simple matter to evacuate a banking floor or the retail ground floor of a commercial building, one security officer responsible for tenants in a major high-rise office building discovered that simply notifying all the tenants that a bomb threat had been received would take more than an hour and a half.

A BOMB PREVENTION POLICY

Government booklets are available that offer guidelines from which policies can be established to cope with bomb threats.[2] Generally, the security program should include the following:

1. Determine what bomb search and bomb disposal services are available from local police, fire, and other governmental agencies; how they are to be contacted in an emergency; what procedures they recommend; and whether they will survey your premises to identify areas that might offer opportunities for bomb concealment.[3]
2. Establish strict procedures for the control (and inspection, if necessary) of packages and materials going into critical areas such as vaults, tellers' sections, elevators, public rooms and restrooms, as well as heating, air conditioning, electrical and communications areas, fuel and storage areas, and crawlspaces above ceilings. All rooms, halls, and occupancies having a wall common to a vault or computer room should be included in "critical area" precautions.
3. Develop a positive means of identifying personnel for whom access

---

[2] Office of the Provost Marshal General, Department of the Army, the Pentagon, Washington D.C. 20315. Also Defense Civil Preparedness Agency, Department of Defense, Washington, D.C. 20315.

[3] Where local police do not have bomb disposal units there is access to an Explosive Ordnance Disposal unit of the Army. One such unit is designated for each region of the United States.

to critical areas is authorized, as well as means for excluding those not authorized.

4. Instruct personnel as to why they should be alert and why they should promptly report the presence of suspicious persons or objects (like unidentified parcels) to designated supervisors.
5. Provide for frequent physical checks (or for surveillance) of critical areas to ensure that unauthorized persons are not hiding, loitering, or reconnoitering. Lock accessible unoccupied spaces such as telephone equipment and machinery (elevator and air conditioning) rooms.
6. Take adequate protective measures for safeguarding records essential to the business, including duplication of records or computer tapes if their loss would seriously hamper operations. Be sure to store duplicate records off premises. In one bombing, a company's 24-hour computer operation was undamaged, but structural damage to the building prevented resumption of operations for several weeks.
7. Instruct all personnel, beginning with telephone switchboard operators, as to the sequence of actions to be followed in the event a bomb threat call is received. Operators should seek to learn from the caller, if possible, the location(s) of the explosives, the reason for the attack, and the name of the party calling. Voice recorders should be interfaced to switchboard lines to facilitate the taping of such messages. Procedures established must include notifying authorities, alerting evacuation supervisors or floor wardens and the company fire brigade, signaling evacuation, securing assets, commencing a search, and turning off fuel and nonessential[4] power supplies.

Other protective and deterrent measures include closed-circuit TV surveillance, metal detection units at critical points, pick-resistant lock cylinders protecting unattended areas, and visitor pass and identification systems. Intruder motion-detection alarm systems, like adequate safe and vault structures, are as essential to defense against a closed-period bomb attack as they are against burglary attack.

The decision and responsibility for bomb threat response must be delegated. Security officers whose powers and responsibilities are spelled out in clearly defined corporate policy are able to proceed in a rapid and efficient manner. Where corporate, company, or facility policy is lacking, the general discussion of possible bomb threat policy will evoke many emotional and unfulfilled (not fun-filled) hours of discussion with officers and executives who dislike even the contemplation of a problem so distasteful. Assistance and support in motivating policy planning may be available from local law enforcement; many police departments have bomb squads, bomb disposal units, and public relations officers who can furnish charts, photographic

[4] Loss of electrical power to a computer could cause as much damage as a bomb, depending upon the individual installation.

slides, and physical dummies of explosive and incendiary devices. Solicit their cooperation, where possible, in presenting bomb threat issues directly and squarely to executives responsible for establishing bomb threat response policy.

One final word: The author strongly recommends that security officers traveling to company plants in other cities do not carry dummy incendiary or explosive devices with them for training purposes. Explaining such suitcase items to airline personnel and fearful fellow passengers can be an embarrassing experience at best. At worst, you can find yourself repeating your explanations to airline security people, sky marshals, airport security, local police, and the FBI—long after your plane has departed!

46

Commercial Office Building Security

Building Security Blocks

Shortly after commercial business hours one spring evening late in the 1960s, a security guard in a big-city high-rise office building received a telephone call saying a bomb had been planted in an elevator shaft of the building. A pre-established plan was promptly implemented to alert tenants still at work and to seal off the elevators[1] until a thorough search could be made.

The bomb exploded before the search could be concluded. The damage was extensive, and months passed before the necessary repairs could be completed.

This building did not house government facilities or a firm manufacturing war material. It was a commercial office building owned by a major financial institution identified by activists as an "establishment" target.

The building was almost new and well constructed, and the security provided was outstanding. One might understandably wonder if the attack could not have been prevented or its effect lessened, but the answer is, "Probably not"—at least at that time.

EVALUATION OF RISK

The extent of vulnerability to criminal activity will vary from building to building, but the following factors offer a basis for evaluation.

Access into and out of the Building

If the criminal can enter and leave through unsupervised entrances and exits without being delayed by pedestrian traffic, he will rate the building

[1] Due to the standard "service core" design of high-rise buildings, elevator shafts are necessarily close to the most probable areas for bomb placement (rest rooms, utility rooms, and so forth). As a result, elevators should not be used for evacuation.

a prime target. If the crime contemplated requires heavy or bulky equipment, as in a vault burglary attack, the criminal will be particularly encouraged by accessible and unsupervised freight entrances, freight elevators, and unprotected stairwells by which he can bring in the tools of his trade without arousing suspicion. These unsecured points of access also offer criminals the important alternative exits the professional seeks.

Proximity of Building to Similar Structures

A highly concentrated, downtown commercial business area guarantees a heavy stream of traffic. Employees, messengers, clients, vendors, and delivery personnel flowing in and out create a degree of congestion that provides "cover" for the criminal. For the criminal wishing to avoid public lobby entrances, particularly those manned by security guards or building personnel, adjacent buildings connecting by interior passageways or unsecured doors or windows only a few feet away from unsecured openings in an adjacent building provide other access advantages.

Environment of Building

A building in a city having a high crime rate, or located in close proximity to an urban ghetto, a campus, a government complex, or a park area, is statistically more likely to be attacked. Therefore, security in such buildings should be high.

New Concepts in Development

Commercial developers are designing complexes that include mall areas and hotel spaces in addition to commercial offices. The problems associated with access control to the commercial areas require new approaches, addition of security personnel, closed-circuit TV, and improved access control systems.

Kind of Business Occupancy and Class of Visitors

Enterprises that may have increased probability of attack include branch banks, some government agencies, foreign consulates, international airline offices, war-associated companies, and places of entertainment. Individual tenants and visitors who might attract criminal attention include politicians, diplomats, scientists, gamblers, bail bondsmen, prostitutes, and criminal syndicate leaders.

CRIME CONSEQUENCES

The effects of successful criminal attack in commercial buildings include *physical injury* to victimized tenants and visitors; *major building damage* (the cumulative cost of removing graffiti, replacing broken glass, repairing doors, and replacing equipment stolen or damaged by vandals can be as great as the cost of a bomb blast); *civil damages* for negligence based on building management's failure to take reasonable precautions to protect the lives and property of tenants and visitors; *loss of rental income* as frightened tenants move to safer sites such as suburban high-rise office buildings; and *increased employee turnover* (with its resulting inefficiency and wasted training time) as employees seek safer places to work.

There is no doubt about it—in few U.S. cities can building management afford to procrastinate much longer in regard to security. As urban crime rates rise generally, crime in high-rise buildings accelerates. And as law enforcement concentrates its primary efforts on protecting the citizen in the street and in his home, the criminal will inevitably turn to the high-rise office building as a more inviting arena for his operations.

Clearly, building management must make positive efforts to protect its assets: the building structure, the occupancy ratio, and rental income. Once the necessity is recognized, building management can readily reduce vulnerability to an acceptable (and profitable) level. Tenants will pay higher rent in a well-secured building and will stay longer in safer, securer surroundings. Indeed, in recent years many building leaders have preplanned security into new buildings, particularly those tailored for the needs of a specific industry. The success of these projects is stimulating a trend toward incorporating building security and procedures in future building, both generally and to meet specific needs.

INITIATING THE SECURITY PROGRAM

To achieve effective security in an office building, four steps must be executed in sequence. First, the building owner or management team must establish which single individual shall have the responsibility for security and the authority (with the approval of the board of directors or the building owner) to prepare and implement a security program. Second, their designee, the security officer, must analyze, by a physical inspection of the building (or plans), the overall vulnerability and the specific risks represented by individual tenants. Third, expert advice may be sought for the security analysis and must be obtained in regard to guard services, alarm systems, and security hardware. Fourth, the security officer should complete his "blueprint for security" with the development of an overall plan incorporating open-hours access control, alarm systems for restricted areas, the means to be used in securing the building during closed periods, and sound security procedures for tenants as well as for the effective functioning of building guards.

Let's examine in detail the steps essential to the development of a total security plan for an office building. The following sections discuss the most important steps.

Access Control

It is impossible to control access completely where thousands legitimately pass in and out each day. Regardless of age or size, commercial office buildings offer opportunities for many forms of criminal attack including vandalism, riots, bombings, burglary, robbery, rape, assault, sneak theft, arson, industrial sabotage or espionage, fraud, and the occasional fake personal injury staged by an employee or visitor.

Thus, the most difficult problem in commercial building security is that of controlling lobby access during open-for-business hours. Multiple street entrances, multiple elevator banks, and escalators to floors above or below street level all complicate access control. The volume of foot traffic is apt to be heavy throughout the day and overwhelming during peak hours. Under these circumstances and in risk locations, several security guards could be necessary simply to deter vandals, to provide limited surveillance to deter suspicious individuals, and to check unauthorized visitors in restricted building areas.

In high-risk buildings, tenant employees and building personnel should be issued (and show) ID cards including photographs, and arrangements should be made to accept delivery and messenger services at a street-level reception area rather than permitting these visitors unrestricted access to other floors of the building. Relatively simple procedures and a wide range of access control devices can be utilized to exclude the unwanted visitor in all but the most sophisticated situations. The basic interior access control rules are as follows:

1. Never admit a service person without identifying him by his credentials and by confirming, with the supervising officer of his firm, the fact that these credentials and his errand are valid.
2. Never permit any previous visitor unquestioned access to the premises when no one has requested his visit.
3. Service personnel necessarily admitted to areas where critical records or valuable stocks exist should be escorted to and from the area and supervised while within the area.

4. Customers and officials accorded special privileges should be denied access to critical areas or escorted within them.
5. Keys should be issued only to those who must have access and only for those specific points within the premises necessary for that individual. Keying of locks should be changed periodically and keys maintained under proper control. Lock cylinders should also be rekeyed whenever a key-holding employee has been terminated for cause or a key has been lost.

In smaller buildings having only one entrance and a single bank of elevators, a single security guard may perform the control function since his post can be located to permit him to check everyone entering through the public lobby. Automated identification and other automatic access controls are easily adapted to such circumstances, with employees and tenants of the building using the automatic access equipment, freeing the security guard for the screening of visitors. This is well accepted in practice because the guard appears to be functioning as a receptionist and maintaining an information desk service.

To be effective, access control must be maintained throughout the entire open period. This necessitates not only luncheon and break relief for the guard but also a second shift to ensure coverage from early arrivals to late departures.

Where an entire floor or several floors is occupied by a single major tenant, employee access control and visitor identification for the tenant may be controlled at a receptionist position on each tenant floor. Indeed, in some high-rise buildings individual doors opening into public hallways are kept locked. Visitors must go to a reception point on each floor for identification and be met by an employee who acts as an escort.

Since the cost of a single security guard (including fringe benefits) is estimated at $10,000 to $12,000 per year, closed-circuit television is often substituted for additional guards or utilized as backup for limited guard forces. Closed-circuit TV is used at key points to improve security in critical areas and on individual floors to ensure the safe flow of employee, tenant, and visitor traffic from lobby to destination. Of course, since in most applications someone must supervise the monitor(s) and respond when necessary, closed-circuit TV is not a total labor-saving system.

Tenant Premises

To provide a competent level of security, the overall building security program must have the cooperation of tenants. Since failure of the tenant to provide security within his own premises can seriously affect the building's security program, every effort must be made to obtain tenant cooperation. Today, most tenants can be "sold" on cooperation since effective building security means reducing theft of office equipment, petty cash, and employees' handbags and wallets and less chance of physical attack against employees. Tenants should, and usually do, recognize that a safer place to work means less employee turnover, higher morale, and better use of working time.

The building management security officer must identify the person within each tenancy to whom that tenant's security responsibilities have been delegated. He should arrange to meet with this individual to review the tenant's security (and particular risk) and to acquaint him with the building security plan in general terms. Conflicts are best ironed out prior to the tenant's commencing his occupancy within the building.

When new security programs are established or existing plans amended, the tenant's security representative should be promptly advised as to the changes and the reasons for them. Each tenant's security officer should supply and maintain an up-to-date list of the names and telephone numbers of responsible management people to be contacted in the event of an emergency affecting their premises. He should also be required to supply a list of personnel authorized to enter during closed periods. Both lists should be periodically checked to be sure that they are still entirely current.

Some tenants may elect to keep corridor doors locked. Others may provide an enclosed reception or lobby area within their premises with a receptionist to receive and identify visitors and employees before they are admitted to work areas. In this arrangement, an electric strike or lock release may be used to release the interior door from the receptionist's desk, or the person to be visited must provide an escort from the reception area. In high-risk applications, it is desirable to wire the electric strike latch circuit by a method that permits the remote release of the tenant's inner door only when the exterior door is closed and latched. In such high-risk installations, the receptionist should be separated from the entrance foyer by bullet-resistant glass. A special pass-through device can allow the receptionist to receive packages and letters safely.

If solid panel exterior doors are required and an interior double-door security foyer arrangement is not possible, a wide-vision peephole and voice communications link will permit employees to identify visitors before opening the door. This arrangement of course cannot approach the security of the safely overseen double-door security foyer. Where safety codes permit, dead bolt locks should be installed on all extraneous or little used tenant corridor doors because snaplatch locks are vulnerable to several common types of criminal attacks.

When the building houses tenants engaged in high-risk businesses, the building security officer should make every effort to coordinate building security with the security program of the tenant. Appropriate cooperative efforts include ensuring that the hours during which the building provides public area security will cover the tenant's scheduled open time; promptly admitting (but care in identifying) alarm company guards responding to burglar alarm signals from the tenant's premises during closed periods;[2] permitting the high-risk tenant to secure his premises with non-master-keyed high-security locks, using closed-circuit television to monitor building corridor(s) adjoining the tenant's premises; alarms on fire stair and freight elevator doors signaling in the lobby; securing freight elevators with power-off locks; and stopping unauthorized passenger elevator service to the tenant's floor during the closed period.

In return for those services, the high-risk tenant should be prepared to develop and maintain his own security against robbery, theft, and burglary. The high-risk tenant should be as aware as the building security officer that his high-value status may attract more criminals to the building, visits that could lead to burglary and robbery attacks against other building tenants.

Warranties from Private Security Contractors

Contracts and agreements with alarm contractors and suppliers of security equipment for the building should be carefully reviewed by building management counsel and the terms of the contract clearly understood by the building security officer. Security contractors should be required to report in writing all visits to the building, the reasons for such visits, the time they were within the building premises, the type of work performed, and procedures relating to the use of building keys. Logs of alarm report/response should be maintained so that building management can spot and correct situations where equipment trouble or tenant error is producing false alarms.

Shipping and Receiving Areas

Building shipping and receiving docks should be supervised by a security guard or by building personnel capable of maintaining security procedures and assigned full time to the freight-handling function. Receiving security measures should include the following:

- Fencing or partitions to restrict access to merchandise, equipment, and raw materials;
- Allowing no drivers beyond the receiving window or loading dock entrance;
- Separating telephone and restroom facilities for waiting drivers in large commercial buildings;

[2] An uninstructed night building guard admitted an impersonator posing as an alarm serviceman 27 times in 2 months. Indications are that the impersonator was actually visiting the unprotected telephone terminal box. Fifteen high risks, including a branch bank, were located in the building, and all alarm lines were labeled.

- Manning freight elevators within the building at all times except when the elevator is secured by power-off locks;
- Requiring tenants into whose premises freight elevators open to supervise their floor's loading dock, including the receipt or dispatch of materials at the elevator. This can be assisted by fencing or partitioning to create a secured freight reception area, by use of closed-circuit TV and alarms, and by adequately controlling access to and from the elevator.
- Requiring a record of any material leaving the building through the freight area, either by a pass from a tenant (signed by an authorized individual) identifying the size and nature of the outgoing package or shipment or by completion of a log entry listing the pertinent information (name and signature of the individual, tenant releasing the shipment, number of packages, tenant's waybill number, and so on);[3]
- Prohibiting access from shipping and receiving areas into fire stairwells or building plant and equipment areas, except in emergencies;
- Securing all openings between the freight area and the building by adequate key-operated locks. Closed-circuit TV and alarms are also used at these points.

Video-recorded closed-circuit television is an effective tool for supervising receiving and shipping docks during the open-for-business period and may deter theft by both "visitors" and employees. Large convex mirrors can increase the area overlooked by guards and shipping personnel at fixed stations.

SECURING BUILDING PLANT, EQUIPMENT, AND RESTROOM AREAS

Restrooms accessible from public corridors and lobbies should also be kept locked, and since the number of tenants' employees and visitors using keys to these facilities will be many, provisions should be made for frequent lock cylinder changes. Restrooms should be regularly checked by guards (at a minimum, at the close of each day's business), to check for packages that could conceal a bomb and for hide-ins waiting for night to launch a closed-period criminal attack. More frequent daytime sight checks of the restroom latch and strike provide some assurance against jamming to keep the latch from securing the door.

Doors to building heating, air conditioning, electrical, plumbing, elevator machinery, and telephone equipment should be kept locked at all times, as should be utility closets and supply rooms on each floor. Only security

---

[3] Tenant passes are sometimes also required for packages going out through office building lobbies.

personnel and a limited number of authorized building maintenance persons should be assigned, or have access to, keys to these doors. Where possible, the locks securing these doors should not be included in any master key system. Similar care should be taken to secure elevator shafts, trap doors, drop ceilings, and equipment panels.

These measures substantially reduce vulnerability to explosive or incendiary attack in these areas, as well as expedite effective building searches. Not only do these areas offer concealment for bombs, but also attacks here could "knock out" the entire building operation.

Hide-in attackers also utilize these spaces. For these reasons, such untrafficked areas and access points should be secured around the clock by dead bolt locks having pick-resistant cylinders. In addition, a strict key control and accountability system should be established and maintained. Lock cylinders should be changed at frequent intervals, particularly when a key-holding employee is terminated and certainly when a key is lost. Naturally, this task will be easier if equipment and utility rooms are not keyed to the building's master key system.

Telephone equipment rooms in commercial buildings are extremely vulnerable. Besides bomb attacks and wiretapping, the compromise of alarm telephone circuits of high-risk tenants is done here. Keys to these rooms should be kept under the strictest control, and both the identity of persons claiming to be telephone or alarm company employees and their assignment should be verified each time through calling their company before they are granted access. Telephone terminal circuit diagrams should be secured by the telephone company away from the premises (see Chapter 37).

Generally, outside services personnel should not be admitted to building plant and equipment areas without proper identification. They should also log in and out, and the log should include their employee identification number, time of arrival and departure, nature of their visit, and so forth.

When the building is considered to be a likely target for bomb attack or sabotage, a building security guard or maintenance employee should accompany the outside serviceman while he works in critical areas. If the building has a security center manned during the open period, closed-circuit TV surveillance of critical building plant and equipment areas offers an efficient alternative for supervising the activities of most outside service people. It is impossible to overemphasize the necessity for safeguarding these vital building "organs." Failure of heating, air conditioning, or elevator service or structural damage may result in the immediate loss of rental income.

Cleaners

Business concerns prefer to avoid interruption in employees' work activities by having cleaning performed during the closed period. Like many other conveniences, the presence of cleaning personnel in a closed building and within the tenants' closed premises seriously weakens any security program.

Building management should provide tenant cleaning services only during the open period, and regulations for tenants should include the requirement that the tenant may engage his own cleaning service provided this service is performed during the tenant's normal business hours. In either case, personnel engaged as cleaners or admitted to perform a cleaning service should be screened as a condition of the maintenance contract. In addition, they should be bonded—an incentive for the maintenance company and its insurer to conduct an adequate background investigation. Other building cleaning services such as window washing and floor waxing should be performed under the direct supervision of the building security officer.

Stairwells and Towers

To the extent permitted by applicable municipal safety codes, fire exit doors should be secured against entrance to intermediate floors from the fire stairs or to the stairs from the exterior of the building. Where possible, egress from stairwells should be limited to street-level public lobby exits that can be supervised by security personnel because fire stairwells are a favorite escape route for criminals.

Doors opening onto roofs, skylights, and other hatches should be locked[4] during both the open and the closed periods. Rooftops are frequently accessible from adjoining buildings, and rooftop appurtenances provide cover where criminals can hide until it is time for a closed-period burglary attack.

Window-washing equipment housed on the exterior of the building or at roof level should have locked manual operation controls as well as power-off locks. This equipment could otherwise be used for vandalism or to gain access to unprotected windows opening into the premises of high-risk tenants. Fire exit doors and stairwells should be subject to frequent patrol by security guards to discourage intruders and to be sure door lock mechanisms and strikes have not been tampered with.

Parking Lots and Garage Areas

Exterior parking lots and building garage areas should be extremely well lighted. In high-crime areas, parking should be supervised and watched by security guards or closed-circuit TV (with immediate guard response) during both open and closed periods. Employees working late should be given par-

---

[4] During the open period, fire exits should be locked to the outside but unlocked from the inside for emergency exit.

ticular attention while between the elevator and their automobiles. If the building is not well secured, night worker escort should begin at the office. Tenant personnel should be warned against using fire stairwells and any poorly lit or lightly traveled routes to the parking area.

Parking areas are also vulnerable to attack by explosives. For example, an "armed" vehicle can be driven into the parking building, parked, and left with sufficient time remaining for the perpetrators to travel a safe distance before the time-delayed explosion takes place.[5] Periodically changed tenant car identification stickers assist in identifying unauthorized cars.

Elevators

Automatic elevators should be equipped with emergency signals that, without stopping the elevator, will alert a security guard to a problem. The alarm-actuating devices should lock in to enable security officers to identify the specific elevator involved and should be designed to minimize the chance of false alarms due to curiosity. A simple wiring change can also cause the elevator alarm to sound if the door is held or propped open longer than a predetermined 1 or 2 minutes, facilitating traffic and deterring disabling the elevator by this means.

When floor lock-out controls are installed at the elevator control panel to secure individual floors from elevator access during closed hours, the lock switches should have UL-listed pick-resistant cylinder inserts. Similarly, elevator control units should have locked cover plates, and headless screws or similar security fasteners should secure elevator equipment panels against tampering and disabling. Provision must be made for the manual or key-controlled operation of passenger elevators in the event of emergencies but only under fire department or building personnel control (never under automatic operation, which can hold the elevator open at a fire-involved floor).

As many passenger elevators should be shut down at the close of the business day as possible and power to these elevators switched off. If at all possible, elevators left operable should be manned. In one new high-rise building, during closed hours one can only exit to the manned lobby; the elevator cannot be directed to another floor. If a tenant wishes to go to his office during closed hours, he must present to the lobby security guard a coded identification card that is checked through a computer. The lobby is monitored by video-recorded closed-circuit TV cameras. The guard then activates one elevator to go to the authorized floor only; it cannot be taken to another floor. This procedure can be completely automated if traffic in closed hours warrants the expense. The freight elevator is manned by a guard around the clock, and if the guard is called away by an emergency,

---

[5] A bank headquarters was saved when a guard became suspicious of a car parked next to the building. The car contained 150 pounds of dynamite and a timing device.

he locks the elevator against operation. Fire stairwells are alarmed, and the flights leading to the exits are covered by closed-circuit TV.

In addition, certain major tenants in the building have extended the building access control system to use the identification card for after- and before-hours entry to each floor's office area. Each entry is automatically recorded.

BUILDING EXTERIOR/PERIMETER SECURITY

Commercial office buildings rarely retain their original floor plans over the years. Security features incorporated into the original design are often distorted or eliminated by alterations, while structural additions or changes may increase accessibility. Tenant alterations such as interior stairwells and penthouses contribute weaknesses. In the latter case, precautions must be taken to deny intruders entry into the building from the roof or an adjacent offset as well as to make certain the tenant is aware of the security problem his alterations have created.

Perimeter Security Survey

Window and door grilles protecting accessible ground-level openings must be checked to determine if they are properly installed and rechecked at intervals thereafter. Are bolts and hinges on the inside? Are they still in good condition, or have rust and masonry deterioration weakened the physical security they are intended to provide?

Are there permanent or temporary ladders against or affixed to the exterior of the building? What doors or windows are accessible to exterior ladders or fire escapes? Are divider spikes or barbed wire barring access from adjoining buildings still intact?

If local exit alarm devices are installed on emergency doors, have the batteries that power their horns or sirens been changed within safe time limits? Are the exit alarms key locked in the on position at all times? Are building perimeter doors checked at the close of business to ensure they are locked and secured to the outside? Is ground-floor lighting, exterior and interior, maintained at proper levels to permit police and passersby to detect intruders in sight through street-level glass? Finally, are tenant doors and accessible windows actually or only apparently secured?

In recent years, there has been an increased use of UL-approved burglary-resistant glass in new building construction for street-level doors, facades, and windows. While this material, consisting of thin sheets of a tough plastic sandwiched between the plate glass, is not burglary proof, it is burglary resistant and will prevent entry by all but the most determined (and unhurried) criminals.

While there are lighter, less-expensive UL-listed burglary-resistant plastic glazing materials, most—if not all—are easily defaced and therefore unsuitable for exterior glazing. Sharp instruments, acid, and paints will permanently mark these plastics, but minor scratches can be buffed out.

EVACUATION PLANNING

In large buildings, maps showing evacuation routes are desirable in public areas (and large tenant areas) on each floor. These maps would, of course, be in addition to compliance with local building codes requiring signs that indicate the location of emergency stairwells. On the evacuation maps, different stairwells can be color coded or identified by letters or numbers, "floor wardens" identified, and instructions given in both English and a foreign language if suitable. These floor evacuation plans are of the utmost value in facilitating prompt and safe building evacuation under emergency conditions. The development and periodic detailed review of these plans assist building management executives in the prudent examination of their responsibilities in evacuation from present-day security problems to the physical condition of stairwells and fire escapes.

SEARCH AT CLOSING

Just prior to securing the building at the end of the business day, guards should carefully search and secure, or check the securing of, all building plant and equipment areas, stairwell doors, and other entrances from public lobbies or corridors. Restrooms should be searched and checked to be sure they are locked. Tenants' premises already closed, whether occupied or not, should have corridor doors locked.

Searches by tenants within high-risk locations such as banking operations and fur and jewelry stores are necessary to rule out lock-in intruders who stay behind for a burglary or early-morning ambush attack. Individuals found in the building after the close of business should not be regarded simply as vagrants or vandals. Criminals use any excuse as a pretext for casing premises prior to attack. Strangers lacking confirmable reasons for their presence should be required to furnish positive identification, and police assistance should be requested to confirm the identification and to determine the purpose of the intruder's visit to the premises.

PATROL

During the closed period the building should be patrolled with continuing checks of doors and search of critical areas other than in tenants' premises.

The security guard should be alert for smoke, fire, gas, water leaks, and other emergency situations as well as the possibility of intrusion. Closed-circuit television can supplement or shorten guard tours.

SECURITY CENTERS

Where guards are used to secure a building, a suitable security enclosure is desirable. This might include the construction of a security center of bullet-resistant glass permitting the security guard both safety and the widest range of supervisory vision.[6] Security rooms should have nonkey push button combination locks or pick-resistant cylinders (with tight key control). More commonly, electric latch releases allow the security guard on duty to admit a visitor seeking access to the security center after identification. Some form of outside override must be provided for emergencies, however, since high-security fail-safe features lock the release automatically upon power failure. Where relief or egress might be denied, water, electric power, and restroom facilities should be included within the secured perimeter of the security center.

SUPERVISION OF SECURITY SYSTEMS

So far, our discussion has concentrated on access control for areas vulnerable during the open period and methods for securing the building—and floors within the building—during closed hours. There are approximately 120 closed-period hours per week, or three 40-hour tours. Using the standard formula of four to four-and-a-quarter full-time guards to cover three weekly 40-hour tours (the fourth guard is required to cover, for example, long weekend tour hours, holidays, sickness, and vacation relief), we can estimate the annual cost of one security guard per shift for the standard 3-shift closed period at $60,000 to $75,000.

Building management has various options: the use of employee guards or contract security guard services, periodic contract patrol service, a central station burglar alarm system with armed response or a police-connected burglar alarm system, or alarm devices (burglary, fire, air conditioning, and so on) supervised at a security center in the building. Generally speaking, when more than one security guard is needed for any of the closed-period tours, the economics of a proprietary system and security center are attractive.

This is neither an in-depth study nor a commentary on the problems, responsibilities, and advantages inherent in establishing a proprietary security force, but unless building management employs a full-time, experienced

[6] One such lobby-level security center is inconspicuous due to a facing material that provides a mirror effect that can be seen through from the inside.

security officer to handle this assignment, the supervision of the employee guard force presents special problems. Guards, whether directly employed or provided by a security contractor, should be trained in the handling of firearms, self-defense, civil defense, the laws of arrest for security personnel, and practical security procedures. Due to the competitive nature of the contract guard industry, the all-inclusive rates for contract service are not much higher than the cost to building management of employing security guards at prevailing wages plus employee benefits, uniforms, and equipment. Of course, when security guards are contracted, the liability potential is shared with an insured contractor.

Where guards are needed primarily during open hours, protecting the secured building during the closed period by means of remotely supervised alarm systems may be satisfactory. Wherever service is available from one or more central station alarm contractors, building management can contract for the monitoring of sprinklers, heating and air conditioning systems, pumps, and so on as well as for burglar alarm and fire alarm service. While most UL-approved fire and burglar alarm systems must necessarily be separated and each monitored by an individual leased telephone circuit, certain economies can still be achieved by obtaining both fire and intrusion alarm services from a single alarm contractor.

For closed-period supervision of stairwell doors, roof hatches, and other vulnerable openings, alarm contractors can provide special "zone annunciators" at a point of entry such as the lobby. While the entire intrusion alarm system signals over one leased telephone circuit to the central office, the zone annunciator at the building pinpoints the source of the alarm for the alarm company guard responding to the premises, permitting an effective search. When central station service is employed, the leased telephone circuit facilities may also be used to provide for the transmission of holdup alarms during the open period and for the protection of secured safes, vaults, and other high-risk points during the closed period.

The advantages of central station service in a commercial building include the cost savings accruing from the elimination of a security guard on duty at the premises during the closed period, the higher level of security provided by approved central station alarm systems, and the shifting of some liability to an experienced, approved contractor. The disadvantages include the elapsed time between the receipt of an alarm signal and the arrival on the premises of an alarm company guard (with or without police assistance) and the inability of alarm company servicemen to take corrective action with regard to closed-hours failure of heating, air conditioning, or alarm-monitored industrial processes.

PROPRIETARY SYSTEMS

When the security force required to protect the building reaches the 'round-the-clock level, employing one security guard or more on each tour, a proprietary alarm center becomes economically feasible, costing less to install and maintain than contract central station alarm systems and service. A proprietary system can be as simple as an alarm annunciator panel to which are connected fire alarm devices and intruder-detection equipment protecting doors and windows, vaults, and so forth. The proprietary panel may also monitor industrial systems processes. Many incorporate closed-circuit television. In some buildings locating the supervisory panel in the building engineer's facility might be effective; in another application, the panel might be installed at a reception desk in the building lobby. Regardless of location, the supervisory panel and its component equipment should be physically as well as electrically secured against attack. For these reasons, in most instances the security center is best located away from the lobby or, if located in a public area, housed in a bullet-resistant glass and steel enclosure.

The supervisory panel in a lobby security center facilitates a more economic deployment of security personnel during the open period. The lobby guard then serves two functions. If the building is of substantial size or the security level should be high, however, a lobby security center cannot be recommended.

If the decision is taken to establish a proprietary security system, the advice and services of experienced manufacturers who specialize in the design and installation of this special console-type equipment are essential. Detailed preliminary bids that incorporate all features desired should be obtained from more than one contractor. Each bidder must be able to design, manufacture, install, and service the equipment. The costs developed by the bids, together with those of later modifications or additions, and the hard realities of budget limitations are facts essential to finalizing the system specifications. Design of the system should consider both present and possible future needs for fire, intrusion, industrial process, and other desirable supervisory elements, two-way communications (both intercom and radio), and space for expanding the closed-circuit-television-monitoring capability.

The system should incorporate the following features:

- A printout unit (sealed against tampering) that automatically records the opening and closing time for all protected points, registers all alarm conditions and the time each is received, and records the time at which service is restored;
- A stand-by power supply capable of operating the system for 24 hours or more, in the event of sustained power failure;
- Provision for the remote supervision of alarm devices and systems—that is, the capability of connecting the alarm systems to a central station or a police department;
- Provision for a "delinquency unit" that, if not activated, will automatically report to a remote central station or a police headquarters the presumable inability of the security guard on duty to function as intended. A delinquency alarm signal should result in a response having

the priority of an "officer needs help" call. The proprietary center should also include a holdup or emergency signaling device by which the guard can silently summon aid if necessary;

- Provision for locating signaling alarm points by a graphic display to speed an appropriate response in large buildings. Consideration should always be given to the potential for supervising alarm signals from other buildings owned or managed by the same company. Obviously, such arrangements allow more efficient utilization of existing security manpower;
- Incorporation of remote two-way intercom stations if the building is in the planning stages. These remote stations will enable security guards investigating alarm conditions to report back to the security center promptly and in detail. These intercom stations may be used to monitor sound emanating from the area under alarm conditions and may also be used to facilitate evacuation in fire, bomb threat, or other emergencies;
- Radio communications equipment for immediate communication with security guards and key personnel. This equipment is often expanded to include coded paging and other features useful to both security and building management.

To summarize, the advantages of a proprietary system are the following:

- Cost savings,
- Day and night security supervision and control,
- Immediate response to and investigation of alarm conditions.

If manpower costs are excluded, a proprietary system generally costs less than complete central station service. Further, it offers superior security communications and remote closed-circuit TV surveillance at significant savings in building security manpower. Remote access control can be incorporated into the original console design or added at a future date.

The primary disadvantage of the proprietary alarm center is that most (but not all) such systems do not provide as sophisticated electronic circuitry and as high a degree of security as do line-security-equipped central station systems commonly employed for the protection of safes and vaults. Sometimes building management considers the possibility of extending proprietary intrusion alarm system services to tenants within the building. While this move may be practical and attractive to tenants, it is not prudent for high-risk applications.

Most tenants whose stocks are in the "most wanted" categories must have UL-approved alarm service in order to meet insurance requirements. While there is a UL standard applicable to proprietary monitoring equipment, such service would not normally satisfy an insurer of a high risk. Further, while building management could furnish part of the security protection for such a tenant, with the balance provided by an alarm company, in the event of a loss a dispute as to the division of responsibility could very well arise. Special liability insurance should be purchased to cover the building management's risk if the decision is made to provide alarm supervisory services for tenants at the proprietary security center. A more detailed discussion of proprietary systems, including centrally monitored closed-circuit television, appears in Chapter 47.

SPECIAL RISKS IN COMMERCIAL BUILDING SECURITY

Computer Installations

Computer installations constitute substantial security risks for both tenants and building management. Computer security planning must prevent vandalism, theft of records (both printed and magnetic tape), commercial espionage, bombing, and a number of physical hazards inherent in computer design.

Access control limiting the persons authorized to enter a computer room, badging to indicate into which computer area the employee may go, pickup and delivery at a point outside the computer room, surveillance of exterior computer room walls, protection against tunneling below the floor in older installations, fire-resistant tape libraries, and closed-period fire and intrusion alarm systems are all needed to reduce the vulnerability of computer operations. Additional "insurance" against loss is achieved by the duplication of key programs and records and the storage of the duplicates in separate (and remote) safes or vaults. Naturally, careful background checks of employees with access to the computer room are vitally necessary.

This discussion does not deal with the risk of theft of computer information by "hacking" or wiretapping. This is a problem for the tenant rather than building management since the "action" generally takes place away from the building. The possibility, however, is one of the reasons telephone rooms should be secured and access to them strictly controlled.

The schedule of hours worked in the computer area presents a special problem for building management. In the interest of maximum efficiency, most computers are operated on a two- or three-shift basis, sometimes 7 days a week. This requires that computer personnel be admitted to and exit from the building at hours when other tenants are closed for business and it would otherwise be possible to secure the building completely. Under these circumstances, additional building security may be required for which the computer tenant must expect to pay increased rental costs. Also, if it is possible, elevators serving the computer area during otherwise closed hours should be programmed to travel only between the computer floor and the lobby or manned parking garage.

Extreme care should be taken to limit as far as possible the number of duplicate keys (building entrances, elevator controls, and so on) assigned to second- and third-shift computer operations employees. Manning the lobby eliminates the need for keys, at substantial expense, but this expense is in part offset by increased building security as well as the elimination of the cost of rekeying critical access points whenever the tenant discharges a keyholder or a key is lost.

Computers are vulnerable to lightning, fire, and smoke, and their associated magnetic tapes are readily damaged by humidity and high temperatures. It is common practice to air condition computer rooms separately and to wire the air conditioning control units to register alarm signals in the event the air conditioning should stop. (Air conditioning should automatically stop in the event of fire, and fire dampers in the ducts should close.) Smoke or combustion detectors are installed in computer air conditioning ducts and in the under-the-floor electrical conduit section to detect smoke or fire at the earliest moment.

Computer rooms do not usually have conventional sprinkler systems because water damage could be as destructive as fire. Carbon dioxide and halon extinguishing systems perform the same function, but require a local alarm for personnel evacuation. Automatic fire detection systems are usually incorporated into computer installations and may readily be wired to signal remotely as well as in the computer room.

In any event, all computer room areas should be equipped with portable halon, carbon dioxide, or dry powder fire extinguishers designed for electrical fires. A liquid extinguishing agent should not be available. Most computer room fires—statistically—are wastebasket fires due to smoking materials and can be effectively handled by portable extinguishers.

Branch Banks

Financial institutions are usually located on the ground level of the commercial building, with access directly from the street or through an entrance opening from the building lobby. Bank parking is sometimes provided adjacent to or within the building and additional security provided in this area. In recent years attacks against night depositories, resulting in some damage to the building exterior, have been rising in frequency.

Where there is to be a banking tenant, building floor load-bearing capacities must be adequate to support the weight of the vault(s) and bank vault door(s). The branch bank's receiving and shipping of currency exposes building occupants and visitors to danger; an armored car hijacking or robbery involves several men, all armed and dangerous. Bank cash receiving and loading platforms should be within the building, and special security precautions for this area should be incorporated at the planning stage.

In some instances, operations centers for large financial institutions are housed in commercial (multi-tenant) buildings. These centers present special problems. For example, computer operations invariably run two or three shifts, 7 days a week, creating the access problems discussed earlier. Bank personnel commonly move between floors occupied by the banking tenant by way of the stairwells. This movement necessitates a modification of fire stair door locks to permit entry to the banking tenant's floors from the stairwell side. (Where building management does not modify stairwell door locks to facilitate tenant-authorized access from the stairs, personnel soon jam the door latch or strike to facilitate travel from one floor to another.) Stairwell alarms (and signs announcing their presence) located above and below these major tenant floors will deter unauthorized travel into the unsecured stair door area. When financial operation centers are being planned into the design and construction of a commercial building, a separate secured section of the building should be earmarked for this use, including provision for additional space to accommodate growth.

Other Tenants Affecting Building Security

Certain business operations present special security problems that result from their image, the type of visitor attracted to the operation, or their hours of business. Businesses that require special security consideration include recreational services, parking garages, hotels and motels, theaters, restaurants, dance studios, taverns, airline offices, utility companies, offices of military hardware manufacturers, foreign diplomatic offices, travel agencies, international government offices (including official tourist agencies), government welfare offices, bail bondsmen, hospitals, medical centers, and psychiatric clinics. The security risk involved ranges from the handling of intoxicated individuals to the mentally disturbed, the saboteur, and the anarchist. Preestablished security rules cannot be applied to these situations. Building management must recognize a security "red flag" in these tenants' security requirements.

APPLICABLE OFFICE BUILDING SECURITY PROCEDURES

Where adequate security procedures are lacking, even the finest alarm systems and structural security hardware are impotent against criminal attack. The following elements are essential to a formal security program.

General

Procedures should be written and all building management and security personnel indoctrinated as to their individual responsibilities. Tenants should be advised in writing of building security requirements they must meet, particularly when their occupancy presents special security problems.

Building Hours

It is essential to establish building open-for-business schedules, hours during which building services will be provided for tenants, and visitors will be freely admitted. These hours should be posted as well as included in the tenant's lease. Rules governing the building, security, and schedules for weekends, holidays, and vacation shutdowns, if applicable, should also be carefully detailed. Tenants should be required to state the hours and the nature of their business, and any change should require tenant and building management agreement. It is important that tenant security responsibilities be incorporated in the lease.

Closed-Period Access

Access outside of "open" hours should be restricted to a single entry point, and depending upon the level of security maintained within the building and the nature of the security risk in general, tenants may be admitted in one or more ways. None of the following can be considered high security.

If a security guard is on duty throughout the closed period, tenants presenting authorized identification cards should be admitted by the guard after signing a log with written information pertinent to their visit and permitted to exit after signing out. The identification cards must be prepared and issued to tenant employees formally identified as being authorized by their firms to re-enter the building during the normally closed period. More security would be added if each log entry were to be countersigned once a week or month by the tenant/employer to ensure that the tenant knows which employees enter after hours.

Where no guard is posted, access control can be accomplished by an electronic access control system in which an identification card releases an electric strike, permitting the authorized card holder to enter the building. Problems with this type of control include the facts that these cards may be loaned to unauthorized individuals; most access control locks of this kind can be tampered with; and in the absence of any printout (which is recommended), the visit will not be recorded.

An even less sophisticated access control involves the issuance of special keys that permit key-holding tenant personnel to release an electric door latch strike.

Finally, the assignment of a building door key to unlock the designated entrance door will permit tenants access during the closed period. However, once a number of building keys have been issued, security reaches zero level as far as preventing unauthorized access to unsecured or insecure areas is concerned.

Access Control by Badging

In more sophisticated installations, identification and access control may be accomplished by assigning employees and visitors special identification badges. When such an ID program is employed, the badges should include a color photograph of the individual and be laminated in such a way that the identification card information or picture cannot be altered without detection. Badge access control systems may be further improved by color coding identification cards by zones, thereby limiting the areas into which employees may go.

Badge access identification systems are suitable for supervision by closed-circuit TV, security guards, or receptionists or supervisors assigned this specific responsibility. Where visitor identification cards are issued, these should be dated, color coded, prenumbered, carefully logged, and recovered before the visitor leaves the premises.

Badge access control can be sophisticated by the introduction of information invisibly embedded in the individual's identification card, which can then be used to actuate door releases at predesignated points of entry. Here, the identification code information can limit employees' access to certain areas and through certain doors, and the use of the card can be centrally recorded.

When considering electronic access control for high-risk applications, the system that is contemplated should include other control features as follows:

1. It should be possible to eliminate or nullify specific cards immediately.
2. The individual's authorized level of entry should be easily changed but only by supervisory action.
3. In highly critical locations, an alarm should occur locally or remotely when an attempt is made to enter through a control point with an invalid card or if an attempt is made to tamper with the lock or "card reader."

For those considering the "ultimate," beyond systems requiring a push button code as well as a card, there are systems available that combine magnetically coded information with fingerprint characteristics. This system requires that the individual wishing access through an electronically controlled point insert his identification card and place his finger in a "reading" unit; the fingerprint is then matched with the fingerprint on file and coded in the ID card. If all match, the individual will be admitted. Even systems employing voiceprint comparison are believed to be within the capability of modern technology.

Whatever the means used, it cannot be too often repeated that access control is of vital importance. Remember, this is also the means by which a premises structure, safe or vault, and alarm system is cased in planning tonight's burglary or tomorrow's robbery.

PIONEERING: A CAUTION

Alarm system protection for commercial buildings is a relatively new field for many alarm companies and security equipment suppliers. The conventional equipment traditionally used to protect individual stores, warehouses, and factories is not always the most suitable for building security. While new alarm devices and systems presently being developed may serve the special needs of building management more efficiently and more economically, the security officer is warned that, historically, pioneering in the area of alarms can raise problems not obvious under demonstration and test conditions. Such problems often "wipe out" the anticipated economies and efficiencies of the new and different "mousetrap." Finally, building management's security policy, equipment, alarm systems, security procedures, and contingency plans should be incorporated into a confidential manual that will serve as a basis for the execution of the security program.

Building management is staffed with experts in the field of architecture, engineering construction, and maintenance. Under the circumstances, management will be strongly tempted to "go it alone" in planning a security program or to rely, in whole or in part, on the recommendations of potential suppliers. These sources of knowledge should not be turned off, but in security, "90 percent accuracy" means that one out of ten attacks will succeed. Building management can better afford to purchase expert consultation than to suffer a one-in-ten crime loss experience. Unbiased expert opinion of their specific needs can then be fed to the alarm contractor or equipment supplier who knows best how to apply the right hardware and procedures.

47

Proprietary Alarm System Centers

With Propriety

A proprietary system is usually one in which a company's or a facility's alarm devices and surveillance monitoring equipment are supervised at a point (usually also a communication center) in or immediately adjacent to the protected premises. In some instances, proprietary systems are also connected to remote central station or police alarm supervisory services. In other instances, facilities at some distance are monitored from a remote proprietary center, with the responding guards stationed at or near the monitored facility.

Chapter 46 discussed proprietary systems for commercial office buildings. The basic principles of proprietary systems are the same, however, whether designed for the protection of retail, wholesale, or manufacturing premises, for public buildings, or virtually any other large risk.

THE WHAT AND WHEN OF PROPRIETARY SYSTEMS

Proprietary systems are used to supervise burglary, holdup, fire, sprinkler (waterflow), and industrial process alarm devices, as well as for central monitoring of closed-circuit television, for remote supervision and operation of controlled access points, and for radio communication to and from security personnel and vehicles, as well as other security, safety, and service functions. Proprietary systems may be in operation only during open-for-business hours, only during closed periods, or (more commonly) around the clock.

MANPOWER KEY TO CHOICE

Generally speaking, proprietary alarm systems are more expensive than commercial central station service except where other factors require that manpower be present at the site during the periods alarm supervision is needed. Thus, we find proprietary systems most often employed in conjunction with large manufacturing and warehouse facilities, central banking or corporation headquarters, urban complexes, and public buildings with one or more of the following needs:

- Where supervised access control is needed when in-person supervision rather than remote access control systems is required by the volume of traffic or by the need for personal inspection of incoming and outgoing packages and loads—for example, warehouses stocking valuable and/or highly resalable merchandise, precious metals refining and manufacturing, factories subject to the pilferage of costly tools, and facilities that may be targets for sabotage, theft of secrets, and so forth;
- Where yard security and surveillance are necessary either to protect stocks that must, by their nature, be stored outside a protected premises or where vehicles loaded with materials for delivery are parked;
- Where control of traffic or the presence of a guard is necessary for the safety of personnel, property, or visitors to the facility;
- Where internal surveillance is necessary in conjunction with closed-circuit TV in order to prevent theft and to maintain operational efficiency;
- Where restricted security areas (as, for example, classified government contract work) require on-site security personnel;
- Where fire insurance requires a watchman on the premises during the entire closed period and/or periodic internal tours of the facility by security personnel, whether or not this includes the registration of watch tour signals at strategic locations.

In addition, when machinery, equipment, and processes require around-the-clock supervision, central monitoring of these operations and processes may make the addition of alarm supervision practical. Services that can be provided from a proprietary center include plant surveillance, fleet dispatching, paging, radio communications, and so forth.

THE SINGLE GUARD

When a proprietary system is utilized only during the open-for-business period, it may be staffed by one or more security guards. However, the operation of a proprietary system or center with a single security guard leaves management's hands virtually tied in the event of emergencies; the security guard cannot be dispatched to other areas within the plant to investigate improper entry or exit, to search incoming vehicles, to supervise multiplant access points, for instance.

Further, if a proprietary system is operated during the closed period by a single guard on duty, the guard is powerless to prevent losses through hit-and-run attacks, to apprehend intruders, to render first aid, or to assist the police in the search of the premises. He may also be subject to diversionary attempts to lure him away from the target zone and may in certain circumstances be rendered helpless by plans involving the holding of others as hostages and so on.

Actually, it is not possible to operate even a single shift of a proprietary system with a single guard since that individual will require relief periods, luncheon breaks, and illness and vacation period replacement. Key maintenance personnel or nonsecurity dispatchers may be substituted to provide the additional service required. However, this arrangement—the single guard relieved by nonsecurity personnel—is at best semiprofessional and should not be considered for any serious risk. If a single guard is the requirement, it is generally better to contract for his services from a contract guard service organization that will assume the responsibility for vacation and illness coverage. Too, the contract guard organization expects its personnel to man their posts with little or no time away from their assigned duties.

HOURS OF OPERATION

Whether a proprietary system is to be operated on a single shift basis or around the clock may also be controlled by other factors such as the existence of a second or third work shift, a 24-hour computer center, fire and/or theft insurance requirements, the value and nature of stocks outside the premises, difficulty in reliably securing a large multi-entrance plant, openings that cannot be secured (railroad sidings, for example), and the manufacturing environment. For instance, it is very difficult to maintain electrical alarm systems properly in manufacturing environments like foundries where acids and other corrosives attack alarm devices and wiring, resulting in so high an incidence of false alarms as to require on-site screening of alarm signals.

ECONOMICS OF CHOICE

The cost of installing, maintaining, and operating a proprietary system must be compared with the alternative of remote (central station) contract supervision of, and response to, all necessary alarm systems and industrial process functions. Proprietary systems are usually more economical than remote central station services when large or multi-plant complexes are concerned, but the direct comparison of costs (proprietary system purchase and maintenance vs. central station installation and annual service) is improper unless the cost of manpower labor (security guards vs. central station guard response) is carefully considered.

In making the choice between proprietary and remote supervisory systems, a great deal of planning and future projection—as well as expertise (equipment suppliers, insurers, and independent consultants)—must be employed. Even in operations having two or three shifts, there are many instances when remote central station or police supervisory alarm systems are more economical than the proprietary system if the presence of security guards would otherwise be unnecessary during the early-morning hours, weekends, holidays, and vacation shutdowns.

Central Station Backup

Further, in some high-risk situations, even where the proprietary system is manned on a 24-hour basis, the responsibility for security against burglary (and in some instances robbery) of high-value targets (generally safes and vaults) is wisely placed in the hands of a central station contractor. When this is done, there should be dual annunciation of alarm signals at the central station and at the security center, and under no conditions should house security have the capability of arming or disarming the system without evoking an alarm signal at the central station. Dual operation (Chapter 19) meets UL certification requirements (proprietary systems do not) and is not as vulnerable to physical or hostage attack as the proprietary security center may be.

Proprietary Central Station

In addition to providing in-plant or multi-plant security for a single location or for closely grouped locations, a proprietary system may also be used as a central station linked by alarm telephone circuits to alarm systems at more remote locations. Branch banks and high-value chain retail outlets would be logical applications. When there is a need for prompt 24-hour guard response to remote locations, the economics of supervising remote points are very much in favor of expanding the operation of the proprietary center as compared to central station service for each remote location. However, one must reckon with the responsibility (in addition to needed experience and know-how) involved in providing one's own protection for high-value targets, insurance company requirements, and the arrangements and staffing necessary for prompt response to the remote location at all times on receipt of an alarm signal.

POINT-BY-POINT PROTECTION

Rapid advances have been made in recent years in the development of proprietary systems equipment for supervising alarm devices. Some of this new equipment affords a relatively high degree of security against skilled compromise attack for in-house alarm circuits as well as for leased alarm telephone circuits. Systems recently developed also provide individual annunciation and/or supervision of a great number of individual alarm protected points, a capability the conventional central station or police-connected intrusion alarm system lacks. These proprietary systems can supervise each stairwell door, each loading door, each office, and so on rather than just the alarm circuit protecting a number of these points. Proprietary supervisory equipment usually achieves this degree of supervision at a lower cost per point than could be achieved in any other way. This is due in part to the utilization of multiplex transmission circuits and digital signaling interrogation.

MICROWAVE APPLICATIONS

Over relatively short distances (25 miles on a point-to-point line-of-sight transmission basis) some proprietary systems can utilize microwave signal transmission and reception to provide a wireless remote supervisory capability. Microwave systems may also be employed to transmit closed-circuit TV for supervision at a remote point. Differences in terrain can be overcome by repeater and reflector stations, but these units substantially increase cost. This use of microwave signaling for dual alarm supervision has been experimentally employed as supplementary protection for certain high risks in those sections of the United States where alarm systems with line security have been compromised.

CONSIDERATIONS OF CHOICE

In analyzing the merits of proprietary supervision as opposed to remote contract service supervision, from a practical standpoint one should base his cost calculations and need comparisons solely on the necessity for proprietary service. Once the necessary objectives are determined (for example, the need for a radio communications center or for closed-circuit TV surveillance) and the economics of the matter lean toward the proprietary system, then one may begin to weigh the benefits in improved security or in cost savings that may accrue from the versatility of a proprietary security center.

CLOSED-CIRCUIT TV IN THE PROPRIETARY CENTER

There has been a steady and logical increase in the use of closed-circuit TV to monitor operations, exits, high-value storage, parking lots, and corridors, providing the surveillance of a guard at a fraction of the cost of a manned post. The increased use of closed-circuit TV rises in part from the development of equipment capable of operating under normal to limited lighting conditions at substantially lower costs. Auxiliary remote controls to "pan" the camera or to "zoom in" for a close-up view are also less expensive now.

Closed-circuit TV cameras are often used with remote lock releases to man remote building entrances, viewing both the person at the door and the employee and visitor identification he presents. Thus, one security center operator may supervise more than one entrance, especially at nonrush hours. Indeed, closed-circuit TV can be a valuable aid to a security force dispatched from a proprietary security center.

Auxiliary to the improved closed-circuit TV monitors is electronic switching, which automatically selects from one of several cameras in sequence, displaying each scene for a limited period of time (10 seconds or so) before automatically shifting to the next closed-circuit TV camera in the schedule. Thus, the security center operator is constantly observing many areas. These systems also provide for "holding" a given closed-circuit TV picture for closer study should something be occurring.

One should not, however, let his closed-circuit TV imagination run away with him. There is a limit to the number of closed-circuit TV cameras a single security operative can effectively monitor, as well as a limit to the period of time closed-circuit TV can sustain the operator's attention. After an hour or two there is a real question whether the security operator would actually see an intruder crossing the path of a relatively still TV stage. Another disadvantage of closed-circuit TV lies in the limitation of what can be distinguished on the monitor (for example, note-passing holdup scenes have gone unnoticed). For this and other reasons, the location and use of closed-circuit TV by a single console operator should be carefully planned and definitely limited in scope.

Some solutions to these closed-circuit TV limitations are the rotation of console operators at the end of each hour and the use of two operators at the console at all times. In high-risk (bank money dock) situations, a second smaller console having fewer cameras to monitor concentrates on the risk situation, while the master console watches those scenes as well as many others. Alarm sensors can also be utilized to call attention to activity in normally unoccupied areas such as vacant plant areas, exits, fire stairs, or corridors after open hours.

Notwithstanding the necessary precautions, the combination of closed-circuit TV with a proprietary system offers a definite advantage in security manpower utilization.

PROPRIETARY SYSTEM REQUIREMENTS

Considerations for a proprietary system, in addition to those described in Chapter 46, should include the following:

1. The supervision of intrusion devices should assure that there is virtually no chance that alarm signals may be missed, improperly interpreted, or poorly investigated. Provision should be made to require that an alarm device that has been activated may be reset only by a visit to the point of protection (as opposed to the ability to restore the circuit from the security center). The security center should be able to silence only the audible annunciation (but not the visual annunciation) of the alarm until proper investigation permits the restoration of the protected point. Circuitry must be fail-safe—that is, alarm in the event of power failure, line loss, and so on.
2. Where closed-circuit TV monitoring is included in the proprietary center system, experience indicates that space should be provided to permit the later addition of more monitors at the center as plant expansion and new applications may require. Further, the installation of closed-circuit TV coaxial connections throughout the facility in advance of need will allow the temporary installation of closed-circuit TV surveillance as conditions dictate.
3. Security centers should be adequately lighted and provided with standby power for that purpose as well as to maintain all security equipment in normal operation.
4. The design of the console should permit maximum efficiency on the part of the console operator under the specific conditions of the individual operation. While progress in standardizing proprietary supervisory equipment design has reduced costs and space requirements and assures that a proprietary system can be in operation in a shorter period of time than custom design permits, the use of standard proprietary equipment sometimes presents disadvantages that can be overcome by custom-engineering console components.
5. The proprietary center should be self-supporting, including provisions for food, water, weapons, communication, first-aid supplies, and rest and sleeping facilities. Holdup alarm signal devices should connect directly into remote central stations or the appropriate police and fire stations. Unlisted private telephone circuits are a must, as are "logging" tape recorders that provide a permanent record of all incoming and outgoing console communication, both telephone and radio. In addition, a digital paging service should be established to provide that security personnel on duty in the proprietary center will always be able to contact management supervisors, even when they are away from their residence. These centers are more versatile and efficient in operation if they can be developed as the hub of plant security, access control,

and intercommunication facilities. Quite often the security center is equipped to transmit emergency signals and messages throughout the plant.

6. If closed-circuit TV surveillance is used, a videotape recorder should be available to provide a semipermanent record of critical activities to permit a review after an event has occurred and as a backup for security guards who are often expected to maintain supervision over a numerous array of closed-circuit TV monitors.
7. If a proprietary center is only in operation part time, alarm central station signal systems should protect the center from intrusion during the closed period. Since valuable and highly confidential security records are frequently kept in the security center, which usually includes the security office, line security should protect the central station alarm system circuit.
8. If unattended electronic access control units are in use, supplementary remote controls for access should be installed in the security center. Similar provisions may permit the remote supervision of metal detection equipment employed to detect large masses of metals.
9. The operation of a proprietary system and/or security center also requires the training of personnel, the development of a written security policy, a security procedures manual, and provisions for standby personnel who can man and operate the proprietary center in an emergency.

EXPERT ADVICE ESSENTIAL

If this sounds as if the development of specifications for and the operation of a proprietary center is a complex, tricky business—it is. When management is considering this step, independent experts in the field should be called upon for assistance in preparing specifications and in evaluating proposals from potential equipment suppliers or service contractors. Further, management and security personnel should personally visit existing proprietary systems and interview personnel operating these systems to obtain firsthand information and comments concerning their capabilities and shortcomings. Every step in the operation of a proprietary system requires planning, perseverance, and propriety.

48

There Are Two Sides to An Alarm Contract

A "Must Read" Subject!

CHANGING TIMES

In recent years, contractual agreements applicable to burglary and fire alarm services have been subject to extensive revisions and expansion to reflect, in part, the era of consumerism and the changes in alarm technology and related services. However, disclaimers and additional warranty limitations emphasize the alarm contractors' position that they are not insurers of a subscriber's property or assets.

This chapter addresses some of the major alarm contract provisions that should be of primary concern to the alarm system subscriber. Since both the scope and precise language of agreements vary among contractors, the reader is urged to review specific agreements with his attorney to better understand the particular conditions or limitations that govern alarm system installation, maintenance, monitoring, and response services. Further, the subscriber should review the provisions of the alarm contract with his insurer to determine if there are conflicts between conditions of insurance and any liability assumed by the subscriber by the execution of the alarm contract.

MAINTENANCE AND REPAIR OF THE ALARM SYSTEM

Most alarm contracts include a clause that states:

> The expense of any extraordinary maintenance and repair of said alarm systems shall be borne by the Subscriber.

Damage to alarm system wiring devices and control units may occur as the result of burglary, fire, explosion, building renovations, or carelessness on the part of employees of the alarm subscriber working on the premises.

The cost of such repairs or replacement may be significant. For example, the inflation rate would tend to double the replacement cost of an alarm system every 5 to 10 years. The alarm user should arrange to include the alarm system under his standard fire or broad-form insurance coverage. Such additional coverage usually is achieved at modest increases in insurance premiums.

Most alarm contracts provide that expense of all normal maintenance and repair is to be borne by the alarm contractor. While it is true that certain maintenance may be necessary simply to keep the alarm system in operating order, lack of preventive maintenance and permanent repairs will, over a period of time, result in a system deterioration that may be the cause of false alarms, as well as expose wiring and terminal points to criminal attack. It is suggested that the alarm subscriber physically inspect the alarm devices and wiring periodically to be sure that any temporary repairs made by guards responding during the closed periods have been permanently repaired (on the next business day) and that all temporary splices have been soldered and bare wiring reinsulated without delay.

Similarly, electrical foil applied to windows and other surfaces should be inspected for wear and tear and periodically recoated with special lacquers or varnish to protect the foil against breaks due to window washing, for example. In addition, the alarm contractor should be asked to inspect the entire system and to adjust, repair, or replace sensors and wiring that no longer perform to standards, at least on an annual basis. The subscriber should request a letter signed by an alarm company supervisor certifying that the inspection has been performed and that the entire system does then still meet the extent of protection expressed in the original contractual agreement, as well as any UL certification standards that may exist in relation to the alarm system(s) in service.

In addition, when a new alarm installation is contemplated, consideration should be given to placing alarm wiring in a conduit and/or concealing insulated wiring in pipe shafts, above drop ceilings, and so forth to reduce the wear-and-tear exposure open wiring will receive. Generally, the small additional cost involved in concealing the alarm wires and protecting them in a conduit is a relatively small investment over the long term but one that will significantly improve the reliability of the entire alarm system. Some building codes now require that alarm wiring be Teflon coated if not installed within an approved conduit. The reader should make certain that the alarm contractor will meet all applicable codes.

Note: Some alarm contracts contain a clause limiting the alarm contractor's liability for repairing alarm systems as they age. An example reads:

> All repairs, maintenance, and replacement of lead wires, conduit, or other nonrecoverable equipment unsuited for reuse shall be at the Subscriber's expense after two (2) years from the date service is initially operative, and the contractor will notify the Subscriber if the contractor finds such work is necessary for the proper performance of the system set forth in the Schedule of Protection.

A subscriber facing this liability has additional incentives to negotiate the initial installation of alarm system wiring in a protected conduit or, at the least, concealed in walls or above dropped ceiling areas where there is less exposure to damage. Similarly, consideration should be given to concealing alarm contact magnets and switches inside doors and frames.

LIMITATION OF LIABILITY

Most alarm contractors have, at the advice of counsel and their insurers, considerably expanded the limitation of liability clauses contained in their contracts. One example reads:

> It is understood that the Contractor is not an insurer, that insurance, if any, shall be obtained by the Subscriber, and that the amounts payable to the Contractor hereunder are based upon the value of the services and the scope of liability as herein set forth and are unrelated to the value of the Subscriber's property or the property of others located in the Subscriber's premises. THE CONTRACTOR MAKES NO GUARANTY OR WARRANTY, INCLUDING ANY IMPLIED WARRANTY OF MERCHANTABILITY OR FITNESS, THAT THE SYSTEM OR SERVICES SUPPLIED WILL AVERT OR PREVENT OCCURRENCES OR THE CONSEQUENCES THEREFROM, WHICH THE SYSTEM OR SERVICE IS DESIGNED TO DETECT. The Subscriber does not desire this contract to provide for full liability of the Contractor and agrees that the Contractor shall be exempt from liability for loss or damage due directly or indirectly to occurrences, or consequences therefrom, that the service is designed to detect or avert; that if the Contractor should be found liable for loss or damage due to failure of service or equipment in any respect, its liability shall be limited to a sum equal to ten percent (10%) of the annual service charge, or $250, whichever is the greater, as liquidated damages and not as a penalty, as the exclusive and complete remedy, and that the provisions of this paragraph shall apply if loss or damage, irrespective of cause or origin, results directly or indirectly to person or property from performance or nonperformance of obligations imposed by this contract or from negligence, active or otherwise, of the Contractor, its agents, or employees.

While this clause defines the limitation of liability as a sum equal to 10 percent of the annual service charge or $250, whichever *is the greater,* some contracts read "whichever is the *lesser.*"

Most contracts also contain as part of the limitation of liability clause a section that reads:

> Subscriber agrees that the Contractor shall not be liable for any of the Subscriber's losses or damages irrespective of origin, to person or property, whether directly or indirectly caused by performance or nonperformance of obligations imposed by this contract or by negligent acts or omissions by the contractor, its agents, or employees.

It further agrees:

> The amounts paid by the Subscriber are not sufficient to warrant the Contractor's assuming such liabilities or any risk of consequential or other damage. THE CONTRACTOR WILL, HOWEVER, BY AMENDMENT GIVE THE SUBSCRIBER THE OPTION TO PAY AN ANNUAL SERVICE CHARGE CONSONANT WITH ADDITIONAL LIABILITY. UNLESS THE SUBSCRIBER HAS ELECTED TO PAY SUCH INCREASED ANNUAL SERVICE CHARGE BY EXECUTING AN AMENDMENT TO THIS AGREEMENT, THE SUBSCRIBER DOES NOT DESIRE HIS CONTRACT TO PROVIDE FOR SUCH INDEMNIFICATION BY THE CONTRACTOR, AND THE SUBSCRIBER DOES HEREBY WAIVE AND RELEASE ANY RIGHTS OF RECOVERY AGAINST THE CONTRACT THAT IT MAY HAVE HEREUNDER.

Thus, if the subscriber agrees to pay some reasonable additional annual service fees, the contractor then agrees to obtain a higher limitation of liability coverage applicable to this contract, and the amount and condition that apply will be stipulated in the amended agreement. This is not insurance that covers a subscriber's loss of property but a higher limit of liquidated damage that is the maximum amount the contractor may be required to pay to the subscriber in the event the subscriber sues the contractor for losses suffered as a result of the contractor's failure to perform in accordance with the contractual agreement and the court decides in favor of the subscriber.

There are pros and cons to this issue. If the limits of liability are increased substantially, an alarm contractor may afford special attention to the installation, service, and supervision of the alarm system as well as in notification and response to alarm signals. This, in and of itself, may be sufficient reason to opt for an increased liability limit since effective alarm system supervision is paramount and the subscriber's own insurance is presumed to provide adequate coverage against crime losses. Conversely, the subscriber's election to purchase a higher limit of liability may be viewed by the court as strengthening the contractor's position as to limitation of liability in cases where a subscriber's loss exceeds the newly defined limits.

One contractor has offered a $10,000 limitation of liability or one year's annual service, whichever is less. In examining that proposal, it is noted that most alarm subscribers pay, on the average, a much lower annual service rate. Therefore, this agreement would not substantially improve the subscriber's position. In those instances where the subscriber's premises are protected by extensive and numerous alarm systems, annual service rates do sometimes equal or exceed the $10,000 amount. However, it is important to the subscriber to consolidate all contractual agreements covering a single location in one contract to relate that total annual charge with the liability limits.

In any event, the author notes that subscribers encounter significant difficulty in their efforts to negotiate increases above the standard liability limit. In some cases, the additional annual service rates quoted by the alarm contractor are unrealistic. It is suggested that counsel be retained to assist in these negotiations if the subscriber elects to obtain a contractual increase in the limits of liability.

Hold Harmless Clause

Almost all alarm contracts now include a clause that reads:

> Subscriber agrees to and shall indemnify and save harmless the Contractor, its agents, and employees, for and against all third party claims, lawsuits, and losses alleged to be caused by Contractor's performance, negligent performance, or failure to perform its obligations under this Agreement.

The subscriber and his counsel are urged to evaluate this condition as it relates to both the subscriber's liability for the alarm company's actions and any subrogation rights imposed on the subscriber by his insurer as a condition of insurance.

Understanding of Limitations of Liability

A standard clause in alarm contracts now seeks to strengthen further the alarm contractor's position as to the limitation of liability involved. Usually this clause reads:

> The Subscriber hereby acknowledges that he has read and understands this entire Agreement, including the terms and conditions on the back of this page.

We can only comment that if the contractor's liability insurer feels this clause is necessary, then it is essential that the subscriber's counsel read and advise the subscriber as to the contractual contents and limitations.

LEASED SYSTEMS AND SERVICE

The conventional practice in the alarm industry provides that:

> The Contractor installs and maintains during the term of the Agreement an alarm system specified in an attached Schedule of Protection which includes transmission boxes and wire connections necessary to transmit signals from the premises of the Subscriber to the Contractor's central station (or a police station), and the Contractor will maintain such system in good working order with the understanding that the entire system, including all devices, instruments, appliances, and all connections, wires, conduits, foils, screens, cabinets,

contacts, or any other materials associated therewith, is and shall be and remain the personal property of the contractor.

While such leased agreements are practical in most cases (since the subscriber is usually a tenant and the length of occupancy is a short-term factor), the subscriber who owns his premises or who holds or contemplates a long-term occupancy might well be advised to consider, as an alternative, the outright purchase of the aforementioned system together with the exercise of a contract to provide maintenance and supervision of the alarm system.

When the alarm system is leased, the subscriber will agree to pay a sum related to the cost of installing and connecting the system, which is commonly called an *installation* or *advance service charge*. Usually this sum reflects the alarm contractor's costs of nonusable materials and the labor of installation. However, some contractors also price their installation rates to include the cost of reusable equipment such as motion-detection sensors, alarm control instruments, and so forth.

OUTRIGHT PURCHASE

As previously noted, subscribers who contemplate a long-term use of an alarm system with no foreseeable major changes in the premises layout (as it would relate to security requirements) should evaluate the long-term costs of an outright ownership of the alarm system versus the conventional lease arrangement. Most alarm contractors will quote either arrangement, except that some alarm contractors will not agree to sell their alarm control equipment and/or high line security devices. This is both understandable from a security standpoint and acceptable from the subscriber's viewpoint since a change to another alarm contractor's supervisory central station service would nearly always necessitate a change in the alarm control and line security equipment.

The advantages of outright purchase to the subscriber are the following:

- A net cost saving over a long term (three or more years of system use),
- The position of flexibility or negotiation that permits the subscriber to change alarm-monitoring and maintenance service contractors with less recurring expense,
- Possible tax advantages (depreciation, investment credit).

When a system is purchased outright, the contractor will usually include in the quotation a warranty period that may include parts only or the parts and the labor to make replacements. In any event, the warranty will be limited to equipment defects as opposed to wear and tear. The term of warranty may vary from a minimum 90-day period to 1 year. The alarm contractor will usually propose, if requested, a separate agreement providing for maintenance beyond the warranty period and remote station monitoring of alarm signals (and guard response, if requested). This contract price should be for a smaller amount during the initial year than in later years since it must relate to outright purchase warranty. In subsequent years, the contract service rates should continue to be lower than those that might be proposed under the conventional lease agreement since the alarm contractor will have obtained his cost of capital equipment (for example, motion-sensing devices) and profit in the outright purchase price.

The subscriber who negotiates an outright purchase of an alarm system can obtain the usual UL certificate that may be applicable to the extent of the system and service, providing that he does maintain a service contract with an alarm contractor who is a UL-approved agent.

AUTOMATIC CONTRACT RENEWAL

Most alarm contracts written in conjunction with leased or purchased alarm system installation and services cover periods varying from 1 to 5 years and contain a clause that automatically extends the contract on expiration of the initial term on a year-to-year basis, subject to written cancellation notice by either party within 30, 60, or 90 days of said expiration date. Since it is usually necessary for an alarm subscriber to maintain an alarm system as a condition of insurance and the time required to replace an alarm system installation may take a month or more, any alarm subscriber contemplating a change to other alarm services should review the terms of his existing alarm contract and plan for any such changes several months in advance of the expiration date.

AUTOMATIC RATE INCREASES

Many alarm contracts written today are for a 5-year term but include clauses that permit the alarm contractor to increase annual service charges at the expiration of the first year of the agreement or on any anniversary date thereafter. These clauses also permit the alarm subscriber to terminate the agreement with proper written notice if, on any anniversary date within the initial 5-year term, the alarm contractor invokes his option to increase the annual service charges.

Such provisions are sometimes negotiable and may be modified in one or more of the following ways:

- To provide that the contract rate may not be increased during the term of the agreement,
- To ensure that any increase proposed by the contractor will be within an agreed-upon percentage,
- To provide for fixed increases at specific times during the contract period,
- To ensure that the contractor must provide more advance notice (for example, 90 days) if an increase is proposed. This modification provides the subscriber with improved latitude to negotiate with the existing contractor or to exercise his option and to seek the services of another alarm contractor.

CANCELLATION PENALTIES

Most alarm contracts require the payment of cancellation charges if the alarm subscriber, for one reason or another, discontinues service prior to the expiration of the initial contract period or any subsequent renewal period. Since most alarm subscribers are tenants and thus subject to leases of varying terms, relocation due to urban development, or changes in population centers, it would be in the alarm subscriber's best interest to negotiate the terms of the alarm contract to coincide with the expiration of existing leases. Similarly, since subscribers may be forced to terminate their business for reasons beyond their control, it would also be advisable to negotiate an amendment to this clause of the alarm contract to provide that, if the business is discontinued at this location for reasons beyond the alarm subscriber's control, the alarm contract may be terminated without penalties on 30 days' written notice.

INSTALLATION

Charges

Most alarm contractors request installation charges be paid on execution of the contract. However, this clause is usually negotiable, and modifications of standard agreements may include 50 percent down with the balance on completion of the installation, for example. An alternative might tie the down payment in with the start of the installation work to reduce the likelihood of delays in progress on the job. In addition, some contractors may request a percentage in advance, followed by progress billings related to the percentage of the work completed.

In any event, it is suggested that the subscriber negotiate to withhold a small percentage of the installation charge to be paid within 30 days of the date the alarm system is placed in service. This arrangement serves as an incentive for both parties to cooperate in the completion of the installation and to the elimination of any defect that may arise as a result of defective sensors, installation errors, or alarm telephone circuit problems.

It is also advisable to include a mutually agreed upon date when the installation being completed is activated and central station monitoring is in effect. This is particularly important to a high-risk alarm subscriber whose insurer may not provide insurance coverage unless and until the alarm system and related services are fully operational.

Installation by Others

Some alarm contracts include a clause that states that any installation charge quoted in the agreement is based on the contractor performing the installation with its own personnel. It continues:

> If for any reason this installation must be performed by outside contractors, said installation charge shall be subject to revision.

This situation may occur in new construction or during major renovations where union jurisdictional problems arise. Under those circumstances, the installation costs may escalate by 100 percent or more. The subscriber is advised to determine in advance of negotiation of the agreement if there is any possibility of such circumstances arising and, if so, to negotiate appropriate limits applicable to such charges.

ADVANCE ANNUAL SERVICE CHARGES

Alarm contractors traditionally provide for payment of the annual service charge in advance. The amount to be paid will vary, however, from monthly to quarterly or even annual charges paid in advance on the contract effective date. This is a negotiable item, and in most cases, it is to the subscriber's advantage to agree to pay monthly or quarterly in advance.

SCHEDULE OF PROTECTION

The Schedule of Protection should define the specific points to which the sensors are to be applied and the extent of coverage to be provided by the system. The schedule should also describe the separation of systems or zones and state specifically the extent and number of UL certificates that will be issued in conjunction with the system installation and remote monitoring service.

It is important for the subscriber to be certain he fully understands the Schedule of Protection and that it satisfies his security requirements as well as those of his insurer. A sales proposal letter in which an outline of protection may be stated is not a substitute for the Schedule of Protection as a part of the contractual agreement.

TAXES, ASSESSMENTS, AND LICENSE FEES

In recent years, many municipalities have enacted ordinances that require that alarm systems be installed by permit or license and/or that the alarm contractor pays licensing fees to the municipality. In addition, certain sales and use taxes may also apply to alarm system installation and annual service charges. While this additional expense must necessarily be borne by the alarm subscriber, a check should also be made to determine if any ordinances permit a municipal government to assess charges for alarm signals resulting in police response to the premises. If such is the case, the agreement between the alarm subscriber and the contractor should be clearly worded to fix the responsibility for the cost of charges incurred, on the one hand, by carelessness on the part of the subscriber and, on the other hand, the fault of the alarm contractor, false alarms due to equipment and system defects, or telephone circuit failures.

Some municipal ordinances also provide for termination of police response to alarm or trouble signals in the event the number of unnecessary alarms initiated from a specific premises exceeds a stated acceptable limit. The subscriber should determine in advance if such practices exist and/or should negotiate an understanding with the alarm contractor as to the role the alarm contractor will play in compliance with any such statutes, particularly in assisting the subscriber in meeting the conditions imposed by the municipality for the prompt restoration of police response should such conditions arise.

ALARM DEVICES FOR TEMPERATURE CONTROLS AND INDUSTRIAL EQUIPMENT

It is practical to install alarm devices that will be activated on failure of heating and air conditioning systems, sump pumps, and other automatic equipment that functions during the closed periods. As a matter of fact, an early warning of a flood or freezing condition may be of great value in reducing losses due to water damage or conditions that make it impossible for employees to perform their work.

While these devices may be remotely supervised at a central station, it is important to note that most central station alarm contractors do not render guard or on-site investigation services in response to alarm signals of this nature. Instead, the contractual agreement provides that the alarm contractor contact a representative of the alarm subscriber to report the nature of the alarm signal received. Accordingly, the subscriber must make certain that at least one supervisory employee is able to be reached at all times during closed-for-business periods and that telephone contact numbers furnished to the alarm contractor are maintained on a current basis. Today, many subscribers arrange for digital paging services to provide a means wherein individuals designated to respond to alarm or trouble signals are more likely "reachable" whether at home or away from the residence but within the range of the digital paging service.

THE ARREST CLAUSE

Alarm contractors usually include a clause in the agreement that, in effect, states that any citizen's arrest made by the agents of the alarm contractor on the subscriber's premises will be made with the alarm contractor performing as an agent of the subscriber. In addition, the subscriber will bear any and all liability that may relate to false arrests or other conditions of that nature.

In some instances, this clause may involve a substantial liability. Here again, the alarm subscriber may be able to negotiate the deletion of this clause from the contract or to obtain special insurance applicable to this liability. In some instances, alarm contractors may be willing to delete this clause only if it is amended to read in effect that their agents will not detain or arrest any persons found in the premises in the normal course of their response to an alarm condition.

OPENING AND CLOSING REPORTS

For many years, most central station alarm contractors have, on request, agreed to furnish to an alarm subscriber a written or printed record showing the exact times when individual alarm circuits were opened and closed, as well as the time of receipt of alarm signals and the subsequent restoration of the circuit. Usually such reports are mailed to the subscriber on a weekly basis. However, in recent years, some alarm contractors have adopted a practice of furnishing such reports only when the alarm subscriber agrees to pay an additional annual service charge for the service. This information is often well worth the additional charge, particularly in those instances where a firm may operate a number of branch locations, using limited supervision at the branches.

Some alarm contractors offer computerized central station service. In such a case, the subscriber should require that the records furnished be generated by the computer rather than as a manually generated report or other recreated format.

UNSUPERVISED OPENING AND CLOSING

In order to provide a more competitive service rate structure for central station supervision of alarm systems, some alarm contractors have devised contractual agreements that provide for an alarm system that is key controlled by the alarm subscriber and that does not transmit alarm signals at opening or closing time to the central station. The circuitry usually involves the addition of a type of alarm-shunting device that permits the alarm subscriber to enter or depart the premises without transmission of an alarm signal or the restoration signal. It is similar in nature to the conventional police-connected local alarm.

While this form of service may be more economical, it may not be possible to obtain central station UL certification for systems employing this type of shunt device, and as such, this system may not meet the insurance company's requirements. Shunt-type systems also involve security weaknesses that may increase the vulnerability of the system to compromise or defeat of the alarm telephone circuit.

NO-GUARD RESPONSE

Alarm contractors, striving to offer a wide variety of competitive services to their prospective subscribers, have developed contracts that provide for supervision of the alarm system at a remote central station without guard response to investigate an alarm. Under these conditions the service charges are somewhat lower than those charged for conventional guard response, and the alarm contractor's sole responsibility is to notify the police and/or the alarm subscriber on receipt of any alarm signal.

This is not a desirable security arrangement and should not be considered unless the distance from the central station to the protected premises is so great that guard response takes a considerable period of time. A no-guard response service places the responsibility for investigation of the alarm signal squarely on the alarm subscriber's shoulders and may delay the prompt repair of alarm system defects when such are found to have been the cause of the alarm. Central station service without guard response may be certifiable as a local or police-connect alarm service providing that the extent of the protection at the premises, including an approved bell-type annunciator, otherwise meets the UL standards for such certification.

KEY OR NO-KEY ALARM SERVICE

Alarm contractors will normally offer to retain the keys to the premises under a security seal program at the central station. This move permits guards responding to alarms to enter the premises, conduct a proper search, and restore the alarm in most instances. A no-key response limits the alarm contractor's efforts to one of an external search of the premises to determine whether a forced or surreptitious entry has occurred and limits the alarm contractor's ability to search or restore service properly unless and until a representative of the alarm subscriber is contacted and reaches the scene to admit the alarm contractor to the premises.

Today many subscribers are located in shopping malls, plazas, industrial parks, and high-rise buildings where it is virtually impossible to search the exterior perimeter walls of the premises or the ceilings and rooftops to determine if there is evidence of forced entry into the premises. Accordingly, if a subscriber chooses not to provide keys to the premises to the alarm contractor, it is essential that a subscriber's representative be available at all times during the closed periods who must be able to respond promptly to the premises on notification from the alarm company.

Some alarm contractors confine the guard response where keys are not furnished by the subscriber to an inspection of the exterior of the premises from the guard's vehicle. In many instances, as described earlier, such inspection would not be effective. Further, some contractors stipulate that if keys are not furnished and the subscriber requests the alarm contractor to retain the guard at the premises until the subscriber's representative arrives, an additional charge will be made for such services. It is important for the subscriber to be aware of such potential additional charges and to determine precisely what the rates and conditions are for such services.

Similar charges may be made for labor incurred as a result of the subscriber's failure to set the alarm properly or maintain the equipment. It is noted that some alarm contractors presently charge rates approximating $75 per manhour for such response, including travel time to and from the location as well as the time spent by the guard or serviceman at the premises. Again, the subscriber should be aware prior to negotiation of the agreement what these rates are and the impact they may have on his overall costs of alarm service.

ACTS OF GOD

Most alarm contracts include clauses that permit the alarm contractor to terminate service without penalty or liability, other than temporary or permanent cessation of monthly service charges, when "acts of God" make it impossible for the alarm contractor to continue to supervise the alarm system. In addition to fires, explosions, floods, and so on that may damage or destroy the alarm system at the subscriber's premises, other conditions that may prevent the alarm contractor from maintaining service include damage to alarm telephone circuit cables between the subscriber's premises and the central station premises. Under these conditions the alarm subscriber may find himself without alarm services and, under certain conditions, his insurance coverage void until remote central station supervision is restored.

VAULT ALARM SYSTEMS

Most alarm contractors now include a clause in the terms and conditions section that states:

> The Subscriber represents that any vault to be protected by the Contractor hereunder by sound or vibration detector systems has the minimum construction characteristics prescribed by the Underwriters' Laboratories, Inc.

Thus, the subscriber should furnish the vault construction specifications to the alarm contractor with a request that the contractor confirm in writing that said form of vault construction is adequate for the application of the contractor's sound- or vibration-detection devices in accordance with UL standards. If there is a question, the contractor might submit the vault structural specifications to UL for their evaluation and opinion.

TESTING INTRUSION-DETECTION DEVICES

Alarm contracts now include a clause under terms and conditions that reads:

> The Subscriber agrees to test any ultrasonic, passive infrared, microwave, capacitance or other electronic equipment designated on the Schedule of Protection prior to setting the alarm system for closed period, according to procedures prescribed by the Contractor, and to notify the Contractor promptly in the event that such equipment fails to respond to the test. The Contractor shall make such repairs as shall be necessary as soon after receipt of notice as is reasonably possible.

This is a very important clause. It emphasizes the fact that the alarm system is not designed to permit the alarm contractor to test the sensitivity or other performance characteristics of such devices from the central station. It is therefore essential that the subscriber learn precisely how such tests are properly made and make certain that the contractual agreement includes the necessary equipment to permit the subscriber to perform such tests. In addition, the subscriber should maintain a written record (log) that details the dates on which such tests were performed, any deficiencies noted, the time and date the alarm contractor was notified of the defects, and the date and time the contractor's representative effected adequate repairs or adjustments to correct the defect.

Some insurance conditions limit or void the insurance coverage under circumstances wherein the subscriber is aware that an alarm system is inoperative. Extreme care should be taken to establish an agreement requiring that the alarm contractor make repairs immediately when notified and/or that the subscriber's representative remain in charge of the premises in a way that satisfies an insurer's conditions.

DISCONTINUANCE OF SERVICE

Most lease-type alarm agreements now provide that when alarm services are discontinued for one reason or another the alarm contractor has the right to abandon and/or remove all or part of the alarm system. They further specify that the alarm contractor will be under no obligation to repair or redecorate the premises in conjunction with the removal of the equipment. In most instances this clause proposes no serious problem to the subscriber. If, however, there are specific obligations incumbent on the subscriber in conjunction with his lease of the facilities, the subscriber may wish to negotiate a different agreement with the alarm contractor.

NO EXPRESSED OR IMPLIED WARRANTY

Alarm contracts may be amended by change in the original contract language or by the addition of riders. Most alarm contracts hold that there is no expressed or implied warranty related to any verbal agreements made between representatives of the alarm company and the subscriber. All changes or modifications should be in writing and should be initialed or signed by duly authorized representatives of each party. Generally, it is held that sales engineering representatives of alarm contractors are not legally responsible to sign or amend that company's contractual agreements.

SUBSCRIBER'S TERMS AND CONDITIONS

The foregoing discussion addressed the terms and conditions that most commonly appear in the alarm contractor's formal agreement and the related Schedule of Protection. However, we note that from time to time subscribers, on advice of counsel and/or their insurers, do make additional efforts to amend or extend such contracts via amendments or riders that require the alarm contractor to perform in a specific way or to provide specific additional services and notification. The following sections discuss such areas of consideration.

Priority Response

The contractor agrees to notify promptly the subscriber's representative(s) at the telephone number(s) furnished in the event that the telephone alarm circuit link serving subscriber's premises is fully or partially impaired in such a manner that the contractor cannot or possibly cannot receive alarm or trouble signals from the subscriber's premises. Further, the contractor agrees to notify promptly the subscriber's representative(s) in any other circumstance wherein the conditions for receiving signals at the central station or the ability of the central station to respond normally to such alarm signals is impaired or destroyed.

Changes in Alarm Systems

The contractor will promptly notify the subscriber by letter in any instance where the contractor's employee or agent modifies the alarm system central station receiving equipment or alarm sensors or other components of the alarm system installed at the subscriber's premises to materially reduce the level or the extent of the protective service as represented in the Schedule of Protection of this agreement.

Annual Inspection

The contractor agrees to furnish at least one formal annual inspection of the alarm system installed at the subscriber's premises. This inspection will be performed by a competent service technician who will test, adjust, repair, and/or replace sensors and other alarm system components so that on completion of this inspection the alarm system will perform to the level and extent as originally provided in the Schedule of Protection. The contractor will furnish a written report signed by the service supervisor confirming that the inspection has been performed and that the system does conform with the contractual agreement.

Issuing UL Certificates

The contractor agrees to issue the UL certificate(s) described in the Schedule of Protection to the subscriber immediately upon completion of the installation of the alarm system. Further, the contractor agrees to notify the subscriber in writing immediately upon any change in UL standards that would result in the cancellation or downgrading of any UL certificate described in the Schedule of Protection.

Alarm Telephone Transmission Circuits

The contractor will advise the subscriber at the time of execution of this agreement as to the length of time required to obtain the necessary alarm telephone circuit from the utility providing such service. The contractor will use due diligence in ordering the necessary circuits.

Insurance

The contractor warrants that a current liability and/or errors and omissions insurance policy is in effect. Further, the contractor will notify the subscriber in the event its ability to obtain such insurance coverage is impaired or such policy is cancelled. A copy of a current Certificate of Insurance provided by the contractor's insurer is furnished as an addendum to the contract in force.

Local or Police-Connect Alarm Service

The contractor will provide service at the subscriber's request on a 24-hour, 7-day-a-week basis. Usually, local or police-connect alarm contracts provide that service will be rendered within 24 hours following notification by the subscriber during the contractor's normal business hours, Monday through Friday.

Record Retention

The contractor warrants that all records prepared in connection with service provided to the subscriber will be retained on file at the contractor's premises for a specific (for example, to cover the statute of limitations) period of years from the date of preparation and that these records, documents, memorandums, and so on will be made available for the subscriber's review upon request by the subscriber's authorized representative.

Subscriber's Keys

The contractor warrants that any keys to the building or to the subscriber's premises furnished by the subscriber will be adequately safeguarded at the central station in accordance with existing UL standards.

THE NEED FOR COUNSEL

The decision to contract for burglar alarm services is based on the necessity to protect property and other assets that are in peril of criminal loss. Normally, the prospective alarm system subscriber recognizes that property and assets are not fully insurable or that, without burglar alarm protection, they may be uninsurable. Clearly, this major decision requires the subscriber to determine precisely whether the extent of alarm protection and the services provided, as defined in the alarm contract form, achieve his objectives.

When a prospective subscriber is not experienced enough to determine if the alarm system will deter burglary or, at least, substantially reduce the extent of loss, he should obtain expert advice. Similarly, if the subscriber, like the author, is not trained in law, he should engage legal counsel to advise regarding alarm contract conditions and liabilities and any recommended changes in the form of agreement. Similarly, existing subscribers might well ask their attorneys to review contracts in effect and, where appropriate, to recommend execution of new agreements to replace those that are, under present law, invalid or contentious.

49

The Alarm Industry in the Twenty-first Century

A Vision of the Future

HOLMES'S CRYSTAL BALL

After 25 years in business, the inventor of the burglar alarm, Edwin Holmes, was so confident of its future, he sold his 25 percent interest in the newly formed American Telephone and Telegraph Company to devote his full energies to the improvement and growth of the alarm business. After 50 years, Holmes observed, "The challenge to the security world, an industry older than telephone service, was to continue to improve its product and service to prevent crime."[1] During my 25-year privileged association with the alarm industry, references to Mr. Holmes's vision never failed to amuse my audiences who viewed the communications industry as a Golden Boy and, until 1984, AT&T as the pillar of strength and vitality from which all communications must grow.

But Look What's Happening

The telephone industry entered a period of transition and less predictable growth, whereas alarm industry studies, prepared by Predicasts, Inc., Cleveland, Ohio, in 1984, reported that 1983 sales of security equipment were four times the 1973 levels. This extraordinary growth spanned a decade that included a major recession and a leveling off in the burglary crime rate. Further, Predicasts forecasts that security equipment sales will triple in the next decade. This phenomenal growth trend supports Holmes's prediction that businessmen and citizens in residence have accepted the burglar alarm as a necessity of life!

---

[1] *A Wonderful Fifty Years.*

On with the Predictions

If the alarm industry does indeed improve its product and service to gain the complete acceptance of subscribers, insurers, and law enforcement agencies, there may well be an alarm system in every business and abode by the turn of the century. You and I hope to be there on January 1, 2000, to say "We told you so."

MEETING THE REQUIREMENTS

To achieve complete acceptance, a burglar alarm system must meet these objectives:

1. The system must deter the burglar or absolutely detect an intrusion into the specific protected area.
2. The sensing system must perform this function free of any unnecessary signals that cannot be positively identified as the result of a condition other than intrusion.
3. The medium used to transmit alarm signals must be equally reliable and fail-safe.
4. Control units designed to transmit and annunciate alarm signals should be fully dependable and versatile. They must provide the subscriber options like monitored fire and life safety devices as well as the economic advantages of energy management and data communications.
5. Response to alarm signals must be prompt and effective. Loss must be prevented or kept within acceptable levels. The subscriber should be able to equate the quality of response practices to a recognition of an improvement in his personal safety.

To achieve these objectives, changes in technology and system engineering concepts are imperative—and they are happening! Most alarm system components in demand today did not exist a decade ago. Of particular importance, computer technology affords a means by which a sizeable number and variety of sensors may be programmed, tested, activated, interrogated, and supervised by a reliable control unit installed within the protected premises. In turn, actual alarm signals may then be transmitted to a compatible central station computer with the capacity to monitor all signals and to provide response data specifically tailored to the loss prevention requirements of each alarm system. Similarly, rapid advances in electronics now permit the manufacture of smart dual and redundant sensors at affordable costs.

PRIORITY NUMBER 1: ELIMINATION OF UNNECESSARY ALARMS

The key to complete acceptance of an alarm system is total reliability. When a burglar recognizes the alarm system will detect his attack and promptly signal police or private agents who will respond swiftly to prevent loss and apprehend him, he will truly be deterred. However, unnecessary alarm signals cause the subscriber, alarm company personnel, and police to lose confidence in a system quickly. They also significantly add to the cost of the alarm service. Clearly, unnecessary alarms must be eliminated.

Nationwide action by municipalities and law enforcement agencies to license, regulate, and fine alarm companies and subscribers serves to highlight the problem, but the emphasis on assessments or fines for unnecessary alarm response is more often a form of double taxation than a cure of the disease. Similarly, statutes that permit police to curtail or delay response to the premises of subscribers whose alarm systems are noted for excessive unnecessary alarms address the effect rather than the cause and tend to encourage burglarious attack. Cooperative action by industry associations, individual alarm companies, and law enforcement agencies will help lead to improvements in alarm system installation, inspection, and maintenance standards that will address the problems created by inexperienced, careless, or unscrupulous alarm contractors.

However, in the author's opinion, improvement in sensor reliability and development of fail-safe applications, together with easy-to-operate control units, will solve the unnecessary-alarm problem. And, these achievements lie solely within the province of the alarm industry; its equipment suppliers; agencies like UL who provide the basis for equipment design, manufacturing, and system standards; and insurers having a major interest in the efficacy of an alarm system.

ORIGIN OF UNNECESSARY ALARM SIGNALS

Most unnecessary alarms are caused by careless actions on the part of the alarm user, changes in the environment (for example, air turbulence, temperature change, noise, humidity), or by malfunctions of sensors, premises signal circuits, or control equipment. In defending its position in the face of law enforcement charges of irresponsibility, the alarm industry has spent considerable time evaluating the percentages of unnecessary alarms attributed to each of these factors. Although it was necessary to identify and quantify the causes, it is more essential—yes, imperative—that the industry engineer alarm systems and equipment that eliminate all unnecessary alarm causes. Further, placing the blame on a careless subscriber will not improve either consumer or police acceptance levels. Subscriber-caused unnecessary alarms must be eliminated by control design that will prevent the subscriber from turning the system on or off at any time those actions would result in an unnecessary alarm. To achieve these objectives, we suggest consideration to the following factors.

System Redundancy

To eliminate or reduce unnecessary alarms caused by environmental factors within a premises, today's installer can select from a variety of sensing devices with different detection characteristics to provide a combination of dual monitoring sensors that will perform satisfactorily in each specific environmental application. As discussed in Chapter 8, for example, an ultrasonic sensor teamed up with a passive infrared device can be utilized to operate alarm free in an environment where, on occasion, air turbulence or temperature changes would otherwise create an unnecessary alarm condition if only a single sensor were utilized. Similarly, both ultrasonic and passive infrared sensors are available with dual sensing elements that preclude unnecessary alarms as a result of changes in a small portion of the protected area or those environmental disturbances that are short in duration.

By integrating dual sensing concepts into a strategically engineered analytical control circuit, a smart sensing system is achieved. Such a system also provides the user and/or the alarm-monitoring computer station with information covering both equipment malfunction and environmental problems that may then be subject to effective corrective action the next business day to eliminate a repetitive unnecessary alarm condition.

Similarly, alarm contact switches, shock sensors, and other protective devices and wiring can be engineered and installed to achieve trouble-free performance. In considering a new alarm system installation, the additional cost of a totally redundant system is modest when compared to the long-term cost savings in alarm response fees of $50 to $100 or more currently assessed by municipal ordinance—and some alarm contractors.

The Microprocessor Control Unit

The application of microcomputer technology to alarm control units offers a means by which unnecessary alarms resulting from the careless operation of the system can be eliminated. This application requires refinements to provide an automatic control against actions that cause unnecessary alarms. Such features must include the automatic test of each component of the alarm system to assure that environmental or component defects do not exist at the moment the system is to be activated. Further, premises control unit displays and annunciation must provide for reporting alarm signals created by one part of a dual sensing device during the closed period, time delay exit and entry features, and verification of the remote station monitoring circuit at closing time. In addition, the control unit should have the capacity to supervise strategic intrusion engineering concepts wherein an alarm signal transmitted by one device is treated as an early warning rather than one requiring initial response, and a subsequent alarm from a backup sensor requires an actual alarm response.

Installation and Maintenance Training

Redundant sensing systems and structured computer controls will, in theory, eliminate the burdensome unnecessary alarm load and further reduce alarm-monitoring and response costs. However, there is still a need to assure the quality of both system installation and service as well as the proper operation of the system by the subscriber. To achieve these objectives, the skills of the installation and service technicians should be expanded. The equipment manufacturer or supplier should provide full installation and maintenance training services for every alarm technician permitted to install or service their product. These training levels are hoped to emulate factory service training standards like those in use in the appliance industry.

The alarm contractor, the municipality, and the alarm standards agencies have a further responsibility to inspect alarm systems to be certain they are properly installed and maintained. Finally, the subscriber should contractually agree to designate only qualified personnel to be trained and to operate the alarm systems and, failing this, should contract to pay significant additional fees applicable to unnecessary alarms resulting from the careless operation of the system.

Alarm Signal Transmission

While failures in alarm signal transmission circuits also contribute to the unnecessary alarm load, the alarm industry's attitude toward telephone circuit troubles may be influenced by its concern over excessive increases in telephone alarm circuit charges and direct competition by telephone companies who install, service, and monitor alarm systems. To the observer, it seems obvious the restructured telephone industry will require and obtain increased revenues for services, including the special circuits leased to the alarm industry. We also believe the alarm contractor experiencing unnecessary alarm problems due to deterioriation of copper transmission circuits must take the initiative to convert subscriber services to more reliable and compatible telephone transmission circuits such as AC-multiplex, derived channel,[2] and digital communicator links. It is not practical to expect a restructured telephone company to replace poor-quality McCulloh or direct-line transmission circuits that are no longer compatible with the basic service offered by the utility. Nevertheless, we anticipate some telephone companies serving viable urban centers will continue for many years to provide direct wire circuits which enable the telephone companies to achieve a profitable revenue from a "plant" which is highly depreciated.

REVOLUTIONARY CHANGES IN ALARM SIGNAL TRANSMISSION?

Digital Communication Circuits

Within a 5-year period, the growth of digital transmission circuits using existing subscriber telephone circuits has been phenomenal. Over 40 regional or nationwide independent digital central stations, averaging 2 years in operating experience, now compete for this lower-cost alarm-monitoring service. In addition, many conventional central station contractors also offer digital communication-monitoring service. However, telephone companies are now mapping strategies for increasing revenues from a basic telephone circuit when it is used for the transmission of alarm data. Some insiders predict the promulgation of tariffs wherein the cost of digital communication alarm service will equal or exceed charges for other types of alarm transmission circuits.

The use of digital communicator transmission circuits also portends additional costs for subscribers since increases in tariffs, whether flat rate or measured time increments, will likely be included in the subscriber's regular phone bill. In that form, it will be difficult for the subscriber to determine the full cost of this alarm transmission circuit and to compare that cost with other forms of alarm transmission service.

At present, digital communication transmission circuits do not include a line security system that is satisfactory for use in alarm systems serving high-risk subscribers. Further, the evolution of regional and nationwide digital monitoring stations has created a dual security team wherein a local contractor installs and maintains the equipment at the premises, and a digital central station provides the monitoring service. When this condition exists, it is incumbent on the subscriber to contract for and obtain effective services from both contractors.

---

[2] A number of regional local access telephone companies are offering derived channel alarm circuits. These circuits utilize special telephone company equipment to transmit alarm data over the subscriber's voice grade telephone line. This system does not interfere with voice transmissions and does provide line security. The special engineering and equipment result in additional charges for this service and permit the telephone company greater control over the data transmitted, making the telephone company a more direct partner in furnishing the alarm service.

RF-Multiplex Circuits

While it is important to explore ways to reduce unnecessary alarms resulting from poor-quality direct-line or McCulloh alarm transmission circuits, the integrity of the circuit must also be considered. RF-multiplex and derived channel systems include interrogate-response line security features that make those alarm transmission mediums more valuable than digital communicator or McCulloh circuits. Use of digital communications combined with radio (wireless) transmission to provide redundant signal transmission has not to date achieved a level of line security that is recognized by UL for Grade AA certification. RF-multiplex, derived channel, and line-security-equipped direct-line transmission circuits do meet this standard.

Star Gazing?

While it is folly to predict the ultimate medium of alarm signal transmission during a period of deregulation and restructuring in the communications industry, there are other transmission methods that may one day be both cost-and security-effective, as described in the following sections.

Radio Transmission

In use for many years, radio (wireless) transmission has not been proven superior to telephone alarm transmission methods. Some of the reasons for this are that radio transmission is limited to 15-to-25-mile transmission ranges, the number of channels available is limited (the FCC recently increased the number of channels via allocations in the 900 MHz range), and its vulnerability to both interference and compromise attack (assuming extensive use of this medium) is unknown.

Closed-Circuit TV

The use of closed-circuit TV cable transmission systems to carry alarm signals is controversial. There are legal issues that include alarm industry rights to use municipally regulated cable TV systems, joint ventures between alarm contractors and cable TV operators who do offer such services, and a general consensus that closed-circuit TV cable systems must include two-way transmission capability, a higher degree of 24-hour reliability, and immediate service capability if cable TV alarm signal transmission is furnished.

Data-Processing Circuits

Commercial data lines used to transmit information from remote terminals to central computers may be adapted to provide for simultaneous transmission of alarm signals over long distances. This method is of special interest to financial institutions and other multi-location companies who operate proprietary central alarm monitoring stations. As an alternative, alarm signals might also be multiplexed from a computer center to a private central monitoring station.

Fiber Optics

Fiber optic alarm signal transmission is a most promising medium. The reliability and integrity of this type of alarm signal transmission are superior to other mediums since fiber optic circuits are immune to electromagnetic and electrostatic interference, and if the jacket cable is penetrated in an effort to compromise the alarm circuit, the attack creates an immediate alarm condition. Presently, cost and availability of fiber optic circuits are limiting factors. However, as this medium expands, costs may be reduced substantially.

Satellites and More

As the technology is fine tuned, satellite, microwave, and cellular telephone transmission systems may also be used to transmit alarm signals. Reliability and capital costs will be key factors in an evolution of these mediums to alarm signal transmission use. However, as these mediums are predominantly controlled by the communications industry, the subscriber's cost for such services will most likely approximate or exceed the present level of cost for other transmission methods.

FUTURE OF WIRELESS SENSING SYSTEMS

The author believes the alarm industry will gradually shift to a wireless sensing system technology. The improved reliability and integrity of wireless sensors (see Chapter 32) provide the alarm industry with an opportunity to expand its capacity to meet the predicted alarm system growth rates. Wireless sensors require considerably less time and skill to install and service, thereby addressing the industry's present limitations in terms of the manpower required to achieve rapid growth. Further, the related lower labor costs will permit the alarm contractor to reduce alarm system selling prices, thereby fueling market growth. Most important, contractors utilizing the wireless sensor technology have an opportunity to maximize profits since unit installation and service cost estimates will be more accurate than the estimates provided in conjunction with conventional hard-wired systems.

However, before this crystal ball enters orbit, suppliers of wireless sensing equipment must address the need for a broader range of sensors operating at low power levels and premises signal transmission methods that are immune to externally generated interference. The principle of redundant sensing remains a requirement although single power supplies may be adequate to serve both sensors. Finally, there is a need for modular plug-in design to permit replacement service by technician or subscriber at lower cost. Overall, the future for wireless sensing systems appears bright.

ONE PICTURE IS WORTH A THOUSAND ALARM SIGNALS

Miniaturization and improvement in the reliability of closed-circuit TV cameras, switching, sequencing, and video recording equipment will permit development of the use of closed-circuit TV cameras monitored at remote station to deter burglary as well as robbery and theft. The present factor limiting the use of this medium is signal transmission, which may be by microwave wireless transmission, coaxial cable, or conversion of video signals to audio signals that are then transmitted over conventional telephone circuits and reconstructed as video, or pictures. The latter technique, sometimes referred to as *slow scan,* provides limited-quality reproduction of camera outputs at 10- to 60-second intervals.

The use of coaxial cable is currently cost-prohibitive, and costly microwave transmission systems have been limited in range to approximately 2 to 3 miles. However, this long-shot burglar alarm system concept has exciting possibilities if manufacturers can reduce equipment cost, increase microwave signal transmission ranges, or utilize fiber optics. Someday a central station, on receipt of an alert signal, will view critical protected areas within the premises and take fully effective response actions. Smile, Mr. Burglar, you're on camera now.

Using a video burglar alarm system, the intruder may be detected by changes in the camera field of view, by conventional sensors, or by a combination of these methods. Sensor redundancy requirements could be significantly reduced while achieving a 100 percent elimination of unnecessary alarms insofar as police, alarm company agents, or subscriber response are concerned.

STRUCTURE OF THE ALARM INDUSTRY

In recent years the alarm industry has been affected by acquisition and merger mania. Nationwide companies constantly strive to expand by acquisition or installation of bridging and satellite facilities for retransmission of alarm signals from suburban areas to regional computerized central stations. New nationwide alarm companies have been formed by venture capitalists who select and acquire, at sometimes extraordinary costs, strategically located existing independent central station companies. Both European and Asian conglomerates have taken a direct plunge via this route. In addition, as the alarm industry fears, some telephone companies have entered the alarm field, and undoubtedly more will follow.

As analysts now peg security as a growth industry, one may expect continuing change and growth in the alarm central station segment. This growth may well lead to dominance by a number of major corporations furnishing a variety of nationwide security services. However, we believe there will always be a place in the alarm industry for the independent alarm contractor who, as a member of the community, demonstrates excellence in the quality of alarm system installation, maintenance, and central station monitoring functions. After all, the most successful alarm contractor, Edwin Holmes, proved a pioneer could succeed in that fashion. Let's get together on December 31, 1999, and see what's happened.

50

The Consultant's Role

Consult!

"Here it comes," says our reader, "the commercial I've been expecting. The author has been trying to scare the living daylights out of us to convince us we lack the experience necessary to handle our own security problems. That's what he must be selling—consultation services."

WHY A SPECIALIST?

That's not the objective, but the reader has a point. Regardless of whether the security officer is from the ranks of law enforcement or military or federal security, shanghaied from personnel and industrial relations, assigned the responsibility on top of operations management, or even a thoroughly competent, broadly experienced security professional, no one person (including this author) is—or can be—expert in every phase of security. Security officers with law enforcement education and experience are often the best equipped and best informed in general, but they rarely have had the opportunity to school themselves in the intricacies of alarm systems and components and the why of related security procedures. The purchase of a proprietary alarm system is, at best, a once-in-a-decade experience, but even the wrong choice of an alarm contractor can lock the company into a virtually unbreakable association due to lack of budget for a brand new installation. Clearly, failure to consider utilizing specialized independent consultants to provide the necessary experience for the wisest choice may be worse than penny wise and pound foolish.

Besides startup costs and operational problems, a loophole in the alarm security system may be the opening through which financial disaster enters. It can be the peg on which the insurance underwriter hangs his decision to deny or to compromise a loss claim, and it can permit mysterious uninsured theft.

No one in a position of security responsibility is anxious to expose what management could regard as a professional weakness. Most security officers are expected by their bosses to know everything and anything in the field of crime prevention, detection, investigation, apprehension, plus more law than company lawyers. After all, if the security officer needs security help, maybe we selected the wrong man!

Not so. Each security job is multi-faceted. Most security decisions, policy, and operating procedures necessarily evolve from the operations of the particular company, the manner in which the business is conducted, the products manufactured/distributed, the way in which profit—the heart of the business—is developed, the location, the personnel policies, and even (and, sometimes, particularly) the philosophy of top management.

THE CONSULTANT AS INTERFACE

In addition, basic alarm decisions involve values, critical areas, critical processes, and competitive information that management may be reluctant to disclose to the alarm contractor or security equipment suppliers. The independent consultant (having no ties to any alarm product or service) serves not only as a disinterested information resource but also as the go-between, filter, and interpreter.

Security and management personnel tend to think that the security consultant specialist, like the specializing surgeon, will charge prohibitive fees. Not so. The electronic alarm security consultant is likely to have obtained his training from practical experience (and, sometimes, misfortune) and is not likely to have invested an additional 8 to 10 years in formal learning. Through his practical experience, he is likely to have developed a keen sense of the operational problems and priorities of management, as well as a far broader knowledge of applications and experience, and of security requirements. Unlike the specialist in the medical field, the consultant necessarily sees the forest and not just the trees.

The alarm security consultant, like the accountant or the attorney, must offer long-term service and dependability; the constantly changing context of security makes periodic re-examination and evaluation essential to the security "total."

SELECTION OF A CONSULTANT

The alarm security consultant should not be employed by or receive fees of any kind from alarm service contractors, equipment suppliers, patrol service agencies, investigators, or other vendors in the security field. He should be forthright and candid in assisting management in their choice of such contractors to ensure that they will have the capability to furnish the needed services. The consultant should assist management in the preparation of the basic specifications from which the security equipment or services contractor will develop his proposal. Finally, the consultant should assist in evaluating proposals as to their cost-effectiveness and return on investment in terms of one concept of security versus another.

In selecting an electronic alarm security consultant, as in choosing any other consultant, management should determine the range of security services offered (for example, burglary, employee theft, robbery, fire detection, and closed-circuit TV surveillance), the experience of the individual (which should be readily available), his professional reputation, and through direct contact with other clients of the consultant, the extent of the services provided by the consultant and the degree of satisfaction felt by those clients.

Appendix

The Security Audit

The prevention of burglary, robbery, and theft requires correct application of physical barriers to control access, delay intrusion, and minimize loss and alarm sensing systems to detect intrusion and transmit alarm signals to central monitoring stations where personnel will effect prompt response by police officers, alarm company agents, and subscriber personnel. The following security checklist is provided to assist the reader in the analysis of an existing or planned retail, financial, or commercial facility. Using relevant sections as a guide, the reader can grade the level of protection. For the most part, a "no" answer to any question represents a defect in security that should be evaluated in regard to the risk involved.

The checklist includes some reference to the area of employee theft prevention in the belief that dishonest employees may also be involved directly or indirectly in robbery, burglary, or thefts committed by outsiders. Also, some checklist questions cover fire extinguishing and detection systems as well as industrial process alarm devices and systems. Again, the intent is to assist the reader in evaluating the security levels as they may relate to vandalism, sabotage, and arson and the dangers related to response to industrial process alarms during normally closed for business periods.

A security supervisor should use the checklist to audit the security program to assure the continuation of a deterrent system in relation to changes in operations, plant renovations or expansion, increased inventory values, new products, and other factors that demand day-to-day security diligence. Suggested intervals between audits and identification of the individual performing the security audit will assist in maintaining a timely audit program.

A specializing security contractor can use the checklist to spot a defect in a total security concept that may result in a crime loss even though his product or service may be adequate. For example, the most sophisticated alarm system is not good enough to protect a fur inventory unless the merchandise is stored in a vault that will resist penetration long enough to permit the arrival of police in response to an alarm signal from the premises.

The checklist may also be used as a training device for company supervisory personnel newly assigned to security responsibilities. The questions asked provoke a need to understand why the answer should be "yes" and permit more knowledgeable supervisors to provide these explanations. If the answers are not obvious, reference to the text may assist you in finding the answer. In the checklist D = daily; W = weekly; M = monthly; Q = quarterly; A = annually.

The Security Checklist

	Suggested Security Check Intervals					
Subject Area	*D*	*W*	*M*	*Q*	*A*	*Assign To*
PHYSICAL SECURITY						
Exterior						
Is yard area completely fenced?					x	
Is gate motorized for remote control?					x	
Are gate locks UL-certified burglary resistant?				x		
Are gate lock code numbers obliterated?				x		
Are gate locks secured to the gate hasp in locked position during the open-for-business period?	x					
Is perimeter fence in good physical condition (no breaks or sags)?					x	
Does shrubbery present a place for concealment of individuals or merchandise?				x		
Are you careful not to place materials of any kind directly against the fence (or the building)?		x				
Is employee parking restricted to areas outside the yard area or at least separated from the building and/or truck materials storage areas by a secondary fence?				x		
Are yard gates locked at the end of the regular work period?		x				
Are gasoline pumps locked at all times when a supervisor is not in attendance?		x				
Are delivery trucks checked on return to be sure all material is moved back into the secured premises?	x					
Are trucks kept locked at night?	x					
Is tractor removed and pin lock installed if it is necessary to leave a loaded trailer overnight in yard area?	x					
Is there a provision for securing vehicles (and contents) returning after normal business hours?	x					
Are the yard area and building perimeter adequately lighted at night?		x				
Are energy cost-saving sodium vapor lights in use?					x	
Are exterior lights automatically controlled by photoelectric cells to conserve energy?				x		
Are the photo cells operating properly?			x			

The Security Checklist (*continued*)

	Suggested Security Check Intervals					
Subject Area	*D*	*W*	*M*	*Q*	*A*	*Assign To*
Are building perimeter door hinges mounted on the exterior side, welded, or otherwise protected against removal of hinge pins?				x		
Show windows						
Where high-value merchandise is kept in show windows (or interior showcases) during nonbusiness hours is UL-listed burglary-resistant glazing material installed?				x		
Or is interior grille or guillotine in use?				x		
Are show window section joints properly protected against "spreading and fishing" during the day as well as at night?			x			
Are trimstrips or other fasteners securing "joints" tamper resistant?			x			
Where show windows project beyond building lines, are bulkheads or ceilings burglary resistant?				x		
If external grilles are installed, are they burglary resistant?				x		
Do they provide visibility for police or passersby to see what's going on inside?				x		
Are external grilles secured on sturdy tracks and locked with a UL-listed burglary-resistant padlock?				x		
Glass entrance doors						
Is the glazing material UL burglary rated?					x	
Or is a grille-gate-type delay barrier installed inside the door?					x	
If delay barrier is attached to door frame, is it locked in place?	x					
Are UL double deadlocks in use during closed period?	x					
Mall-type premises entrance doors						
If sliding section, can one or more sections be moved or removed by first removing track stops?					x	
If pull- or roll-down grille, is UL-listed burglary-resistant locking device in use?		x				
Can electrically operated grille be closed manually if power fails?					x	
Other perimeter doors						
Are doors heavy-duty steel or wood?					x	

The Security Checklist (*continued*)

Subject Area	*Suggested Security Check Intervals*					
	D	*W*	*M*	*Q*	*A*	*Assign To*
Are overhead doors constructed of heavy-duty material instead of glass and masonite insert panels?					x	
If electrically operated, can doors also be closed manually?	x					
Windows						
Are all glass windows protected by steel bars installed on the inside and secured with tamper-resistant fasteners?		x				
Can security sash be substituted for existing windows?					x	
Can some windows be bricked up, welded shut, and so on? (This may also permit elimination of some alarm sensors at corresponding cost savings.)			x			
Will substitution of burglary-resistant glazing material reduce replacement costs due to vandalism?			x			
Are movable windows equipped with adequate locks?					x	
Are movable windows locked at night?	x					
Vents and other openings						
Are all vents protected by steel bars installed on the inside and secured with tamper-resistant fasteners?		x				
Have any new vent openings exceeding 96 square inches been added but not alarm protected?		x				
Can old skylights be permanently sealed over (and alarm sensors eliminated)?				x		
Are there old coal scuttles or other street hatches leading into the basement that can be permanently sealed?			x			
General						
Is building structure physically sound?					x	
Have any weak temporary walls/partitions been created?	x					
If the premises is not freestanding, are common (party) walls structurally weak?					x	
Do doors and frames fit properly?		x				
Do party walls extend to ceiling or roof line?					x	

The Security Checklist (*continued*)

	Suggested Security Check Intervals					
Subject Area	*D*	*W*	*M*	*Q*	*A*	*Assign To*
Selecting a site			As required			
Is there physical evidence of prior forced entry?						
Do the police have records of prior forced entry?						
Is it a high-crime area (or likely to become so)?						
How long will it take police to respond?						
How long will it take alarm company guards to respond?						
How long will it take management personnel to respond?						
Will it be dangerous for management personnel to respond?						
What kind of labor market does the area offer?						
Is there adequate and safe employee parking?						
Is there adequate and safe public transportation?						
Will existing employees be willing to relocate?						
Will the move precipitate labor problems?						
How accessible (expressways, etc.) is the area?						
How satisfactory are public services (water, fuel, electric, telephone, etc.)?						
What types of alarm system supervision are available?						
What statutes apply to alarm systems, pre-employment screening, and so forth?						
Building a facility			As required			
Will employee parking area be fenced separate from work yard areas?						
Will employees enter through controlled gates?						
Is there open visibility all around the building perimeter?						
Is there open visibility all around the fence line?						
Is employee parking area protected (fencing, lights)?						
Are zoning, building, and safety codes determined in advance?						
Interior						
Are work areas physically separated from office and/or visitor areas?			x			
Are dividing doors locked?						
Is access restricted to authorized individuals?						

The Security Checklist (*continued*)

Subject Area	*D*	*W*	*M*	*Q*	*A*	*Assign To*
	Suggested Security Check Intervals					
Are keys assigned?						
If electrically locked, are individuals controlling entry properly instructed?						
In the office						
Is there an entry foyer?					x	
Is entry electrically controlled? Do locking devices function?		x				
Is there a bullet-resistant reception window?					x	
Is it locked, properly secured?		x				
Is there an intercom or telephone communication device? Is it functional?		x				
Is there a pass-through? Is it adequate for mail, packages?					x	
Are instructions to visitors/salesmen posted?				x		
Are typewriters, calculators, and so on secured to desks? Are serial numbers recorded?				x		
Is the office safe still fire resistant?					x	
Is the office safe lock functional?		x				
In retail/showroom areas						
Are show/wall/window cases well constructed?					x	
Are tops or panels loose?		x				
Is there evidence of tampering?	x					
Are cases/drawers equipped with locks?					x	
Are locks operating properly?	x					
Are there barriers (gates) to restrict customers and/or visitors access from employee work areas?					x	
Are gate locks operating properly?	x					
Are notices to customers/visitors posted? Adequate?				x		
Stockroom/cage areas						
Are they adequately constructed?					x	
Is roof or ceiling enclosed?					x	
Do they meet insurance and/or government requirements?				x		
Are doors, gates adequately secured, locked?	x					
Are doors equipped with self-closers?				x		
Are self-closers operating properly?	x					
Are cage bolts tamper-resistant?				x		
Are cage skirts installed?				x		

The Security Checklist (*continued*)

	Suggested Security Check Intervals					
Subject Area	*D*	*W*	*M*	*Q*	*A*	*Assign To*
Is cage securely anchored?				x		
Are closets/cabinets used for high-value storage adequate, equipped with locks?				x		
Shipping/receiving areas						
Are overhead doors secured, padlocked?	x					
Are overhead door tracks secure?		x				
Is shipping area separate from receiving? Fenced?				x		
Are fenced enclosures high enough?					x	
Do fence gates function properly?		x				
Are fence gates secured, locked?	x					
Is there a pedestrian door for drivers?					x	
Is there a pay telephone for drivers?					x	
Is there a restroom for drivers?					x	
Is shipping/receiving area well lighted?				x		
Are driver/visitor instructions posted?				x		
Is there good security visibility in the area?	x					
Is there a will-call foyer?				x		
Is the will-call area physically secure, locked?				x		
Is there a will-call pass-through?					x	
Is dock space provided?			x			
Is there a barrier/grille to secure openings/chutes into storage area?					x	
Is there a rail siding? Do rail cars make roof accessible, conceal entry?				x		
Safes and vaults						
Is the safe securely anchored in place?					x	
Is the view of the combination dial restricted from customers/visitors/passersby?				x		
Is a safe UL labeled as fire resistant still fire-resistant?					x	
Do key/combination locks function properly?		x				
Is there a vault day gate?					x	
Is day gate lock functional, secure?		x				
Is access to safe/vault entrance restricted by enclosure, fence, and so on?					x	
Is safe/vault door burglary resistant?					x	
Does safe/vault meet insurance and/or government requirements?					x	
Is there a vault emergency ventilator?					x	
Is there a vault door emergency escape mechanism? Operable?				x		

The Security Checklist (*continued*)

Subject Area	*Suggested Security Check Intervals*					*Assign To*
	D	*W*	*M*	*Q*	*A*	
Is the premises sprinklered?					x	
If not, would a sprinkler system reduce fire insurance premiums?					x	
Computer/data processing areas						
Is the area fully enclosed?					x	
Are door locks adequate?				x		
Is the door locked when unattended?						
Is there a day access control lock?	x			x		
Is there a disk/record storage file, vault, or safe?					x	
Does it meet required fire/safety insurance standards?				x		
General						
Are there any new holes/openings in interior partitions?		x				
Are tow motors, forklifts, dollies, stored/charged in a secure area?					x	
Are they equipped with locks?				x		
Are they locked at night?	x					
Is there a proper storage area/room for flammables?				x		
Is it secured, locked?				x		
Are all areas functional?				x		
Is there an orderly layout?				x		
Do supervisors and employees have good visibility all around?			x			
Are aisles wide enough?				x		
Are employee lockers and lunchroom areas separated from work/storage areas?					x	
THEFT PREVENTION						
Locks, Keys, and Combinations						
Locks						
Are perimeter door lock cylinders UL listed as burglary resistant?					x	
Do lock bolts have at least a 1-inch throw?					x	
Are strike guards installed to reduce vulnerability to jimmying?					x	
Have exterior handles been removed from emergency-only exits?					x	
Do lock cylinders require keying from both sides?				x		

The Security Checklist (*continued*)

	Suggested Security Check Intervals					
Subject Area	*D*	*W*	*M*	*Q*	*A*	*Assign To*
Are padlocks UL-listed burglary resistant?			x			
Are critical area locks changed periodically?					x	
Keys						
Is there a key control policy?					x	
Is there a key control log?					x	
Is the log up to date?			x			
Are employees required to sign for keys?			x			
Are employees required to report missing, lost, or stolen keys in writing?			x			
Are duplicate keys kept in a locked cabinet?	x					
Is the locked key cabinet secured in the vault?			x			
If some locks are keyed alike, is there a security weakness created by a change in operations or personnel?				x		
Are all keys accounted for?			x			
Do rules require employees always to carry keys on their person?		x				
Are padlock key codes obliterated (when installed)?				x		
Are forklift keys adequately controlled?				x		
Are alarm keys adequately controlled?				x		
Are day annunciator keys adequately controlled?				x		
Combinations: Safes and Vaults						
Is the combination known to any individual who has no need to know?				x		
Are combinations immediately changed when this condition exists?				x		
Are combinations changed periodically? At least every 2 years?				x		
If dual combinations/key locks exist, is knowledge split between two employees?					x	
Do rules prohibit employees putting combinations in writing?				x		
Are "common" numbers (for example, Social Security and date of birth) prohibited?				x		
Access Control						
Identification for Employees						
Are employees required to wear a badge?					x	
Are employees required to show an ID card?					x	

The Security Checklist (*continued*)

Subject Area	*Suggested Security Check Intervals*					
	D	*W*	*M*	*Q*	*A*	*Assign To*
Does either include a photo?					x	
Are duplicate badges or ID cards kept in a locked file?					x	
Are badges/IDs issued by number, controlled, and logged?	x					
Are lost or stolen badges cancelled?	x					
Are lost or stolen badges reported promptly?	x					
Are badges color coded to restrict individual access to unauthorized areas?				x		
Identification for Visitors						
Are all unknown visitors adequately identified? By telephone communication to their employers?		x				
Are visitors assigned badges?				x		
Is there a visitor log?				x		
Is it legible? Is name printed in addition to signature?		x				
Is the log maintained and retained?		x				
Procedure						
Are visitors escorted?	x					
Are drivers restricted to the receiving area?	x					
Are employees required to enter/depart through specific supervised points?				x		
Are safes, vaults, and day gates closed and locked at break, lunch times?	x					
Is the shipping and receiving area always supervised when open?	x					
Are employees always subject to package inspection, metal inspection?					x	
Are visitors always subject to package inspection, metal inspection?					x	
Are rules covering inspections posted? Signed by an employee?					x	
Are entry foyers controlled?				x		
Are employee relatives/friends restricted from access to the premises?				x		
Are job applicants restricted to a designated office area?				x		
Are push button combination locks used for access to cages, computer rooms, and so forth?				x		

The Security Checklist (*continued*)

Subject Area	*Suggested Security Check Intervals*					
	D	*W*	*M*	*Q*	*A*	*Assign To*
Are such combinations changed frequently?				x		
Are card key-type access systems in use?					x	
Are cards controlled?				x		
Do cards have restrictions limiting access to critical areas?				x		
Are will-call customers restricted to an entry foyer?				x		
Are employees asked to report unidentified visitors?				x		
General theft prevention						
Are all openings (movable windows, vents) fine screened?					x	
Are screens frequently inspected (on a random day and time basis)?		x				
Are there day annunciator systems on all emergency-only use doors?				x		
Are the annunciators loud?				x		
Are they supervised?	x					
Are battery-operated annunciators changed at 6-month intervals?				x		
Are devices tested and inspected physically?	x					
Is there another way to remove materials undetected?				x		
Are employee lockers subject to inspection?				x		
Is this rule in writing? Posted?				x		
Is there an employee purchase/discount plan?					x	
Are items purchased by employees filled by a supervisor and delivered only at the employee exit?				x		
Are cleaning personnel subject to the same access control procedures as other employees?				x		
Are cleaners always supervised?	x					
Are aprons, gloves, work clothes subject to inspection?				x		
If there is a night shift, are the same rules in effect?		x				
When some employees are assigned overtime, are the same rules in effect?		x				
Are night cleaners limited in authority to control alarms?				x		

The Security Checklist (*continued*)

Subject Area	*Suggested Security Check Intervals*					
	D	*W*	*M*	*Q*	*A*	*Assign To*
Dock Areas						
Are items received immediately checked and moved to a permanent storage area?	x					
Are receiving shortages promptly reported? Is there followup?		x				
Are returned goods promptly moved from the dock?	x					
Are goods moved to a cage or other controlled access enclosure?				x		
Is the receiving clerk checked by a supervisor?				x		
In the shipping area, is staged merchandise enclosed to restrict driver access until loaded?	x					
Are all valuable items shipped in sealed containers?				x		
Is the area continually supervised?				x		
Are shipping labels and customers' invoices double checked?				x		
Are will-call orders promptly documented, suspicious calls verified?	x					
Are new customers cleared before shipping?			x			
Do drivers have access to other merchandise?	x					
Do trucks or rail cars remain locked overnight?			x			
If so, how are the cargoes protected?			x			
If there is a night shift in shipping, is it adequately supervised?			x			
Are these employees safe from attack?				x		
Are all returning drivers' collections received, checked, and immediately deposited in an alarmed safe?	x					
Are all trash, cartons, barrels, and so on kept clear of the dock area?	x					
Are hiding places checked frequently?	x					
Are outsiders restricted from the loading dock and yard areas?	x					
Does any dock employee make outside phone calls?	x					
Has any dock or driver employee refused transfer or promotion?	x					
Does any employee refrain from discounted employee purchase on higher-priced but commonly used items?	x					

The Security Checklist (*continued*)

Subject Area	*Suggested Security Check Intervals* D	W	M	Q	A	*Assign To*
Inventory control procedures						
Is a physical inventory taken at least annually?					x	
Is it subject to outside auditor participation?					x	
Are the auditors' procedures effective?					x	
Are spot physical inventories taken at least monthly?			x			
Are controls covering issue of shipping documents adequate?					x	
Are sales and shipping records verified?		x				
Are all credits and discounts subject to a supervisor's approval?		x				
Are shortages reported promptly to all authorities?	x					
Are all invoice/shipping copies accounted for?	x					
Are all multiple-item orders shipped in one sealed container?				x		
Note: Expand this section to cover individual accounting procedures applicable to protection of assets other than merchandise.						
Closed-circuit TV						
Does camera cover the shipping/receiving area?					x	
Are lighting and picture quality satisfactory?	x					
Do closed-circuit TVs cover employee entrance, visitor reception, entry to stockrooms, and vaults?					x	
Is closed-circuit TV output continuously monitored?	x					
Is there a time-lapse video recorder in use?					x	
Are tapes reviewed by supervision? At least at random?	x					
Is all equipment functioning properly?		x				
Are monitors restricted from casual viewing by work force?					x	
ALARM SYSTEMS						
Burglary Systems						
Equipment and Procedures						
Are contact switches, lacing or foil, wiring, and motion-detection sensors inspected visually?	x					
Are motion-detection mounting brackets secure?	x					

The Security Checklist (*continued*)

Subject Area	*Suggested Security Check Intervals*					
	D	*W*	*M*	*Q*	*A*	*Assign To*
Do detectors face in proper direction?	x					
If there are photoelectric or infrared beams, are units firmly mounted, guards intact?	x					
Have obstructions (partitions, cartons, racks, curtains, and so on) been installed or stored to reduce or eliminate motion-detection sensor coverage?	x					
Have new openings (doors, windows, skylights, vents) been created?	x					
Has critical inventory been relocated or added in unprotected areas?		x				
Are walk-tests performed? By two supervisors? Are logs maintained? Defects corrected?		x				
Is circuit wiring free of temporary splices?		x				
Are unnecessary alarm devices/sensors still in service?				x		
Have disconnected alarm devices/sensors been physically removed?				x		
Are alarm control units located within protected areas?				x		
Is there UL-approved pseudorandom high line security in operation?				x		
Is a standby power supply part of the system?				x		
Are standby power batteries fully charged?			x			
Are AC outlets used to supply power to alarm devices/sensors on a separate circuit breaker?				x		
Are alarm control keys removed from control units and shunts? Are they kept on the person?	x					
Storage cage or stockroom						
Is the cage or stockroom properly protected by motion-detection sensors?				x		
Are cage or stockroom doors equipped with alarm contact switches?				x		
Is this alarm system on a separate circuit or combined with a vault system?				x		
Do racks, partitions, or merchandise located adjacent to the cage block motion-detection coverage?		x				

The Security Checklist (*continued*)

Subject Area	*Suggested Security Check Intervals*					
	D	*W*	*M*	*Q*	*A*	*Assign To*
Vaults and safes						
Does the alarm system completely protect the vault?				x		
If the vault door contains less than 1½ inches of solid steel, is it alarmed properly?				x		
Is the vault alarm control unit mounted properly on the exterior vault wall to permit closed-period troubleshooting without opening the vault?				x		
Are safes used for high-value storage properly alarmed?				x		
If the safe has double doors, are both equipped with alarm contact switches?				x		
Is the safe or vault on a separate alarm circuit?				x		
If the safe is protected by a proximity, or capacitance, alarm system, are insulating blocks installed under the safe?				x		
Are any metal objects placed on or close to the safe?	x					
Are office/record/computer disk safes or vaults equipped at least with alarm contacts?				x		
Perimeter of the premises						
Are all accessible perimeter doors, windows, and vents equipped with proper alarm devices?			x			
Are motion-detection devices and beams on a separate circuit to permit perimeter opening alarm devices to be turned on when only a few individuals are on hand?				x		
Are doors or windows leading from warehouse to office equipped with alarm devices installed at least on the warehouse side?				x		
Is the office on a separate alarm circuit or at least equipped with a time delay shunt?				x		
If the computer department works overtime or on a second shift, is there a separate alarm circuit to provide for the protection of employees working inside?				x		
Is there a separate alarm system covering the truck bay (for early dispatch/late returns)?				x		

The Security Checklist (*continued*)

Subject Area	*Suggested Security Check Intervals*					
	D	*W*	*M*	*Q*	*A*	*Assign To*
Alarm-related procedures						
Does the alarm company furnish reports of alarm openings and closings?		x				
Are these reports reviewed for compliance with company policy?		x				
Does the safe or vault alarm system open only after the full work force is on hand?		x				
Does the safe or vault alarm system close prior to work force departure?		x				
Does the alarm company furnish a written report of all alarms?		x				
Are false alarms investigated and causes eliminated promptly?		x				
Are repairs made promptly? Are they permanent?		x				
If the alarm contractor holds keys to the premises, does he furnish key seal reports?		x				
Are specific company supervisors listed for alarm notification/response?			x			
Are specific company supervisors' residence telephone numbers up to date?			x			
Is there a weekend, holiday, vacation duty roster?			x			
Do supervisors have paging devices? Are they operative?				x		
Do supervisors verify alarm calls before leaving the safety of their residence?	x					
Is the alarm contractor required to dispatch police on all alarms?			x			
Is the alarm contractor required to dispatch police on all telephone circuit troubles?			x			
Do special openings require a letter or visit to the central station?			x			
Do special openings occur frequently? Are they justified?		x				
Do written instructions to the alarm contractor conform alarm schedules with business hours, days of the week, holidays?			x			
Is there an emergency disaster response plan?				x		
Does the alarm contractor have a priority notification list if central station emergencies oc-						

The Security Checklist (*continued*)

	Suggested Security Check Intervals					
Subject Area	*D*	*W*	*M*	*Q*	*A*	*Assign To*
cur? Is your vault system on this list?				x		
Are there two opening and closing schedules for perimeter alarms?				x		
Has all alarm telephone circuit identification (sleeves, tags) been removed from terminal boxes or pouches in or near the premises?				x		
Does the alarm contractor test and inspect all systems at least annually?					x	
Does the alarm contractor issue a written report certifying all is in order?					x	
Are all applicable UL certificates current and accurate?				x		
Is there a complete Schedule of Protection in the company files? Is it correct?					x	
If an alarm system is inoperative, do procedures provide for manning the premises?				x		
When responding to alarms, do police remain on hand and thoroughly search?			x			
Holdup Alarm Systems						
Equipment and procedures						
Is there a fixed button in the vault?				x		
Are there fixed buttons at the reception desk, in shipping, and at the switchboard?				x		
Are there wireless devices for use by supervisors responsible for opening, closing, responding to alarms, and shipping?				x		
Does the wireless signal transmission range reach their parking spaces?			x			
Are all holdup devices operative, tested monthly, and logged?			x			
Are wireless batteries replaced at 6-month intervals and logged?				x		
Do employees understand procedures restricting use of holdup devices?			x			
Are such procedures in writing?			x			
Are new employees indoctrinated immediately?	x					
Do holdup devices operate quietly?			x			
Is the holdup signal circuit silent (no bell or siren)?			x			
Do the alarm company and the police have a						

The Security Checklist (*continued*)

Subject Area	*Suggested Security Check Intervals*					
	D	*W*	*M*	*Q*	*A*	*Assign To*
prearranged investigation/response procedure?			x			
Is it a safe procedure?			x			
Is the holdup alarm circuit combined with a vault or premises circuit for economical service?				x		
Is there a visual annunciator to alert management when a device has been tripped?				x		
Are all holdup devices designed to lock in when tripped? Do they require a special reset key? Is the key kept only by a supervisor?				x		
Are all false alarms resolved immediately?	x					
Fire-Signaling Systems						
Manual alarms						
Do they meet statutes and codes?				x		
Are they tested to codes?			x			
Are "use" instructions clear?				x		
Are employees instructed in evacuation procedures? Are maps in place and exits marked?		x				
Automatic detection alarms						
Do they meet codes?				x		
Are they tested monthly?			x			
Have alterations or additions created coverage problems?		x				
Are false alarm causes corrected immediately?	x					
Is computer room properly protected?				x		
Is records vault properly protected?				x		
Automatic extinguishing systems						
Do they meet codes and insurance requirements?				x		
Are they tested monthly?			x			
Are they water-flow tested?			x			
Are wet lines adequately protected against freezing?			x			
Is there a low-temperature alarm?				x		
If sprinkler system water surges are probable, has a corrective circuit been installed?				x		
Are gate valves alarmed?				x		
Are gate valves properly locked open?	x					
Are merchandise and racks, and so forth kept at least 18 inches from sprinkler heads?		x				

The Security Checklist (*continued*)

	Suggested Security Check Intervals					
Subject Area	*D*	*W*	*M*	*Q*	*A*	*Assign To*
Is the water tank equipped with a low water–low temperature alarm? Is it tested?				x		
Is the fire pump equipped with an alarm device?				x		
Do AC vent devices operate properly? Are they tested?			x			
Fire safety						
Are flammables and explosive materials properly stored? Do they meet codes?		x				
Are alarm devices that are installed in explosive area specifically sealed to prevent fire or explosion?				x		
Are extinguishers properly located?		x				
Are extinguishers inspected as required?			x			
Are fire extinguishers installed on trucks? Do they have the correct devices? Are these tested?		x				
Are fire exits clear of obstructions and properly equipped?	x					
Are fire exits locked from outside?	x					
Are special fire doors unobstructed?		x				
Are fire drills conducted?				x		
Are no-smoking rules properly posted?		x				
Industrial Process Alarm Systems						
Equipment and procedures						
Are such alarm systems on separate alarm circuits?				x		
Do procedures require that a supervisor respond? With police?				x		
Are water detectors installed at all low points?				x		
Are boiler flame or low-temperature devices properly located and tested?				x		
Are air conditioning and heating temperatures automated? Remotely supervised?					x	
Are other industrial process devices available?					x	

Index